My Darling Winston

My Darling Winston

THE LETTERS BETWEEN WINSTON CURCHILL AND HIS MOTHER

DAVID LOUGH

PEGASUS BOOKS

NEW YORK LONDON

My Darling Winston

Pegasus Books, Ltd.
148 West 37th Street, 13th Floor
New York, NY 10018

First Pegasus Books hardcover edition October 2018

ISBN: 978-1-68177-882-2

10 9 8 7 6 5 4 3 2 1

Printed in the United States of America
Distributed by W. W. Norton & Company, Inc.

To Felicity, a brilliant mother to our five children

CONTENTS

FOREWORD

by Randolph Churchill

I VERY MUCH welcome the first publication of these letters between my great-grandfather, Sir Winston Churchill, and his mother, Jennie, as a correspondence in their own right. I believe that history has under-appreciated the role of Jennie Jerome (as she was known at her birth in America) in shaping the early years of her son, Winston, and the influence she had on the life of a great statesman. Nothing illustrates better how she did it than these letters.

Jennie Jerome and her American ancestors, who were of early pioneering stock, are legends in my family history. My great-grandfather loved the stories of supposed Iroquois antecedents, which we are now told are untrue. But Jennie's father, the fabulous Leonard Jerome, created a spark of energy in her, because Jennie was beautiful, talented and captivating. So much so that when, aged nineteen, she met the young Lord Randolph Churchill when they were guests on board HMS *Ariadne* in 1873, he proposed to her just two days later. Although Jennie's parents did not think that the second son of a duke was good enough for their daughter, the young couple were very much in love. They married in 1874 and Winston was born later that year.

Jennie had to bring Winston up almost single-handed once he was a teenager, because his father, Lord Randolph Churchill, was so ill and away so much. He died when Winston was barely twenty. Thereafter Jennie was completely on her own, and Winston was a handful.

But, then, Jennie was no ordinary Victorian mother, as David Lough makes clear in his Introduction. She combined a naturally warm and vivacious personality with considerable talents. She was a concert-standard pianist and was fluent in several languages, skills she had acquired during a childhood spent in New York, Trieste and Paris. This equipped her to survive the shock of marrying into the stiff, male-dominated world of the Victorian upper class and, indeed, to carve out a position among its top politicians, soldiers and intellectuals.

Jennie kept this position after her husband died and used her network of friends to pull all sorts of strings on Winston's behalf; at the same time, she tried to smooth his rougher edges without blunting his exuberance. Jennie also passed a spark of strong American independence onto Winston, which was to manifest itself in the darker years ahead when Britain 'stood alone' and then later alongside her American allies after he persuaded them to enter the war. I love the tribute Winston gave his mother when he addressed the joint houses of Congress in December 1941 and said: 'I wish indeed that my mother, whose memory I cherish, across the vale of years, could have been here to see.'

The striking intimacy of their long correspondence will give pause to those who assume their relationship was distant or strained. For his mother's eyes only, Winston confided his innermost thoughts on his strengths and weaknesses, on the senior generals and politicians of the day, and on his early attempts to devise his own political philosophy. Jennie told him whenever she thought he was wrong, at the same time describing evocatively the gilded lives of the Victorian and Edwardian elites among whose country estates she moved effortlessly as a popular guest.

All this we can now read in an exchange of sparkling letters spanning forty years. David Lough has assembled a wonderful collection that takes us through mother and son's shared successes and failures, love and disappointment, exhilaration and despair.

The result is not just wonderfully entertaining; it also sheds important historical light on a relationship that was pivotal in the growth of my great-grandfather's personality, political philosophy and moral courage.

RANDOLPH CHURCHILL
Crockham Hill

INTRODUCTION

————

W INSTON CHURCHILL and his mother Jennie Jerome[1]
exchanged more than a thousand letters in the forty years
between his sixth birthday and her death. Jennie was better at keeping
her son's letters than he was at keeping hers, especially while he
was fighting as a young man in north-western India, the Sudan and
southern Africa. Nevertheless, I estimate that at least three-quarters of
their letters survive; although many have found their way individually
into biographies of either mother or son, they have never before
appeared as an uninterrupted correspondence between the two.

I have had to omit some letters for reasons of space, but the
majority of these omissions date from Winston's days at boarding
school when he had to write a weekly letter home and he followed
the schoolboy's well-worn formula of weaving appeals for more
pocket money or parental visits into tales of sporting or academic

————

1   Jennie became known formally as Lady Randolph Churchill on her marriage
to Winston's father, Lord Randolph Churchill, in 1874; then as Mrs George
Cornwallis-West during her second marriage between 1900 and 1914, before
reverting to the name of Lady Randolph Churchill, including during her third
marriage to Montagu Porch from 1918 until her death in 1921. To her children
she was always Mamma; to the remainder of her family and close friends she was
Jennie, which is how I refer to her in this book.

achievements. I have included a representative but far from exhaustive sample of the genre.

The many attractions of the letters exchanged between Winston and his mother Jennie struck me while I was researching an earlier book, *No More Champagne: Churchill and His Money*. It is not just the entertainment that two natural writers provide us as they express themselves to each other without reserve; nor is it just the historical light that each shines on the ruling elite at work and play in the years before the First World War, when Jennie in her own right was as well known a public figure as her son.

There are two additional attractions. The first is the insight that the letters offer into the curious mind of Winston Churchill as he develops his adult personality. By the time he was a teenager, his father Lord Randolph Churchill was seriously ill with a disease that doctors at the time treated as syphilis, although modern medical opinion is not so sure. So it was Jennie who took the strain of bringing up their difficult son and his brother Jack, six years younger.

Soon after Winston's twentieth birthday, his father died and Jennie became a single parent. From this moment onwards, she helped him to develop his education and his philosophy towards life. He confided intimately in her while testing out his increasingly assertive views about the military, social and political figures or controversies of the day. She was able to respond in kind because, being both well educated and socially well connected, she knew all the leading actors whom her son was precociously judging.

The second attraction is the almost operatic quality that the Churchills' letters bring to the universal story of a mother's invincible love for a son, counterpointed by her gradual decline from the vibrant, young giver of life in the child's early days to the lonely, elderly burden that she felt herself to be in her later years.

In the first act of the drama, this mother struggles to cope with a wayward child while losing her husband inch by inch, in public, to a terrible disease. Following his death, the second act sees her subsume her ambitions into those of her son, deploying her many great gifts to advance his career. Then, in the third act, just as their joint endeavours are bearing fruit, she falls for the charms of a young suitor half her age. Despite many warnings against the alliance she marries him while her son stands loyally by.

After an interval, in the fourth act her attractions fade, the new marriage cracks and her life crumbles. By the time she calls on her son for help, he is too busy and successful to give it. It takes a serious check to his career in the final act to revive their intimacy and provide a fitting coda to their correspondence as he goes off to war. He survives; yet she meets a tragic end soon afterwards and her son arrives at her deathbed just too late to say goodbye. The curtain falls.

When Winston Churchill was born in 1874, letter-writing was the standard way for family members and friends to keep in touch with one another. The invention of a self-adhesive stamp in 1840 had transformed the popularity of the post by allowing the writer of a letter, rather than its reader, to pay for its delivery. Between 1837 and 1874, the number of letters posted in Britain rose from 67 million a year to more than a billion. For the price of a red penny stamp (a little more than we pay today in real terms), the Royal Mail delivered a letter of up to half an ounce in weight to almost any part of the country on the day after postage. London houses could receive six to twelve deliveries a day.

After 1870 there was the alternative of sending a telegram, but its first nine words cost six times as much as a letter. In addition, its contents had to be transcribed at each end by clerks in post offices nearest to the sender and receiver. It therefore offered no assurance of privacy. The abbreviated language of a telegram could also cause misunderstandings, so even the extravagant Churchills preferred to write a letter in most circumstances.

Proper Victorian letter-writers, of whom Jennie was one, spent the first hour or two of each day after breakfast in the bedroom attending to their correspondence. The owners of the country houses that they visited prided themselves on the quality of the crested note-paper provided to their guests. Their young sons learned the habit of letter-writing as soon as they left home at the age of eight. Every Sunday their boarding schools would set an hour aside for them to write a letter home, under supervision.

Letters could be gossipy and intimate, their contents (by convention) to be absorbed only by the reader unless he or she was invited by the writer to share them more widely. In some cases, the reader might be asked to burn the letter after reading it; Winston asked his wife Clementine to burn several letters, but he only asked his mother to destroy one.

Jennie's ancestors had emigrated from Britain to its colonies in North America as early as 1710. The founding fathers had set out to establish a less patriarchal society than the one they had left behind; thus, when Thomas Jefferson drew up the laws of Virginia, he consciously rejected the incorporation of primogeniture and male entail, the twin pillars of English aristocratic society. So far as American inheritance laws existed at all after 1800, they treated sons and daughters alike, including those born outside marriage.

Most well-to-do American parents used very different methods of bringing up their children from the Victorian elite in Britain. The authoritarian controls of the latter gave way in America to a more relaxed relationship between the generations, in which mothers played a more influential role in bringing up their sons than they did in Britain.

The country's rapid economic growth required its children to assist their parents as soon as they were sufficiently able-bodied to do so. Values that shaped America's culture, such as personal autonomy and success, also infused the attitudes of parents towards their children. As a result parents encouraged displays of initiative, gave their young more independence and employed a less rigid approach to discipline.

By contrast, English parents of the Victorian era imagined their children to inhabit a state not of 'childhood' but of 'defective adulthood'. Children learned to eradicate their defects over time by acquiring rules of behaviour which would breed a moral rectitude that led in turn to social and economic success.

When Winston was born, British law still subordinated the role of the mother to that of the father. It was the father who owned the family's property and who was legally responsible for the welfare of his children. As portrayed in John Galsworthy's novel *The Man of Property* (1906), the archetype of the Victorian father was authoritative and wise, benignly exerting his influence over the whole family, yet remote from his children, who lived, ate and slept in a separate part of the house.

By the time Queen Victoria came to the British throne in 1837, wealthier parents had acquired the habit of delegating the teaching of these adult rules to a servant – the nursery nurse or 'nanny', who ruled over the nursery, a suite of rooms on the top floor of the house, usually filled by pieces of furniture not required elsewhere in the ancestral home.

More than 100,000 nannies were in service in Britain in 1874, when *The Times* each day carried advertisements for an average of twelve new such positions.[2] Unlike governesses, nannies usually came from working-class homes and occupied a strange middle ground in the domestic household, part servant and part *in loco parentis*. Relationships between a mother and her nanny ranged between a genuine partnership in bringing up the child and cases where the nanny seized effective control.[3] In most families, however, the nanny acted as the child's *de facto* mother, deferring only briefly to his or her real mother during a daily visit downstairs at teatime to its parents' drawing room. The nanny took responsibility for the child's clothes, food, sleep, play, health and behaviour.

Today it is difficult to conceive how tens of thousands of British mothers handed over the care of their young, almost from birth, to

2   J. Gathorne-Hardy, *The Rise and Fall of the British Nanny*, pp. 189–90.
3   *Idem*, p. 126 *et seq*.

women of whose background they often knew little. In part, perhaps, it was a way of coping with the risk of infant mortality, still a defining feature of life for the Victorian social elite. When Winston was born in 1874, diseases like diphtheria, smallpox, measles, rubella, polio and meningitis still killed more than 7 per cent of children born to the British aristocracy in the 1870s before they reached the age of one and probably as many again before they reached the age of five.[4] Children were of limited use to the dynastic family until they reached adulthood.

Jennie had warmed more to her gregarious father, Leonard Jerome,[5] than to her mother, Clara, during her childhood years. These were split between New York and Trieste, the summer playground of the Austro-Hungarian court on the Adriatic Sea, where Leonard spent two years as the American consul. Jennie's father pursued many enthusiasms in his life – money, horse racing, sailing, the opera and women among them – yet he always seemed to have time for his three daughters.

It was the difficulty of dealing with the extra women in Leonard's life that led his wife Clara to leave him behind in New York and return to Europe with their three girls in 1867, when Jennie was thirteen. Clara had developed a fascination for the European aristocracy while the family lived in Trieste. On their way home through Paris, the self-styled emperor of France, Napoleon III, and his empress, Eugénie, had greeted the Jeromes warmly and invited them to return. Clara took him at his word, generously funded by Leonard who crossed the Atlantic regularly to visit his family in the French capital in between tending to his business affairs in New York.

The family's idyll in Paris lasted only three years until 1870, however, when the fragile French Second Empire crumbled following

---

4   C. Corsini and P.P. Viazzo, eds, *The Decline of Infant Mortality in Europe, 1800–1950*, citing Hollingworth's British peerage series.

5   Leonard Jerome combined newspaper proprietorship and share dealing on Wall Street (see People, p. 566).

military defeat by Prussia. As the invading troops closed in on the capital, the Jerome women escaped by one of the last trains to the north coast. From there they crossed the Channel to England, where Leonard installed them at Brown's Hotel in London, an altogether drabber city than Paris. To allow them to escape the city's pollution in the summer, he rented a seaside cottage for them each year in the sailing resort of Cowes on the Isle of Wight.

There, in August 1873, the nineteen-year-old Jennie unexpectedly encountered Lord Randolph Churchill, second son of the duke of Marlborough. Twenty-one years old and newly graduated from Oxford University, Lord Randolph was slim, fashionably dressed and sported a large moustache. Destined for a career in politics by family expectation and personal ambition, Lord Randolph exuded an air of impulsive, excitable energy. Within seventy-two hours of meeting Jennie, he had proposed marriage and she had accepted.

Lord Randolph found his fiancée a complete contrast to the daughters of the English aristocracy whom he was used to meeting. Where they had been tutored inside their own home by a single governess, Jennie had already lived in New York, Trieste, Paris and London and had attended a private school in America followed by a *lycée* in Paris. She was widely read, spoke two languages and was a gifted musician. Above all, she could converse with him as an equal.

Further differences between the American and British backgrounds of the couple became apparent well before their wedding. For example, when the two families discussed the financial settlements that each would make for the marriage, Jennie's father Leonard was at a loss to understand why the income from the capital sum handed over by the Jeromes should go only to Lord Randolph. 'My daughter ... is an American and ranks precisely the same as you,' he told his future son-in-law.[6] They compromised halfway the day before the wedding took place in Paris on 15 April 1874.

---

6   7 April 1874 Leonard Jerome letter to Lord Randolph Churchill, Blenheim Papers.

Jennie Jerome, shortly before her marriage
to Lord Randolph Churchill, 1874.

By the time the newlyweds settled down to life in London, Lord Randolph had already been elected member of Parliament for the family-controlled seat of Woodstock, next to his ancestral home of Blenheim Palace, in Oxfordshire. Aspiring politicians and their wives were expected to take part in a seemingly endless round of entertaining while parliament was sitting in London, but Jennie needed no persuasion to play her full part as a hostess; she threw herself enthusiastically into her husband's social and professional world, quickly finding that it absorbed her.

So when a first child, a son whom they named Winston, arrived after only seven months of marriage, he presented an awkward choice between her instincts as a mother brought up in America and her duty as the new wife of a British aristocrat immersed in the world of politics. There may have been a brief tussle in Jennie's mind, but she soon employed a nanny, Mrs Everest,[7] to look after Winston: the British approach to parenting offered an attractive route by which she could still conform to the expectations of her new tribe while her children were young.

Little evidence survives of the way that Jennie and Mrs Everest divided the duties of mother and nanny. Jennie's diary of January 1882 (the only year for which it survives) records her reading and giving lessons to the seven-year-old Winston.[8] The fact that Mrs Everest stayed with the Churchill family for seventeen years, much longer than the normal tenure of a nanny, also suggests that she and Jennie established one of the more satisfactory partnerships.

Winston was two years old when his family moved to Dublin, taking Mrs Everest with them. The move was forced on the family by a serious falling out between Lord Randolph and the Prince of Wales (the future Edward VII). Lord Randolph, in an attempt to prevent his elder brother, the marquess of Blandford, from being named in a

---

7 'Mrs' Elizabeth Everest, who remained with the Churchill family until 1893 (see People, p. 578).

8 P. Churchill and J. Mitchell, *Jennie, Lady Randolph Churchill*, pp. 108–9.

divorce suit, threatened to reveal compromising letters written by the Prince some years earlier. The outraged 'Bertie' announced he would no longer visit any house in London which admitted Lord Randolph and Jennie. The prime minister, the earl of Beaconsfield (the former Benjamin Disraeli), had to step in to defuse the scandal by proposing that Lord Randolph's father, the duke of Marlborough,[9] serve as viceroy of Ireland and take his son with him as his private secretary.

Years later Winston wrote of his memories of his mother during that spell in Dublin: 'My picture of her in Ireland is in a riding habit, fitting like a skin and often beautifully spotted with mud ... My mother always seemed to me a fairy princess: a radiant being possessed of limitless riches and power.'[10]

During Lord Randolph's frequent trips home to keep in touch with the political world at Westminster, Jennie was seldom short of male company, often hunting in the company of young men in military uniform to whom she would be attracted throughout much of her lifetime. One young officer in the Coldstream Guards, Edgar Vincent (later an eminent diplomat as Lord D'Abernon), provided a different perspective of her from that of her son when he described her impact at a reception given in the Vice-Regal Lodge:

> a dark lithe figure ... appearing to be of another texture to those around her, radiant, translucent, intense. A diamond star in her hair, her favourite ornament – its lustre dimmed by the flashing glory of her eyes. More of the panther than of the woman in her look, but with a cultivated intelligence unknown to the jungle.[11]

The Churchill family moved back to London in March 1880, a few months after Winston's fifth birthday. On his return to full-time politics at Westminster, Lord Randolph revealed a sharper edge to his

---

9 John Spencer-Churchill, the 7th duke, who died in 1880.
10 W. Churchill, *My Early Life*, p. 4.
11 R. Foster, *Lord Randolph Churchill*, p. 34.

oratory, honed by his contact with genuine poverty in Ireland. More aware of the hidden costs of social division, he became a mordantly effective speaker both inside and outside the House of Commons; together with friends he formed a 'fourth party' to articulate the case for a more compassionate form of Conservatism, soon dubbed 'Tory democracy'.

Politics became a shared obsession of both Lord Randolph and Jennie. 'Our house became the rendezvous of all shades of politicians,' Jennie wrote. 'Many were the plots and plans which were hatched in my presence.'[12] She proved a valuable asset at her husband's side, attracting many of the leading political figures of the day.

The controversy surrounding Jennie's record as a mother concerns whether she neglected Winston and Jack during this period when they were young children. Sylvia Henley, a cousin, told Winston's youngest daughter, Mary Soames, that even by the standards of their day Jennie and Lord Randolph had been 'pretty awful' parents.[13] Winston himself fuelled the fire when he wrote a passage in *Marlborough: His Life and Times* that seemed to convey an authenticity born of personal experience:

> It is said that famous men are usually the product of an unhappy childhood. The stern compression of circumstances, the twinges of adversity, the spur of slights and taunts in early years, are needed to evoke that ruthless fixity of purpose and tenacious mother-wit without which great actions are seldom accomplished.[14]

Furthermore, he would write in his autobiographical volume *My Early Life* that, while his mother had 'shone for me like the Evening

---

12 Mrs G. Cornwallis-West, *The Reminiscences of Lady Randolph Churchill*, p. 126.
13 M. Soames, interview transcript with author Jon Meacham, *Franklin and Winston: An Intimate Portrait of an Epic Friendship*, 16 November 2004.
14 W. Churchill, *Marlborough, His Life and Times*, p. 33.

Star', he had 'loved her dearly but at a distance'.[15] Many have interpreted that distance as lasting throughout his mother's life, although the passage appears at the beginning of the book, set in the context of his earliest years.

Jennie's niece and biographer Anita Leslie provides the picture that best fits her record as a mother from the evidence of her correspondence with Winston: 'She loved and hugged [her sons] as babies, she forgot about them as schoolboys, she rallied to their side as young men and slaved during their early years of endeavour.'[16]

If we accept that Jennie 'forgot' about Winston during his schooldays, the ease with which they took up the striking intimacy of their correspondence after Winston left school suggests that she must have forged a stronger bond in his pre-school years than was typical of Victorian parents.

During Winston's years away at boarding school, however, there is ample evidence that Jennie had other preoccupations and kept a distance from her son that was more typical of the Victorian elite than of its American counterparts. There is no sign that either she or Lord Randolph inspected Winston's first boarding school before they sent him there just before his eighth birthday in 1882. As he arrived in the middle of the school term, the selection of St George's School in Ascot bears the hallmark of haste, caused by his parents' imminent departure to spend two months in America.

St George's was a fashionable and suitably exclusive establishment that prepared its pupils for Eton, Harrow and Winchester, the public schools of choice for the sons of the British aristocracy, but its headmaster ran a brutal regime. Within eighteen months of Winston's arrival his health had broken down so seriously that Mrs Everest and the family doctor combined forces to persuade his parents to remove him.

They chose a gentler establishment on the south coast near

---

15 *Idem.*
16 A. Leslie, *Jennie: The Life of Lady Randolph Churchill*, pp. 304–5.

Brighton, where the doctor lived. The school, which enjoyed no formal name, was run by two elderly spinsters, the Misses Thomson, in a house on Brunswick Road in Hove. Jennie and Lord Randolph both wrote to Winston there from time to time, although never as regularly as he would have wished. Jennie travelled to the school once in February 1885, but his father did not visit Winston until March 1886, when he contracted pneumonia and almost died.

This period of Winston's schooling coincided with the brief phase of Lord Randolph's career in which his brand of progressive Conservatism became increasing influential in the party and his star rose rapidly, although he was already experiencing the first signs of ill health. He entered the cabinet as secretary of state for India in June 1885, when he was thirty-six and Winston was ten.

On this first occasion Lord Randolph stayed in office for only seven months until the minority Conservative government lost power in January 1886. Back in opposition, he led the party's resistance to Prime Minister William Gladstone's policy of Home Rule for Ireland, which the House of Commons rejected at the end of June. The Conservative leader Lord Salisbury, on being asked by Queen Victoria to form another government, requested an immediate dissolution of parliament. In the general election campaign that followed, Lord Randolph played what was acknowledged to be the leading role in winning a decisive majority for the Conservatives over all other parties. He emerged as the second most important figure in the new government formed by Lord Salisbury, holding the twin posts of leader of the House of Commons and chancellor of the exchequer.

On this second occasion Lord Randolph lasted in office for only five months. Just before Christmas 1886 he ostentatiously resigned over the opposition of some cabinet members to his plans to cut military spending. Lord Randolph's expectation had been that his actions would trigger a crisis from which he would emerge preeminent; but his budgetary proposals had caused such unease among his colleagues that Lord Salisbury calmly accepted his resignation, making no attempt to persuade his chancellor to change his mind.

Lord Randolph Churchill, in his short-lived prime.

Jennie was devastated. She had thrown herself behind her husband's career, yet he had not consulted her before making the move which had brought it to a sudden halt. Their marriage had already been under strain before this development, following which Lord Randolph left England for several months in early 1887 to lick his wounds and nurse his health overseas.

Still only thirty-three years old, Jennie kept up her social round. She found that many men were ready to fill the gap left by Lord Randolph's absence and by the doctors' diagnosis of his illness. A series of discreet affairs followed, in the course of which Jennie displayed her continuing attraction to dashing young officers. Among them was a young scion of a princely Austro-Hungarian family, Count Charles Kinsky,[17] who had first visited England in the late 1870s. He returned in the early 1880s as an attaché (and probably an intelligence agent) at the Austro-Hungarian embassy in London. When he won the Grand National steeplechase in 1883 on his own horse Zeodone at the age of twenty-four, Kinsky became a prize catch for London's hostesses. The short but confident and trim aristocrat could pick and choose between the many women who vied for his attention and it was Jennie to whom he was attracted more than anyone else. Kinsky and Jennie would each have other flings over the coming years, but their relationship proved a lasting love affair.

The turmoil in Jennie's personal life now took over from politics as her chief distraction from Winston's many appeals for more attention. Neither of his parents, for example, made it to Brighton in November 1887 to celebrate his thirteenth birthday.

Winston entered Harrow School in April 1888. Jennie paid more visits to Harrow, only a half an hour's journey by train from central London, than she had to Brighton, yet she still turned down most of Winston's requests for her presence.

---

17 Count Karl 'Charles' Kinsky (see People, p. 568).

She is most vulnerable to charges of neglecting her son in the summer of 1891 when he was sixteen years old and his father had left to spend nine months in southern Africa leading a gold-prospecting expedition that was designed to improve the family finances. Jennie took advantage of her husband's absence to spread her own wings at a time when her affair with Kinsky was its height. Her letters of the time carry an air of distraction; for example, when Winston was struggling with acute toothache and appealed to his mother to go with him to the dentist in London while the tooth was extracted, Jennie stayed with her party of house guests at the Newmarket races and sent her younger sister Leonie instead.

Still, soon after leaving Harrow, Winston would lament his mother's absence in words that are unusual for a twenty-year-old son: he would miss 'my own one love to talk to'.[18]

Mother and son were drawn together by the last stages of Lord Randolph's illness, which became so severe by the summer of 1894 that Jennie took him away for a long journey around the world to avoid its horrors.

In November 1894, just before his twentieth birthday, Winston learned from the family doctor that his father was terminally ill. The tone of his letters to his mother changed: 'Now about yourself. Darling Mummy ...'

Two months later, after her husband's death in January 1895, Jennie responded in kind. She declared that she would centre her ambitions on her sons; she changed the greeting at the top of her letters from the 'Dearest Winston' which she had used in his schooldays to 'My darling boy', 'My darling Winston' or just 'Darling Winston'. She cast off the vestiges of a Victorian parent, reverting to the easy intimacy more typical of her American upbringing. From this point onwards, Winston wrote in *My Early Life*, he

18 3 August 1894, WSC letter to JSC, CAC, CHAR 28/19/33–4.

and his mother 'worked together on even terms, more like brother and sister than mother and son'.[19]

Well, not quite. Jennie was quite capable of issuing firm parental guidance or strictures on her elder son's behaviour and attitudes, or of remonstrating with him fiercely when she thought it necessary. Jennie's elder sister Clara told Anita Leslie:

> [Jennie] could be a terror, but for that fatherless youth she was just right. Never flattering or possessive, she tempered his steel. And though everyone called her selfish she cherished his ambition, when better informed, more detached observers failed to discern greatness.[20]

Jennie suggested and supplied much of the reading material that Winston wanted after he decided that he had missed out on a 'liberal education'; she found literary agents, newspaper editors or publishers for him when he needed them; she spoke to top generals or politicians to ease his career path; she checked out the credentials of lecture agencies that wished to engage him; she 'boomed' (as she put it) his books and articles among her wide circle of friends; she arranged his first political engagements; she found his first houses and decorated them for him; she lent him her personal secretary and recruited his servants. She also acted as the first sounding board for the early political philosophy that Winston expounded in his letters to her from India, to which he travelled in 1896 as a subaltern in the army, aged twenty-one. She encouraged him to express himself, yet criticized him when she thought his conclusions too simple.

The mail between England and India left weekly and they wrote to each other almost every week. Letters took sixteen days to make the journey, travelling by land across Europe to southern Italy, then by sea to Bombay (now Mumbai) and on again overland to Bangalore

---

19 W. Churchill, *My Early Life*, p. 62.
20 A. Leslie, *Jennie*, p. xiii.

(now Bengalaru) where Winston was billeted. If either he or Jennie was away from home (and Jennie frequently 'visited' friends at their country estates), the letters had to be forwarded, adding extra days to their journey.

Hence any favour that Winston asked of his mother had to wait at least five or six weeks for a response. Seen from his end of the correspondence, she may have taken a long time to react to his many requests. I have ordered the letters, however, in the sequence that Jennie would have read or written them; seen from this perspective, she answered the great majority of her son's many requests promptly, patiently and to great effect. Her own social preoccupations rarely caused her to miss the weekly mail in the three years Winston spent in India.

The emotional intimacy of the correspondence while Winston was fighting on India's north-western frontier, in the Sudan or in southern Africa, faded after 1900 when his mother remarried. It did not help that she chose a man of her son's age, a young officer called George Cornwallis-West. Winston and Jack shared private misgivings about her decision, yet stood loyally by their mother, coached by her own adage: 'Remember that a son should always seek & find extenuating circumstances for his Mother.'[21]

Even after her second marriage Jennie featured surprisingly often in Winston's life for a son who was now twenty-five years old and a busy new member of Parliament. He was still a bachelor and looked to his mother for practical help with his clothes or furniture or secretarial arrangements; for Jennie's part, her son provided the opportunity to relive through him the life on the edge of politics which her husband's impulsiveness had denied her fifteen years earlier.

—

21 5 January 1917, JSC letter to GCW; P. Churchill and J. Mitchell, *Jennie*, p. 242.

Jennie believed, like the playwright George Bernard Shaw, in the age of the 'new woman' who could match any man in her education and was therefore equipped to be as bold or enterprising. She was one of the first homeowners to install electricity in a London home; she founded and edited an expensive literary magazine; she raised large sums of money from her network of wealthy friends to help good causes; she wrote magazine articles, two plays and a book; and she played the piano at private concerts.

The list of men who are thought to have slept with Jennie is long and often distinguished. She is supposed, for example, to have featured at the top of the Prince of Wales's list of mistresses for two years from 1895 to 1897. If this is correct (their correspondence is too discreet to confirm it), she displayed with the future king the same talent that she exercised with other former lovers: the ability to remain on friendly terms with them and to tap them for continuing favours, including towards her sons Winston and Jack.

She was 'an incredible mixture of worldliness and eternal childhood, in thrall to fashion and luxury,' wrote Edward Marsh, the man of many parts who became Winston's private secretary in 1905, 'yet never sacrificing one human quality of warm heartedness, humour, loyalty, sincerity or steadfastness and courage'.[22]

Jennie had her critics who claimed that she was selfish, talked too freely, was extravagant and sometimes short-tempered – all faults later laid at her elder son's door. The similarities between their characters have struck public and private observers alike. Just after Winston had moved to the Admiralty as first lord in 1912, the *Daily Express* observed Jennie organising a theatrical pageant at Earl's Court:

> As one realized the enthusiasm with which she has approached her work and complete grasp that she has of all the details, one began to understand how very much Mr Winston Churchill is the son of his mother ... He certainly owes to his American

---

22 E. Marsh, *A Number of People*, p. 154.

Jennie in Ireland, in the riding habit remembered by Winston.

mother the superb energy and thoroughness with which he astounded the Board of Trade, appalled the Home Office and is delighting the best elements at the Admiralty.

Anita Leslie encapsulates the link between Jennie and her son that fills their correspondence of forty years: 'Winston she completely understood. Hot-headed ambition, the thirst for fame, that gallivanting in the cannon's mouth, the bullying of publishers, the nagging of generals – all that lay in Jennie's province.'[23]

The letters begin in 1881 when Winston was not quite seven years old. A year earlier Jennie had told her mother that he was 'a most difficult child to manage'.[24]

---

23 A. Leslie, *Jennie*, pp. 394–5.
24 10 July 1880, JSC letter to C. Jerome; A. Leslie, *Jennie*, p. 70.

EDITORIAL NOTES

Abbreviations: Throughout the editorial text linking the letters I refer to Winston Churchill as Winston and his mother as Jennie. The headings of each letter and the footnotes use the initials by which they often signed themselves to each other once Winston was an adult, WSC and JSC.

I have left without elucidation the simple abbreviations that Jennie and Winston each used sometimes (although not always) for common words such as 'vy' for very, 'shd' or 'sh^d' for 'should' and 'wh' for 'which'.

For other abbreviations which they use, I provide the full form of the words abbreviated in square brackets after their first use in each chapter: e.g. 'S.H. [Salisbury Hall]'.

'Conservative and Unionist' Party: After 1845 the Tory group in British politics officially became known as the Conservative Party, although many people still used the term 'Tories' as a form of shorthand. Between 1895 and 1905 the party formed governments with the help of Liberal Unionists (those Liberals who opposed Home Rule for Ireland); it then changed its official name to the Conservative and Unionist Party between 1909 and 1922. Although its members were often known as Unionists throughout these years, for simplicity I have called them Conservatives – or Tories for short.

Dates: Where Jennie or Winston included dates in the body of their letters, I have left their format as they wrote it, including the writer's abbreviations such as 'Sept^r'.

Jennie and Winston each used different methods at different stages of their lives to date their letters (or sometimes forgot to include a date at all). I have adopted a standard format of date at the head of letters, as for example '1 September 1900'.

If Jennie or Winston omitted part or all of a letter's date, I have included the missing component within square brackets, wherever it has been possible to deduce it, e.g. '1 September [1900]'.

If the writer headed a letter just by a day of the week, yet it is possible to deduce the rest of the date on which it was written by the letter's contents or by postmark on its envelope, I have shown the date within square brackets followed by the day its author specified e.g. '[1 September 1900] Saturday'.

If the writer did not date a letter at all, in almost all cases I have adopted the date attributed to it by the Churchill Archives Centre and shown this within square brackets e.g. [1 September 1900]. I have over-ridden the archival attribution only in a very few cases where the content or context of the letter has convinced me to do so.

Ellipsis [...]: An ellipsis indicates that I have omitted a passage for reasons of space. I have not, however, included an ellipsis if post-scripts are omitted.

Footnotes: I have used footnotes to provide a brief and immediate explanation of the first reference in the letters to any person, place or event. If the person or place appears often in the letters, the first footnote ends 'see People' or 'see Places', followed by a reference to the fuller information about them then appears in the Appendix.

Greetings and sign-offs: JSC and WSC both varied the greetings and salutations they used at the beginning and end of their letters. I have shown them as written in each letter, although I have sometimes shortened a long sign-off to conserve space.

Money values: I have left each reference to a sum of money in its original form. For any amount of £ sterling mentioned before 1914, the simplest method of converting to a similar value today is to multiply the sum by 100. During the First World War, this multiplier should fall gradually until it reaches approximately 50 by the end of the war in 1918.

Punctuation and paragraph breaks: I have followed the punctuation used by each of Jennie and Winston, unless the sense of the sentence is difficult to grasp without making an editorial change.

Jennie often wrote in the style of a 'stream of consciousness', separating her phrases or sentences by a dash rather than by a comma or full stop. Nor did she necessarily start a new topic by switching to a new paragraph that started on a fresh line; often she just left a slightly wider gap than normal between her sentences to signal a change of subject.

I have adopted a policy converting her dashes into a full stop if they clearly separate sentences, for example if she started the next phrase with a capital letter. I have also inserted a paragraph break, starting on a fresh line, in those places where she left a longer gap than usual gap between sentences and switched topic.

Occasionally I have also inserted a paragraph break into Winston's letters where I feel that this helps comprehension by breaking up a long block of text.

1

HIS MOTHER'S SON

1881–90

'*Mice are not caught without cheese*'

THE YOUNG Churchill family returned to London from Dublin in March 1880. Although the Prince of Wales did not immediately lift his social boycott of the Churchills that had originally sent them into 'exile' (see Introduction, p. xxii), Lord Randolph rejoined the world of politics at Westminster with a perspective broadened by his exposure to abject levels of poverty in Ireland.

His elder son, Winston (WSC), now five years old, had a new younger brother Jack, born in February. Their mother Jennie (JSC) delegated the care of both boys to their nanny, Mrs Everest, who was in her early forties when she joined the family after Winston was born. Sometimes called 'Oom', 'Woom', 'Womany' or simply 'Everest' by her charges, she accompanied them when they travelled without their parents to visit her sister, who lived at Ventnor on the Isle of Wight, or their grandparents, the duke and duchess of Marlborough, who lived at Blenheim Palace in Oxfordshire.

There are two candidates for the first surviving letter from Winston to his mother. Both are thought to have been written in 1881, when he was six: one probably from Blenheim and the other from Ventnor. (Sadly, none of Jennie's letters to Winston during this period have survived, except one written in April 1889.)

— WSC to JSC —

[1881] Monday   [Ventnor]

My dear mama

I am so glad you are coming to see us. I had such a nice bathe in the sea to day.

love to papa, your loving son
winston

— WSC to JSC —

[1881]   [Blenheim][1]

My dear Mamma,

I am quite well and getting on very nicely with my lessons. Baby [Jack] is quite well. I am enjoying myself very much with love and kisses
Your affectionate
W.S. Churchill

— WSC to JSC —

1 April [1882]   [Blenheim]

Dearest Mama

It was such a lovely day yesterday that we went for a drive. I am enjoying myself here very much. It is so much nice being in the country. The gardens and the park are so much nicer to walk in than the Green

---

1   Home of the dukes and duchesses of Marlborough, near Woodstock in Oxford-shire (see Places, p. 578).

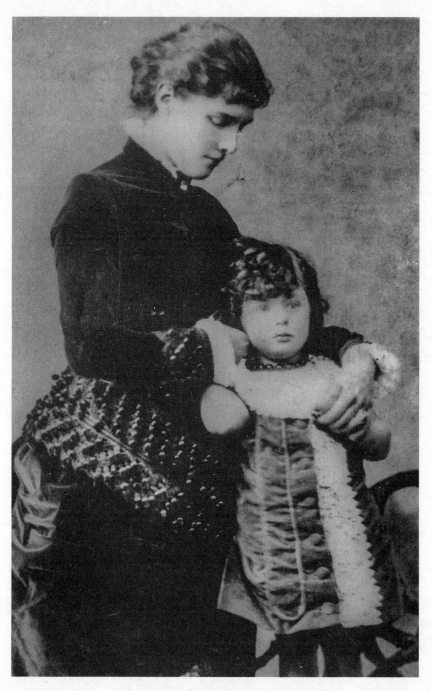

Jennie and Winston, aged four.

Park or Hyde Park. Baby is very well and sends you his love. I have been playing out of doors at making encampments which is great fun. I pretend to pitch a tent and make the umbrella do for it.

With best love to you and Papa, Ever your loving son
Winston

———

I N NOVEMBER 1882, Winston's parents sent him away to board at St George's School, Ascot, twenty miles west of London. Prep schools set aside a fixed time each week when boys would sit down to write a letter home to their parents, supervised by a member of the staff. He or she was there not only to maintain order, but to keep an editorial eye on the content of the letters being written home.

— WSC to JSC —

[3 December 1882]   St George's School, Ascot

My dear mamma

I hope you are quite well. I am very happy at school.

You will be glad to hear I spent a very happy birthday. I must now thank you for your lovely present you sent me. Do not forget to come down on 9th Dec^er.

With love and kisses I remain your loveing son,
Winston kisses xxxxx

———

B Y THE end of 1882 there were already signs that the regime at St George's was affecting Winston's health. The family doctor advised that he should spend a week by the sea before returning to the school in January 1883.

— WSC TO JSC —

[17 June 1883]   St. George's School, Ascot

My dear Mamma

I hope you will come and see me soon. Did Everest give you my flour I sent you. Give my love to my ants, and tell them not to forget to come down.

I am comeinge home <u>in a month</u>.

...W...I...T...H
love & kisses, I remain your loving Son
W.L.S. Churchill

— WSC TO JSC —

[November 1883]   St George's School, Ascot

My dear Mama

I hope you are quite well. The fireworks have been put off till next week. [...] I am in the singing class there is Humpty Dumpty, The lion & four wolves, Euclid, Softly falls the moonlight, The voice of the bell, Wilow the king, old daddy long legs.[2]

With love & kisses I remain your loving son
Winston

O N 9 March 1884, the Prince of Wales finally met the Churchills again at a dinner hosted by the attorney general, Sir Henry James. Prime Minister William Gladstone,[3] the chief political opponent of Lord Randolph, was a fellow guest.

---

2 'Humpty Dumpty' was set to music by James Elliott in his *Nursery Rhymes and Nursery* Songs, published in 1870. Musical copyright guides contain references to 'Softly Falls the Moonlight' (G. F. Briegel) and 'Old Daddy Long Legs' (George Wheeler), but not to the other songs.

3 William Gladstone was at the time in his second spell (of four) as prime minister (see People, p. 573).

Gladstone's government was pressing through parliament a reform bill that would abolish 'rotten boroughs' such as Lord Randolph's Woodstock constituency. He announced defiantly that at the next general election he would stand instead in Birmingham, a centre of radicalism represented by three Liberal members.

— WSC TO JSC —

16 March 1884   [St George's School, Ascot]

My dear Mama

I hope you are quite well. Mrs Kynnersly[4] went to Birmingham this week. And she heard that they were betting Two to one that Papa would get in for Birmingham.[5]

We all went too a sand pit the other day and playd a very exciting game. As the sides are about 24 feet high, and a great strugle, those who got out first kept a fierce strugle with the rest.

With love & kisses I remain your loving son
Winston

———

WINSTON'S SCHOOL report of March 1884 described his general conduct as 'very bad – is a constant trouble to everybody and is always in some scrape or another. He cannot be trusted to behave himself anywhere.'[6]

---

4   Wife of the headmaster of St George's School, Ascot.
5   In November 1885, Lord Randolph narrowly failed to win election in Birmingham; he was subsequently elected in the London constituency of Paddington.
6   R. Churchill, *WSC*, 1C1:94.

Albert Edward, Prince of Wales.

8 June 1884   [St George's School, Ascot]

My dear Mama

I hope you are quite well. It is very unkind of you not to write to me before this. I have only had one letter from you this term. Now though; I will have m[o]y point you must come down and see me on June 24ᵗʰ as it is a grand day with us we have a whole Holliday and I want you to come down to see me, let Everest come and Jack.

With love and kisses I remain your loving son
Winston

———

W INSTON DID not return to St George's School after the summer holiday of 1884. His health and general morale had declined since he had moved there and in *My Early Life* he recalled that 'a serious illness' in the summer holidays had precipitated his removal. Nanny Everest is said to have pointed out to Jennie the physical marks on his body caused by past beatings.

Corporal punishment was an integral feature of the disciplinary life of Britain's prep schools until the second half of the twentieth century. The headmaster of St George's School, a clergyman by the name of Revd Herbert Sneyd-Kinnersley, stands out, however, as a particularly brutal exponent of these beatings, according to accounts written later by some of Winston's contemporaries at the school.

To help restore him to proper health, his parents sent Winston to a school in Brighton, run by two elderly sisters, the Misses Thomson. It was recommended by the Churchills' new doctor, Dr Robson Roose, whose own sons attended the school; he promised to keep an eye on Winston for his parents.

— WSC to JSC —

28 October 1884   29 Brunswick Rd, Brighton

My dear Mamma

I hope you are quite well. I am quite happy here. I have been very extravagant. I have bought a lovely stamp book and stamps, will you please send me a little money. Good bye dear Mummy.

With Love And kisses, I remain your loving son.

Winston xxxxx

D R ROOSE'S task was no sinecure. In mid-December the ten-year-old Winston and a fellow pupil became involved in a fight that ended in Winston sustaining a minor stab wound. Jennie broke the news of the incident in a letter to Lord Randolph as he travelled to India: 'I hope I shall be able to manage him,' she told her husband, who was to be away another five months. 'I mean to make him do a little writing etc every morning.'[7]

— WSC to JSC —

21 January 1885   29 Brunswick Rd, Brighton

My dear Mamma,

I hope you are well. I am getting on pretty well. The Play is on the 11th of February 1885. You must be happy without me, no screams from Jack or complaints. It must be heaven upon earth. Will you try and find out for me what day Dr Rouse [sic] is going to take me to see Dr Woaks [Woakes][8] write and tell me. Will you tell me what day the mail goes to India, because I want to write to him [Lord Randolph].

With love and kisses I remain, your loving son,

Winston

7   18 December 1894, JSC letter to Lord Randolph; P. Churchill and J. Mitchell, *Jennie*, p. 128.
8   Edward Woakes, an aural surgeon, who practised at 78 Harley Street in London.

J ENNIE VISITED her son in Brighton on 12 February. 'I thought he looked very pale and delicate,' she reported to her husband. 'He told me that he was very happy & I think he likes the school.'[9]

— WSC TO JSC —

9 May 1885   29 Brunswick Rd, Brighton

My dear Mamma,

I hope you are quite well. Have you recovered your good health again as I expect you were rather frightened when the shaft went into your leg.[10]

I am looking for another letter from you. I recd a nice one from Papa this morning, he sent me a half dozen autographs I have been busy distributing them to-day everybody wanted one, but I should like you to send me a few of yours too. I must now say Good-bye.

I remain your loving son
Winston

L ORD RANDOLPH returned from India in April, still in poor health, then left again almost immediately to spend a month in France. For the first time Dr Roose referred Lord Randolph that summer to a neurological expert, Dr Thomas Buzzard.

In June 1885 Lord Salisbury appointed Lord Randolph to the cabinet of his new minority Conservative government as secretary of state for India. At the time ministers had to seek re-election as a member of Parliament in their constituencies on their first appointment to the cabinet. Jennie undertook most of the campaigning on her husband's behalf.

---

9   13 February 1895, JSC letter to Lord Randolph, *idem*, p. 129.
10   I have been unable to unearth details of the incident.

— WSC to JSC —

9 June 1885   29 Brunswick Rd, Brighton

My dear Mamma,

I hope you will accept my scribble. The weather is doubtful and there has been a sharp wind today. I like riding better than anything else so I know you will allow me to continue it.

You know that Postal Order you sent me, I could not get it cashed at the Post Office because it was crossed out, so I am going to send it back to you. [...]

I hope you will come and see me, the time is slipping away and if you do not come quickly it will not be worth coming at all. [...] Give my love to my aunts and Everest. [...]

With love and kisses, I remain your loving son,
Winston

B Y T H E end of the summer holidays of 1885, Winston was nearly eleven years old. He wrote from a house near Cromer, on the Norfolk coast, to which the Churchills had sent their children with not only their nanny but a governess, whose task was to administer some schooling.

— WSC to JSC —

2 September [1885]   Chesterfield Lodge

My dear Mama,

[...] I am not enjoying myself very much. The governess is very unkind, so strict and stiff, I can't enjoy myself at all. I am counting the days until Saturday. Then I shall be able to tell you all my troubles. I shall have ten whole days with you. [...]

With love and kisses I remain your loving son,
W. Churchill

THE MINORITY Conservative government proved short-lived; it fell on 28 January 1886. Ten days later, on 8 February 1886, a group of 'Revolutionary Social Democrats' organized a protest meeting of unemployed people in London's Trafalgar Square; after it was over, a section of the crowd broke windows and looted shops as they moved down Pall Mall, up St James's Street and along Piccadilly.

— WSC TO JSC —

14 February 1886   [29 Brunswick Road, Brighton]

My darling Mummy,

I trust you will not be the object of any malice at the hands of the London Mobs. I have a little plan to ask, namely:- to let Oom [Mrs Everest] and Jack stay a little longer. It makes me feel happy to think that my Oom and Jack are down here, so you will let them stay here, wont you?

With much love I remain, your loving son
Winston

THREE WEEKS later, Winston fell seriously ill with pneumonia. His parents both visited him in Brighton, in his father's case for the first time since Winston had joined the school eighteen months earlier. Their son spent a month convalescing in London.

In June of the same year, Lord Randolph was instrumental in bringing down the Liberal government of William Gladstone over the issue of Home Rule for Ireland. Lord Salisbury[11] became prime minister again; this time Lord Randolph was the government's most prominent minister in the Commons, serving as both chancellor of the exchequer and leader of the House of Commons.

The autumn brought a bout of marital *froideur* between Lord Randolph and Jennie, in the middle of which their son, now just

11 Robert Gascoyne-Cecil, marquess of Salisbury (see People, p. 573).

short of his twelfth birthday, introduced a new tone into his correspondence with his mother.

— WSC to JSC —

5 October 1886   29 Brunswick Rd, Brighton

My dear Mamma,

I have much joy in writing "Ye sealed Epistle" unto thee. I will begin by informing you the state of the weather after that, I will touch on various other equally important facts. I received your letter and intend to correspond in the best language which my small vocabulary can muster. The weather is fearfully hot. […] Last night we had a certain Mr Beaumont give a lecture on Shakespeare's play of *Julius Caesar*. He was an old man, but read magnificently. […]

I remain, Your loving son
Winston S. Churchill

— WSC to JSC —

14 December [1886]   29 Brunswick Rd, Brighton

My darling Mamma,

I hope you will not think my demand unreasonable, but nevertheless I shall make it all the same. Now you know that you cannot be watching a juvenile Amateur Play in the borough of Brighton, and at the same time be conducting a dinner party at,

2 Connaught Place
London.

If you go up to town in time for the dinner party you will not be able to see the Plays, but simply distribute the prizes and go.

Now you know I was always your darling and you can't find it in your heart to give me a denial, "I want you to put off the dinner party and take rooms in Brighton and go back on Monday morning. … You know that mice are not caught without cheese. […]

This petition I hope you will grant.

Love to all. I remain your loving son
Winston S. Churchill

———

THAT AUTUMN Lord Randolph had signalled his intention
to prune the government's military spending, always a risky
enterprise for a Conservative chancellor. Meeting internal resistance, he resigned suddenly on 23 December, expecting the prime
minister, Lord Salisbury, to back him by asking him to stay. Instead
Salisbury allowed the resignation to stand and calmly replaced
him with a former banker and Liberal Unionist politician, George
Goschen, whom Lord Randolph had 'forgotten' in his political
calculations.

He had given Jennie no warning of his resignation, which came
as a blow to her own social and political ambitions. The strain in
the Churchills' marriage lasted until February 1887, when it was
temporarily resolved before Lord Randolph set off on another long
journey through France, Italy and northern Africa.

— WSC TO JSC —

17 May 1887   29 Brunswick Rd, Brighton

My dear Mama,

I had the pleasure yesterday morning of receiving an Epistle from
thee, and in return intend to gladden the heart with one from me. I am
quite well. Rather a blunt sentence but you will think it very satisfactory,
I have no doubt. [...] mind & come down on 21st.

Love to all I remain, Your loving son
Winny

———

THAT SUMMER the first of many battles of will broke out in the
letters between Jennie and her elder son; it concerned Winston's

wish to return home for the celebration of the golden jubilee of Queen Victoria's accession to the throne on 20 and 21 June 1887.

— WSC ᴛᴏ JSC —

[11 June 1887]   29 Brunswick Rd, Brighton

My dear Mamma,

Miss Thomson does not want me to go home for the Jubilee because she says that I shall have no place in Westminster Abbey and so it is not worth going. Also that you will be very busy and unable to be with me much.

Now you know that this is not the case. I want to see *Buffalo Bill* and the Play you promised me. I shall be very disappointed, disappointed is not the word I shall be miserable, after you have promised me, and all, I shall never trust your promises again. But I know that Mummy loves her Winny too much for that.

Write Miss Thomson and say that you have promised me and you want to have me home. […] Don't disappoint me. If you write to Miss Thomson she will not resist you. […]

Love and kisses, I remain Yours as ever, Loving Son,
Winny

— WSC ᴛᴏ JSC —

[? 12 June 1887] Sunday   29 Brunswick Rd, Brighton

My dear Mamma,

[…] I am writing this letter to back up my last. I hope you will not disappoint me. I can think of nothing else but Jubilee. Uncertainty is at all times perplexing write to me by return post please!!! […] I must come home, I feel I must. Write to Miss Thomson after this principle so: [draft letter provided] …

Please, as you love me, do as I have begged you.

Love to All
I remain as ever, Your loving son
Winny

For Heavens sake Remember!!!

— WSC to JSC —

[15 June 1887]   29 Brunswick Rd, Brighton

Dear Mamma,

I am nearly mad with suspense. Miss Thomson says she will let me
go if you write to ask for me. For my sake write before it is too late.
Write to Miss Thomson by return post please!!!

I remain, Your loving son
Winny

— WSC to JSC —

[19 June 1887]   29 Brunswick Rd, Brighton

My dear Mamma

I am much better now though not very happy I am so dull and want
to come home so badly. I have not got much time.

Thanks for your letter. Won't forget the 21st. I shall have a lot of
news good and bad to tell you. Weather cold, & changeable. [...]

Good Bye. Much love I remain our loving son
Winny

WINSTON WAS on balance the winner of this tussle. He was
allowed to return home on 21 June, the second day of the
queen's jubilee celebrations and the day of her procession through the
streets of London. He did not return to school until two days later
and it is clear from his next letter that the visit did not go entirely
smoothly.

— WSC to JSC —

[24 June 1887]   29 Brunswick Rd, Brighton

My dear Mamma

I arrived hear [sic] alright yesterday, and took a cab to the school,

Winston (right) with Bertie Roose, the doctor's son (left), and Jack.

at which I arrived at 7.15. I am settling down alright now, though rather dull at first. [...]

I hope you will soon forget my bad behaviour while at home, and not to make it alter any pleasure in my summer Holidays. I telegraphed to Everest as soon as I arrived at the station. All serene. [...]

Please be quick and send me the autographs 6 of yours & 6 of Papa's.[12]

With much love, I remain as ever, Your loving son
Winny

———·———

I T WAS not long before plans for Winston's summer holidays did indeed turn into a new bone of contention between mother and son. He heard that his mother planned to hire a young German tutor to give him extra coaching.

— WSC TO JSC —

[July 1887]   [29 Brunswick Rd, Brighton]

My darling Mama,

I hear that you are going to get a tutor for me. I will just endeavour to trace an outline of my day – get up at 6 a.m. lessons till breakfast & lessons till 12. 12 AM go out for walk in town with the tutor. 1–4 lessons. 4–5 walk. 5 tea. 5.30–6.30 preparation. That is a sketch of my happy holidays.

I shall be miserable, utterly miserable. [...] I shall have to work until I am knocked up. We boys have 9 months hard work 8 hours a day. But only 3 months holidays, and 'tis hard that we should have to work in them. [...]

I would not mind at [sic] tutor under the following terms

I.   That I may always have my meals with you or Everest

———

12 WSC conducted a brisk trade in selling his parents' autographs for cash to his classmates.

II. That I need not walk with the aforesaid animal unless I like

III. That I don't do a stroke of work

IV. That I may have the right complaining to you in anything I don't like and you will rectify the same.

If not I cannot be happy. I will try & be a good boy if you will consent to rid me of the tyranny of this stealing, lying, catchpenny German blackguard.

I know you have too much love for me to do me the unkindness of letting him tyrannise over me. Do you think he will like to stand about while I catch butterflies? [...]

Please send me the autographs, book, & 5/-.[13]

I do love you mama so much. I know I am not right in writing to you in this way but I must do something.

Love and kisses, I remain Your loving son
Winston

— WSC to JSC —

[late July 1887]   [29 Brunswick Rd, Brighton]

My dear Mamma,

I am told that "Mr Pest" is going to be my tutor in the Holidays. Now as he is a Master here and I like him pretty well I shall not mind at all, on one condition v.i.z. "Not to do any work" I give up all other conditions except this one I never have done any work in my holidays and I will not begin now. [...] When I am doing nothing I don't mind working a little, but to feel that I am forced to do it is against my principles. [...]

I remain Your loving son
Winny

---

13 WSC had requested a copy of either *She* or *Jess*, both by H. Rider Haggard; 5/- was for a present to his teacher.

— WSC to JSC —

[14 July 1887]   [29 Brunswick Rd, Brighton]

My dear darling Mummy

I received your letter yesterday evening & I was very pleased to get the Autographs + 5/-. But I did not enjoy the letter quite so much, nevertheless I deserved it, I know. I promise you I will be a very good boy indeed in the Holidays. [...]

You may have thought me unaffectionate

But I always was & always will be, Your loving son
Winny

— WSC to JSC —

22 October 1887   29 Brunswick Rd, Brighton

Dearest Mother,

I am quite well – quite happy – in fact all that could probably be wished. Please try and get Father to come down to the Distribution of prizes as well as yourself. [...] I should like to come home for my birthday but then I should sacrifice any chance of a prize. I finished the 1st Book of Euclid to-day.

I suppose you are coming down for my birthday, I also suppose that we are going to have a party, are we not?!!!!! [...]

"The Examinations are drawing very near" I am glad of that as there is always some excitement then & I am hoping to have the success that is due to a long term of hard work. I can conscientiously say that I have learnt more in this term than I had learnt in the preceeding ones. [...]

Thank Father from me for his letter & autographs. Will you send me some more of yours not merely the initials but the full name "J.S. Churchill" as there is rather a demand for them here. I must now end this epistle as I shall not have time to do some Latin prose. Love to all

I remain Ever your loving son
Winston S. Churchill

JENNIE ENTERTAINED busily at home that autumn as part of her husband's attempt at a political comeback, but to little effect. By this stage Lord Randolph's interests leaned more towards horse racing, when his deteriorating health allowed.

Neither of Winston's parents visited him on his thirteenth birthday (30 November). Just before Christmas, they left their children behind while they spent six weeks in Russia and Germany, visits arranged by the Rothschild banking family. In Russia they were treated almost as royalty, fêted at court by the family of the tsar.

— WSC TO JSC —

14 December 1887   29 Brunswick Rd, Brighton

Dearest Mother,

Miss Thomson told me your plans before your letter arrived. I am very disappointed at hearing that I must spend my holidays without you. But I am trying to make the "best of a bad job". We shall not be able to have a Party of course. [...] I shall see you on Saturday and I have no doubt that you will try your best to make me happy.

I remain, Your loving son
Winston

— WSC TO JSC —

12 January [1888]   46 Grosvenor Square[14]

Dearest Mother,

Grandmamma has kindly allowed us to sleep here until you come back. I do long to kiss you my darling Mummy. I got your kind letter yesterday. How I wish I was with you, in the land of the "Pink, green, & blue roofs."

We have been staying at Blenheim lately – it was very nice. Everest is much better – thanks to Dr Roose. My holidays have been chopped

---

14 The London home of the dowager duchess of Marlborough.

about a good deal but as I expect an *exeat* [weekend leave] in the term I do not wish to complain. [...]

I remain with Love and Kisses, Your loving son
Winston S. Churchill

B Y EARLY 1888, Winston was thirteen years old, the age at which children of the British moneyed classes moved from their 'prep' school to their 'public' school, where they would normally remain until the age of eighteen. Lord Randolph had attended Eton, but he chose its close rival, Harrow School, for Winston. The school stood on a hill north-west of London, so its cleaner air was expected to benefit his son's still delicate health.

Winston had to gain a place at the school by passing an entrance exam in March 1888. Boys at Harrow lived in houses under the care of a housemaster, the choice of whom was therefore important.

— WSC to JSC —

7 February 1888   29 Brunswick Rd, Brighton

Dearest Mother,

I received your letter this morning, it was so nice to see it without a Russian stamp on it. I am longing so, to see you & Papa, it is such a long time since I saw you. I hope it has been arranged which house [at Harrow] I am to go to; I want to go to "Crookshank's"[15] as I know a boy there & would like to be with him. I am working hard – very hard – to get in – I only hope that my efforts will be rewarded. Mr Best says that I am certain to pass the Entrance [...]

Love to all, I remain Your loving son
Winston S. Churchill

---

15 Revd J. A. Cruickshank was housemaster of Church Hill at Harrow until 1891; the house was demolished in the 1920s to make way for the school's memorial to pupils who died in the First World War.

— WSC TO JSC —

16 March 1888   [29 Brunswick Rd, Brighton]

Dearest Mother,

I have passed, but it was far harder than I expected. I had 12 or 13 lines of very, very, hard Latin Translation and also Greek Translation No Grammer in which I hoped to score no French – no History no Geography the only things were Latin & Greek Trans. [...] However I am through which is the great thing. [...]

Harrow is such a nice place – beautiful view – beautiful situation – good swimming bath – a good Gymnasium – & a Carpentering shop & many other attractions.

You will often be able to come & see me in the summer it is so near to London you can drive from Victoria in an hour & 15 minutes or so. [...]

"My funds are in rather a low condition the Exchequer would bear replenishing." I am very tired so I must conclude.

With love & kisses I remain, Your loving son
Winston S. Churchill

———

WINSTON MOVED to Harrow School at the start of the summer term in April 1888. He started in a small boarding house run by Mr. H.O.D. Davidson, a married man in his mid-thirties who had himself been educated at Harrow.

— WSC TO JSC —

[20 April 1888]   [Harrow]

My dear Mamma,

I am writing according to promise. I like everything immensely. [...] Boys generally bring back hampers. I shall to have to find my breakfast. They only do that in large houses. At tea a boy had a chicken and jam and those sort of things. If you will send me a

1 chicken

3 pots jam

1 plum cake

I think that will be all. I am afraid I shall want some more money. [...]

With love & kisses I remain Your loving son

Winston S. Churchill

— WSC TO JSC —

[14 May 1888]   [Harrow]

My own Mummy,

I have been so naughty in not writing to you, but really the days simply fly & I have had a good deal of work outside school. However I have some news. I joined the Corps [army cadet force] as you know & attended my drills punctually. On Saturday I went with the corps to Rickmansworth & we fought Haileybury [a rival public school] it was very exciting. The plan of battle was (as far as I could make out) like this [sketch attached].

Mr Davidson's house at Harrow, 1888. Winston is standing on the left.

As I had not got a uniform I only carried cartridges. I carried 100 rounds to give away in the thick of the fight consequently my business enabled me to get a good view of the field. It was most exciting you could see through the smoke the enemy getting nearer & nearer.

We were beaten & forced to retire. [...]

With love and kisses, I remain Your loving son
Winston S. Churchill

— WSC TO JSC —

[27 June 1888]   [Harrow]

Dearest Mother

I read your letter the other day. My reports this week are:

Mathematics. 'Churchill has done decidedly better in the last week.'

Form Report. 'Conduct decidedly improved. Work irregular.'

I think I shall be higher this week 2nd or 1st. [...] Don't be cross with me any more. I will try and work, but you were so cross you made me feel quite dull. [...] I will try to work harder. Do come down Mamma on Saturday – I am not lazy & untidy but careless & forgetful. Good Bye My Mummy.

I remain, your loving son
Winston S. Churchill

— WSC TO JSC —

[October 1888]   [Harrow]

Dearest Mother,

Thank you very much for letting Jack and Everest come down.

Please try to come on Saturday & not to put it off. Come by train arriving at 2.30. Do try to come early because it spoils my afternoon to wait at the Railway Station.

Let me have a line to say whether you can come or not.

I want you to bring a nice hamper <u>the other boys have them</u>. [...]

I remain, Your loving son
Winny

7 November 1888   [Harrow]

Dearest Mamma,

I am going to write you a proper epistle, hoping you will forgive my former negligence. On Saturday we had a lecture on the

'Phonograph'

By 'Col Gouraud'.[16] It was very amusing he astonished all sober-minded People by singing into the Phonograph

'John Brown's Body lies – Mouldy in the Grave

And is [sic] soul goes marching on

Glory, glory, Halleluja'

And the Phonograph spoke it back in a voice that was clearly audible in the 'Speech Room'.

He shewed us it in private on Monday. We went in 3 or 4 at a time.

His boys are at Harrow.

He fought at Gettysburg.

His wife was at school with you. [...]

With love and kisses, I remain
Winston S. Churchill

———

A FTER CHRISTMAS, Jennie travelled to Paris to stay with her sister Leonie. There she pursued her relationship with Count Charles Kinsky.

[March 1889]   [Harrow]

My darling Mummy,

I am so delighted to hear that you have come home. I had been

---

16 Colonel George Gouraud, United States Army, who was Thomas Edison's agent in Europe after 1873 and introduced his invention of the phonograph at a press conference in London on 14 August 1888.

feeling quite dull at your protracted delay. However I am now sure that you are once again in 'Merry England'. Do try and come & see me soon. I am looking forward to a visit very much. I am rather, or rather my funds are rather low. However, I do hope that you will not go off to Ireland without seeing me.

Good Bye Mummy, With love & kisses I remain, Your loving son,
Winston S. Churchill

P.S. getting on very well in class.

WINSTON RETURNED to Harrow at the end of the Easter holiday, transferring to a larger house run by the headmaster, the Revd J. E. C. Welldon.[17]

— WSC TO JSC —

[15 May 1889]   [Harrow]

My dear Mamma,

I am very sorry I have not written to you before. I have written to Papa to thank him for sending me £7.2.6. for my Bicycle. I am getting on very well in Welldon's. All the boys are so kind and nice. I want a few more pictures and some white curtains. I have to pay for my breakfast and I have a 10/6 subscription to pay so I would not mind a little more cash.

Do try and come down soon I believe Saturday is a whole holiday. [...]

With much love I remain, Your loving son
Winston S. Churchill

ON WEDNESDAY 19 June Winston fell off what his mother supposed was his newly acquired bicycle, hitting the back of his head.

------

17 James Welldon became headmaster of Harrow School, in 1885, the year in which he was ordained as a priest (see People, p. 577).

— WSC to JSC —

[21 June 1889]   [Harrow]

My dear darlingest Mummy,

I am very well – considering. The fact is nothing what ever would have happened if I had been on any bicycle but I got on a tricycle to try it (please forgive the pun) and as I was used to a bicycle I turned too sharp [diagram] and then I went to sleep "or ever I reached the bottom".

I feel much better now. But I felt very sick yesterday & had a bad headache. They made rather a fuss but I suppose it amuses them. Thank you so much for sending Everest down to see me. She was a "great" big boon.

But I almost hope to see your face tomorrow. It is fearfully dull – mayn't read or anything & nothing to do but sleep (& grumble). If you don't come, send Womany [Mrs Everest]. In fact I should so like it, if you could let her come in the morning, whether you come or not.

I know you will think my requests exorbitant but it is so terrifically dull to lie & twiddle my thumbs all day that I hope you will give the "amendment" a "Second Reading".

And so Good Bye my dear mama, Much love from your ennuyéd
Winny

I N THE summer of 1889 Lord Randolph decided that his elder son should follow a career in the army. According to Winston's account in *My Early Life* Lord Randolph's decision followed a rare visit to the nursery, where he was impressed by his son's collection of 1,500 miniature soldiers, drawn up in battle formation. Winston acknowledged that his father might also have felt that his son did not show sufficient academic promise for a university education or a career in the law. In September, Winston therefore joined Harrow's army class, which prepared its members for the army's entrance exams.

— WSC to JSC —

[28 September 1889]   [Harrow]

My dear Mamma,

    I got your letter all right, I have joined the 'Army Class'. It is rather a 'bore' as it spoils your half Holiday: however we do French & Geometrical drawing which are the two things most necessary for the army. [...]

With love and kisses I remain, Your loving son
Winston S. Churchill

— WSC to JSC —

[5 October 1889]   [Harrow]

My darling Mummy,

    It is more than a fortnight since I have heard from you. In fact I have only had one letter this term. It is not very kind my darling Mummy to forget all about me, not answer my epistles. However remiss I may have been in the past in my correspondence, you must never scold me again about it. I have many requests to make. In the first place I beg that you will give me some money. [...]

    Please write to me soon and send me 'oof' [money] as I want to come up to town on Tuesday.

With much love, I remain your loving son
Winston S. Churchill

A LETTER OF 28 October from Winston asked his mother to arrange appointments with a doctor and a dentist in London so that he could have tea with her in between them. Its postscript betrayed a growing talent for bending others to Winston's will: 'P.S. Millbanke is writing this for me as I am having a bath'.[18]

---

18 28 October 1889, WSC letter to JSC (in the hand of J. Millbanke), CAC, CHAR 28/18/19–21.

Winston sent no further letter for a while, provoking the following reaction from Jennie in the first of her letters to her son that survives.

— JSC ᴛᴏ WSC —

[November 1889] Monday   2 Connaught Place

Dearest Winston

I suppose when yr exchequer is at a low ebb I shall have the pleasure of hearing from you.

Your affectionate
Mother

— WSC ᴛᴏ JSC —

[November 1889]   [Harrow]

Dearest Mummy

Not at all my darling Mummy, my Exchequer is quite full at present. I don't want anything for a wonder (except a hamper which is always welcome). I have written to ask Papa to come down tomorrow. <u>Don't go to Mashonaland</u>[19] it is very dangerous.

Goodbye my darling sceptical Mummy
Your loving son
Winston S. Churchill

———

WINSTON'S HONEYMOON with the authorities at Harrow had come to an end and he was placed on 'reports', the school's system for keeping a close track of boys with unsatisfactory work or behaviour. For help in fighting his corner, he turned to his mother rather than his father.

---

19 WSC's appeal suggests that his parents were already considering an expedition by Lord Randolph to prospect for gold in Mashonaland, southern Africa; he left (without JSC) in April 1891.

Jack, Jennie and Winston, 1889.

— WSC to JSC —

[November 1889]   [Harrow]

My dear Mamma,

You know that you spoke to Welldon, when you came down last, about taking me off reports. Well he said to you he would do so of course the moment I got a good report I am on still. [...]

I hope you don't imagine that I am happy here. It's all very well for monitors & Cricket Captains but its quite a different thing for fourth form boys. Of course what I should like best is to leave this [hell of a][20] place but I cannot expect that at present. But what I want you to do is to come down and speak to Welldon on Tuesday. Please don't be afraid of him because he always promises fair & acts in a very different way. You must stick up for me because, if you do not nobody will. [...] Now

---

20 Later crossed out.

you know Mamma that you told me to rely on you & tell you everything so I am taking yr advice.

> *Good Bye my own Mummy, Hoping to see you on Tuesday,*
> *I remain, Your loving son,*
> *Winston S. Churchill*

— JSC to WSC —

[25 January 1890] Saturday   2 Connaught Place

Dearest Winston

We were delighted to hear that you had yr remove [promotion in class] & I do hope that you will continue to work. You ought to feel much encouraged & full of ambition. We are off at 3 oc [o'clock] & I fear will have a fearful tossing as it is blowing a gale.[21] Everest will go & see you next Tuesday – as she has a great deal to do today. Will you, you naughty boy! explain to me where the economy comes in, of sending 2 letters in one envelope – & at the same time telegraphing next day to Everest – when a letter wl^d have done as well? Mind you write at least twice each week, & write to Jack. Goodbye darling – best love

> *Yr loving Mother*
> *JSC*

— JSC to WSC —

7 February 1890   Grand Hotel, Monte Carlo

Dearest Winston

[...] Papa returns to London tomorrow – but stops a night in Paris. I daresay if he is not too busy with his parliamentary work, & you write & ask him, he might go to see you next Saturday. I am so pleased that you are working up – it must be a great feeling of satisfaction to you – it certainly is to me! [...]

> *Goodbye darling – mind you write.*
> *Yr loving*
> *Mother*

---

21 WSC's parents were due to cross the English Channel by ferry to France.

THERE FOLLOWS a first hint of Winston's artistic talent.

— WSC TO JSC —

12 March 1890   [Harrow]

My dear Mamma,

How are you? How is poor Uncle Moreton.[22] How is Grandpapa?[23] [...] I am getting on in drawing and I like it very much. I am going to begin shading in Sepia tomorrow. I have been drawing little Landscapes and Bridges and those sort of things. [...]

Well good bye
With much love, I remain, Ever your loving son
Winston S. Churchill

LORD RANDOLPH was now increasingly ill (and absent), so Jennie continued to play the role of mentor towards her son that Victorian society would normally have expected of a father. Lord Randolph had sent his son £5 at the beginning of June. Winston did not acknowledge it until 8 June when he started his letter to his father: 'Thanks awfully. I was quite astounded – stricken "all of a heap in fact".'[24]

— JSC TO WSC —

12 June 1890   2 Connaught Place

Dearest Winston

I am sending this by Everest, who is going to see how you are getting on. I would go down to you – but I have so many things to arrange about the Ascot party next week that I can't manage it.

---

22 Moreton Frewen, married to JSC's elder sister Clara (see People, p. 566).
23 JSC's father, Leonard Jerome, who moved from New York to the seaside air of Brighton, England, in October 1889 (see People, p. 566).
24 [8 June 1890] WSC letter to Lord Randolph, CAC, 1C1:203–4.

I have much to say to you, I'm afraid not of a pleasant nature. You know darling how I hate to find fault with you, but I can't help myself this time. In the first place your father is very angry with you for not acknowledging the gift of the 5£ for a whole week, and then writing an offhand careless letter.

Your report which I enclose is as you will see a <u>very</u> bad one. You work in such a fitful inharmonious way, that you are bound to come out last – look at your place in the form! Yr father & I are both more disappointed than we can say, that you are not able to go up for yr preliminary exam: I daresay you have 1000 excuses for not doing so – but there the fact remains. If only you had a better place in your form & were a little more methodical I would <u>try</u> to & find an excuse for you.

Dearest Winston you make me very unhappy – I had built up such hopes about you & felt so proud of you – & now all is gone. My only consolation is that your conduct is good and you are an affectionate son – but your work is an insult to your intelligence. If you would only trace out a plan of action for yourself & carry it out & be <u>determined</u> to do so – I am sure you could accomplish anything you wished. It is that thoughtlessness of yours which is your greatest enemy. [...]

I will say no more now – but Winston you are old enough to see how serious this is to you – & how the next year or two & the use you make of them, will affect your whole life – stop & think it out for yourself & take a good pull before it is too late. You know dearest boy that I will always help you all I can.

Your loving but distressed
Mother

– WSC to JSC –

[19 June 1890]   [Harrow]

My darling Mummy

I have not written till now because I can write a much longer letter. I will not try to excuse myself for not working hard, because I know that what with one thing and another I have been rather lazy. Consequently when the month ended the crash came I got a bad report & got put on reports etc. etc. That is more than 3 weeks ago, and in the coming months I am <u>bound</u> to get a good report as I have had to take daily reports to Mr Davidson twice a week and they have been very good on the whole.

And then about not answering Papa's letter – I did that very evening & I gave it to the Page to put in the Pillar box & a 1^d [for postage] for him at the same time.

I could not put it there myself because it was after Lock-up. He I suppose forgot and did not post it until several days had elapsed. My own Mummy I can tell you your letter cut me up very much. Still there is plenty of time to the end of term and I will do my <u>very best</u> in what remains. [...]

Good Bye, my own,
With love I remain, Your own
Winston S. Churchill

2

TRIALS WITH A TEENAGER

1890–92

'Too busy with your parties'

WINSTON RETURNED to Harrow for the new school year in September 1890, two months before his sixteenth birthday. In December he was due to sit the army's preliminary exam, the first stage required for admission to the Royal Military College at Sandhurst, which trained all young officer cadets.

In the same month, Jennie set off without her husband on a tour of her friends' Scottish country estates, a progress that became a regular feature of her social calendar each September and October until the outbreak of the First World War. It usually lasted for between six and eight weeks, taking in half a dozen estates.

Given Lord Randolph's frequent absences and ill health, she was now becoming used to acting virtually as a single parent to their children.

— JSC ᴛᴏ WSC —

[September 1890] Friday 19   Invermark, Brechin[1]

Dearest Winston

I hope you enjoyed yr play Tuesday night – & that you two got back to school all right – & are now settling down to your work. I was so sorry to leave in such a hurry – hardly had time to say goodbye to you & Jack. [...]

Darling Winston I hope you will try & not smoke. If only you know how foolish & silly you look doing it you w^d give up, at least for a few years. If you give it up & work hard this term I will get Papa to get you a gun & a pony & perhaps next season there will be something to shoot at Banstead.[2] Anyhow dear – I will do my best to get you some sport & make you enjoy yourself – but you must do something for me in return. Now mind you write me a nice long letter & tell me all you do. I want you _so_ much to get on. Don't forget to brush your teeth! & think of me.

Your loving
Mother

— WSC ᴛᴏ JSC —

[21 September 1890] Sunday   [Harrow]

My dear Mamma

I have just recd your letter. Thank you very much. I will leave off smoking at any rate for 6 mths because I think you are right. [...]

Good Bye my darling Mummy, With ever so much Love
I remain, Your loving son
Winston S. Churchill

---

1   Estate of the Dalhousie family in Angus (see Places, p. 580).
2   Property near Newmarket racecourse, rented by the Churchills (see Places, p. 578).

— WSC to JSC —

[13 October 1890]   [Harrow]

My dear Mamma,

I have not written before because I did not know your address.
I wish I were with you. Mind & bring the shooting hat home & one for
Jack too. […]

I have had a tremendous hamper from Fortnum & Mason sent
anonymously. It must have cost at least £3.10s. I rather suspect Lady
Wilton,[3] who has answered a letter I wrote.

I am working very hard & I hope to pass my Preliminary [exam]
in at least 3 subjects. […] But I am afraid I shall fail in arithmetic &
Algebra & Geometrical Drawing. […] Still I have a good 2 months to
go before me and am working 'to some purpose'.

> *Good bye my darling Mummy, With much love & many kisses*
> *I remain, Your loving son*
> *Winston S. Churchill*

— WSC to JSC —

[November 1890]   [Harrow]

My darling Mama,

I hear that you are greatly incensed against me! I am very sorry –
But I am very hard at work & I am afraid some enemy hath sown tares
in your mind. I told you I thought I should not pass my Preliminary
on account of my being put under a master with whom I hated & who
returned that hate. Well I complained to Mr. W. [Welldon] & he has
arranged all things beautifully. I am taught now by masters who take
the greatest interest in me & who say that I have been working very
well. […]

I have been working very hard & if not slanged too much stand a

---

3   Elizabeth, formerly countess of Wilton, widowed 1885; childless, she styled
    herself 'your deputy mother' in letters to WSC (see People, p. 569).

very fair chance & I have much the best chance of knowing. [...] Besides if you want to give me a chance please let me know the extent of the evil of which I am accused. [...]

Good Bye my darling Mummy, With love from
Winny

———

T HE RESULTS of the examination arrived in the middle of January 1891: Winston passed in all subjects.

— WSC TO JSC —

[21 January 1891]   [Harrow]

Darling Mummy,

I skated today on Ducker.[4] It is very wet a quarter of an inch of water all over, but the ice is beautiful, quite clear & very very slippery. [...]

I have had to buy a lot of things for my room. Do come down tomorrow, like a darling. I am very anxious to talk to you on a lot of subjects before you journey to Monte Carlo. Please come down & skate part of the time, but come alone, because I find there are several things which I want to talk to you about. [...]

I remain, Your loving son
Winston S. Churchill

— JSC TO WSC —

[22 January 1891] Thursday   2 Connaught Place

Dearest Winston

I am very sorry not to be able to get to you today, but Grandpapa

---

4   In the Harrow vernacular, 'Ducker' was the school's irregularly shaped swimming pool, built in 1866.

is not quite so well[5] & Grandmamma has asked me to go back there this afternoon. If possible I will go to see you on Saturday or Jack & Everest will go.

Dear boy, I do hope you are sticking to yr work & are not spending all yr money. [...]

With best love Yr loving
Mother

— WSC TO JSC —

[late February/early March 1891]   [Harrow]

Darling Mamma,

I do not know where you are, nor how grand papa is, nor how Jack is, nor when you return from Brighton, if you are there, nor anything. Please write to me by return of Post dear Mummy. Will you send me a P.O.O. for £1 if you please. Do write to me.

I remain, Your loving son
Winston S. Churchill

———

I N APRIL 1891 Lord Randolph left England at the head of a gold-prospecting expedition to southern Africa organized by the Rothschilds. He would be away until January 1892.

Jennie used his long absence to spread her social wings, often spending time hosting parties of her friends at Banstead, a manor house close to Newmarket and its racecourse, which the Churchills had rented with the financial help of the dowager duchess of Marlborough.

---

5   Leonard Jerome died in Brighton on 3 March 1891 at the age of 73.

— WSC to JSC —

[April 1891]   [Harrow]

Darling Mummy,

My face is swelled up double its natural size through toothache. I have made an appointment with Pritchard [a London dentist] for Tuesday. I have got some money of my own which you gave me, but want you to send me journey money for Tuesday. [...]

As it will play old Harry with my Finances to pay this sum. I have paid my debts & relinquished Betting. I have lost your address so I have to send this through Auntie Clara [Frewen].

Please send me the "oof" in time.

Will you be in town on Tuesday? Write & let me know.

Good bye my darling,
With love & kisses I remain, Your tooth tormented – but affectionate – son
Winston S. Churchill

— JSC to WSC —

[29 April 1891] Wednesday   Banstead

Dearest Winston

I am <u>so</u> sorry to hear you have a toothache, & I hear from Everest that the dentist cannot see you until tomorrow. Perhaps he will pull it out. I don't want to lecture on the subject – but I am sure if you wl^d take a little more care of yr teeth you wl^d not suffer so much. Quite apart from the "pigginess" of not brushing them!! However I do hope darling that you are better. I am quite settled here & like it very much. The Curzons[6] & Lady Kaye[7] are with me, and tho' I do not go to the races, I see people & it is pleasant. [...]

Write to me often my darling. Yr loving Mother
JSC

<u>So</u> glad you have yr remove.

---

6 Richard Curzon, later Earl Howe, and his wife Georgiana, née Spencer-Churchill (see People, p. 563).
7 American-born wife of Sir John Lister-Kaye, a soldier.

— JSC to WSC —

[10 May 1891] Sunday   Banstead

My dearest Winston,

I am so sorry to hear that you have had such a bad time with yr teeth. I expect you will have to have one out – otherwise am glad to hear that you are well & happy.

Grandmama Marlborough[8] has been very seriously ill with influenza & bronchitis, but she is better now. We have all been very much worried about her – you must write & tell her you are glad to hear she is better.

Everything is going on well here. I am expecting a few people for the races this week. [...]

Write to me my darling & tell me all you do. I will go and see you the first time I go to town in about a fortnight. I hope you are working hard.

Yr loving Mother

— WSC to JSC —

[19 May 1891]   Harrow

My darling Mummy,

I wrote to you on Thursday and you did not answer. I am well & all right, but have just been in the deuce of a row for breaking some windows at a factory. There were 5 of us & only 2 of us were discovered. I was found, with my usual luck, to be one of these 2. I've no doubt Mr Welldon has informed you of the result. [...]

Please come & see me on Thursday or Saturday, anyway please send me a little money to keep the exchequer solvent. Please send £1 by next post as I am absolutely '*oofless*'.

Good Bye my darling Mummy.
With much Love, I remain, Your loving son
Winston S. Churchill

---

8   Frances Spencer-Churchill, widow of the 7th duke of Marlborough (see People, p. 565).

O N 9 June the dentist lanced an abscess on Winston's tooth; two days later he warned his mother that the tooth would have to be removed and asked her to accompany him to the dentist in London when this happened. He repeated his request on 13 June.

— WSC TO JSC —

[13 June 1891]   Harrow

Darling Mummy,

I have got an appointment for 4.30 on Thursday afternoon with Doctor Braine.[9] Do come up & write & tell Welldon you will look after me & "give me Tea."

I have no more pain. Please do come I shall not like going alone at all.

Good Bye my darling, With love & kisses
I remain, Your loving son
Winston S. Churchill

— JSC TO WSC —

[18 June 1891] Thursday   Oakley Court, Windsor[10]

Dearest Winston,

I am so sorry I could not go up to meet you today but it was impossible.

I hope you went to Aunt Clara's. She promised she would look after you. Write here & tell me how you got on with yr tooth.

I shall try & see you one day next week – The weather at last is warmer.

Goodbye & bless you – Yr loving Mother
JSC

---

9   Dr Charles Carter Braine, anaesthetist at the Royal Dental Hospital from 1890.
10 Victorian Gothic mansion, owned by the estate of Lord Otho Fitzgerald; rented out since the death of his wife in 1883.

Mrs Clara Jerome (seated, left) with her daughters
(from left to right) Clara, Leonie and Jennie.

— WSC to JSC —

[19 June 1891]   Harrow

Darling Mummy,

I had my tooth taken out very successfully. I remembered nothing
but went to sleep & snored throughout the whole performance. Do
send me some money as I am awfully hard up owing to journey money
for dentist. I am coming up to town on Thursday by the 3.30 to have
another out, do try and come. Auntie Clara was very kind.

Goodbye Your loving son
Winston S.C.

— WSC to JSC —

[21 June 1891]   Harrow

Darling Mummy,

Do come up & meet me on Thursday. I come by the 3 o'clock from
Harrow. I am very well. I like the Dentist and think him a much more
capable man than Pritchard. Please send me £1 as I have had to pay an
old Bicycle debt of 10/- that I had quite forgotten.

Also I have to pay 8/- as my share of those windows we smashed.
Please send it to me before Tuesday as I have to pay the 8/- then.

Goodbye my darling Mummy, Ever your loving son
Winston S. Churchill

— WSC to JSC —

[25 June 1891]   Harrow

Darling Mummy,

So sorry you could not come. Have got to pay some of that
'Window Smashing stupidity.' 8/-. Various other items; Will explain ad
lib. Please give me 30/- shall be awfully delighted.

Excuse Telegraphic communication as the Post leaves in 10 minutes.
[...]

Ever your loving son
Winston

— JSC to WSC —

[28 June 1891] Sunday   Compton Place, Eastbourne[11]

Dearest Winston,

I shall be up by one but fear I shall just miss you – I do hope yr face is better & that the abscess has burst. Auntie Leonie promised to look after you today. I wish you were here – such a lovely place – just 15 mts from the sea. It is blowing somewhat but we are going for a long walk notwithstanding. I shall hope to see you tomorrow. If not let me know when the Eton & Harrow match takes place.

Yr loving Mother
JSC

— WSC to JSC —

[29 June 1891]   [Harrow]

Darling Mummy,

It was a pity you could not come to see me on Sat. I did not expect you & so was not disappointed. Mr Searle says there is every chance of my being allowed to come to your concert,[12] however we can talk it over at 'Lords'. [...]

I have copied our Papa's letter and sent it to Jack.

Good Bye my darling Mummy, with love & Kisses
I remain, your loving son
Winston S. Churchill

WINSTON'S REFERENCE to 'Lord's' (as he should have spelled it) concerned the annual cricket match between Eton and Harrow which was played on the Friday and Saturday of the second

---

11 Owned since 1858 by the duke of Devonshire who laid out the new town of Eastbourne in the southern part of the estate.
12 JSC often performed as a pianist at private concerts.

weekend of July (in 1891 it fell on 10–11 July) at the headquarters of the sport, Lord's cricket ground in St John's Wood, London. The fixture had become one of the main events of the capital's social season each summer.

– WSC to JSC –

3 July 1891   [Harrow]

My darling Mummy,

Please do all you possibly can for me. Think how unhappy I should be being left at Harrow when 90 out of every hundred boys are enjoying themselves. You promised me I should come. It is no special exeat but a regular holiday given in the Summer Term to every boy whose conduct has been such to merit it. I was terribly frightened when I got your letter [missing] this morning. The Possibility of my not being able to come being to my mind entirely out of the question. Could you not ask Grandmamma Marlborough to let me stay with her (at least).

I managed all right about Speech day (having taken the precaution of writing & of telegraphing) Mummy darling if you knew or had known how much I was looking forward to my 'Lords' I am sure you would have endeavoured to avoid that Engagement, or make some provision for my holiday.

It will be a poor time indeed for me if I have to go to Lords, Friday & Saturday as a Harrow boy & answer my name every 2 hours & not leave the ground etc (as 100 other unfortunates usually have to do.) [...]

Where is everybody?

No one has written to me to tell me any news for a long time. Where is Everest.

Do try my Darling Mummy to please your loving son
Winston S. Churchill

———

THE CHURCHILL family's financial difficulties had forced Jennie to rent out their house at Connaught Place for the summer while

Lord Randolph was away. When she was in London, she stayed officially at Moreton and Clara Frewen's home in Aldford Street, although Moreton commented to Clara who was in Paris: 'Jane [Jennie] is here – at least I suppose she is – but she is on the fly and I see nothing of her.'[13]

Without her own London base, Jennie spent time at Banstead or was easily tempted by an invitation to join a house party at a country estate, even if its date coincided with a fixture in her children's school calendar. Such a clash occurred over Harrow's 'Lord's weekend', when Winston had earned the right to stay overnight in London as a reward for good conduct, whereas Jennie had accepted an invitation to spend the weekend with the Comte de Paris at Stowe House in Buckinghamshire, which the *comte* had leased.

– JSC to WSC –

[5 July 1891] Sunday   Banstead

Oh! Dear oh! Dear what an ado!! You silly old boy I did not mean that you would have to remain at Harrow only that I cl^d not have you here, as I am really obliged to go to Stowe on Saturday. But I shall see you on Friday & can arrange something for you. I shall be at Aunt Clara's. Perhaps she can put you up too. I will write & let you know. [...]
Goodbye my darling. Write to Aldford Street where I go tomorrow.
Your loving Mother

– JSC to WSC –

[6 July 1891] Monday   18 Aldford Street

Dearest Winston,
It is all right. Grandmama Marlborough will put you & Jack up Friday night & I suppose you go back Saturday evening? Write & tell me. I am trying to arrange for a coach – for Lord's –

---

13 July 1891, M. Frewen, letter to C. Frewen, Frewen Papers, Library of Congress.

You must come here the first thing – & mind you make yrself <u>very</u> smart –

Yr loving mother
JSC

W INSTON SPENT Friday 10 July at Lord's with his mother. On the Saturday Charles Kinsky came to the rescue by taking Winston to the Crystal Palace where 100 fire engines and 3,000 firemen paraded in front of the emperor of Germany before a display of fireworks.

Once Jennie had navigated the demands of 'Lord's weekend', she had to deal with her son's demands for the school holidays which were due to start in late July and last until the middle of September.

— WSC TO JSC —

[14 July] 1891   [Harrow]

My darling Mummy,

Mr Welldon told me last night that he had written to you about my going to spend "at least 4 weeks" in France. His ideal of course is a 'family' one of his own 'specials'. I told Papa when he came down that I ought (in Mr W's opinion) to go, but he said "utter nonsense, if you like I'll get a German scullery maid for Banstead". I'm sure you would not like me to be away the greater part of the holidays with some horrid French Family. It would be perfectly – well unpleasant. Besides practically there is no hurry. I have very nearly 3 years at the outside limit. [...]

Of course it is (as says Welldon) entirely in your hands. But I am sure you will not send me to any such abominable drudgery with your free consent.

Even if the worst comes to the worst you could send me to some of your friends & not to the 'respectable creatures'. A governess would I am sure answer all the immediate colloquial requirements. As Papa

Jennie flanked by Count Charles Kinsky (left) and Lord Dudley.

absolutely veto'ed the idea & as I beg you to let me have a bit of fun.

I remain Your loving son
Winston S. Churchill

P.S. Really I feel less keen about the Army every day. I think the church would suit me better. Am well, safe, & happy. [...]

— JSC to WSC —

[July 1891]   [no address]

Dearest Winston,

<u>Too</u> sorry to have missed you – you ought to have wired. Write to me fully about next week – do you want money?

Yr loving Mother

— WSC to JSC —

[24 July 1891]   [Harrow]

My darling Mummy,

I am so sorry I missed you. I did send a telegram but I thought you were staying at 18 Aldford Street. I can't tell you how happy I am to hear that I am not to go abroad for the holidays. [...]

About the Camp [for army cadets]. [...] The board & Lodging is to cost 30/- a week, but I expect the food will be passing meager so as I shall have to amuse myself in the afternoons, Money will be most agreeable. [...]

Ever your loving son
Winston S. Churchill

— JSC to WSC —

[July 1891]   18 Aldford Street, London

Dearest Winston,

I thought it was something about money – I send you the £1.1.0. you want & will reserve my lecture for tomorrow!

Affectly
Mother

J ENNIE, WINSTON and Jack spent most of the holiday together at Banstead, much of it in the company of Kinsky, whose affair with Jennie was then at its height. A 'nice young man from Cambridge' gave the boys some light tuition for four weeks.

Winston returned to Harrow two days late in September because, as Jennie wrote to her husband, he 'conveniently worked himself into a bilious attack ... honestly he is getting a bit too old for a woman to manage. [...] Winston will be all right the moment he gets into Sandhurst. He is just at the 'ugly' stage – slouchy and tiresome'.[14]

– WSC to JSC –

[19 September 1891]   [Harrow]

Darling Mummy,

Welldon wants you to write to him & 'explain' why I did not come back Thursday. 'The Doctors Certificate' says he 'accounts for Wed'. I told the animal I understood that if you telegraphed, it was sufficient. "Nay" saith he. But I see & he says he does not want to make a row. So he proposes that you should write him a letter saying that I was unable to 'favour him with my presence' on account of – anything. Twiggez-vous?

Don't say anything about the Theatre or that would make him rampant. [...]

With much love & many kisses
I remain your dull homesick exiled darling
Winston S. Churchill

– WSC to JSC –

[22 September 1891]   [Harrow]

My Darling Mummy,

I am quite settled down & happy now. My room is very pretty & I

---

14 25 September 1991, JSC letter to Lord Randolph, Blenheim Papers.

have not bought any pictures, only 1 pr of candlesticks (second hand) a mantel board, & a curtain for my bed. These are all necessities. I have been allowed to leave off German & take up Chemistry instead. I am so glad, it means that I can safely declare that I will pass next June. [...]

With love & kisses I remain
Your loving son
Winston S Churchill

— WSC TO JSC —

[27 September 1891]   [Harrow]

My darling Mummy,

Why have you not written to me, as you said you would, in answer to my 3 letters! I think it is very unkind of you because I am very dull here, and am working very hard. I don't know whether you have made the appointment I asked you to for Tuesday or anything. If Everest did not write to me I should hardly imagine there was such a place as Banstead. [...]

I suppose you are busy with your 'race party' & so have not time to send me a line. I have been back 10 days & you have not sent me a single word. If you have not time to write you might telegraph, that takes very little time.

Please darling mummy do write to your Loving son
Winston S Churchill

— WSC TO JSC —

[28 September 1891]   [Harrow]

Darling Mummy,

Oho! Aha! What did you say? Every letter I wrote – eh? You would answer – was it not so? And now Behold I have written 3 long epistles & not one single SOLITARY LINE have I recd. [...]

I am going to sell my bicycle for a Bull-dog. I have known him some time & he is very tame & affectionate. [...] He is a celebrated blood dog

& worth a £10. I have never had a decent dog of my own & Papa told me he used to have a bulldog at Eton so why not I at Harrow. [...]

I have asked credible judges about the dog & they all say he is a very good animal. So please write my mummy & give your gracious consent. [...]

Good bye my bird, With much love I remain your ever loving son
Winston S. Churchill

— JSC TO WSC —

[29 September 1891]   Banstead

Dearest Winston,

I confess that I have been very remiss about writing – but I have been too busy. Do as you like about yr bicycle but it wl^d be wiser I think to keep it – a dog is sometimes a nuisance. I can only write you a hurried line as the post is off, but I will do so shortly & tell you the news. [...]

Goodbye my darling. Will write again.
Yr loving
Mother

———

THE BULLDOG had to find another home. Jennie visited Winston at Harrow early in October and gave the still absent Lord Randolph a positive account of his son's appearance and behaviour. Winston wrote frequently to his mother in October, largely without success, so he contacted the family cook at Banstead, Mrs Keen, directly about sending him some extra food at school.

— JSC TO WSC —

28 October 1891   Banstead

Dearest Winston,

Since seeing you I have been so busy I have not had time to write.

I have been very remiss I confess – but dear child your letters always have the same refrain "please send me money". You do get through it in the most rapid manner. Here is a P.O.O. for £1.

Mrs Keen informs me that you have sent an "order"? for ducks etc. The house being full of people she hasn't time to cook them until the end of the week. You ought to have written to me to ask. I was horrified to hear from Everest that you had had another tooth out. It is <u>too</u> silly of you & you will regret it. Send me the address of the dentist who did it as I wish to see him & give him a piece of my mind. [...]

I have just had a wire from Papa who is very well & returns by Tuli & Mafeking.[15] I will write again.

Best love, Yr Loving
Mother

— WSC to JSC —

[early November 1891]   [Harrow]

My darling Mummy,

Thank you very much for the P.O. You however 'slang' me wrongfully. The money I wrote for was only in reality my expenses for two journeys up to town. As for the ducks – you have got plenty at Banstead, so why should I be without. I only wrote for the duck because the pheasants that were sent me were in such bad condition. Therefore *chère maman* be not wrathful without a cause. [...]

Enclose a Photo & Remain Ever your loving son
Winston S. Churchill

---

15 Tuli and Mafeking lay close to the meeting point of Mashonaland (now Zimbabwe), Bechuanaland (now Botswana) and the Cape Colony. Mahikeng (its official name) is now the capital of the North-West Province of South Africa.

− JSC to WSC −

[10 November 1891]   Iwerne Minster House, Blandford[16]

Dearest Winston,

I told Everest to send you a sovereign when I left London on holiday. I have just received yr report which is not quite as satisfactory as I cl^d wish. You <u>must</u> try & have a better one next term as Papa will be back & will expect glowing accounts of yr work.

Well you old Puss – I will try & get you both up for the 21st. I go from here to Doveridge, Derbyshire on Saturday to stay with L^y Hindlip[17] – but I shall return to London Friday 20th. I have had a telegram from Papa saying that he leaves Capetown in the *Mexican*[18] on the 9th of Dec, therefore he will be here about the end of the month.

I had a day's hunting yesterday – which was great fun – but at first I was so 'blown' that at the 3rd fence, I cut a lovely somersault – I shan't be able to chaff you any more about yrs.

Goodbye best love, Write here
Yr loving Mother

− JSC to WSC −

15 November [1891]   Doveridge Hall, Derby[19]

Dearest Winston,

Did you ever get the sovereign I told Everest to send you – also some pheasants from Banstead? [...]

I hope you are sticking to yr work & that yr next report will be a

---

16 Home in Dorset of George Glyn, Lord Wolverton, whose young son Freddie became a close friend of JSC (see Places, p. 580).
17 Georgiana, married Samuel Allsopp 1868; succeeded as Baron Hindlip 1887 (see People, p. 568).
18 RMS *Mexican*, launched 1883, owned by Union Steamship Co. and operated between Southampton and Cape Town.
19 Recently purchased by Lord Hindlip; demolished 1938.

really good one. Have you read *The Light that Failed?*[20] I like it. Bless you old puss.

Yr loving
Mother

———

A NOTHER BATTLE of wills was looming between mother and son, this time over the Harrow headmaster's recommendation that Winston should spend the Christmas holidays with a family in Paris in order to improve his language skills.

— WSC TO JSC —

[mid-November 1891]   [Harrow]

My darling Mummy,

I got your letter this morning. I recd the £1 for which I return many thanks. They tell my Report this month is much better than last. Please write to Mr Welldon & say that you would very much like me to come up for the Wedding[21] as I have been asked by Grandmamma etc etc.

I am so glad Papa will be home by Christmas or thereabouts. I must certainly go to France during the holidays, but I beg and Pray that you will not send me to a vile, nasty, fusty beastly French "Family". [...]

Your loving son
Winston S. Churchill

— WSC TO JSC —

[22 November 1891]   [Harrow]

My darling Mummy,

I got to Harrow all right in good time. It was very 'bad luck' having to go just as the fun was commencing. It is still worse having to look

———

20 Written by Rudyard Kipling when he was 26, first published 1891.
21 The wedding of Lady Sarah Spencer-Churchill (WSC's aunt) to Lt. Col. Gordon Wilson (21 November 1891).

forward to such a time as you and Welldon seem to be planning out for me next Christmas. [...]

Your loving son
Winston S. Churchill

P.S. It was awfully bad luck having to go, just as I was making an impression on the pretty Miss Weaslet. Another 10 minutes and ...!?

— WSC to JSC —

[6 December 1891]   [Harrow]

My darling Mama,

I had written a long letter to you but on second thoughts I decided not to send it. I hear Papa will be nearly a fortnight later coming back. Mr Welldon is in consequence very keen on my going to Paris straight from here. Darling Mummy, I shall think it will be very unkind and unnatural of you if you allow him to do me out of my Christmas. [...]

Please don't you put pressure on me. Welldon got very angry last night when I told him I couldn't give up coming home. He said "very well then you must give up the Army." That is all nonsense. But Mummy don't be unkind and make me unhappy. I have firmly made up my mind not to go abroad till after the 27th. If you in spite of my entreaties force me to go I will do as little as I can and the holidays will be one continual battle. I am sure Papa would not turn me away from home at Christmas or indeed at any time. If you do all you possibly can to make things nice for me I will go after the 27th and return so as to have 4 days with Papa.

Please don't be unkind, Ever your loving son
Winston S. Churchill

— JSC to WSC —

[8 December 1891] Tuesday   London

Dearest Winston,

I was beginning to wonder why you had not written. My dear boy

I feel for you in every way & can quite understand your anxiety & desire to be at home for Xmas, but quite apart other considerations, the tone of your letter is not calculated to make one over lenient. When one wants something in this world, it is not by delivering ultimatums that one is likely to get it. You are old enough not to play the fool, & for the sake of a few days pleasure, give up the chance of getting through yr exam: a thing which may affect yr whole life. [...]

Of course if you don't "intend" going abroad till after the 27ᵗʰ & have "firmly" made up yr mind to return here for the inside of a week, I suppose that wlᵈ give you about a fortnight at Versailles. If possible I will come & see you on Thursday. Meanwhile I will think it over.

You can be quite certain my darling that I will decide for what is best, but I tell you frankly that I am going to decide not you. If you have to go, I shall see if it is possible to make it up to you in another way. I count on you helping me & not making a useless fuss – I will let you know what train I come by Thursday – until then bless you & work so that Papa may see a good report.

Yr loving
Mother

— WSC TO JSC —

[9 December 1891]   [Harrow]

My darling Mamma,

I received your letter this morning. I hope that you will come down tomorrow as it is so much easier to explain things. You ought not however to be so sarcastic to me since it is I not you who have to make the sacrifice. You say that "You tell me frankly" very well Mamma I only told you frankly my intentions. Not intending or wishing to overcome you

"I merely stated frankly" that I would throw every obstacle in the way of my going abroad before the 27ᵗʰ.

You say it is for you to decide. I am required to give up my holidays – not you, I am forced to go to people who bore me excessively – not you. You were asked to give up a short part of the year to take me abroad – you promised – refused & I did not press the point.

I am very much surprised and pained to think that both you & Papa should treat me so, as a machine. [...]

Please do have a little regard for my happiness. There are other and higher things in this world than learning, more powerful agents than the Civil Service Commissioners.

With Love & kisses, I remain, Ever your loving son
Winston S. Churchill

— JSC TO WSC —

[15 December 1891] Tuesday   2 Connaught Place

Dearest Winston,

I have only read one page of yr letter and I send it back to you – as its style does not please me. I confess after our conversation the other day I did not expect you to go back on yr word, & try & make everything as disagreeable to yrself & everyone else as possible. My dear you won't gain anything by taking this line. Everything that I can do for you to make things as smooth & palatable as possible I will do – more I cannot promise. [...]

Write to me a nice letter!

Yr loving
Mother

— WSC TO JSC —

[16 December 1891]   [Harrow]

My darling Mummy,

Never would I have believed that you would have been so unkind. I am utterly miserable. That you should refuse to read my letter is most painful to me. There was nothing in it to give you grounds for rejecting it. I am glad however that I waited 3 hours before answering or I would have sent you something that would have startled you. I can't tell you how wretched you have made me feel – instead of doing everything to make me happy you go and cut the ground away from under my feet like that. Oh my Mummy!

I made up my mind I would write no letter to you of any length in future as in my letters length I can perceive [is] a [reason] for your not reading it. I expect you were too busy with your parties and arrangements for Christmas. I comfort myself by this. As to the style – it was rather good. A letter of mine to *The Harrovian* [magazine] has recently been accepted & pronounced good.

[...] Darling Mummy – I am so unhappy but if you don't read this letter it will be the last you'll have the trouble to send back. [...]

I am more unhappy than I can possibly say. Your unkindness has relieved me however from all feelings of duty. I too can forget. Darling Mamma if you want me to do anything for you, especially so great a sacrifice don't be so cruel to

Your loving son
Winny

– WSC TO JSC –

[December 1891]   [Harrow]

My darling Mummy,

[...] Do attend to my letter. I am so wretched. Even now I weep. Please my darling Mummy be kind to your loving son. Don't let my silly letters make you angry. Let me at least think that you love me – Darling Mummy I despair. I am so wretched. I don't know what to do. Don't be angry I am so miserable. [...]

Please don't expect me to go on Monday if [Welldon] doesn't let me come till then. [...]

Good Bye my darling Mummy.
With best love I remain, Ever your loving son
Winston

WINSTON LOST this tussle. He crossed to France before Christmas; to compound his misery, he had to travel second class. On 18 December Jennie wrote to Lord Randolph: 'He makes as much fuss as though he were going to Australia for 2 years.'[22]

— WSC TO JSC —

[22 December 1891]   [Versailles]

My darling Mummy,

I was too tired to write last night. We travelled 2nd class but notwithstanding a horrible smell of Brandy & beer on the boat, I was not sick. *Au contraire* I slept all the time. [...]

Fatigue, the passage, The strange food, The cold, home sickness, the thoughts of what was behind & what before nearly caused me to write a letter which would have been painful to you. Now I am better & I think that I will wait here my month though not one day more. [...]

I have already made great progress in French. I begin to think in it, in the manner in which the first part of my letter is written. [...] Of course I would give much to return, if you wish it I will come tomorrow – but considering all things I am prepared to stay my month. [...]

Goodbye my darling Mummy
With love I remain Your loving son
Winston

— WSC TO JSC —

[27 December 1891]   [Versailles]

My darling Mummy,

Monday 3 weeks I come home – at least my month is up. I will remind you of the promise you made me at Harrow of an extra week [at home] if I gave up my Christmas. A promise is a promise & as I have

22 18 December 1991, JSC letter to Lord Randolph, Blenheim Papers.

fulfilled my part I rely on you my darling mummy to do the rest. I know you won't chuck me like that.

I am longing to return. I think if all is well I shall be home on Monday 3 weeks. I count the hours. I won't travel 2nd again by Jove. [...]

> Goodbye my darling Mummy
> Hoping to see you in 3 weeks 21 hours, I remain your loving
> Winston S. Churchill

EARLY IN January 1892, Lord Randolph arrived home from his expedition to southern Africa, sporting a beard.

– JSC to WSC –

Sunday 10 January 1892   Canford Manor, Wimborne[23]

Dearest Winston,

Yr letter received today was very short – you do not tell me anything either of yr visit to Mr de Breteuil[24] or to the Hirschs.[25]

[...] Papa is very well & in great spirits but his beard is a "terror". I think I shall have to bribe [him] to shave it off. Dearest boy don't be so lazy & neglectful about writing – you only seem to do so when you want something – & then you are very prolific with yr pen! I don't know when yr time is up. You must find out. I will write again shortly.

> *Best love*
> *Yr Mother*

---

23 Home of Lord Wimborne and his wife Cornelia, sister of Lord Randolph, in Dorset (see Places, p. 579).
24 Marquis Henri de Breteuil, former soldier and at the time MP in France (see People, p. 567).
25 Maurice Hirsch, a wealthy German-born banker, and his wife, Clara Bischoffsheim, who lived in Paris (see People, p. 568).

— WSC to JSC —

[14 January 1892]   [Versailles]

My darling Mummy,

Il faut que je vous explique quelque choses. You addressed your letter to me à Paris. Result sent back and again forwarded by Edney. I had not rec'd a letter from you for a fortnight when it arrived.

[...] I want either to come home Monday and see Jack and go on to France with you and Papa or – to wait here for Papa. I don't mind much which only you might easily bring Jack here too; But I am of course counting, my Mummy, on you to fulfil your promise which was more than anything the reason of my coming here willingly. [...]

With love and kisses I remain, your loving son
Winny

3

COPING WITH A CADET

1892–4

'What a goose you are – write!'

WINSTON RETURNED to Harrow in January 1892, now aged seventeen. He was soon deploying his language skills, newly acquired in France, to enliven his letters home, albeit with an undertone of irony.

His father's absence of nine months in southern Africa had not made their relationship any closer. Doctors continued to treat Lord Randolph's illness as syphilis, a condition known at the time as 'general paralysis of the insane'. It was thought to be a progressive disease, of which Lord Randolph was considered to be entering a more acute phase. Easily irritated, he found his elder son lazy, slipshod and careless with money.

Jennie tried to steer a middle course between her husband and Winston, staying loyal to the former while offering the latter sympathetic refuge from the harshest strictures of his father. Winston was due to sit the entrance exam for the Royal Military College at Sandhurst in July 1892.

— WSC ᴛᴏ JSC —

[January 1892]   [Harrow]

My dear Mamma,

I am deeply grieved to find how fierce you are. I am very sorry I did not write sooner, but the truth is that (here follows customary excuse) I am getting on all right in every way and am very happy and 'contented loike'. Now you want a long letter and I have very little to say.

I will send you *The Harrovian* that contains the answer to my letter. It is very feeble. I shall cut it in pieces in my retort. [...]

Votre lettre est foudroyante, inouie, pyramidal. Je vous demande pardon et je vous remercie pour la cinquantaine de francs, dont je vous ai parlé.[1]

Ton fils qui t'aime
Winston de Montéglise[2]

— WSC ᴛᴏ JSC —

[7 February 1892]   Harrow

My darling Mummy,

Thank you very much for your letter. I am working very hard for my Special Remove. I do hope I shall get it, but some horrid master has been saying that the army class get too many Removes. I am making much progress in my fencing and have beaten the others.

I am getting terribly low in my finances. You say I never write for love but always for money. I think you are right but remember that

---

1 'Your letter is terrible, extraordinary, sharp. I am sorry and I thank for the fifty francs for which I asked you.'
2 *Montéglise*: a linguistic play, in French, on 'Churchill'.

you are my banker and who else have I to write to. Please send me *une peu.*

> *J'espère que vous êtes en bonne santé, comme votre fils devoué.*[3]
>
> *Winston S. Churchill*

— WSC TO JSC —

[February 1892]   Harrow

Dear Mamma,

Many thanks for your kind letter and more for your kinder "2 quid". [...]

Il neige! Il fait un froid de loup. Je suis en bonne santé. Les armes marchent très bien.[4]

> *With much love I remain, Your loving son*
>
> *Winny*

EARLY IN March, Jennie left her husband behind in England while she spent a month in Monte Carlo, popular for its winter sunshine and casinos. While she was there, pickpockets relieved her of her purse in the casino.

— WSC TO JSC —

[16 March 1892]   [Harrow]

Darling Mamma,

I am terrified by hearing that you have been robbed of your purse. C'est Dommage, because at the same moment I must put in a request for 'un peu plus d'argent'.

I am quite well. I am very sick with you for going away like that.

---

3 'I trust that you are in good health, as is your devoted son.'
4 'It is snowing. It is bitterly cold. I am well. [Literally] The weapons [arms] are working well'.

I am awfully excited about the fencing which comes off on Tuesday. [...]

Don't go to that Casino. Invest your money in me, its safer. Darling Mummy don't slang me about the shortness of this letter. You are a bird. [...]

Good Bye my darling Mummy. Best luck and much love,

From your loving

Winston S. Churchill

— WSC to JSC —

[24 March 1892]   [Harrow]

Darling Mummy,

I have won the Fencing. A very fine cup. I was far and away first. Absolutely untouched in the finals. I have written to Papa. The oranges were luscious. [...]

Ever your loving son

Winny

— JSC to WSC —

[28 March 1892] Monday   Grand Hotel, Monte Carlo

Dearest Winston

I am delighted you won the fencing prize – you must write and tell me all about it. I am in a great hurry, as they are waiting dinner for me, but I feel I must send you my "congrats"! You will have to teach me. Jack seems to have had a nice exeat.

Best love – Yr loving

Mother

— WSC to JSC —

[27 March 1892]   [Harrow]

My darling Mama,

I am quite well and working as only I can work. My fencing is now my great employment out of school as now that I represent the School it behoves me to 'sweat up'.

I have become awfully wily and am sure I shall completely settle you on your return from the sunny south.

Give my love to Lady W [Wilton] and take for yourself all the affection that can be expressed by your loving son
Winston S. Churchill

PS I'm 'stoney'.[5] If you could replenish the exchequer it would indeed be Tara-ra boom-de-ay.

— JSC TO WSC —

[3 April 1892] Sunday   Paris

Dearest Winston,

I shall be home on Tuesday night, & shall hope to be able to go to Harrow on Sat & see you. You dear – How have you been going on? – Paris is very cold, snowing this morning – I feel it doubly coming from the land of oranges & lemons! [...]

Best love – Yr loving Mother
JSC

— JSC TO WSC —

[May 1892] Monday   Banstead

Dearest Winston,

Here is a P.O.O. for 30/-. Yr wants are many – & you seem a perfect sieve as regard money. I shall be delighted to see [you] tomorrow – wire what time you come. No more at present, as I shall see you I hope so soon.

Yr loving Mother
JSC

---

5   Short for 'stony broke', slang for 'out of money'.

W INSTON FAILED at his first attempt to pass the entrance
exam to Sandhurst, finishing 390th in a list of 693 candidates.
He returned to Harrow in September to make a second attempt at
the exam in December. Jack, now twelve years old, accompanied him
for the first time to Harrow, where the boys shared a room. Their
mother had already left for her annual pilgrimage around her friends'
Scottish estates.

— JSC TO WSC —

[24 September 1892]   Invermark, Brechin

Dearest Winston,

I hope that both you & Jack are settled & comfortable at Harrow.
Do write & tell me all about it, & what you find your room wants. I do
hope you mean to work hard – I was rather chaffed here as to yr having
been "ploughed" [failed the Sandhurst entry]. I suppose I made too
much fuss over you & made you out a sort of paragon. However it will
be all right if you put yr shoulder to the wheel this time. I shall write a
line to Mr Welldon as soon as I can.

I am so much better here you would not know me – I can walk quite
briskly & can stay out in the open air all day without getting tired. Poor
Banstead is empty now. What a pity we forgot to be photographed as I
wanted. We are going out, L^y Hindlip & I, to see a grouse drive today.
We drive as far as we can & then get on ponies & walk to the grouse
boxes – little mounds of earth thrown up. We sit in the ditch, & the
birds fly over – such a pace. I thought of you & if you cl^d ever get any –
once you are in Sandhurst you must practise all sorts of shooting. [...]

Yr loving
Mother

— WSC TO JSC —

[September 1892]   [Harrow]

Dear Mamma,

We have now quite settled down. The room is very beautiful. We purchased in London sufficiency of ornaments to make it look simply magnificent.

I got my remove & when you come down to Harrow you will see yours truly in 'Tails'.⁶ [...]

Your loving son
Winston. S. Churchill

JENNIE BECAME seriously ill late in October, almost certainly with a form of peritonitis. At the time surgical removal of the appendix was not an option for treating the disease.

— WSC TO JSC —

[21 November 1892]   [Harrow]

My dear Mamma,

I hope you are better and out of pain now. We arrived back last night (Sunday) and did not have to do any work for the next morning. Mr Welldon was most kind and said we might come up when you wanted us in future. He also asked after you a great deal. [...]

I remain Ever your loving son
Winston S. Churchill

WINSTON FAILED his second attempt at the Sandhurst entrance exam in December, this time placed 203rd out of 664 candidates. He had done well enough for the headmaster of Harrow to recommend that he transfer before a final attempt to a crammer in London which specialized in preparing its pupils for this one exam. Run by a former army officer, Captain Walter James,⁷

------

6   Formal dress, now usually 'morning dress', then worn as uniform by older boys at Harrow.
7   Co-editor of the Wolseley Series of military books, from 1897.

the crammer was based at his house in Lexham Gardens in South Kensington, London.

Before Winston could take up his place at Captain James's establishment, he injured himself badly while playing at Canford Manor in Dorset, the home of his aunt, Lady Wimborne.[8] Trying to avoid 'capture' by his brother Jack and a friend, Winston jumped off a bridge across a ravine, expecting to break his fall with the help of a tree. Instead he fell 29 feet onto hard ground, rupturing a kidney and remaining unconscious for three days.

He convalesced partly in London and partly in Brighton, where his mother wrote to him while he stayed at the home of his Aunt Lilian,[9] recently widowed by the death of her husband, the 8th duke of Marlborough.

– JSC TO WSC –

[7 February 1893]   50 Grosvenor Square

Dearest Winston,

You <u>are</u> a lazy little wretch! I thought <u>of course</u> I wl^d hear from you this morning. <u>Write</u>.

I hear yr new hat is a "terror"! Aunt Clara said you looked too funny in it. Please send it back to C. & Moore[10] & tell them that it is too big. What a goose you are – <u>write!</u>

Yr loving
Mother

---

8   Née Cornelia Spencer-Churchill, sister of Lord Randolph (see People, p. 564).
9   Widow of Louis Hammersley and of WSC's uncle, the 8th duke of Marlborough, who died in November 1892 (see People, p. 565).
10   Chapman & Moore, hatters of Bond Street.

— JSC to WSC —

[February 1893]   50 Grosvenor Square

Dearest Winston,

Papa was so angry with you for telegraphing to him in that stupid way. Of course we knew all about the fever from Jack & from Mr Welldon – & in any case to write was quite enough. You take too much on yrself young man, & write in such a pompous style. I'm afraid you are becoming a prig!

If possible I will come to Brighton tomorrow for the day & see for myself how you are getting on. I hope you will be able to settle to yr work soon otherwise you will have a scramble for it! Goodbye my darling – I shall hope to see you tomorrow. I am writing to the Duchess, give her my love.

Yr loving
Mother

———

B Y MARCH Winston was fit to attend Captain James's crammer in London; while there, he lived at his grandmother's house in Grosvenor Square, as did his parents. They made few concessions to his presence, so he returned to Aunt Lily's house in Brighton for Easter, while his mother visited the duke of Rutland at Belvoir Castle, then spent a week in Paris.

— JSC to WSC —

[March 1893]   50 Grosvenor Square

Dearest Winston,

Papa and I have gone to Kensington – back after dinner together. Look after yourself this aft:.

Yr ever loving Mother
JSC

If you prefer, arrange a dinner for yourself.

— WSC to JSC —

2 April 1893   Brighton

Dear Mamma,

I got here all right on Friday, and have not so far injured Myself in any way. Aunt Lily put me up in a very comfortable room & I have enjoyed myself immensely; the weather is delightful and the town is crowded with people. [...]

Last night Mr Balfour[11] came to dinner; he is just off to Ireland to "Ulsterise".[12] ...

Ever your loving son
Winston S. Churchill

— JSC to WSC —

[7 April 1893] Friday   50 Grosvenor Square

Dearest Winston,

I go to Belvoir[13] today only – having been put off by Ld Granby's[14] illness. I shall be back here Monday. I hope you are comporting yrself properly – I feel a little nervous at yr visiting alone. I don't want to preach dear boy, but mind you are quiet & don't talk too much & don't drink too much. One is easily carried away at yr age. [...] Papa seems to have had a great reception at Liverpool[15] & his speech is most stirring –

---

11 Arthur Balfour, leader of Conservative Party, previously chief secretary for Ireland (see People, p. 571).
12 Ulster is the northernmost of the four ancient provinces of Ireland; the term was also used more loosely to denote the area of Ireland in which Protestants outnumbered Catholics. On the country's partition in 1921, six of the province's nine counties and two boroughs formed Northern Ireland; the other three became first part of Southern Ireland and then of the Irish Free State when it came into being in 1922.
13 Belvoir Castle in Leicestershire, home of the Manners family, dukes of Rutland.
14 Marquis of Granby is the title given to heirs of the duke of Rutland.
15 Lord Randolph spoke against Home Rule for Ireland in Liverpool on 6 April.

Bless you – hold yrself up & behave like the gentleman you are.

Yr loving
Mother

— JSC ᴛᴏ WSC —

19 April [1893]   Paris

Dearest Winston,

I am sorry not to have been able to write to you before – but I am so "hunted" here I haven't had <u>one</u> moment to myself. I am afraid you did not get to London on Sat: but never mind. When I return we will put that right. [...]

I am enjoying myself immensely, ride & skate go to the races dine and even dance! It is too unfortunate tho' that the weather which was divine – is now rather wet. Write me a line dear, I do hope you are getting on well, & that you are fit. Bless you. Do write

Yr loving Mother
JSC

— WSC ᴛᴏ JSC —

14 June 1893   50 Grosvenor Square

Dear Mamma,

[...] Papa has been very kind to me and Capt James has written to tell him that he thinks I shall pass. I am told his verdict is rarely at fault. [...]

Your loving son
Winston S. Churchill

— JSC ᴛᴏ WSC —

[18 June 1893] Sunday   Sunningdale[16]

Dearest Winston,

[...] I have had a delightful week & won my money. I shall make

---

16 Sunningdale Park near Ascot, home of Major Joicey.

you a pres: of £2. It is hot! I hope you are careful not to get in the sun
– one might really get a sun stroke. [...]

I do hope yr "prognostication" will prove correct & that you will
pass – à demain mon cher enfant. Travaille bien et aime moi encore
plus.[17]

Yr loving
Mother

―――

J ENNIE DID not wish to expose her sons to the severity of their
father's illness during the long summer holidays of 1893; she
therefore arranged for a young Eton schoolmaster, Mr. J. Little, to
escort them on a tour of Europe, while she took Lord Randolph to
two spa resorts in Germany.

As Winston left England, news arrived that he had passed the
Sandhurst entry exam, coming 95th in the list of 389 candidates,
four places too low for automatic entry into the infantry branch. He
qualified instead for entry into the cavalry, which required its officers
(or, more accurately, their parents) to shoulder the extra costs of
providing horses, saddles and other equipment.

His mother wrote to congratulate her son, but warned him that
his father's reaction might be one of scepticism.

― JSC TO WSC ―

7 August 1893   Kissingen[18]

Dearest Winston,

We have just received yr letters & are very pleased to think you are
enjoying yrselves – I am glad of course that you have got into Sandhurst

---

17 'Until tomorrow, my dear child. Work hard and love me still more.'
18 Bad Kissingen in Bavaria on the River Saale, a fashionable spa town frequented
    by the royal families of Austria-Hungary and Russia.

but Papa is not very pleased at yr getting in by the skin of yr teeth & missing the Infantry by 18 marks. He is not as pleased over yr exploits as you seem to be! [...]

Poor Puss! Being so [sea]sick. I can sympathize tho' we had a lovely crossing. We are doing the cure most conscientiously & I think it will do Papa a lot of good. Kissingen is a very pretty place – lots of walks & drives. We get up at 6.30!! & go to bed at 9.30 – drink water – take baths & listen to music. The time passes somehow. [...]

Best love – & look after yrself & Jack.

Yr loving

Mother

TWO DAYS later Lord Randolph wrote to his son: 'I am rather surprised at your tone of exultation over your inclusion in the Sandhurst list. There are two ways of winning an examination, one creditable the other the reverse. You have unfortunately chosen the latter method ...'. He went on to complain of Winston's 'slovenly happy-go-lucky *harum scarum* style of work', warning: 'I no longer attach the slightest weight to anything you may say about your own achievements and exploits.'[19]

— WSC TO JSC —

14 August 1893   Hotel Continental, Milan

Dear Mamma,

I have just got your letters and one from Papa. He seems awfully displeased with me. I can tell you it was a disappointment to me to find that he was not satisfied. After slaving away at Harrow & James' for this Exam, & trying, as far as I could to make up for the time I had wasted I was only too delighted to find that I had at length got in.

After all I <u>am</u> through & my chances are as good as they were

19 9 August 1893, Lord Randolph letter to WSC, *WSC* 1C1: 390–1.

before I tried at all. I begin again on quite new subjects, in which I shall not be handicapped by past illness.

If I had failed, there would have been an end of all my chances. As it is my fate is in my own hands & I have a fresh start. [...]

I will write soon & tell you about our journey, but it don't come in right here.

Ever your loving son
Winston S. Churchill

— JSC TO WSC —

19 August 1893   Kissingen

Dearest Winston,

I was very glad to get yr letter from Milan – you have not written very often & Jack only once – but I daresay you have little time & probably so much travelling is tiring – you have only another week. [...]

By the time we get home you will have been a whole month at Sandhurst – quite the man! I hope you will do well there – & then there will be no question as to how you got in. [...]

Our life here is unchanged – & we have stuck to the Cure religiously. I think Papa is ever so much better, & after Gastein[20] I am sure will be quite well. The heat is very great & makes one very lazy. [...]

Ever yr loving
Mother

— WSC TO JSC —

23 August 1893   Hotel Couronne & Poste, Brigue[21]

Dear Mamma,

[...] I am going to buckle to at Sandhurst & to try and regain Papa's

---

20 Another spa resort, in the Salzburg region of Austria.
21 Described by contemporary guidebooks as a first-class hotel with electric light and central heating, in Brig (French spelling Brigue), which sits in the Valais, in southern Switzerland, at the foot of the Simplon Pass, which leads to Italy.

opinion of me. I will send you a Photograph of myself in my uniform – which I am longing to put on.

When I have been there a day or two I will write you and Papa a <u>long</u> letter & describe everything. I have got a good deal of money in hand (£7) but I don't know at all what my expenses are likely to be on joining & I have had no information. You might suggest an allowance to Papa.

Thanking you once more for your letter and sending you my very best love & many kisses.

I remain Ever your loving son
Winston S. Churchill

————

W INSTON ARRIVED in London on 30 August, the day before he was due to report to Sandhurst. Waiting for him in London was a letter telling him that he had been promoted to the infantry list as a result of some withdrawals. Later the same day he wrote to his father to ask for a regular financial allowance; at the same time he wrote to his mother, appealing for her support.

— WSC TO JSC —

30 August 1893   50 Grosvenor Square

Dear Mamma,

I got your letter this morning. You did not say anything about the absorbing topic – money. I have written a long & respectful letter to Papa to ask him to give me an allowance. Please try & persuade him. It would be much better & cheaper than the present arrangements which are

"Spend as much as I can get"

"Get as much as I can".

I have been very anxiously awaiting a letter from Papa. But I have had none since the one he wrote me on my examination 3 weeks ago.

I hope he will be pleased to hear that I have got into the infantry after all. [...]

> *Good-Bye dear Mamma – I will write to you from Sandhurst on Sunday.*
> *I remain Your Ever loving son*
> *Winston S. Churchill*

———

LORD RANDOLPH compromised by agreeing an allowance of £10 a month, designed to meet only a part of his son's spending while he kept control of the larger outlays. At the same time he refused to authorize 'unrestricted leave' for Winston from Sandhurst at weekends.

— WSC to JSC —

17 September [1893]   [Sandhurst]

My dear Mamma,

Your letter arrived last night, and made me feel rather unhappy. I am awfully sorry that Papa does not approve of my letters. I take a great deal of pains over them & often re-write entire pages. If I write a descriptive account of my life here, I receive a hint from you that my style is too sententious & stilted. If on the other hand I write a plain and excessively simple letter – it is put down as slovenly. I never can do anything right.

Thank you very much for your letter. I am afraid that you have reason to be cross with me for not writing to <u>you</u>. I will not give you cause again. [...]

As to the leave – it is very hard that Papa cannot grant me the same liberty that other boys in my position are granted. It is only a case of trusting <u>me</u>. As my company officer said he "liked to know the boys whom their parents could trust" – and therefore recommended me to get the permission I asked for. However it is no use my trying to explain to Papa, & I suppose I shall go on being treated as "that boy" till I am 50 years old.

It is a great pleasure to me to write to you unreservedly instead of

Winston (left) as an officer cadet at the Royal Military College, Sandhurst.

having to pick & choose my words and information. So far I have been extremely <u>good</u>. Neither late nor lazy, & have had always 5 minutes to wait before each parade or study. [...]

Well I have told you all about my life. I am cursed with so feeble a body that I can hardly support the fatigues of the day; but I suppose I shall get stronger during my stay here. [...]

Ever so much love & more kisses from your ever loving son
Winston S. Churchill

— WSC to JSC —

20 September [1893]   [Sandhurst]

Dear Mamma,

I have written to Papa a letter that I hope will please him. [...] I want you to explain to Papa that on the 6th of October I have to pay the Canteen bill & extra messing account: probably over £4. They only give 24 hours notice & anyone not producing the money is posted on a blackboard. Of course it will come out of my £10 per month. Only I wanted you to remind Papa – so that he should not send it late – as a day would make all the difference. I hope in future months to have a balance – but the expenses of coming here – of carpet & chairs etc. have swallowed that. I have however sufficient to keep me going till the 3rd or 4th of October.

Goodbye my dearest Mamma – I have tried my best to write larger & to do all the many things you have told me to do. I am very happy here & like the place more & more.

Ever your loving son
Winston S. Churchill

— WSC to JSC —

13 October [1893]   [Sandhurst]

Dear Mamma,

I had such a nice letter from Papa, in answer to one I wrote him about his Stalybridge[22] meeting. Will you be in London on Sunday week? If so, I will come up & if you can find me a bed – can stay until Sunday. It has been rather a bore, not being able to go up to town on Saturdays, as all my friends go & have grand fun at the London Pavilion.[23] However I hope to have a little more liberty when you come home. As I have not got a permission from home to have leave when entitled to it you will have to send me a letter explicitly inviting me to come. Such a bore being different from everyone else. [...]

> *Goodbye my darling Mummy. Longing to see you. I remain,*
> *Ever your loving son*
> *Winston S. Churchill*

THE FOLLOWING weekend Lord Randolph allowed Winston to leave Sandhurst to accompany him on an overnight stay with Lord Rothschild, a former school friend, at Tring Park, his estate in Hertfordshire.

Lord Randolph found himself impressed by the change in his son after only a month at Sandhurst, while Winston wrote later in *My Early Life* that he felt he now 'acquired a new status' in his father's eyes. Lord Randolph began to take his son with him on more occasions, yet still drew back as soon as Winston showed any 'sign of comradeship'.[24]

Winston wrote from Tring to his mother, who was away visiting friends.

----

22 Lord Randolph addressed a Unionist meeting attended by 3,000 people at the Grand Theatre, Stalybridge, near Manchester, on 4 October.
23 The London Pavilion theatre, close to Piccadilly Circus, had been rebuilt in 1885: it set a new standard for the variety theatre, with its classic exterior, marbled interior and bright electric lighting.
24 W. Churchill *My Early Life*, p. 46.

— WSC to JSC —

21 October [1893]   Tring Park, Tring

My dear Mamma,

I am so disappointed at not having seen you. What a pity it was. I arrived at Waterloo at 12 o'clock and you left at 11. Papa was very pleased to see me and talked to me for quite a long time about his speeches & my prospects. He seemed very interested in the R.M.C. [Royal Military College] intelligence & gave me a cheque for £6 to pay my mess bill with.

I went to see Grandmamma,[25] who was so sorry you had not been able to see me. From what she said I hear you are going to "visit" for some time to come. [...]

I think Papa seems much better for his rest & far less nervous. Hoping to see you soon.

I remain Your loving son
Winston S. Churchill

— WSC to JSC —

10 December [1893]   [Sandhurst]

Dearest Mamma,

Thank you so much for your kindness – v.i.z. £3. I have been working very hard and today have done an Exam in Tactics. I will refrain from prophesying having been wrong so many times before. Do come down on Friday. [...]

Ever your loving son
Winston S. Churchill

---

25 Lord Randolph's mother, the dowager duchess of Marlborough (see People, p. 565).

WINSTON SPENT Christmas at Blenheim Palace, once again apart from his parents who stayed in London, probably as a result of his father's health.

— WSC TO JSC —

25 December [1893]   Blenheim

My dear Mamma,

I am enjoying myself here very much – though there is plenty of divine service. Every one is very kind and civil to me & Lady Blandford[26] has really gone out of her way to make me comfortable. [...]

There is no sort of party & I am quite alone with Sunny.[27] He is very good company and we have sat talking till 1.30 every night since I have been here. [...]

Hoping you were not bored to death in town – that Papa looked well – and that you had a "Happy Christmas".

I remain, Ever your loving son
Winston S. Churchill

—————

TO HIS mother's relief, Winston rejoined the household at Grosvenor Square before he returned to Sandhurst. Jennie and her mother-in-law never got on.

— JSC TO WSC —

11 February [1894]   50 Grosvenor Square

Dearest Winston,

I hope you are none the worse for yr journey. Let me know how

---

26 Mother of Charles, 9th duke of Marlborough; she and her husband had divorced in 1882 while he was still marquess of Blandford. She remained known as Lady Blandford when he became 8th duke in 1883.

27 Familiar name for Charles Spencer-Churchill, derived from his courtesy title, earl of Sunderland, before he became duke.

you are getting on. I felt so sorry to have you go – you poor thing – particularly when you are not feeling well. I don't know what I w^d have done in G. [Grosvenor] Square without you.

Make a little list of the things you want for your room – & I will see if I have them.

Goodbye – take care of yrself – & write often.

Yr loving Mother

JSC

— WSC to JSC —

13 February [1894]   Sandhurst

My dear Mamma

I am much better today all round. The boils are healing up and I do not think that they will have to be lanced up again. [...]

I am sending you a list of the things I should like for my room. Please let me have what you can – as soon as possible as it is very uncomfortable at present. [...]

Ever your loving son

Winston S. Churchill

PS I found such a kind letter from Papa (6 pages) waiting for me when I got back. WSC

— JSC to WSC —

[20 February 1894] Tuesday   50 Grosvenor Square

Dearest Winston,

I will send on the furniture tomorrow. [...] I am so sorry you had such a bad time with yr tooth but it is all right now I hope. I feel too stupid for words with neuralgia – so forgive this uninteresting letter. Papa arrives this evening. I will write & tell you how he is.

I believe Mr. Gladstone will resign before the end of next week.[28] He is nearly blind.

Yr loving
Mother

— WSC ᴛᴏ JSC —

16 March [1894]   Sandhurst

My dear Mamma

[...] Everything is going on well here – the riding specially, and I hope to satisfy even Papa at the examination at the end of summer.

I am awfully hard up and wish you would send me a sovereign, as I am reduced to almost bankruptcy – having been so often to town. Please do or I shall have to stay here all holidays. [...]

With best love & many kisses I remain, Ever your loving son
Winston S. Churchill

— JSC ᴛᴏ WSC —

[17 March 1894] Saturday   50 Grosvenor Square

Dearest Winston,

I am not going to read you a lecture as I have not time – but I must say you are spending too much money – & you <u>know it</u>. You owe me £2 & you want more besides. You really must not go on like this – think of all yr bills besides! I shall see you on Wed: & we can have a nice talk. Papa is very well & in good spirits. Goodbye old Puss! I am rather X all the same you fleece me!

Yr loving
Mother

---

28   The 84-year-old William Gladstone resigned as prime minister on 3 March and was succeeded by his foreign secretary, Lord Rosebery.

THE IMPROVEMENT in Winston's relations with his father since the previous autumn came to an abrupt halt in April 1894 when Lord Randolph visited his watchmaker in London. He heard that his son had already brought in the valuable gold watch which Lord Randolph had recently given him for two sets of repairs. On the first occasion, the watch had simply fallen onto hard ground; six weeks later, however, Winston had dropped it into a pool of deep water. The Sandhurst fire brigade had helped to recover the watch by pumping the pool dry, but it had rusted badly.

— JSC TO WSC —

[22 April 1894] Sunday   Hotel Scribe, Paris

Dearest Winston,

I am <u>so</u> sorry you have got into trouble over yr watch – Papa wrote to me all about it. I must own you are awfully careless & of course Papa is angry after giving you such a valuable thing. However he wrote very kindly about you so you must not be too unhappy. Meanwhile I'm afraid you will have to go without a watch. Oh! Winny what a *harum scarum* fellow you are! You really must give up being so childish. I am sending you £2 with my love. I shall scold you well when we meet.

Yr loving
Mother

— WSC TO JSC —

24 April [1894]   Sandhurst

My dearest Mamma,

Thank you so much for your letter – which I have just received. Papa wrote me a long letter about the watch and seems to be very cross. I wrote back at once saying how sorry I was and explaining the whole affair & got a letter by return of post – last night. I think that by his letter Papa is somewhat mollified. I hope so indeed. But how on earth could I help it. I had no waistcoat to put the watch in and so have had to wear it in the pocket of my tunic.

Papa writes, he is sending me a Waterbury[29] – which is rather a come down. [...]

It is so dear of you to have written me such a kind letter & for sending me the £2. You are the best and sweetest mamma in all the world. With lots of love & kisses,

I remain Ever your loving son
Winston S. Churchill

– JSC TO WSC –

30 April [1894]   50 Grosvenor Square

Dearest Winston,

How are you? A bird whispered to me that you did not sleep in yr own bed last night. Write to me all about it. I am not sure if Papa wl[d] approve.

[...] I came back Friday evening very sorry to leave Paris which was delightful. I find London cold & dull. Papa is pretty well. When shall I come & spend the day with you?

Yr loving
Mother

– WSC TO JSC –

1 May [1894]   Sandhurst

My dearest Mamma,

I have just got your letter. I should not think that Papa would object to my having stayed with Col Brab[azon][30] at Aldershot. He distinctly wrote to me that he did not want me to come up to London much. [...]

How I wish I were going into the 4th [Hussars] instead of those old

---

29 The Waterbury Watch Co. of Connecticut, USA, had produced cheaper watches than its competitors, with fewer moving parts, since 1879.

30 Colonel James Brabazon, a friend of the Churchills, colonel of the 4th Hussars since 1892 (see People, p. 575).

Rifles. It would not cost a penny more & the regiment goes to India in 3 years which is just right for me. I hate the Infantry – in which physical weaknesses will render me nearly useless on service & the only thing I am showing an aptitude for athletically – riding – will be no good for me.

Furthermore of all regiments in the army the Rifles is slowest for promotion. However it is not much good writing down these cogent arguments – but if I pass high at the end of the term I will tackle Papa on the subject. I hope he is not incensed about the watch anymore. I wish you would send me a line on the subject.

Also I wd be very grateful if you would draw Papa's attention to the date (May 1) as I am not particularly rich owing to the £3 I had to disburse for my watch.

You are a darling mamma – and I hope to see you on Saturday.

With lots of love, I remain, Ever your loving son
Winston S. Churchill

– WSC to JSC –

10 May [1894]   [Sandhurst]

Darling Mamma,

So sorry and disappointed to find you can't come down. Had hoped that you would have been able to spare a day – as tomorrow is the only day in the whole year on which the place is at its best & when every arrangement is made for visitors. If you could come after all I should be so pleased as I am sure you would not be bored. There is an excellent train leaving London at (Waterloo) 11.45 a.m. arriving 1.17.

If you find that it is impossible to come please try and get me a [fancy dress] costume and send it by the <u>guard</u> of the train at 11.45. I will meet it. Try and get a gorilla or something amusing. I do hope you will do so as I have payed 10/- for the entrance and if no costume then I can't ride.

With best love, Ever your loving son
Winston S. Churchill

— WSC ᴛᴏ JSC —

13 May [1894]   Sandhurst

My darling Mamma,

Thank you so much for sending me the [gorilla] dress which I wore
& which did very well. I am having it carefully washed and will send it
back tomorrow night. It was perhaps just as well that you did not come
down after all – for it poured with rain the whole day and I am sure you
would have been very bored. […]

I wonder if you would like to send me a little money as I am desperately short and have had to go about the whole month with a mess
bill of £7.0.0. […]

Ever your loving son
Winston S. Churchill

— JSC ᴛᴏ WSC —

17 May [1894]   50 Grosvenor Square

Dearest Winston,

I am sending enclosed cheque for £2. I don't wish to be disagreeable
but I wish to remind you that this makes £6 I have given you the last
month – in fact more – 2 sent from Paris, 2 paid to Healy & 2 now. I
really think that Papa gives you a very fair allowance & you <u>ought</u> to
make it do. He wlᵈ be very X if he knew that I gave you money. It is yr
own fault if you spend all yr money on food & then have nothing for
other wants. I give you warning I shall not give you any more.

Yr loving
Mother

— WSC ᴛᴏ JSC —

19 May 1894   Sandhurst

Dearest Mamma,

Our letters crossed. I was very glad to get a line from you at last.

Thank you very much for sending me the cheque; which was very welcome – though I think I should have preferred a more gracious letter.

I am considerably better this morning, though they will not let me out of hospital yet. I can't understand what has been the matter – but I shrewdly suspect liver – though with the plain food & generous allowance of exercise I fail to see why. Extraordinary headaches all the week. Such a bore.

Everything seemed very crude here but I judiciously distributed a few half crowns and am consequently looked after "en prince". The other cadets are too loathsome to be described. [...]

Looking for a letter and with best love and lots of kisses, I remain Ever your
loving son
Winston S. Churchill

— JSC ᴛᴏ WSC —

24 May [1894]   50 Grosvenor Square

Dearest Winston,

I have not felt much worried about you as Mr Derenburg[31] told me you dined with him on Sunday & made an excellent dinner. Perhaps you will not have been surprised at my not writing, when you consider the tone of yr letter to me. Yr father wl^d have been anything but pleased at it. However I did not show it to him as you know & as I don't consider it my "nature" to lecture we will say no more about it. My only way of showing my displeasure is by silence! [...]

Now goodbye for the pres. [...]

Yr loving
Mother

---

31 Carl Derenburg performed alongside JSC in a concert in 1894 after a meeting of the Randolph Churchill Habitation (branch) of the Primrose League; Mrs Derenburg was also musical.

— WSC ᴛᴏ JSC —

25 May 1894   Sandhurst

My darling Mamma,

So glad & delighted to get your letter. Am very sorry indeed you are not pleased with my last epistle but can't possibly imagine what I said to anger you. Yesterday I went over to see the Queen's Birthday Review at Aldershot. Very splendid – I saw Col Brab who took me home & gave me lunch with the mess. Do thank him when you see him.

[...] Do come Down on Wednesday and scold me. Am writing again tomorrow – for the present lots of love and kisses.

Your loving son
Winston S. Churchill

4

DYING BY INCHES

1894

'I feel too low to write'

B Y THE spring of 1894, Lord Randolph Churchill's health had declined to the point where he could not live publicly in London. His doctors shared their gloomy prognosis with Jennie, who was keen to protect their children from witnessing the final stages of their father's illness.

The couple conceived the idea of travelling around the world, westwards, for up to a year. The doctors warned that their plan was too ambitious and counselled a more modest trip to Europe instead, with a doctor in full-time attendance. As a compromise, the Churchills kept to their worldwide itinerary, but agreed to take a doctor and curtail the trip if Lord Randolph's condition deteriorated markedly.

They sailed for New York with a Doctor Keith on 29 June. Meanwhile, when Jack's school summer holidays began at the end of July, their sons were to travel around Europe again with Mr Little of Eton.

— WSC to JSC —

10 July [1894]   Sandhurst

My dearest Mamma,

I have not written to you before because there was not much to tell – except that we were very low at your departure. [...] I do hope that you are feeling well and in good spirits – and that the change has already worked wonders with Papa. [...]

I want to say such a lot of things that one can't put down on paper. We both miss you very much indeed. However it will be for the best and if Papa comes back all right I shall not regret your going away. [...]

I suppose you will have left England a month when this letter reaches you – but henceforth you will get one from me every week. I should so like to have a letter from you. Though I should like to hear about the things you do & see I would much rather hear about how Papa is and if you are feeling cheery.

Such a short and stupid letter. Good bye my darling dearest Mummy, excuse my composition and believe how very much I miss you.

With best love and many kisses, I remain, Ever your loving son
Winston S. Churchill

— WSC to JSC —

17 July [1894]   50 Grosvenor Square

My dear Mamma,

[...] Everything goes on fairly well here at G. [Grosvenor] Square. I do the model "son" very well. Church on Sundays and trot in every now and again to see Grandmamma. People are very kind and I have had a lot of invitations to lunch and dinner. [...]

When you write let me know how Papa is and how you are. Goodbye my darling own Mamma. We miss you very much and long to see you back. Do keep well & cheery and we will try to do the same.

Lots of kisses and best love, Ever your loving son
Winston S. Churchill

— WSC to JSC —

22 July [1894]   The Hatch[1]

My dearest Mamma,

I have had a very pleasant week in London. People have been very kind and I have had lots of invitations to dinner to lunch and to dances. [...]

Yesterday Molly Hacket[2] and I made our great expedition to Harrow – quite alone. As soon as we got down there – we received three telegrams with "Congratulations" from young Clay and others. [...]

We have arranged our trip. It will be modified as we go by the funds and by the time we have – but it is roughly this. London – Brussels – Lucerne – Interlaken – Chamonix – Zermatt – Through the Furka pass – Goeschenen – Milan – Venice (if not too hot) – Innsbruck – Salzburg – Vienna.

At Vienna I leave and return by the Orient express to Sandhurst. Jack and Little will go back by easy stages – via Paris.

I have written Papa a long letter on the subject of the Cavalry. I do so hope he will not be angry – or take it as "freespoken" or stupid. I only wrote what I thought he ought to know – namely how keen I was to go into the Cavalry and how I could not look forward with great eagerness to going with even the best Infantry regiment in the world. [...]

Well! good bye! My dearest Mama. You know how Jack and I miss you and how we long for you and Papa to come back.

Keep well and cheerful and write often – to your loving and affectionate son
Winston S. Churchill

---

1 Possibly Hatch House near Salisbury, owned by Lt.-Col. Bennett Stanford Fane.
2 Niece of JSC's friend, Lady Hindlip; Molly and WSC had met at Hindlip Hall in the New Year; since then they had exchanged letters and taken strolls together in London.

— WSC to JSC —

31 July 1894   50 Grosvenor Square

My dearest Mamma,

I got yesterday a letter from Papa dated the 18th – so I suppose you will get this letter in about a fortnight. Today Jack comes up from Harrow, and to-morrow we start for Switzerland. [...]

I can't tell you how glad I am & how happy to find that everything is still well, and that Papa is so much better. Such a nice little paragraph was in the papers last night to say you had started for Vancouver & were everywhere hospitably received.

Goodbye my dearest darling mama; Jack and I think of you very often and miss you so very much. However I think one may say that all is satisfactory so far.

With lots of love & kisses, I remain Ever your loving and affectionate son
Winston S. Churchill

— WSC to JSC —

3 August [1894]   Hotel Britannique, Bruxelles

My dearest Mamma,

We started on the evening of the 1st – crossed comfortable from Dover to Ostende & did not stop – except to change until we reached Antwerp. [...] There was a very fine American Warship *Chicago*[3] lying in the river and we went and examined it as closely as the authorities would let us. [...]

This is now my 10th letter & I hope you have received them all. [...] I am so thankful to hear of Papa's improvement. A great number of people have asked after him and I have had great pleasure in saying how much better he is.

Dearest Mamma – I have seen several of your letters to Aunt

---

3   The USS *Chicago*, a cruiser, was launched in 1885. One of the first first steel ships (known as the ABCD ships) authorized by Congress as the foundation of the 'New Navy' (the others were the USS *Atlanta*, *Boston* and *Dolphin*).

Leonie & to Consuelo [Duchess of Manchester] and sympathise very much with your dislike of the "vegetation". But your last letters were much more cheery and I feel sure that you will end by enjoying the journey. We feel happy – but it is a horrid bore & worse not to have my own one love to talk to. The duchess was getting very *difficile* when we left and it was perhaps just as well as came off here.

However it is all for the best, and will I feel sure turn out well. I have annexed a beautiful photo of you with the star in your hair[4] and one of Papa which I have had framed. Goodbye darling – Jack and I think of you every day and look forward to the time when we shall meet again.

Ever your loving and affectionate son
Winston S. Churchill

— WSC TO JSC —

26 August [1894]   Lausanne

My dearest darling Mamma,

I got while at Zermatt a dear letter from you [missing] – which I think had taken nearly a month finding me. My time with Jack is now nearly up. Either tomorrow or the next day I shall start for London – and Sandhurst.

The Examination result which perhaps you know better than I do at present is just out. Grandmamma sent me a telegram – yesterday. Maximum 1500; Minimum 750. My marks 1140. [...] Grandmamma did not say in her letter what <u>place</u> these marks gave me- but I should imagine that it would be in the first 20. [...]

This place is very pleasant – if only by the way it contrasts with Zermatt. We have come straight from the latter – 5000 feet above the sea – rather cold – shut in on every side by enormous peaks and a very bad and uncomefotable hotel – to Ouchy[5] where the lake is outside the bedroom windows, the water so warm that you can bathe 3 or 4 times a day – and the hotel – the best in Switzerland. [...]

---

4   The photograph appears as an illustration on p. 423.
5   Lakeside resort, south of the centre of Lausanne.

There were several Sandhurst and Harrow boys at Zermatt and they climbed Dent Blanche – the Matterhorn and Rothhorn[6] – the most dangerous and difficult of Swiss mountains. It was very galling to me not to be able to do something too, particularly as they swaggered abominably of their achievements. I had to be content with toilsome but safe mountains. But another year I will come back and do the dangerous ones. […]

I long to see you. Two months tomorrow since you went so the time is passing – surely though slowly.

Best Love & kisses my own darling Mummy – Jack and I miss you so much.

Ever your loving son
Winston S. Churchill

———

BY THE time this letter from Winston reached his parents early in October 1894, they were nearing the end of a stay of five weeks in Japan, then at war with China over the two countries' rival ambitions on the Korean peninsula.

— JSC to WSC —

11 October 1894   Kyoto, Japan

Dearest Winston

I received yr dear letter from [left blank] about a week ago at Tokyo. I was so glad to hear that both you and Jack were well and had enjoyed yrselves in Switzerland – you will have received by now the money I sent you by Aunt Leonie. It seems ages that we have been away – I can't imagine how I shall be able to hold out a year!

I think Japan has done yr Father good – altho' he is not as well as I could wish. For a fortnight he has been much better & then again today without any reason he is not so well.

———

6   Alpine mountains, respectively 4,357m (14,295 ft), 4,478m (14,692 ft) and 3,103m (10,180 ft) high.

Jennie, Lord Randolph (centre) and Dr Keith (right)
in *jurikisha* in Japan, October 1894.

We are to sail from Kobe (3 hrs from here) on Monday next for
Hong-Kong, Singapore & Burmah. ...

We have been 5 weeks in Japan & I have enjoyed it as much as
possible under the circumstances. It is a fascinating place – & everything
interests & amuses one – it is all we know & more. This town used in
old days to be the capital & the Mikado lived here – but now the Court
is removed to Tokyo.

All the finest masks of art are made here, & we have been over
some interesting factories etc. Today we have just returned from an
expedition to Lake Biwa about 8 miles [away]. It does not sound far –
but when one has to be dragged in a *jurikisha* by 2 men – on rough roads
in the hot sun – it becomes an "expedition". It is wonderful how these
men keep up a steady trot for 7 miles without stopping. [...]

Oct 14<u>th</u> As this letter cannot go until 20<u>th</u> I have left it until today
to finish. This is our last day in Japan. Tomorrow we sail from Kobe.

We saw a very interesting sight yesterday – the funeral of the Governor of the province. We went & sat in a shop to see it go by.

First came a lot of policemen, then heaps of enormous buckets of flowers carried on bamboo poles by men dressed in white, then rows of priests in flowing garments & shaven heads – then one man carrying a huge bamboo pole with a long scroll with the deceased's name. Next the hearse – a species of Noah's Ark carried on poles made of beautiful wood inlaid & ornamented with gold, the sliding panels drawn back, so that one cl^d see the uniform & cocked hat laid on the coffin inside. The men who carried it were all in flowing white clothes. The son followed & the daughter dressed in white was in a *jurikisha* – her face enameled like a clown's ghastly white.

Then came men carrying the orders [&] sword of the governor – these men looked too grotesque in European clothes, white cotton gloves & felt hats. More priests, more policemen & lastly officials, friends & relatives – all in *jurikisha*, looking too absurd & hideous – with every shape of awful felt hat. [...]

One does not hear very much of the war here. The Japanese govt: is very secretive and very little is allowed to appear in the papers – but there is no doubt they are having the best of it, & if they can get to Pekin before the winter, & get away again! They will dictate their own terms.

I wonder how you are getting on in Sandhurst? I think of you both so much darlings. Send this letter to Jack with my best love – I hope he is working a little harder at Harrow. His letters are "beautifully few & far between"! but I forgive him. I am sure he is as tall as you are now – he must get on a bit.

I daresay this will not reach you much before yr birthday – I have got you a nice present – a beautiful silver cigarette box inlaid with sword hilt & ornaments very "Japanesey" – but I can't send it – so you must wait.

Goodbye my darling Winston – mind you keep straight in every way. I count on you.

Bless you darling I can't tell you how miserable I am often – so far away from you all – but I shall feel nearer when I am in India – &

perhaps things will look brighter. Tell Jack I will bring him something nice from India.

With much love to you both
Your loving Mother
JSC

———

WHEN JENNIE and her husband reached Hong Kong, she received a telegram from Freddie Wolverton, one of her younger admirers who came from a wealthy family.[7] The telegram told her of his engagement to marry Edith Ward, the twenty-two-year-old daughter of the 1st earl of Dudley. Jennie felt crushed: she had considered Freddie a possible future husband.

— WSC TO JSC —

4 September 1894   Sandhurst

My dearest Mamma,

Here I am back at Sandhurst. There is a great deal to do here this term as they have again increased the hours and made them awfully long. The riding has begun also and I am working so hard at it. I should like nothing better than to win the riding prize. My only chance of persuading Papa to let me go in the Cavalry is, I feel, to do something of that sort. [...]

How I wish I had not been offered that unfortunate infantry commission after the Exams. I should love to go into the cavalry – even with a bad regiment. Grandmamma writes 'Papa will not hear of it.' This is very sad, but I still have hopes that when he sees how anxious I am – he will not force me into the infantry against my inclination. [...]

I find the time very long. It seems ages since you were gone and really it is only 2 months. Poor Papa! I am so delighted to hear he is

---

7   Lord (Frederick) Wolverton was 30 years old and was a partner of the family's private banking company, Glyn, Mills, Currie & Co. (see People, p. 569).

better. I think Grandmamma only lives on his letters. She cares for nothing else in the world but news of and from him. [...]

Well goodbye my own darling Mummy.

Best love from your loving and affectionate son
Winston S. Churchill

— WSC to JSC —

15 September 1894   50 Grosvenor Square

My dearest darling Mummy,

I sit down to answer a letter of yours from San Francisco. 1st you ask me about Finance. I must tell you that it is most unsatisfactory. Coming back from Switzerland I spent a good deal of money & also I payed several bills with my first allowance in cheques. I have not been more extravagant than before you went away, but rather less. Still the sov. [sovereign] & the 2 sovs & the 3 pounds used to make a great difference & now they have ceased altogether.

The consequence of this has been that I 'mortgaged' my allowance for the next month and have had to pawn several of the things I used least. If therefore as the 30th Nov approaches or Christmas draws near you feel as if you would like to commemorate both or either of these auspicious birthdays – a chequelet would above all things fill my heart with joy and gratitude.

Finally let me – to reassure you – state that though I have been cut off from you and Papa for more than 3 months I am not in any way seriously involved but only extremely hard up. So do not worry about me my darling mummy unless you feel you would like to send me a cheque. It would be a welcome stranger & smooth away many difficulties. The mess bills are much lower. I have economized fifty per cent. So much for finance.

My own darling sweet Mama, I have received some beautiful photographs of you and Papa & some for Jack. [...] Travel seems to have affected you very little & I was astonished – when comparing the photographs of last month with the photo with the diamond star to note how little difference there was between the two. I am sure the journey is doing you good & feel quite convinced that you don't really look or feel 100 but make the local beauties 'sit up' on all fours. [...]

And now good bye my darling Mummy. Excuse the badly written scrawl & accept only the love that it is meant to convey. I think of you always & long to kiss you again.

Ever your loving son
Winston S. Churchill

— WSC to JSC —

19 September 1894   50 Grosvenor Square

My darling Mummy,

The news of the first great battles of the [Sino-Japanese] war have just reached us. You must write and give me some news from the spot. I suppose however that Yokohama and Seoul are as far apart as London & Vienna. It must be most interesting however to be so, comparatively speaking, near the seat of war.

I take the greatest interest in the operations both of the fleets & armies. Anything so brilliant as the night attack of Ping Yang[8] is hard to find in modern war. The reports as they have arrived here seem to show that the Japanese concentration was so accurately timed & their assault so skilfully delivered that the celestials had 'no show' at all. [...]

I went out with our paper chase yesterday and had a couple of falls. In the first my horse pecked on landing & fell and at the second I turned a corner at much too rapid pace & so came to grief. I was not at all hurt – which I consider wonderful as I was galloped over both times. [...]

With best love, Ever your loving son
Winston

---

8   The Battle of Pyongyang took place on 15 September. Japanese troops attacked simultaneously from several directions, killing an estimated 2,000 Chinese defenders, compared to their own losses of 102 men.

– JSC to WSC –

4 November [1894]   Government House, Singapore

Dearest Winston

The Govt: bag went this afternoon & the ordinary mail is closed – but the Colonial Sec. is leaving tonight for England, & I am sending this hasty line by him – a P.S. to my long letter. You ought to get it the 7th of Dec:

An unexpected mail has just come in – just caught us before our departure tomorrow & yrs of the 15th & 19th [September] & also one from Jack. Darling boy don't be foolish about the riding – if anything happened to you – who wl^d look after you?

I send you a cheque for £12, a pres: for yr birthday – don't tell anyone. Don't think <u>too</u> much of amusement – how about yr German??

Bless you darling – thank Jack for me for his letter. Send my love to Aunt Clara – & tell her I will write without fail from Burmah. I've been too low to write – she will understand. In haste

Yr loving Mother
JSC

JENNIE SUFFERED a second blow concerning her personal future when she and Lord Randolph reached Rangoon. A telegram reached her there from Charles Kinsky, telling her of his engagement to a young Austrian countess, Elisabeth Wolff-Metternich zur Gracht. He had given up waiting for Jennie to become free and finally submitted to the pressure from his father, Prince Ferdinand, to marry a younger, Catholic woman from the ranks of the Austro-Hungarian aristocracy. 'I <u>hate it</u>. I shall return without a friend in the world & too old to make any more now,' Jennie wrote to her sister Clara.[9]

---

9   18 November 1894, JSC letter to C. Frewen, A. Leslie, *Jennie*, p. 172.

— WSC TO JSC —

21 October [1894]   [no address]

My own darling Mamma,

I was overjoyed to receive yesterday your letter dated Sept 20th [missing]. The first news I had had for 5 weeks. I cannot understand why you have not received any of the numerous letters I have written to you. I have written very nearly 30 letters since your departure. [...]

We are very much disturbed by Dr Keith's last letter which gives a very unsatisfactory report about Papa. I hope however that there is still an improvement and no cause for immediate worry. Poor old Grandmamma is very low. [...]

Of course you know how I should like to come out and join you in India on your way home. I have worked now for 5 years pretty hard for constant examinations and I think I might really be allowed to have 3 or 4 months rest – especially as there is no real work for me to do. Papa has suggested my going to Germany, a prospect which fills me with profound dissatisfaction. [...]

If I don't come out to meet you I shall go and stay with Lady Wilton at Monte Carlo for a little. I don't suppose that Papa would object – as [I] should have my commission and would really be old enough to look after myself. [...]

With best love and kisses I remain, Ever your loving and affection son
Winston

AFTER WRITING this letter Winston prevailed on the family doctor to tell him the full extent of his father's condition.

— WSC TO JSC —

2 November 1894   50 Grosvenor Square

My dearest Mamma,

[...] I persuaded Dr Roose to tell exactly how Papa was – as I thought it was only right that I should know exactly how he was progressing. You see I only hear through grandmamma Jerome who does not take a very sanguine view of things – or through the Duchess who is at one extreme one minute and at the other the next.

So I asked Dr Roose and he told me everything and showed me the medical reports. I have told no one – and I beg you above all things not to write to Roose on the subject of his having told me as he told it me in confidence. I need not tell you how anxious I am. I had never realized how ill Papa had been and had never until now believed that there was anything serious the matter. I do trust & hope as sincerely as human beings can that the relapse Keith spoke of in his last report was only temporary and that the improvement of the few months has been maintained. Do, my darling mamma when you write let me know exactly what you think.

[...] Now about yourself. Darling Mummy I do hope that you are keeping well and that the fatigues of travelling as well as the anxiety you must feel about Papa – are not telling on you. I can't tell you how I long to see you again and how I look forward to your return. Do what you can with Papa to induce him to allow me to come out and join you. [...]

With best love & kisses I remain, Ever our loving and affectionate son
Winston

– WSC TO JSC –

8 November 1894   Sandhurst

My dearest darling Mamma,

I got yesterday a report of Papa from Yokohama. Dr Roose was good enough to let me see it. [...] I am very sorry to hear that so little improvement has been made, and that apparently there is not much chance of improvement. [...]

Do please write and tell me all about him – quite unreservedly. You know you told me to write to you on every subject freely.

Well – all this is very sad to us at home – at least to me – for grandmamma does not know what Dr Keith writes. I fear that much worry will tell upon you – and that the continual anxiety & added to the fatigues of travelling will deprive you of any interest & pleasure in the strange things you see. If I were you I would always try and look on the bright side of things and endeavour perpetually to derive interest from everything. Above all don't get ill yourself. [...]

> *With best love my darling Mummy,*
> *Ever your loving son*
> *Winston*

— WSC to JSC —

25 November 1894   Sandhurst

My darling Mamma,

I was at Dr Roose's on Sunday & he showed me the telegram from Madras [now Chennai] that had just arrived. I cannot tell you how shocked and unhappy I am – and how sad this heavy news makes me feel. I do not know – how far distant the end of poor dear Papa's illness may be – but I am determined that I will come out and see him again. [...]

It must be awful for you – but it is almost as bad for me. You at least are on the spot & near him.

This is what you ought to try and do. Bring him back – at least as far as Egypt & if possible to the Riviera <u>and I with Jack will come and join you there</u>. Darling dearest Mummy keep your pluck & strength up. Don't allow yourself to think. Write to me <u>exactly</u> how he is. God bless you & help us all.

> *Your loving son*
> *Winston*

Write me an answer to this letter by the return mail. Please.

— WSC to JSC —

9 December 1894   Sandhurst

My darling Mamma,

I am so glad to hear of your return. Write to me and let me know what you think and everything. I have written Papa about [the] riding prize – he will be pleased. Your dear letter with cheque arrived exactly on my birthday as it chanced. […]

I do not wish to make difficulties or add to your labours my darling mummy – but I don't intend for one instant to exile myself in Germany with Papa as ill as he is. As soon as I know about the exams I shall go at once to stay with you and him and will of course come sooner if you can arrange it.

Write soon. With best love and kisses My darling dearest Mummy, I Remain,

Ever your loving son

Winston

W INSTON PASSED out of Sandhurst in mid-December 1894; he was now qualified to be commissioned as an officer.

— WSC TO JSC —

17 December 1894   The Deepdene, Dorking[10]

My darling Mummy,

[…] Duchess Lily is very kind – says charming things about you & has apparently been quite informed as to Papa's health. She is very good to me and I am sorry to have to hustle away to Blenheim to-morrow as the shooting is very fair. We killed 132 pheasants this morning of which I was responsible for 20.

I finished with Sandhurst very successfully; leaving many friends and numerous acquaintants. The examinations were after all easy and I think it extremely probable that I have obtained Honours. […]

Although I intend to be most submissive – I am firmly determined not to exile myself in Germany while my father is ill. A telegram will bring me out to you at any time and should Papa not come home before

---

10 Estate in Dorking, Surrey, leased by Lily, dowager duchess of Marlborough (see Places, p. 579).

the end of January I shall come out and stay with you. Keep up a good heart my darling mummy. God bless you & help you.

With best love, Ever your loving son
Winston

J ENNIE ARRIVED home with her husband in time for Christmas. Lord Randolph lasted another month before he died on 24 January 1895. Charles Kinsky had married his bride two weeks earlier.

5

SINGLE PARENT

1895–6

'You really ought to leave no stone unturned'

I N H I S will Lord Randolph left almost all his capital to be bound up in a trust, from which Jennie would receive the investment income each year. Thanks to the success of a gold-mining company in which Lord Randolph had bought shares at the end of his trip to southern Africa, the trust ended up with an unexpectedly large sum of capital, amounting to £55,000.

Jennie also became the sole beneficiary of the marriage settlements that each of the Churchill and Jerome families had created to mark her marriage to Lord Randolph in 1874. In all, her income amounted to £5,000 a year, enough on the face of it to allow a young widow of forty-one to hold her own in the top echelons of London society.

Beneath the surface, however, Jennie's position was not so straightforward. She had no home in London; she had no access to the capital with which to buy one; and her husband had left nothing in his will for their sons, a serious omission in the stratified world of Victorian society where financial prospects and marriage usually went hand in hand. Jennie would have to use her own income to provide her sons with a living allowance, at least until they could earn their own way. Finally, Jennie had lived in style all her life; she was not used to counting the pennies.

Winston worried less about the financial consequences of his father's death. He was more concerned with the pressing issue of whether he could switch from the infantry to win a commission in the cavalry with the 4th (Queen's Own) Hussars. He claimed in *My Early Life* that his father had blessed the switch before he died; yet Winston realized that he had to achieve it, by the combined efforts of his mother and himself. He had put the case for the change to her in writing to her while his father still lay on his deathbed.

— WSC TO JSC —

11 January [1895]   Hindlip Hall,[1] nr Worcester

My dearest Mamma,

I have written to Colonel Brabazon and have stated my various arguments in favour of a cavalry regiment. I have asked him to say whether or not they are correct – when he writes to you – but in case he should not state this clearly I will put them down for you.

1. Promotions much quicker in Cavalry than in Infantry. (60th Rifles slowest regiment in the army).

2. Obtain your commission (3 or 4 months) in Cav much sooner than in Infantry.

3. 4th Hussars are going to India shortly. If I join before "Augmentation" I should have 6 or 7 subalterns below me in a very short time.

4. Cavalry regiments are always given good stations in India

---

1   Another home of Lord and Lady Hindlip.

and generally taken great care of by the Government – while Infantry have to take what they can get.

5. If you want to keep a horse you can do it much cheaper in the cavalry than in infantry – government will provide stabling – forage – and labour.

6. Sentimental advantages grouped under heading of

    a   uniform

    b   increased interest of a "life among horses" etc

    c   advantages of riding over walk

    d   advantages of joining a regiment some of whose officers you know. i.e. 4th Hussars. [...]

> *With best love and kisses I remain,*
> *Ever your loving son*
> *Winston S. Churchill*

———

C OLONEL BRABAZON, almost inevitably reputed to have numbered among Jennie's former lovers, duly spoke to the right people at the top of the army before instructing her to write 'at once' to the duke of Cambridge, the titular commander-in-chief of the forces, to complete the necessary formalities. By the middle of February, Winston had joined the 4th Hussars as a subaltern at their barracks in Aldershot where they were to remain until they moved to India in September 1896.

— WSC TO JSC —

19 February 1895   IV Hussars, Aldershot

My dear Mamma,

This must necessarily be a short letter as I have but little to say and not much time to say it in. [...]

Everybody is very civil and amiable and I have no doubt I shall get on all right with them. My sedentary life of the last three months has

Jennie and Winston in the aftermath of Lord Randolph's death, 1895.

caused me to be dreadfully stiff after two hours riding school, but that will wear off soon.

My room will have to be furnished – but I have made arrangements with a local contractor, who for a small charge will furnish it palatially on the hire system.

There appears to be a very large Harrow element in the regiment – all of whom are very agreeable and nice. The work, though hard and severe is not at present uninteresting, and I trust that the novelty & the many compensating attractions of a military existence – will prevent it from becoming so – at any rate for the next four or five years. [...]

I will write again soon, my darling Mummy – but for the present – this and the assurance of my undying love, must suffice.

With best love, Your ever loving son
Winston S. Churchill

– WSC to JSC –

20 February 1895   Aldershot

My dear Mama,

[...] To my astonishment I find myself in the [*Official*] *Gazette* this morning – so that pay begins and my commission dates from Tuesday.

The riding school is fearfully severe and I suffer terribly from stiffness – but what with hot baths and massage I hope soon to be better. At present I can hardly walk. I have however been moved up in to the 2nd Class recruits which is extremely good. These horses are very different to the Sandhurst screws. Rather too broad I think for me. [...]

They play Bézique here for 3^{d} points – which is a shocking descent from the shillings of Deepdene.[2]

I will write again soon – Now don't criticize my handwriting in

---

2   A game of cards played by two people, popular in 19th century France and introduced to Britain in the 1860s. '3^{d}' and 'shillings' were coins of Britain's pre-decimal currency: 3^{d} was one quarter of a shilling; twenty shillings made £1.

your next. The pens are awful. My own black-edged paper [to denote mourning for his father] arrives tomorrow.

With lots of love your ever loving son
Winston S. Churchill

F OR HER part, Jennie set off in February for Paris, dressed in black and accompanied by her maid and by Lord Randolph's valet. Custom required widows in London to mourn for six months, but, in cases where a social purdah of this length in London failed to appeal, it was acceptable to spend it in Paris instead.

Jennie rented an apartment close to the Champs Elysées, which she started to redecorate before the affairs of Lord Randolph's estate had been properly settled. She therefore found herself short of funds at the same time as Winston was sending a steady stream of requests for money to help himself establish himself in his new life as a cavalry officer. Aunt Lily had at least offered to help out with the cost of buying a charger, or horse for hunting.

— WSC TO JSC —

24 February 1895   East Cavalry Barracks, Aldershot

My darling dearest Mummy,

[...] Everything is going on very satisfactorily and if I have made no friends – at least I can say I have offended no one. Everybody is very civil and the days pass pleasantly enough.

I play a good deal of whist in the evenings – a most uninteresting game – and one at which I have but little luck – the points however are desperately low so I take no harm. [...]

Yesterday I went to London to see Aunt Lily about the charger. She empowered me to give Colonel Brab[azon] *carte blanche* to get a good one. [...]

I went to see Grandmamma – who looked very pale and worn. I 'cowtowed' and did the civil – which I think pleased her very much.

She carped a little at your *apartement* in "the gayest part of the Champs Elysees" but was otherwise very amiable – or rather was not particularly malevolent. [...]

> *Well goodbye my darling Mummy, Best love and many kisses from your ever*
> *loving son*
> *Winston S. Churchill*

— WSC TO JSC —

2 March 1895   Hotel Metropole,³ Brighton

My dear Mamma,

[...] Things have been going very well with me. I am making friends and many acquaintances. [...] This is the more satisfactory – as Col Brab has only just come down – so that I have found my footholds for myself.

The Colonel is going to see the Duchess Lily himself – about the charger. I fear he will be very grasping – but she will not mind paying a good deal – if he is diplomatic and tactful – as I am sure he will be. [...]

I do hope, my dearest Mamma, that you will keep well and not give way to depression. I am sure Aunt Leonie will look after you and make the time pass pleasantly. I look forward to a few days [off] at Easter – and am likely to get them – so you must keep a "fatted calf" for the occasion.

Now to end a long – and I fear stupid letter – Goodbye my dearest Mamma.

> *Best love & kisses from your ever loving son*
> *Winston S.C.*

— WSC TO JSC —

23 March 1895   Aldershot

My dearest Mamma,

[...] The first part of this letter must be devoted to finance. I find, on writing to Cox [Cox & Co., Winston's new bankers] for my pass book

---

3   Designed by the architect Alfred Waterhouse, the hotel opened in 1890.

that he has already paid out of my account the following subscriptions which I enclose.

I do not think that these are all but I believe they form the major part of the subscriptions one has to pay on joining. [...] I hope you will not delay in sending me a cheque for this amount.

I hope to get the bills for outfit etc in, in about three weeks from this date – and then I will send them to you.

Meanwhile I am looking everywhere for a nice cheap 2nd charger – price from 70 – 100 – which, when I find the horse – will probably have to be paid at once.

This recapitulation of expenses probably strikes you as rather heavy – but I may say that I think that the whole of the outfit will be included in the original estimate of £400. [...]

Well goodbye my dearest Mamma. Very best love and many kisses from your
loving son
Winston

———

CLARA JEROME died in England on 2 April 1895, after a short illness. Jennie attended her mother's funeral with both her sons on 14 April before returning to Paris, where Jack joined her for Easter.

— WSC to JSC —

27 April 1895   Aldershot

My dearest Mamma,

I was so glad to get your letter and to learn that, so far, at least, you have escaped the ravages of the influenza.[4] I have got a lot of

---

4   London's flu epidemic of 1895 was the second worst of the decade, as measured by deaths from the infectious disease. It followed a continuous frost from 21 January to 20 February, when little water circulated in the capital's sewage system; the highest number of deaths was recorded early in March (1,448 in a week from respiratory diseases, 473 from flu); the death toll then declined slowly to the end of April.

tiresome financial details to write to you about – which I will get over first.

[...] I am at present very hard up. [...] Would it be possible and convenient to you to pay at present so large a sum as £100–£120? If not I could wait perhaps a fortnight – but it is an awful bore riding other people's horses. I know that you could not pay a lump sum like that out of your income – but I understood my horses etc were to come out of the capital – I mean the money you are keeping back to buy house etc. [...]

If therefore, as I imagine – you have some ready money do lend me a hundred pounds – even if you do not think you will be able to give it to me as you said. The sooner the better – as ponies rise in price every day – and also I cannot go on without any for more than a few days – unless I give up the game [polo], which would be dreadful. [...]

I would point out that had not my personal charms induced the Duchess Lily to give me a charger it would have been 100 or 120 more. [...]

With very best love and lots of kisses I remain, Ever your loving son
Winston S. Churchill

— WSC to JSC —

2 May [1895]   Aldershot

My Dear Mamma,

I am very sorry that things have not been settled as quickly as you had expected. I am still £25 short of my full allowance for this quarter – after deducting from the amount owed to me the £45 you have advanced. [...]

I cannot put it plainer than that. I am absolutely at the end of my funds – so if you can possibly give me a cheque for all – or any part of this sum – I shall be awfully pleased – but if you can't – you can't & that settles it. I agree with you it is dreadfully inconvenient & I hate to have to worry you like this – but my mess bill comes in in a few days and must be paid somehow. [...]

Well good bye my darling Mamma – let me beg you to try and send me a little money, as it is not a case of current expenses but paying deliberately incurred liabilities.

Your ever loving son
Winston

— WSC to JSC —

8 May [1895]   Aldershot

My dearest Mamma,

Very many thanks for the cheque. I will try and manage somehow until 15th when I must pay my mess bill. I am so sorry that things are not going well as regards finance. [...]

Otherwise nothing of note has occurred. Lord 'Bill' Beresford[5] has told the Colonel to get me a charger, price about £200 – so that is settled. But the Colonel does not hurry and I can't very well stir him up. [...]

Your ever loving son
Winston

— WSC to JSC —

16 May [1895]   Aldershot

My dear Mamma,

I quite understand how difficult it is for you and as you cannot arrange anything at present – I must wait. But I do hope that this deadlock will not last more than a very few days. My mess bill is of course unpaid and that will probably involve all sorts of unpleasant explanations and generally speaking is a thing to be very much avoided. [...]

I only write this to show you that things are very difficult with me

---

5   Lord William Beresford VC, married Lilian, former duchess of Marlborough, in 1895 (see People, p. 575).

and in order that you will be as quick as you can. Please send me a line and let me know what prospect there is.

With very best love, Your ever loving son
Winston

— WSC to JSC —

21 May [1895]   Aldershot

My dearest Mamma,

Mr Lumley[6] went with me to Cox's on Saturday and told one of the partners that there was a delay with regard to my allowance. They were very civil and placed £125 at my disposal pending your convenience to pay. So that was settled. [...]

Then with regard to the polo ponies – Messrs Cox have lent me £100 to buy them with and when things become settled then you can give me the £100 and I will pay them back.

With best love & hoping to see you very soon. Ever your loving son
Winston

— WSC to JSC —

23 May [1895]   Aldershot

My dearest Mamma,

I am sorry you find it necessary to be cross with me. I did not know you had paid my allowance into the bank. I thought I had arranged the whole thing myself & indeed I am still uncertain whether or no you have paid any money into the Bank. You see I have had no line from you on the subject or from Cox's acknowledging receipt of your cheque. So I forgot in my letter to thank you.

I have written a good many letters to you lately. Of course they were chiefly concerned with business – but I have always tried to tell

6   Theodore Lumley, partner of Lumley & Lumley, solicitors to the Churchill family (see People, p. 577).

you such news as I had & to write as often as I had the opportunity. I am very sorry you are not satisfied. With regard to the £55 you say I now owe – I must point out that I do not owe you anything until the £60 pounds I paid in subscriptions have been paid to me. And even then it is not 55 but fifty pounds. [...]

However! – to turn to other things – I am going to the Prince's Levee [court ceremony] on Monday. The Colonel is arranging the details for me. Tomorrow is the Queen's Birthday and of course it is here celebrated by much military display. [...]

Well my dearest Mamma, I can think of no more news & I will not bore you with more wants – so I send you lots of love & kisses – & hope you won't again find cause to scold.

Ever your loving son
Winston S. Churchill

– WSC to JSC –

6 June [1895]   Aldershot

My dearest Mamma,

I was delighted to get your letter yesterday evening. I understand altogether how difficult my numerous expenses make things for you – & I hate to have money discussions with you quite as much as you do. You have always been very generous in money matters & can never be sufficiently grateful to you for allowing me to go in the Cavalry.

But – of course you understand that beginning is expensive and that it is almost impossible for me to put down £40 out of £125 a quarter and I thought therefore that if you were going to buy a house & to borrow money to do it – so comparatively small a sum as £40 for a club might be added to your expenses. [...]

So with best love, Ever your loving son
Winston S. Churchill

— WSC to JSC —

17 June [1895]   Aldershot

My dear Mamma,

I am perfectly idiotic this morning. I have begun this letter three times & torn it up as many – so I trust you will excuse both composition and calligraphy.

As I told you the Colonel told Daly[7] to get me a charger – & after some time I received a magnificent animal – which is said to be the finest charger in the army. The horse cost £200 & Duchess Lily has sent a cheque for that amount – which is very generous of her. [...]

The Londonderry's[8] have been entertaining on a most magnificent scale. Enormous balls – 1500 people & political receptions almost daily. I have had a great many invitations & could go to a ball every night did I wish to – but field days & drills make me more eager for bed than anything else. [...]

With best love your loving son
Winston

— WSC to JSC —

23 June [1895]   Blenheim

My dearest Mamma,

[...] I went this morning to Bladon[9] to look at Papa's grave. The service in the little church was going on and the voices of the children singing all added to the beauty and restfulness of the spot. The hot sun of the last few days has dried up the grass a little – but the rose bushes

---

7 Possibly Major Hugh Daly, a cavalry officer; later knighted as a colonial administrator in India.
8 Charles Vane-Tempest-Stewart, marquess of Londonderry, cousin of WSC, and his wife, Theresa (see People, p. 565).
9 Village in Oxfordshire on the southern edge of the Blenheim Palace estate; its churchyard is the burial place of many members of the Churchill family, including JSC and WSC.

are in full bloom and make the church yard very bright. I was so struck by the sense of quietness & peace as well as by the old world air of the place – that my sadness was not unmixed with solace. It is the spot of all others he would have chosen. I think it would make you happier to see it.

Well, my darling Mummy – I will write to you of other matters in a day or two.

With my best love and kisses I remain, Ever your loving son
Winston

———————

A T   T H E beginning of July, Winston suffered his third loss of 1895 – this time of his childhood nanny, Mrs Everest, who had stayed with the family until 1893.

— WSC to JSC —

3 July [1895]   Aldershot

My dearest Mamma,

I have just got back from London. As I telegraphed to you – poor old Everest died early this morning from peritonitis. They only wired to me on Monday evening – to say her condition was critical. That was the first intimation I had of her illness. I started off & got [Doctor] Keith – who was <u>too</u> kind. [...]

Everything that could be done – was done. [...] It was very sad & her death was shocking to see – but I do not think she suffered much pain.

She was delighted to see me on Monday night and I think my coming made her die happy. [...] I shall never know such a friend again. [...] I feel very low – and find that I never realized how much poor old Woom was to me. I don't know what I should do without you.

With best love Ever your loving son
Winston S. Churchill

6 July [1895]   Aldershot

My dear Mamma,

I went yesterday to poor Everest's funeral & Welldon let Jack come up too. All her relations were there – a good many of whom had travelled from Ventnor overnight – and I was quite surprised to find how many friends she had made in her quiet and simple life.

The coffin was covered with wreaths & everything was as it should be. I felt very despondent and sad: the third funeral I have been to within five months! It is indeed another link with the past gone – & I look back with regret to the old days at Connaught Place when fortune still smiled.

My darling Mamma – I am longing for the day when you will be able to have a little house of your own and when I can really feel that there is such a place as home. [...]

With best love and many kisses I remain, Ever your loving son
Winston

———

J ENNIE STARTED house-hunting in August 1895, eventually choosing a property in Great Cumberland Place, on the northern side of Hyde Park. She showed it to Winston in September and told her sister Clara that she hoped to move in by the end of November, once builders had redecorated it 'top to toe, electric light, hot water, etc'. Each of Jennie's two sisters later bought houses in the same street, leading to its re-christening as 'Lower Jerome Terrace'.

Winston had only been with his regiment for six months, yet he was already beginning to chafe at the routine of army life and his lack of education – and to hint at harbouring political ambitions.

16 August [1895]   Aldershot

My dearest Mummy,

[...] I suppose you will have read the speech in which Sunny Marlborough moved the vote of thanks in return for the address. It appears to have been a very good and even brilliant speech & I was told he had a very good delivery – though a trifle too loud for the House. [...]

It is a fine game to play – the game of politics and it is well worth waiting for a good hand – before really plunging.

At any rate – four years of healthy and pleasant existence – combined with both responsibility & discipline – can do no harm to me – but rather good. The more I see of soldiering – the more I like it – but the more I feel convinced that it is not my *métier*. Well, we shall see – my dearest Mamma. [...]

Well au revoir my dear Mamma, With best love and kisses, I remain, Your loving son
Winston S. Churchill

24 August [1895]   Aldershot

My dearest Mamma,

[...] I find I am getting into a state of mental stagnation – when even letter writing becomes an effort & when any reading but that of monthly magazines is impossible. This is of course quite in accordance with the spirit of the army. It is indeed the result of mental forces called into being by discipline and routine. It is a state of mind into which all or nearly all who soldier – fall.

From this 'slough of Despond' I try to raise myself by reading & re-reading Papa's speeches – many of which I almost know by heart – but I really cannot find the energy to read any other serious work.

I think really that when I am quartered in London I shall go and study one or two hours a week with one of [Captain] James' men – a most capable fellow – either Economics or Modern History. If you know what I mean – I need someone to point out some specific subject to stimulate & to direct my reading in that subject. The desultory reading I have so far indulged in has only resulted in a jumble of disconnected & ill assorted facts. [...]

> *With best love my dearest Mamma I remain, Ever your loving son*
> *Winston S. Churchill*

———

JENNIE TRIED to help her son by suggesting that he write a dissertation on the 'supply of army horses'. Winston gave this idea short shrift, but did start to expand his reading. As he did so, the range of his expressions grew, as evidenced in the last, wistful paragraph of his next, important letter, which he addressed to his mother in Switzerland. She was staying with Jack at the Beau Rivage hotel in Geneva, a luxury establishment that had opened in 1865.

— WSC TO JSC —

31 August [1895]   Aldershot

My dearest Mamma,

I write this in answer to your long letter of two days ago. I have considered the subject you suggest "Supply of Army horses". [...] But I am bound to say it is not one which would interest me. It is too technical. It is a narrow question leading to a limited result. A subject more calculated to narrow and groove one's mind than to expand it. [...]

No – my dearest Mamma – I think something more literary and less material would be the sort of mental medicine I need. [...] You see – all my life – I have had a purely technical education. Harrow, Sandhurst, James's – were all devoted to studies of which the highest aim was to pass some approaching Examinations. As a result my mind has never received that polish which for instance Oxford or Cambridge gives. At these places one studies questions and sciences with a rather higher object than mere practical utility. One receives in fact a liberal education.

Don't please misunderstand me. I don't mean to imply any sneer at utilitarian studies. Only I say that my daily life is so eminently matter of fact that the kind of reading I require is not the kind which the subject you suggested to me would afford. I have now got a capital book – causing much thought – and of great interest. It is a work on political economy by Fawcett.[10] When I have read it – and it is very long, I shall perhaps feel inclined to go still farther afield in an absorbing subject. But this is a book essentially devoted to "first principles" – and one which would leave at least a clear knowledge of the framework of the subject behind – and would be of use even if the subject were not persevered in.

Then I am going to read Gibbon's *Decline and Fall of the Roman Empire*[11] & Lecky's *European Morals*.[12] These will be tasks more agreeable than the mere piling up of shoppy statistics. Well – this far and no farther – my dearest Mamma – will I investigate a question which I am sure will bore you in its discussion.

I write this letter – rather a pompous one too – to the Beau Rivage hotel. How I wish I could secrete myself in a corner of the envelope and embrace you as soon as you tear it open! [...]

What frightful losses we have sustained in the last twelve months. Never did misfortunes crowd in one on another. Only a year ago – almost to a day I was at Ouchy [near Lausanne]. Since then three figures, I had known and loved in different degrees and ways all my life – are gone. Time passes too quickly for vain regrets – & it is unprofitable to resist the consolation which it brings – by reviving ones sorrow. We take our turn – some today – others tomorrow. And after all it has gone on for thousands of years. The history of man is the story of

10 *Henry Fawcett, Political Economy,* published by Macmillan & Co. 1865. Professor Fawcett published a shorter digest, *Manual of Political Ecomomy* 1887.
11 Edward Gibbon, *The History of the Decline and Fall of the Roman Empire,* published in six volumes 1776–88; Gibbon was a Whig MP as well as an historian.
12 William Lecky, *History of European Morals, from Augustus to Charlemagne,* published 1869.

innumerable tragedies and perhaps the most tragic part is to be found in the insignificance of human grief. [...]

With best love, I remain, Ever your loving son
Winston S. Churchill

———

CAVALRY REGIMENTS in Britain trained for seven months in the middle of each year, before enjoying five months of winter leave. During this break, most officers hunted several times a week: the sport was considered healthy for cavalry officers. The routine held little appeal for Winston, however, not least because he did not have the necessary funds required for the expensive sport.

Instead, together with a fellow subaltern Lt. Reginald Barnes, he hatched a different scheme for the winter.

— WSC TO JSC —

4 October [1895]   Hounslow

My dearest Mamma,

I daresay you will find the content of this letter somewhat startling. The fact is that I have decided to go with a great friend of mine – one of the subalterns in the regiment[13] to America and the W. Indies. I propose to start from here between the Oct 28 & Nov 2 – according as the boats fit. We shall go to New York & after stay[ing] there move in a steamer to the W. Indies to Havana where all the Government troops are collecting to go up country and suppress the revolt that is still simmering on: after that back by Jamaica and Hayti to New York & so home.

The cost of the [first-class] ticket is £37 a head return – which would be less than a couple of months at Leighton Buzzard[14] by a long way. I do not think the whole thing should cost £90 – which would be within by a good margin what I can afford to spend in 2 months. [...]

———

13 Lt. Reginald Barnes, later Major-General Sir Reginald Barnes (see People, p. 569).
14 Centre of hunting, in Bedfordshire.

Now I hope you won't mind my going my dear Mamma – as it will do me good to travel a bit and with a delightful companion who is one of the senior subalterns and acting adjutant of the regiment & very steady. Please send me a line.

Your ever loving son
Winston

— JSC TO WSC —

11 October [1895]   Guisachan[15]

My dearest Winston,

You know I am always delighted if you can do anything which interests & amuses you – even if it be a sacrifice to me. I was rather looking forward to our being together & seeing something of you. Remember I only have you & Jack to love me.

You certainly have not the art of writing & putting things in their best lights but I understand all right – & of course darling it is natural that you sh^d want to travel & I won't throw cold water on yr little plans – but I'm very much afraid it will cost a good deal more than you think.

N.Y. [New York] is fearfully expensive & you will be bored to death there – all men are. I must know more about yr friend. What is his name? Not that I don't believe you are a good judge but still I sh^d like to be sure of him. Considering that I provide the funds I think instead of saying 'I have decided to go' it may have been nicer & perhaps wiser – to have begun by consulting me. But I suppose experience of life will in time teach you that tact is a very essential ingredient in all things. [...]

Goodbye God bless you dear – Yr loving Mother
JSC

[...] Would you like me as a birthday pres: to pay yr ticket??

---

15 Guisachan, near Inverness, owned by Edward Majoribanks, Lord Tweedmouth, who was married to JSC's sister-in-law, Lady Fanny Spencer-Churchill (see Places, p. 580).

O N 19 October, Jennie (once again back in Paris) wrote to Jack: 'Between you and I, I hope Winston won't get there. I'm afraid it will be a foolish business.'[16] She was to be disappointed.

− WSC to JSC −

21 October [1895]   Bachelors' Club[17]

My dearest Mamma,

The Cuban business is satisfactorily settled. The War Office have given consent & we have this afternoon been to see the head of the Intelligence Department General Chapman[18] who has furnished us with maps & much valuable information.

We are also requested to collect information and statistics on various points & particularly as to the effect of the new bullet − its penetration and striking power. This invests our mission with almost an official character & cannot fail to help one in the future.

When are you coming to London? Do send me a wire to let me know. I must see a little of you before we go. I shall bring back a great many Havana cigars − some of which can be "laid down" in the cellars of 35 Great Cumberland Place. [...]

I remain Ever your loving son
Winston S. Churchill

J ENNIE OVERCAME her reservations about the Cuban expedition in time to ask a new friend, Bourke Cockran, to look after Winston and his fellow subaltern Reginald Barnes when they passed through New York on the way to Miami and Cuba.

She had met Cockran in Paris earlier in the year, when the Irish-born

---

16 19 October 1895, letter JSC to Jack, CAC, PCHL 1/2/39.
17 London club, membership of which was reserved for bachelors.
18 Lt.-Gen. Sir Edward Chapman, shortly to take over command of the Scottish District as a full general.

American lawyer and politician made his way, too, to the French capital after the death of his wife. Born in Co. Sligo in 1854, the same year as Jennie, Cockran had left for New York at the age of seventeen and supported himself as a teacher while he studied the law and involved himself in politics. His eloquence, charm and education soon produced a lucrative practice at the bar and gave him a platform from which he won election as a Democrat to the House of Representatives.

Jennie and Cockran had found much in common to discuss in Paris where they spent so much time in each other's company that their friends assumed that they became lovers. At the summer's end, however, each returned to their own lives in London and New York, where Cockran was about to prove a generous – and influential – host to Jennie's twenty-year-old son on his first visit to North America.

— WSC to JSC —

8 November [1895]   Cunard Royal Mail Steamship *Etruria*[19]

My darling Mamma,

[…] We expect to arrive at about noon to-morrow and so bring a tedious and uncomfortable journey to a close. The weather was fine for the first day but after that we had it rough and stormy – with the spray covering the whole ship & the deck almost under water. Barnes and I were very stubborn and though we had bad moments were never sea-sick – nor did we miss any meal in the Saloon. Rather a fine performance considering that on one occasion there were only 12 people at dinner. […]

I do not contemplate ever taking a sea voyage for pleasure & I shall always look upon journeys by sea as necessary evils – which have to be undergone in the carrying out of any definite plan. […]

With best love and many kisses I remain, Ever your loving son
Winston

---

19 Launched in 1885, RMS *Etruria* ran between Liverpool and New York; in 1888 she completed the westbound voyage in a record time of 6 days, 1 hour and 55 minutes.

Bourke Cockran, Winston's host in New York.

— WSC to JSC —

10 November [1895]   763 Fifth Avenue, New York

My dearest Mamma,

[...] I and Barnes are staying with Mr Bourke Cockran in a charming and very comfortable flat at the address on this paper.

Everybody is very civil and we have engagements for every meal for the next few days about three deep. It is very pleasant staying here as the rooms are beautifully furnished and fitted with every convenience & also as Mr Cockran is one of the most charming hosts and interesting men I have met. [...]

[...] Today I snatch a quiet hour to pen you a line – but I lunch with Eva [Purdy][20] at 1 – call on the Hitts[21] at 3 – the Cornelius Vanderbilts[22] at 5 & dine with Kitty [Mott] at 8 – so you can see that there is not much chance of the time hanging heavily. They really make rather a fuss of us here and extend the most lavish hospitality. [...]

What an extraordinary people the Americans are! Their hospitality is a revelation to me and they make you feel at home and at ease in a way that I have never before experienced. On the other hand their press and their currency impress me very unfavourably.

I have great discussions with Mr Cockran on every conceivable subject from Economics to yacht racing. He is a clever man and one from whose conversation much is to be learned. [...] [incomplete]

---

20 Eva Purdy and Kitty Mott (see below) were sisters, and cousins of WSC (as nieces of Clara Jerome, JSC's mother).

21 Henry Hitt arrived in America in 1665; the family remained socially prominent in Ohio and New York.

22 Grandson of Cornelius Vanderbilt, who founded the family business (first in ships, later railroads). Cornelius senior fathered 13 children; he entrusted the running of the family business to Cornelius junior's father, Billy.

— WSC to JSC —

20 November 1895   Gran Hotel Inglaterra, Havana[23]

My darling Mamma,

I have just arrived here after a comfortable journey from New York. Mr Bourke Cockran procured a private state room in the train, so that the 36 hours we passed there were not as unpleasant as if we had had to travel in a regular compartment. [...]

[...] The General has telegraphed to Marshal Campos [marshal-general of the Spanish forces] to advise him of our arrival. The letters I have got are a free pass everywhere – and they allowed us to bring our pistols through the Customs as soon as I showed them these letters – in spite of the law being very strict on that point.

Tomorrow we start "for the front" or rather to Santa Clara where the Headquarters Staff are. We go by rail via Matanzas and Cienguegos.[24] The journey takes twelve hours as the trains move very slowly on account of the rebels damaging the line and trying to wreck the locomotives. [...]

Gomez the insurgent traitor is marching to meet Marshal Campos at the head of a force – variously estimated at from 50 to 18,000 men. Inaccuracy – exaggeration – and gratuitous falsehood are the main characteristics of the information received through Spanish sources.

[...] Give my best love to Jack. I wish I had his camera here. I was so foolish in not taking it.

> *With lots of love and many kisses. Ever your loving son*
> *Winston S. Churchill*

---

23 Opened in 1875, described by WSC as 'fairly good' (in a letter to Cockran).

24 Santa Clara lies almost in the geographic centre of Cuba. Matanzas lies on the north coast, 60 miles east of Havana; Cienguegos on the south coast, 100 miles south-east of Matanzas. The last leg of the route was 35 miles north-east to Santa Clara.

WINSTON REPORTED on the struggle between Spanish forces and Cuban rebels for the *Daily Graphic*, the newspaper owned by the Borthwicks, who were friends of his parents – it was his first assignment as a journalist. Once back in Havana, he provided a more personal account to his mother.

— WSC TO JSC —

6 December 1895   Gran Hotel Inglaterra, Havana

My dearest Mamma,

[...] Well my darling Mamma, I can't tell what pleasure it gives me to be able to write to you and tell you that we have got back safely. There were moments during the last week when I realized how rash we had been in risking our lives – merely in search of adventure. However it all turned up trumps and here we are.

[...] For eight days we were with the troops in the field. The General gave us horses and servants and we lived with his personal staff. He did himself very well as far as food went and until the cook got shot we suffered very little inconvenience. [...]

After much marching through virgin forest we found the enemy – and he promptly fired at us. Hence forward for the last three days of the column – we were almost continually under some sort of fire or another. I have described it all in my fourth letter to the *Daily Graphic* and so my dearest Mamma it is hardly necessary for me to re-write a long story. Finally on the last day we attacked the enemy's position and advanced right across open ground under a very heavy fire. The General is a very brave man – in a white and gold uniform on a grey horse – drew a great deal of fire on to us and I heard enough bullets whistle and hum past to satisfy me for some time to come. [...]

Our luck has been almost uncanny. Every train, every steamboat has fitted exactly. We missed two trains that were both smashed up by the rebels by about half an hour. We went into a town in which every sort of dreadful disease was spreading and finally if without any particular reason I had not changed my position about one yard to the right I should infallibly have been shot. Added to all this I left a fiver to be put on "The Rush" at 8 to 1 and it simply romped home. So you see my dear Mamma – there is a sweet little cherub. [...]

Longing to see you and Lots of love Your ever loving son
Winston S. Churchill

PS [...] I am going to bring over excellent coffee, cigars and guava jelly to stock the cellars of 35a.[25]

———

O N HIS return to London, Winston launched himself back into the social round that beckoned for young cavalry officers who could boast an aristocratic connection and a famous father. At Lord Rothschild's house, from which he wrote his next letter to his mother, he met two leading politicians who would loom large in his later life – Herbert Asquith and Arthur Balfour. Asquith had been home secretary in Rosebery's administration until June 1895, when he returned to opposition after the Liberals lost the general election to Lord Salisbury's Conservative–Liberal Unionist alliance. Balfour now served as leader of the House of Commons and first lord of the Treasury.

In his letter Winston also drew Jennie's attention to a speech by a third politician, Joseph Chamberlain, one of four Liberal Unionists to be offered posts in Salisbury's cabinet. He would remain secretary of state for the colonies until 1903.

— WSC TO JSC —

26 January 1896   Tring Park, Tring

My dear Mamma,
    [...] We have a very interesting party here. Mr & Mrs Asquith[26] –

———

25 Number of JSC's new house in Great Cumberland Place, London.
26 Herbert Asquith married his second wife Margot, née Tennant, in 1894 (see People, p. 571).

Mr Balfour[27] – the Recorder & Mr Underdown[28] who has great Railway interests in – Cuba – several ladies – ugly and dull – Hubert Howard[29] & myself. Lord Rothschild is in excellent spirits & very interesting and full of information. Altogether – as you may imagine – I appreciate meeting such clever people and listening to their conversation very much indeed.

[…] Mr Chamberlain[30] has made an excellent speech – but one remark rather sticks in my throat. He says that the aspect of the majority of the population of the Transvaal[31] – paying 9/10 of the taxes and having no representation is an anomaly! Rather a mild term this for a man with the history and political principles of Chamberlain. It was for such an 'anomaly' that America rebelled from England & a similar 'anomaly' was the prime cause of the French Revolution. […]

With best love, Ever your loving son
Winston

– WSC to JSC –

1 May 1896   35a Great Cumberland Place

My dearest Mamma,

Many thanks for your letter. I availed myself of the valuable suggestions contained therein and sent a cheque dated May 12. I do trust that you will be able to let me have my allowance by then as if it is late – the cheque will very likely be dishonoured. Sure to be in fact.

---

27 Arthur Balfour, nephew of Lord Salisbury, shared a deep love of music with JSC (see People, p. 571).
28 Emanuel Underdown KC, later a director of the United Railways of the Havana and Regla Warehouses.
29 Son of the earl of Carlisle; like WSC, he visited Cuba in 1895 and reported at Omdurman in 1898 as a special correspondent for *The Times*; he died in the battle.
30 Joseph Chamberlain and Lord Randolph had at first been political adversaries, later colleagues (see People, p. 572).
31 Officially the South African Republic, which remained independent until the Boers' defeat in 1902, when it became the Transvaal Colony of the British empire.

[...] I dined the night before last with Mrs Adair.[32] Such an interesting party. Mr [Joseph] Chamberlain – Lord Wolseley,[33] Mr Chaplin[34] – Lord James,[35] Sir Francis Jeune[36] and in fact all the powers that be. Chamberlain was very nice to me and I had quite a long talk with him on South Africa. [...]

I am making extraordinary progress at Polo – but I want very much to buy another pony. I wish you would lend me £200 as I could then buy a really first class animal which would always fetch his price. [...]

Cox would lend me the money if you would make yourself responsible – at 5% – with pleasure. Do please try and think over it. It is not a question of spending the money – but of putting it into stock – an investment in fact – which though not profitable would produce much pleasure.

Well goodbye my darling Mamma – our finance is indeed involved!! If I had not been so foolish as to pay a lot of bills I should have the money now.

Ever your loving son
Winston S. Churchill

———

I N THE summer of 1896, officers of the 4th Hussars enjoyed a long period of leave so that they could organize their personal affairs before they left for a three-year posting to India in September.

By now Winston was dreading the tedium of India and asked his mother to see if she could pull any strings to alter his posting.

———

32 Cornelia, American-born widow of John Adair, Irish landowner; after he died in 1885, she ran their estate and was a noted society hostess in London.

33 Field Marshall Viscount Wolseley, commander–in-chief British forces since December 1895; resigned 1900.

34 Henry Chaplin, landowner, racehorse owner and politician; then president of the local government board.

35 Henry James, former Liberal Unionist MP, recently ennobled; chancellor of the duchy of Lancaster.

36 Judge advocate general 1892–1905; created Baron St Helier 1905; married Susan, née Stewart-Mackenzie (see People, p. 568).

Jennie (seated), Hugh Warrender, Jack, Aunt Leonie and Winston (seated with dog, possibly Peas) at Cowes, 1896.

— WSC TO JSC —

4 August 1896   Hounslow

My darling Mamma,

I got your letter this morning – but it was not the first tidings I had heard of you at Cowes. "Bino" Stracey[37] told me he had seen you there in great form – all over the place in a launch.

What fun you must be having! I am trying to get away on Thursday as I am very bored here – but there is lots to do … .

37 Probably Sir Edward Stracey, Bt, a soldier and contemporary of WSC, born in 1871.

[...] My dear Mamma you cannot think how I would like to sail in a few days to scenes of adventure and excitement – to places where I could gain experience and derive advantage – rather than to the tedious land of India – where I shall be equally out of the pleasures of peace and the chances of war. [...]

When I speculate upon what might be and consider that I am letting the golden opportunity of my life go by I feel that I am guilty of an indolent folly that I shall regret all my life. A few months in S. Africa would earn me the S.A. [South Africa] medal and in all probability the [British South Africa] company's Star. Thence hot foot to Egypt – to return with two more decorations in a year or two – and beat my sword into an iron dispatch box. [...]

I cannot believe that with all the influential friends you possess and all those who would do something for me for my father's sake – that I could not be allowed to go – were those influences properly exerted.

It is useless to preach the gospel of patience to me. [...] I put it down here – definitely on paper – that you really ought to leave no stone unturned to help me at such a period. Years may pass before such chances occur again. [...]

Your ever loving son
Winston S.C.

6

A LONG WAY APART

1896

'This godless land of snobs and bores'

JENNIE FAILED to secure a change of plans for Winston, so he sailed to India with his regiment on 11 September 1896. Their route took them from Southampton via the Mediterranean Sea, through the Suez Canal and down the Red Sea until they landed three weeks later at Bombay. From there they travelled a short distance inland to a camp at Poona (now Pune) before moving south by train to their barracks in Bangalore, the capital of the state of Mysore (now Karnataka).

Winston and Jennie wrote to each other by almost every weekly mail. Letters usually took sixteen days to be delivered, several days faster than the troops' journey because the mail travelled overland as far as Brindisi in the south of Italy before continuing by sea.

When Winston first arrived in Bangalore, he reported enthusiastically on the city's climate (it lies almost 1,000 metres above sea level) and on his princely lifestyle in the barracks, where he shared a bungalow and its garden with two fellow lieutenants, Reginald Barnes (with whom he had travelled to Cuba a year earlier) and Hugo Baring, a scion of the banking family. Between them the three employed a retinue of twenty-eight servants.

Within weeks, however, Winston became bored with the routine of army life. It was so hot that training had to finish each day by 11 a.m., while polo could not begin until the temperature had cooled at 4.15 p.m. Winston filled the long gaps in between by reading, in an attempt to acquire the 'liberal education' that he felt he had missed. The more he absorbed of the style and vocabulary used by Edward Gibbon and Thomas Macaulay,[1] the more the style of his own letters began to change.

For her part, Jennie moved easily between her friends' country houses, where she was a popular guest thanks to her high spirits, conversational gifts and musical talent. Nevertheless, the loss of a small fortune – £4,000 – preoccupied her soon after Winston left England. She and her sisters had entrusted the sum to Captain James Cruikshank, a thirty-two-year-old man of roguish charm and extravagant lifestyle, whom they had met at a racecourse. Cruikshank posed as a 'company promoter', securing 'investments' in his fraudulent schemes (which often involved railways) from a series of prominent social figures.

By the time Jennie and her sisters 'invested' through him (and Winston contributed a small amount, too), Cruikshank had already been bankrupted twice. For the particular 'Spec' (or 'Speculation') that attracted the Jerome sisters, Cruikshank had worked in alliance with Arthur Cadogan MP, second son of the earl of Cadogan. Jennie and her sisters engaged the leading fraud and libel lawyer of the day,

---

1 Thomas Macaulay, historian and Whig politician, secretary of state for war 1839–41, paymaster-general 1846–8. His 1835 'Minute on Indian Education' helped English to replace Persian as the official language of India.

Sir George Lewis,[2] to represent them in their attempts to recover the money. Meanwhile, she warned her son off getting involved in racing in India.

— JSC TO WSC —

23 September 1896   Invermark[3]

Darling Winston,

I am thinking of you in the Red Sea piping – here it is like Dec[ember] pouring torrents & blowing great guns. I received yr telegram & hope you cl^d make out mine. I have thought of you so much darling boy since we parted at Southampton. [...] You will be glad to hear that there is still a chance of our getting our money back over the Spec. Cruikshank is to see Sir G. [George] Lewis tomorrow & I hope to hear good accounts of the interview.

Before I forget it, I want to talk to you very seriously about the racing pony – it may be dead for all I know, but if it is not I want you to promise me to sell it. I had a long talk with the Prince [of Wales] at Tulchan[4] & he begged me to tell you that you ought not to race, only because it is not a good business in India – they are not square & the best of reputations get spoiled over it. You don't know but everyone else does that it is next to impossible to race in India & keep clean hands. It appears that Col Brab[azon] told the Prince that he wished you hadn't this pony. Sell it & buy polo ponies. I am sure that you will regret it if you don't.

Now my lecture is over. Write & tell me in yr next that you will do as I wish. I had a very nice week at Tulchan but the weather was &

---

2 Sir George not only advised the rich and famous about their legal affairs, but, with his wife Elizabeth, entertained them and the leading cultural figures of the day on a grand scale at his London home (see People, p. 577).

3 Invermark Lodge, near Brechin Castle, Angus; home of the earl of Dalhousie.

4 A fishing lodge on the River Spey, rented by the Sassoons (see Places, p. 581).

is about as bad as it can be. I go to Minto[5] from here & I think I shall not go to Guisachan, but go home. It is not much fun going out to be half drowned. [...]

Darling boy I am longing to hear from you. Mind you tell me all about yr bungalow, & any fresh words you want to use in code. [...] I hear they played a good deal of baccarat at Tranby Croft.[6] I am quite sworn off poker which is a good thing – sixpenny bezique is now my form!

[...] If the Spec is of any good I will see what I can do for you at Cox's – that would be the best thing to settle first – & some bills afterwards. Mind you are careful of what you drink. [...]

Yr loving Mother
JSC

— WSC TO JSC —

18 September 1896   SS *Britannia*[7] (between Malta and Alexandria)

My dearest Mamma,

I write this letter to you today – though we do not reach Port Said till Sept 20 & it cannot be posted till then. [...] This voyage is a very different experience to crossing the Atlantic in a Cunarder last winter. Then the alternative was between lying cold on deck or seasick and miserable below – but now in the blue Mediterranean things are much more pleasant. The ship is comfortable – the food good & the weather delicious. [...] We pass many ships & my telescope is in great demand and constant use. It is a very powerful glass and will be very valuable in India. [...]

---

5   Minto House in the Scottish borders, seat of the earl of Minto (see Places, p. 581).
6   Scene in Yorkshire of a cheating scandal at baccarat in 1890 when the Prince of Wales was visiting; the incident led to a court case at which the Prince was compelled to give evidence in 1891.
7   Launched in 1887, owned by the P&O Steam Navigation Co. (P&O), used mainly on its route to India; troop ship 1895–7.

In strong contrast to these excellent arrangements I must describe to you my first experience of the pitiful parsimony of the Indian Government. We have been presented with long lists of articles to declare and on which duty must be paid. Would you believe it? Even my regimental saddle is liable to [this] excise. It seems to me a disgraceful thing to tax public servants going to India by the order of the Government in this extraordinary manner [...] . It is contrary to the fundamental principle of government – No taxation without Representation. But to impose such a tax on a saddle used only in military employment is so monstrous an act of injustice that you will find it hard to credit it. I expect I shall find many more instances of this same detestable fruit of bureaucracy. I must go to luncheon now – (or is it "tiffin") – to curb my indignation and this letter.

With best and fondest love to you and Jack from Your ever loving son,
Winston S. Churchill

September 20 [postscript in the same envelope]

Tomorrow we arrive at Port Said. The weather is beginning to get hot … . They say we shall experience great heat in the Red Sea. I feel sure I shall stand it well – being very fat with lots to come off. [...] I do hope tomorrow I may hear that the 'spec' has come off.

Best love my dearest Mamma – expect a P.S. tomorrow
Winston

— JSC TO WSC —

1 October [1896]   Minto House, Hawick

Dearest Winston,

I was so glad to get yr long letter [of 18 and 20 September] from Port Said – I wonder how you have fared since but you are like me in not minding heat – I simply loved it. [...] I must say I agree with you, it is monstrous having to pay duty on saddles etc. I will air the grievance when I get the chance. I enclose a copy of letter from Sir G. Lewis. [...]

Dear Ly Randolph,
I saw Capt C. [Cruikshank] on Friday. I did my best to get from
him particulars of the investment of the money, to whom it had been
paid, to what company, & from what sources was to be derived the
profits – but though I pressed him over & over again he avoided
giving any account & I feel satisfied that he has acted dishonestly.
[…] I sent to Rye where Capt. C. lives to make enquiries about
him & I find that he rents a large place from Mr Brookfield MP
for a time & keeps horses & lives in great style – I am afraid this
establishment is kept up upon yr money. […]

I am by the way of going to Blenheim on the 14th to play at a concert but Ld Hindlip has lent me his house at Newmarket & as it is the
Caesarevitch[8] I am going to see if I can get out of it. […] Do tell me in
yr next that you have taken steps to sell the pony. You have no idea how
it worries me – they all tell me that the racing in India is "very shifty
unsatisfactory thing". If you play fair you can't win.

Now my darling goodbye until next week. […] Take care of yrself
& peer into that Bible sometimes, & love me very much. My love to
the Bungalow.

Yr loving Mother
JSC

— WSC to JSC —

21 September 1896   Port Said

My dearest Mamma,
Your wire received. Letters not yet. […] What an atrocious fraud
has been perpetrated on us. I strongly advise your putting the whole
thing in George Lewis' hands. Cadogan should in my opinion be made

---

8   Horse race held at Newmarket each October, named in honour of Tsarevich
    Alexander of Russia (later Alexander II) when he donated £300 to the Jockey
    Club.

to clear himself too. [...] Port Said is a dirty, squalid and uninteresting place[9] and I do not regret that we steam at noon today. [...]

Best love from your loving son

Winston

— JSC to WSC —

8 October 1896   Floors Castle[10]

Dearest Winston,

[...] The papers are full of Ld Rosebery's resignation of the leadership of the Liberal Party.[11] It is a very clever move on his part – as of course he knew he had no chance of the Premiership & the dissensions in the L.P. [Liberal Party] give him a good excuse of retiring. I suppose old Harcourt will take his place, with reversion to Asquith.[12] By the way Mr Brodrick[13] who is here has just brought in the *Truth*[14] with another vicious article. I send it.

I came here last night from Minto for one night & found them all in a great state of mind as one of their visitors L[d] Kensington[15] fell down dead of heart as they were walking back from shooting. The body is here & the family arrive tomorrow. [...]

I go back to London tonight & to Newmarket on Monday. L[d] Hindlip has lent me a house he has & I have asked Leonie & Jack to come. I may have to go to Blenheim on the Wed to play at a concert.

---

9   Port Said, at the northern end of the Suez Canal, was established in 1859 when the canal was built.

10 In Roxburghshire, seat of the dukes of Roxburghe.

11 Archibald Primrose, earl of Rosebery, former prime minister, resigned as leader of the opposition on 6 October 1896 (see People, p. 574).

12 Rosebery was succeeded jointly by Lord Kimberley in the House of Lords and Sir William Harcourt in the House of Commons. Sir Henry Campbell-Bannerman became sole leader of the party in 1898; Asquith did not take over until 1908.

13 St John Brodrick, Conservative MP, under-secretary of state for war.

14 Magazine of investigative journalism, edited by Henry Labouchere MP.

15 William, Baron Kensington, a former court official and Liberal MP.

I hope to get off as it is the Caesarevitch. I am expecting every moment to get a wire about the Spec. Cruikshank was given until last night to pay up & Cadogan swore he intended to pay with profits!! But I have no faith in it. [...]

Now goodbye darling boy. Take care of yrself & work at yr Hindustani. [...]

Yr loving Mother
JSC

———

WINSTON'S EXPERIENCE as an army officer – now of eighteen months' standing – had helped to build his self-confidence as a speaker, as he explained to his mother in his next letter. He had been concerned about a speech impediment that a surgeon would later tell him resulted from a 'tongue-tie' at birth. It appears that the impediment presented itself as a lisp, and a difficulty with expressing words containing the letter 's', rather than as a stutter.

— WSC TO JSC —

30 September 1896   SS *Britannia* (in the Indian Ocean)

My dearest Mamma,

The voyage is drawing to a close & I for one shall be glad to get on dry land again. [...]

Last night we had rather an amusing "Breach of Promise" case in which I was counsel for the defence. To my relief I found myself able to speak without notes or preparation for twenty minutes and as I succeeded in keeping the audience in constant laughter – my harangue was a success. My impediment did not seem to interfere with my articulation at all and of all who spoke I was the best heard. In the army I came like a duckling among chickens – I don't know whether I or they were most astonished to find I could swim.

I am very anxious to hear further news of your speculation and the consequent prosecution. It is hard indeed to imagine a more cowardly

– mean – and contemptible swindle. The burglar who steals a few pounds worth of plate with an honest gemmy is sent to prison for seven years and it will be simply monstrous if those silken-hatted scoundrels are to be left at large to continue their depredations. [...]

Ever your loving son
Winston

— JSC то WSC —

22 October [1896] Friday   35a Gt Cumberland Place

Dearest Winston,

I feel I wrote you such a scrap last week [missing] that I ought to make up for it today – and yet here I am in a great hurry to catch the post.

[...] I was very glad to get your first letter, and to see that you have had such a prosperous journey. I suppose you are settled by now. I enclose a cheque which tho' small is better than nothing. Today the Spec is to be paid up – or proceedings are to be prosecuted at once. I will wire if it comes off.

I am going to Newmarket next week and then to Sandringham[16] and then back here for a short bit. I raced to see Jack [at Harrow] yesterday – very flourishing.

I have agreed to take him away after this term. Goodbye darling. Bless you. All is well here.

Your loving mother
JSC

— WSC то JSC —

4 October [1896]   Poona Rest Camp

My dear Mamma,

[...] I have been so hard worked these last two or three days ... .

---

16 Sandringham House in Norfolk, bought by Queen Victoria in 1862 for the Prince of Wales (see Places, p. 581).

The disembarkation was a tremendous business and as nearly 500 tons of luggage had to be moved we were busy from 4 in the morning till late at night. I found an hour however to run ashore and look at Bombay [...] .

By train from Bombay we reached this place early yesterday. We are installed in tents – which are as you may imagine very hot under the midday sun – but there is a comfortable mews with a verandah, ice & punkahs.[17] The heat is very great ... .

I have engaged a capital Indian servant who is indefatigable in looking after me and who has a very good character for honesty. [...]

What a strange thing it is – that one so easily adapts oneself to change of scene and custom. Here I am the third day in India – looking at natives as if I had seen them all my life and not a bit impressed with a sense of novelty. [...]

Your letter written from Tulchan arrived here this morning. I do hope you will be able to get that wicked thief punished. I have no sympathy for such people. Sir George Lewis will be able (if any one is), to bring the law upon him in the most effectual way.

Now goodbye my dearest Mamma. Best of love and many kisses to you and Jack. Expect another letter shortly. While material is plentiful you may be sure I will write often.

Ever your loving son
Winston

— WSC to JSC —

14 October [1896]   Bangalore

My dearest Mamma,

The mail has just come in – bringing with it your long and welcome letter of the 23rd Sept. I am very glad indeed to hear that there is still some chance of your getting your money back over the 'spec'. At the same time – whether Cruikshank pays or not he is a swindler and a thief

---

17 A large cloth fan, suspended from the ceiling on a frame, operated by a servant or 'punkawallah'.

Winston's bungalow at Bangalore.

– having obtained money by false pretences in the meanest possible
manner. He ought therefore to be prosecuted and also to have his true
character thoroughly published to the world. [...]

As to the racing pony 'Lily'. I have so far heard nothing of it – nor
do I know by what steamer or in what condition it will arrive – but at
the same time I expect it will be here within a fortnight. I do not at all
want to sell it – and I cannot see that it is unwise of me to keep it. Bill
Beresford would not be likely to have given it to me if it was certain to
involve the unpleasant consequences you anticipate. [...]

Of course I shall do what you wish in the matter and if you insist
upon my getting rid of the pony I will sell her – [...]. Let me beg you,
my dear Mamma, to bear in mind that it is one thing for you to say "sell"
and quite another for me to find anyone to buy – except at a ridiculous
price. Also do remember that there is no reason why I should not join
in the sports of my equals and contemporaries – except on the ground
of expense. If you still wish me to get rid of the pony – after you have
considered what I have written here – I will do so, but even then I
should have to wait my opportunity. [...]

I wrote you my last letter from Poona – which we left on the 6th for this place. [...] The journey from Poona was very hot and the rest camps detestable. However after four days of hard work and continual travel we arrived here on Thursday last.

The climate is very good. The sun – even at midday is temperate and the mornings and evenings are fresh and cool. Hugo, Barnes and I are safely installed in a magnificent pink and white stucco palace in the middle of a large and beautiful garden. I will send you a photograph of the bungalow as soon as we are thoroughly settled. For servants we each have a "Butler" whose duties are to wait at table – to manage the household and to supervise the stables: A First Dressing Boy or valet who is assisted by a second D.B.: and a *sais* [*syce* or groom] to every horse or pony. Besides this we share the services of 2 gardeners – 3 Bhistis or water carriers – 4 Dhobies or washermen & 1 watchman. Such is our *ménage*.

I think I shall like this place and shall enjoy the time I spend here. I do wish you my dear mamma you could come out. [...] My writing table at which I now am – is covered with photographs and memories of those in England. The house is full of you – in every conceivable costume and style. My cigarette box that you brought me from Japan – my books – and the other Lares and Penates[18] lie around and I quite feel at home – though 6,000 miles away. [...]

I play Polo three times a week and find the game out here is very easy. As to indulgencies – I am teetotal and practically non-smoker till Sundown – drinking lemon squash – or occasionally – <u>beer</u> – which after all is but a temperance prescription. I am very well indeed and see no reason why I should not continue so. ...

Goodbye my dearest Mamma – With every wish for love and lots of kisses

Ever your loving son
Winston

---

18 Guardian deities of the household, according to Roman mythology.

WRITING NEARLY forty years later in *My Early Life*, Winston expanded further on the virtues of his retinue of Indian servants: 'No toil was too hard, no hours were too long, no dangers too great for their unruffled calm or their unfailing care. Princes could not live better than we.'[19]

— JSC to WSC —

5 November [1896]   Sandringham

Dearest Winston,

I was so glad to get your letter from Bangalore. How I should love to be with you my darling boy. Yr life sounds very pleasant. [...]

Now to answer yr various questions. About the pony [...] I don't want to enter into a long dissertation on racing in India. I am only telling you what the Prince and other people say – and that is that there is very little fair play in India and if you are honest you have very little chance of winning with the best horse. Anyhow you are warned – and remember that any error of judgment will be counted against you. [...]

I came here on Monday – a very pleasant party tho' not wildly exciting [...] . I am going to stay over the Sunday – when the Salisburys, Arthur Balfour & the new Bishop of London Crichton[20] are coming – the latter used to be private tutor to your Father. [...]

Lewis is still at the Creature [Cruikshank] – but I have given up all hope of getting the money back. Darling boy I do not go to London until Monday – but will send photos etc by next mail. Bless you take care of yourself – I love yr letters. When do you begin yr Hindustani?

Yr loving Mother
JSC

---

19 W. Churchill, *My Early Life*, p. 101.
20 Dr Mandell Crichton, editor of *The English Historical Review*; former bishop of Peterborough.

WITH HER letters, Jennie had enclosed further press cuttings from *Truth*, which was widely read in political circles. A series of articles between 25 June and 22 October 1896 had covered a story that the editor, Henry Labouchere, called the 'scandal of the 4th Hussars', concerning the behaviour of five young subalterns in the regiment, among whom he named a 'Spencer Churchill'.

Truth claimed that the five had bullied two candidate subalterns to deter them from joining the regiment; and that they had then organized a betting coup in the 4th Hussars' Subalterns' Cup race at Aldershot in 1895, when they ran a horse under a false name in order to beat the strongly backed favourite.

When the House of Commons debated the allegations, Labouchere claimed that the War Office's inquiries had amounted to nothing more than 'whitewash', in contrast to the National Hunt authorities' investigation which produced a lifetime ban from racing for the horses involved.

— WSC to JSC —

21 October 1896   Bangalore

My dearest Mamma,

Your letter of the 2nd Oct has just arrived [dated 1 October by Jennie]. I am much interested by Sir George Lewis' letter. It removes from my mind all possible doubt that we have been most cruelly swindled. [...] I do beg of you my dear Mamma – not to allow any scruples to stand between you and the discharge of a public duty. I cannot see what question there can be of legal process: criminal process is all that is wanted. The charge of obtaining money under false pretences – seems to me to exactly cover the case. I regret very much not being able to spur you on personally to exact satisfaction.

As I wrote to you at such length last week on the subject of the racing pony I will not revert to it in this letter except to say that you should tell His Royal Highness – if he says anything further about racing in India – that I intend to be just as much an example to the Indian turf as he is to the English – as far as fair play goes. [...]

I see by the forwarded papers that Labouchere has continued his attacks in *Truth*. It seems hard that when we are away in a foreign land and unable to answer or even read immediately any misstatement he may make – such attacks should go on – and that the public should swallow all of them so greedily. [...]

I get up here at 5 o'clock every morning and having eaten *Chota Hasri*[21] or *petit déjeuner* ride off to Parade at 6. At 8 o'clock breakfast and bath and such papers as there are: 9.45 to 10.45 Stables: and no other engagement till Polo at 4.15. This interval I fill – by sleeping – writing – reading or pursuing butterflies – according to inclination. Mess at 8.15 and bed immediately after bring the day to a close. [...]

Ever your affectionate and loving son
Winston S. Churchill

– JSC to WSC –

13 November 1896   35a Great Cumberland Place

My darling Winston,

[...] I came back from Sandringham Monday and have been rushing about as usual – you will be glad to hear that I do not indulge in as much skating as last winter. Cadogan[22] has written to implore me to stop the proceedings for a little – but I wrote him it was out of my hands. I hear Cruikshank is angry at the writ having "a fraud" in the corner – what else cl^d he have expected.

The Marlboroughs have been rather upset by the death of old Mrs Vanderbilt, Consuelo's grandmother – as they are going to have a great party and ball for the Royalties. They are still going to have the party but the ball is given up. I expect the American press will be very nasty – but as they always are it does not matter. I am dining tonight with Mr

---

21 Light meal served shortly after dawn.
22 Arthur Cadogan MP, second son of Earl Cadogan

Arthur Balfour at Willis's[23] and may hear some news. Politics seem to be deadly.

[...] L^d S's [Salisbury's] speech at the Mansion House[24] was very colourless but he can't help himself. [...] [incomplete]

I N BANGALORE Winston enjoyed his garden, his butterflies and polo. Yet a sense of disenchantment with the monotony of army life in India soon seeped into his letters.

— WSC to JSC —

26 October [1896]   Bangalore

My dearest Mamma,

[...] I have been very busy catching butterflies and playing polo. I am amassing quite a fine collection and Hugo & Barnes complain that the bungalow is degenerating into a taxidermist's shop. [...]

I fear you will never see any of your money again – which was invested in the "spec". I do not put the least reliance in any promises those dishonest men may make to gain time. But if you should get anything back – please do what you can for me. I need money out here very much indeed and any sum however small would be very welcome. [...]

You can't think with what pleasure and excitement I look forward to the mail. Do persuade people to write. Aunt Clara, who writes such good letters or Aunt Leonie. Turn on the devoted [Hugh] Warrender;[25] – stimulate Jack and above all write yourself long, long, letters. Every word is thoroughly appreciated out here – in this godless land of snobs and bores.

---

23 Willis's Rooms, King Street, St James's, originally known as Almack's Assembly Rooms; since 1765, a socially exclusive venue for music, dancing, dining and gambling which had always allowed female members.
24 Ceremonial home of the Lord Mayor of London.
25 Hugh Warrender, son of Sir George Warrender; a young admirer of JSC (see People, p. 569).

The regiment is completely isolated. I find no one worth speaking to or looking at – in the social circles of Bangalore. Miss Plowden was here last week – but alas – I never met her in England so forbore to call. [...]

Well my dearest Mamma – I have reached the end of this letter & till next week I will write no more.

Best of love & many kisses, Ever your loving son,
Winston

— JSC to WSC —

19 November [1896]   Panshanger[26]

My darling Boy,

This will reach you about the 30th – no, a few days later – but near enough yr birthday for me to wish you every good wish – darling, I wish I cl[d] give you a good kiss. Meanwhile a cheque will be quite as acceptable £50. I know you are hard up – but so am I & I pray you to consider that it means a great deal to me & you must make it go as far as possible. I haven't my cheque book with me – but I will enclose it in my next.

I will stir up the family to write. I am here since Monday – a big shoot for the Yorks.[27] L[d] & L[y] Cowper[28] my host & hostess are charming people & it is a beautiful house. An enormous party. [...] Lots of people ask after you. Sunny M [Marlborough] is also here – sends you his love & wants you to write to him. You must write to people if you want letters. [...] I always seem to be in a great hurry whenever I write to you but I will make a struggle next time. Goodbye & bless you my darling.

Yr loving Mother
JSC

---

26 Panshanger House, near Hertford, home of 7th Earl Cowper (see Places, p. 581).
27 The duke of York, later King George V; aged 31 at the time of this letter and recently married (in 1893) to Princess Mary of Teck, later Queen Mary.
28 Francis, Earl Cowper, lord-lieutenant of Ireland 1880–82.

W INSTON'S NEXT letter came from Trimulgherry, a suburb of
Secunderabad, which he visited as a member of his regiment's
polo team. Situated on the Deccan plateau, 350 miles to the north of
Bangalore, Secunderabad provided a safe base for British officials and
troops guarding Hyderabad, its troublesome twin city to the south
and capital of the princely Indian state of the same name. Since 1869,
its ruler, known as the Nizam, had been Asaf Jah VI, popularly called
Mahbub Ali Pasha. A whole wing of his palace was dedicated to his
wardrobe – the Nizam never wore the same outer garment twice.

During this visit Winston managed to meet Pamela Plowden,
daughter of most senior British official in Hyderabad, Sir John
Plowden, who had met Lord Randolph and Jennie. Pamela was six
months older than Winston and her striking grey eyes, porcelain-
smooth complexion and dark, tousled hair evidently left a striking
impression.

— WSC TO JSC —

4 November [1896]   Trimulgherry, Deccan

My dearest Mamma,

I write this letter to you from Secunderabad – where I, and the rest
of the polo team are staying – as guests of the 17th Hussars. [...] Ten
miles away is the independent city of Hyderabad containing 300,000
souls and all the scoundrels of Asia. Almost alone among Indian princes
the Nizam has preserved, by his loyalty in the days of [Robert] Clive
and in the mutiny [1857], his independence. British officers are not
allowed in the city – without permission and escort – and native customs
everywhere prevail. [...]

I was delighted to get your letter of the 16th ult [missing]. I cannot
tell you how overjoyed I shall be if any of our money comes back out
of the "spec". I need money out here very badly – esp at first and have
much difficulty in getting along. I cannot however bring myself to
believe in Cruikshank – and until my hands are closed on the specie I
shall regard him as a swindler – & ourselves as his dupes.

Pamela Plowden (right) in 1910, (by then married as Countess of Lytton) at a fancy dress party with Nancy Astor (left) and their host, Earl Winterton.

I was introduced yesterday to Miss Pamela Plowden – who lives here. I must say that she is the most beautiful girl I have ever seen – "Bar none" as the Duchess Lily says. We are going to try and do the City of Hyderabad together – on an elephant. You dare not walk or the natives spit at Europeans – which provokes retaliation leading to riots.

I see there is a [parliamentary] vacancy in East Bradford. Had I been in England – I might have contested it and should have won – almost to a certainty. Instead of being an insignificant subaltern I should have had opportunities of learning those things which will be of value to me in the future. Perhaps it is just as well – that I am condemned to wait – though I will not disguise from you that life out here – is stupid dull & uninteresting. That, as a soldier & a young soldier – no one cares to give you information & you meet very few who could even if they would. [...]

I shall not stay out here long my dearest Mamma. It is a poor life to lead and even its best pleasures are far below those obtainable in England. I meet none but soldiers and other people equally ignorant of the country and hear nothing talked but "shop" and racing. [...]

With best love and many kisses. Ever your loving son
Winston S. Churchill

———

THIS SECOND reference by Winston to his boredom in India, coming after only two months in the country, prompted Jennie to try to engineer for him a transfer to the Egyptian army, using her contacts in high places; but she also offered her son some frank advice.

— JSC TO WSC —

27 November [1896]   Blenheim Palace

Dearest Winston,

I am going to wire to you today, to write <u>at once</u> and apply to the War Office to be allowed to go to Egypt. The chances of yr being taken are extremely remote as the competition is tremendous, but there is an outside chance of Sir H. Kitchener's[29] personal influence being brought to bear and I am going to try it for you.

Should it succeed you must know and remember that it means lighting a paper to the effect that you will serve in the Egyptian Army for 2 years – and there will be no getting out of it if you don't like it. On the other hand, should this fail, you must not let it unsettle you, and make you take a dislike to yr work in India.

Life is not always what we want it to be, but to make the best of it as it is – is the only way of being happy. [...] In my heart of hearts I have doubts as to whether it would be the best thing for you – but Fate will decide. [...] A lot of influence had to be used, through Ld Salisbury and personally with the Sirdar [Kitchener] [...]

I am telling you all this in order that you should realise the difficulties and not be too disappointed if it does not come off. [...]

Am here for an enormous party for the Prince and Princess – everything wonderfully done. Sunny and Consuelo quite at their best. [...] Darling Winston, I can't write more now as I must get up – I am enclosing £25. I will send the other £25 next post.

Bless you my darling, Ever yr loving Mother
JSC

— WSC to JSC —

12 November [1896]   Bangalore

My dearest Mamma,

I received your letter of 22nd Oct – just as I was leaving Secunderabad – after a pleasant and successful week. We won the polo Tournament after three hard matches. [...]

Your letters – my dearest Mamma – are indeed short. I get none except yours – so my mail does not take me long to get through.

---

29 General Sir Herbert Kitchener, then *sirdar* (commander-in-chief) of the Egyptian Army (see People, p. 576).

However I would far rather have a short letter than none at all so please don't miss the mails. [...]

Mr Labouchere's last article in *Truth* is really too hot for words. I fail to see any other course than a legal action. He distinctly says that five of us – mentioning my name – were implicated in a *coup* to obtain money by malpractice on the Turf. You must not allow this to go unchallenged as it would be fatal to any future in public life for me. [...] The N. H. [National Hunt] Committee furnished the W.O. [War Office] with a letter expressly vindicating us from any charge of dishonesty or dishonourable behaviour. Consult a good lawyer – not Lewis he is Labby's [Labouchere's] lawyer. [...] I feel very strongly about this my dearest Mamma. Until something is done to contradict what appeared in *Truth* Oct 22 I appear in a very unpleasant light. [...] I leave matters in your hands – but in my absence my dearest Mamma – you must be the guardian of my young reputation. [...]

I dined with the Plowdens at Hyderabad and enjoyed myself very much. A civilised dinner with ladies present is delightful in this country after nearly 3 months of messes and barbarism. [...]

I also went through the city of Hyderabad on an elephant with Miss Pamela – who sent many messages to you and who is very beautiful and clever. Nice people in India are few & far between. They are like oases in the desert. This is an abominable country to live long in. Comfort you get – company you miss. I meet few people worth talking to and there is every temptation to relapse into a purely animal state of existence. [...]

With best love – I remain Your ever loving son
Winston

– WSC to JSC –

18 November [1896]   Bangalore

My dearest Mamma,

I have received your letter of Oct 30. I had no trust in Cruikshank. He is a fraud and we shall never see our money again. Prosecute him unremittingly however and have at least your revenge. [...]

I hope you will take steps about the racing article in *Truth*. I trust you my dear Mamma to resent any particularly offensive insinuations he may make – in my absence. He is a scoundrel and one of these days I will make him smart for his impudence. His attacks on us do harm. [...] We are but ground game and within easy range of his invectives. Therefore do muzzle him if you can. [...]

I shall not learn Hindustani. It is quite unnecessary. All the natives here speak English perfectly [...] .

Existence is peaceful if uneventful – comfortable if dull. If I can only get hold of the right people my stay here might be of value. Had I come to India as an MP – however young & foolish, I could have had access to all who know and can convey. As a soldier – my intelligent interests are supposed to stop short at Polo – racing & Orderly Officer. I vegetate – even reading is an effort & I am still in Gibbon.

The newspapers when they arrive are out of date and one gobbles up a week's *Times* in a single morning. [...] You must get people to do things for me. To ask me to visit them etc. etc. Well goodbye my dearest Mamma – I feel exceptionally stupid today and fear this letter is not very bright or interesting. [...]

With best love to you and Jack (Who never writes)
Ever your own
Winston S. Churchill

– JSC TO WSC –

11 December [1896]   35a Gt Cumberland Place

Dearest Winston,

I read some interesting accounts of yr polo match in *The Field*[30] which I send you. It must have been great fun & very exciting. Yr last letter of the 18th Nov seems rather depressed. I have not heard as yet from Kitchener.

---

30 First published as a weekly country sports magazine in 1853.

I have been very busy arranging things for Jack. I went to see Welldon & had a long talk with him as to his future. I am much against his going in the Army. I can't afford to put him in a smart cavalry regiment & in anything else he wl^d be lost & unhappy. Besides at the best it is a poor career. I think he might do [better] at the Bar [as a barrister]. He has plenty of ability & common sense, a good presence & with perseverance & influence he ought to get on. The City he hates. He is going to leave Harrow this term, spend a year or more in France & Germany, then study Greek for 6 months with a tutor & go to Oxford. He seems to like the idea.

I had it out with Welldon about you. He declares he was not thinking of Labouchere's attack & all that business when he wrote to you – but only of your habit (which in this case has cost you a good deal) of putting yrself so much forward. However <u>no one</u> pays any attention to anything in *Truth* so you need not worry. [...]

Goodbye & bless you my darling. I am going to the Londonderry's at Wynyard[31] next week & will write to you from there.

Yr loving Mother

JSC

JACK MAY have liked the idea of Oxford and hated the City – but he was to end up in the City, working at first as 'private secretary' to a family friend, the eminent banker and financial adviser to the Prince of Wales, Ernest Cassel.[32]

---

31 Wynyard Park in County Durham, English seat of the marquess of Londonderry (see Places, p. 581).
32 Cassel was at the time a neighbour in Grosvenor Square of the dowager duchess of Marlborough (see People, p. 567).

– WSC TO JSC –

24 November [1896]   [Bangalore]

My dearest Mamma,

Your letter of Nov 5 reached me this morning. It is the first answer it has been possible for me to get to any letter written from Bangalore. Do you see what a long way we are apart – and how slow correspondence is even in these days of steam. I am very glad you do not insist on the immediate sale of the pony. I shall not keep her a moment longer than necessary – as I am very anxious to realize the money invested in her. [...]

The weather has changed during the last few days and we have had the – to us – agreeable spectacle of grey skies with heavy clouds. We had also 36 hours of rain which comes indeed as a blessing to thousands. It may indeed enable the winter crop to be sown and hence terminate the famine two months sooner. The natives of nearly the whole of India are now experiencing the sufferings of scarcity. [...] The poverty of the people is extreme – and the "bunniales" or grain merchants unscrupulous to a degree. Availing themselves of the scarcity of wheat they organize rings & corners & raise the price to an extraordinary degree. The result is riots and infuriated mobs looting their shops – riots which can be suppressed only by the free use of the military & by frequent firing on the crowds – resulting in the death of many poor starving creatures. [...]

Civilisation builds railways & dykes & bridges; it irrigates & educates and affords security; but no matter how much you increase the food supply you never quite get up to the demand – because the more fertile you render the soil the more prolific does the population become. Till the wit of man discovers or invents some efficient check upon the population of this country our attempts to make it more prosperous will be as successful as trying to fill a sieve. [...]

Please send me a good cheap edition of Macaulay's *History of England*. I am approaching the end of Gibbon and another month will see the end of a long and delightful companionship.

I am so glad you like my letters. I expend a great deal of time and thought on their composition and if they please you both will be well spent. Do write long letters & make Jack continue his efforts. Letters from England are here so precious that even bills are welcome.

Ever your loving son
Winston S. Churchill

7
EGYPT OR INDIA?

1896–7

'*All my political ambitions
shall be centred in you*'

THE TIME that letters took to travel between England and India complicated attempts by Jennie and Winston to agree whether he should stay in India or transfer to Egypt. When they exchanged telegrams to overcome the problem, their attempts to use as few words as possible in order to economise sometimes only heightened the confusion.

For Winston, the question boiled down to whether service in India or Egypt would afford the better stepping stone towards a career in politics; he no longer expected to spend his whole career in the army.

Jennie did nothing to discourage a switch of careers; indeed, the prospect of helping her son's political ambitions excited her after the premature end of her husband's ministerial career. She now regretted having cut short her political activities in the Primrose League,[1] yet she still enjoyed warm relationships with almost every leading figure in the Conservative and Liberal parties. Her contacts within the royal family were also impeccable at a time when this still counted in the world of Victorian politics.

Moreover, Jennie was never afraid of calling in these contacts on her son's behalf when the time was right. First, however, she realized that Winston needed to make up for his weak education and to acquire a reputation in the army for reliability, whether in India or Egypt.

— JSC to WSC —

17 December 1896   Wynyard Park, Stockton-on-Tees

My dearest Winston,

I have just received yr telegram. "Right" may apply to my letter telling you about my writing to Kitchener, or my cheques. I have not as yet heard from Kitchener – but am beginning to look out for an answer. [...] I am passing a very pleasant week here altho' it is rather a boy & girl party. There is 7 or 8 degrees of frost & snow on the ground – so the hunters are in despair.

I am beginning to worry about going to St Moritz – it is so far & expensive & I want to go later to Rome to see that statue Waldo Storey[2] is making of yr Father. Old Jim Lowther[3] is here, & we have long talks about politics – he is in great admiration of Rosebery's Edinburgh speech.[4]

---

1 Lord Randolph was a founder of the Primrose League in 1883. The League's aim was to spread the principles of Conservatism (the primrose being the favourite flower of Benjamin Disraeli). JSC became a member of its Ladies Grand Council in 1885.
2 Anglo-American sculptor, art critic and poet, who lived in Rome for much of his life.
3 James Lowther, Conservative MP for Thanet; previously chief secretary for Ireland 1878–80; died unmarried.
4 On 10 December 1896 Lord Rosebery had spoken at a meeting to raise funds for a memorial to Robert Louis Stevenson.

They say that Ld R. is going to marry Lady Dudley[5] – I don't believe it. I don't think much of a woman whose children dislike her. [...]

I don't know how soon I may hear from the Sirdar – but I will wire & if he takes you, you will have to square yr Colonel – but I don't suppose you wl^d join them until the end of March. In any case when you receive this make enquiries & find out how much money you will want & answer by return – should you be taken – as I shl^d have to find it for you & it cannot be done in a moment. [...]

Cruikshank's last is to say that he won't pay unless we withdraw action. I wired today to the effect that if his bank gave a date & a guarantee as to paying the money which wl^d satisfy Sir G.L. [George Lewis] we wl^d withdraw but not otherwise. I must go to tea now, so goodbye my darling boy. I hope you keep well. [...]

Bless You, Yr loving Mother
JSC

– WSC to JSC –

2 December [1896]   [Bangalore]

My dearest Mamma,

I have been much exercised in my mind by the arrival, last Friday, of your telegram. I await expectantly fuller details. My views are these. I am not going to be a professional soldier & therefore during my military career I will either [aim] to enjoy myself or see active service. This place is not as agreeable to live in as England – but on the other hand it is pleasant and comfortable: I have lots of ponies – polo – interests and friends. I look forward with eagerness to the Amballa[6] tournament in March and to seeing more of this great country.

---

5 Georgina Ward, dowager countess of Dudley, widow of the earl whom she had married in 1865 when he was 48 and she was 17. She did not marry Lord Rosebery, whose first wife Hannah (née de Rothschild) had died in 1890.
6 Or Umballa, city in northern India, close to the border with Punjab.

Now if your telegram means – Kitchener's staff or something extra in that line – or if you have heard of an advance in the spring or even in the autumn of next year or any chance of action whatever – then I should like very much to go to Egypt. But if it simply means transfer to Egyptian service and soldiering in that country on the chance of something turning up in the future I am for staying with my regiment. [...]

A year ago today I was undergoing the most thrilling experience of my life – in Cuba. The 2nd December was the date on which we had our battle – & on which I was for 4–5 hours under fire. [...] How quickly the year has passed. The events of that day – my thoughts and feelings at almost every instant – the whole scene – is as vividly recalled to my memory as if only a week had intervened.

It is for days like that – days which punctuate as it were the monotonous drawl of existence – that I wld live. "Better fifty years of Europe, than a cycle of Cathay."[7] [...]

I am glad to think that Cruikshank is annoyed by the application to his conduct of the word "fraud". It augurs well for the degree of inconvenience which he will experience – should he get as he richly deserves – six months imprisonment. [...]

With best love & kisses, Ever your loving son
Winston S Churchill

– JSC TO WSC –

24 December [1896]   Blenheim

Dearest Winston,

Here I am with Jack until next Monday – & very pleasant it is altho' mostly family Wilsons,[8] Norah & Lilian,[9] L^d & L^y Churchill,

---

7 From Alfred, Lord Tennyson, *Locksley Hall*, 1842.
8 WSC's aunt, Lady Sarah Spencer-Churchill, married Lt.-Col. Gordon Wilson in 1891.
9 Daughters of the 8th duke of Marlborough (who died in 1892), at the time aged 23 and 21 respectively.

Ivor Guest,[10] etc, & last but not least the old Duchess. Between you & I she is not making herself pleasant to me & we have not exchanged a word – but I do not mind & perhaps it is as well. To the world we can appear friends, anything of the kind in private is impossible. Sunny & Consuelo are charming in their own house.

It is very cold, 12 degrees of frost, all hunting people cursing. I envy you yr rose garden & sun. If you don't go to Egypt (which I am beginning to think is more than doubtful, as I am told Kitchener won't take anyone under 27) I will come & stay with you next year D.V. [*Deo Volente*, or God willing].

[...] Darling Boy how I wish that you were with me & that we cl^d have a good talk about everything. I am glad that you are beginning to like India & that it won't be distasteful to you to remain there, if the Egyptian plan fails. There are drawbacks to everything of course – meanwhile in the intervals of polo & military work I hope you will find time for reading. Think how you will regret the waste of time, when you are in politics & will feel yr want of knowledge.

I am looking forward to the time when we shall live together again & all my political ambitions shall be centred in you. I often think I ought to make an effort now & not allow myself to drift out of old "P.L's" [Primrose Leagues] & things. [...]

Everyone has asked after you & say nice things – *à le demain prochain* darling – Bless you & a Happy Xmas & New Year.

Yr loving Mother
JSC

P.S. The £50 was a present for yr birthday.

———

F OR THE first time in this correspondence, Winston now sent a letter that rehearsed an overtly political view, albeit on a military matter. His preference for a strategy of spending on a strong

10 Ivor Guest, son of Lord and Lady Wimborne (see People, p. 563).

navy rather than on the army would remain in place for several decades.

— WSC to JSC —

8 December 1896   Bangalore

My dearest Mamma,

[...] I got your letter written from Panshanger when out snipe shooting last Sunday [6 December]. I am indeed grateful for the £50 – which will be very welcome and help me far more than any present – "in kind" [...]

My impatience to get your letter is increasing every day. I hear it is decided to make a further advance this next year and I hope I may find that you have enabled me to participate in it. [...]

I read a stupid speech of Lord Lansdowne's[11] on the army – of which he advocates an increase. [...] I hoped no one would be so foolish as to advocate the expenditure of more money on the army. It is a shocking thing that we should be compelled to have a 'hundred million budget' every year and you may be sure that the strain of taxation is not without its effect on the prosperity and happiness of the nation. I believe that it is necessary for us to have an unequalled navy: A fleet strong enough to render us superior to a combination of any two powers & with an ample margin for accidents. I would support taxation to almost any extent necessary to attain this end. With such a fleet an army does not become a necessity for defence. [...] Given the unquestioned command of the sea – there is no part of our Empire which our present army could not protect – and without such command there is no part which two such armies could maintain. [...]

With best love and many thanks for your noble and generous present.

Ever your loving son

Winston S. Churchill

---

11 Henry Petty-Fitzmaurice, marquess of Lansdowne, secretary of state for war; previously governor-general of Canada 1883–8, viceroy of India 1888–94; later secretary of state for foreign affairs 1900–5.

— WSC to JSC —

16 December 1896   Bangalore

My dearest Mamma,

I have received your letter of 27 Nov – about the Egyptian business. As it seems certain a further advance is intended – please do your best. I have applied (now three weeks ago) – to the Adjutant-General, Simla[12] – to be noted for 'Special Service' in Egypt. I am also forwarding an application – which I believe – goes direct to Egypt – to be appointed to the Egyptian army. I shall regret leaving India – but I should never forgive myself if an expedition started next year and I felt that it was my own fault I was not there. [...]

I start however on Thursday night for Madras whence I go by boat – (P. & O.) [Peninsular & Oriental] to Calcutta [now Kolkata] – arriving in time for the races which begin on Christmas day. Hugo Baring is coming too and we have engaged our berths. It is a long journey to make for so short a time – as far in point of time as America is from England. [...]

Ever your loving son
Winston

— WSC to JSC —

23 December 1896   Continental Hotel, Calcutta

My dearest Mamma,

[...] Calcutta is very full of supremely uninteresting people endeavouring to assume an air of 'heartiness' suitable to the season. There was a ball last night at the Viceregal Lodge – to which we were asked – but, as you know I do not shine on the parquet and I therefore availed myself of the good excuse my leg afforded.

---

12 Administrative capital of the British Raj in India during the summer months, lying in the foothills of the Himalayas.

Winston as a cavalry subaltern in Bangalore, 1896.

The races begin tomorrow and on Friday (Christmas day) there is a horseshow. Saturday is however the big day – when the Viceroy's Cup – the great race of the Indian Turf – is run. So you see we are indeed in the vortex of gaiety. It is strange however that the moment I get into an Indian Club – or into any situation where I am confronted with [the] spectacle of the Anglo-Indian at home – I immediately desire to fly the country. It is only in my comfortable bungalow – among my roses – polo ponies – & butterflies – that I feel that philosophical composure – which can alone make residence in India endurable. [...]

I see the papers full of pictures of the Blenheim festivities: Sunny gloating over the Prince's marksmanship the most prominent. The whole business appears to have been very satisfactory – and is bound to do Marlborough a great deal of good. There is always a great name to be made by the judicious application of wealth – and he is just the person to do it.

This is a very great city and at night with a grey fog and cold wind – it almost allows one to imagine that it is London. I shall always [be] glad to have seen it – for the same reason Papa gave for being glad to have seen Lisbon – namely – "that it will be unnecessary ever to see it again".

I revolve Egypt continuously in my mind. There are many pros and cons – but I feel bound to take it if I can get it. To-day with cold and quinine I feel that England would be the happiest solution of the question – as to where I should soldier. [...] Two years in Egypt my dearest Mamma – with a campaign thrown in – would I think qualify me to be allowed to beat my sword into a paper cutter & my sabretache[13] into an election address. Such a stupid letter – but how can I help it! Ammoniated quinine![14]

Ever your loving son
Winston

---

13 Flat satchel strapped by cavalry officers to their belt.
14 Medicine used against fever in Victorian times, particularly in the tropics.

— JSC to WSC —

15 January 1897   35a Great Cumberland Place

Dearest Winston,

Yr letter from Calcutta found me here – very glad to be at home after all my visiting – standing on one's hind legs <u>always</u> is somewhat of a trial. I hope you have got rid of your cold & did not part with too much of yr money! [...]

I am giving a dinner tonight – Devonshires,[15] Arthur Balfour, old Staal[16] etc – a good many of us are going on to Niagara[17] afterwards where there is a masked ball. Parliament opens next Tuesday & with it the season & the same old round. If I can afford it I shall go abroad for March, it is too odious in London then.

I hope you have the books by now. I can quite understand what you say of the Anglo-Indian Society, it must be odious. I don't like this plague spreading as it is doing & what with the famine India seems in a bad way.[18]

I hope to have some more interesting news to tell you in my next. This is rather an apology for a letter!

Yr loving Mother
JSC

W INSTON WROTE his next letter in a train on the way back to Bangalore from Calcutta. For the first time he mentioned a fellow soldier, Lord Fincastle (a courtesy title for the twenty-four-year-old Alexander Murray, later earl of Dunmore), an aide-de-camp

---

15 The duke and duchess of Devonshire.
16 Georges de Staal, Russian ambassador to Britain 1884–1902.
17 The Niagara Hall ice rink, near St James's Park.
18 A bubonic plague, originating from the yellow-breasted rat, had spread since the 1850s from the interior of China to reach Canton by 1894 and Bombay by 1896, probably via Hong Kong. Over the next 30 years, India would lose 12.5 million people to the plague.

to the viceroy of India. Fincastle had served briefly the previous year in the Sudan, hence his ownership of the fez that so suited Winston.

Later in 1897 Fincastle reported for *The Times* about the fighting on India's North West Frontier, while Winston wrote for the *Morning Post*; they would compete to produce the first book on the fighting. Winston won that race, but Fincastle was awarded the Victoria Cross. He was to die reporting on the Battle of Omdurman for *The Times* in 1899.

— WSC TO JSC —

1 January 1897   Sioni in the train

My dearest Mamma,

I hope you will excuse a letter in pencil. This train jolts so terribly that ink results only in bad language and illegibility. Hugo and I are on our way back from Calcutta Races – 4½ days ceaseless rattle & bang in the train. We had a very pleasant week. The Misses Kennard's[19] were there – just arrived from England – very pretty & charming. [...]

Your last letter was most satisfactory. I hope I shall be able to go to Egypt especially after the Polo Tournament is satisfactorily decided. The Elgins[20] are very unpopular out here and make a very poor show after the Lansdownes. The evil that a Radical Government does lives after it. All the great offices of the state have to be filled out of the scrappy remnant of the Liberal Peers. [...]

I hope Egypt will come off. I tried on Fincastle's fez:- I look splendid! I am looking forward to getting back to my ponies and roses at Bangalore.

Well goodbye my dearest Mamma, Ever your loving son
Winston S. Churchill

---

19 Probably Victoria and Winifred Kennard, daughters of Colonel Edmund Kennard, a former MP and cavalry officer.
20 Victor Bruce, earl of Elgin; viceroy of India since succeeding the marquess of Lansdowne 1894. Both had been Liberal peers (see People, p. 571).

— WSC to JSC —

7 January 1897   Bangalore

My dearest Mamma,

Your letter of the 17th Dec has just come. I have missed the one before it as it was forwarded to Calcutta and we left before it arrived. However I shall get it in the middle of this week. We safely ended our long though not unpleasant journey in the train arriving here early Sunday morning. I find the garden increased greatly in size and beauty. We have now over 50 different kinds of roses. [...]

On the 15th the regiment goes to a camp exercise which will be interesting and novel though we shall have a great deal to do. I do not know where we shall be as we move all over the country – but your letters, directed here will be forwarded. As to money for Egypt, if it comes off, which I pray it may, I do not anticipate any expense, except my passage as my Indian uniform will do with a few minor alternations. In any case I can always cash a cheque on Cox immediately and if you pay the money in as soon as you hear from me by letter, you [they] will meet it.

[...] Well, my dearest Mummy, I hope we may meet in Cairo but I begin to fear from your silence that the answer is adverse. Perhaps however as the Sirdar has been up at Dongola[21] your letter will have been delayed. [...]

I must fly my dear Mamma as I have just been let in to pay the Squadron.

Your ever loving son
Winston S. Churchill

———

WINSTON'S BROTHER Jack forwarded a letter that Major-General Sir Herbert Kitchener, the *sirdar*, had sent his mother

---

21 Now the northern province of Sudan, then part of Egypt; scene of a victory by General Kitchener over the forces of the Mahdi, 1896.

on 30 December 1896; it was noncommittal about the prospects of a transfer: 'I will note your son's name for special service and if he wishes to serve in the Egyptian army he should send in his application through his Colonel to the A.G. [Attorney General] Egyptian Army Cairo. I have however at present no vacancies in the cavalry but I will have his name put down on the list.'[22]

– JSC TO WSC –

29 January 1897   35a Gt Cumberland Place

Dearest Winston,

I was so sorry to have missed the post last week – but Jack explained to you how hurried I was at the last moment. He sent you a copy of the Sirdar's letter. How much that means I cannot tell – but I think it looks promising. Anyhow for the present you will remain where you are which I daresay you will not mind. [...] How little one hears of any of the Generals in time of peace. There is really very little honour & glory to be got out of the Army. A moderate MP gets better known in the country & has more chance of success than a really clever man in the Army. [...]

The "Spec" prosecution is coming to a head – Aunt Clara saw Sir G.L. [George Lewis] yesterday & he made her sign a lot of questions which Cruikshank will have to answer. I'm afraid there is little chance of our getting our money back.

[...] Well goodbye my darling. I envy you yr rose garden, it must be delightful. I enclose Simpson's[23] bill which you might settle. I wonder if you have received the butterfly nets etc.? & the books?

Bless you darling. With best love, Yr loving Mother
JSC

---

22 R. Martin, *Lady Randolph Churchill*, vol. 2, p. 81.
23 London restaurant on the Strand.

J ENNIE HAD sent to India each volume of Thomas Macaulay's *The History of England from the Accession of James the Second.* Winston was following her injunction to read more if he wanted a career in politics. He had almost finished Edward Gibbon's *The History of the Decline and Fall of the Roman Empire*, before putting it aside temporarily while he tackled William Winwood Reade's *The Martyrdom of Man* and Plato's *Republic*.

Published in 1872, *The Martyrdom of Man* offered a profoundly secular history of the Western world, influenced by the ideas of Charles Darwin and political liberalism. William Gladstone denounced the book as 'irreligious', yet it impressed many at the time, including Winston who was forming his political and philosophical ideas.

— WSC TO JSC —

14 January 1897   Bangalore

Dearest Mamma,

Once more the mail day comes round & I sit myself down to write you my weekly letter. I returned yesterday from Madras where I stayed for two days to play polo with the garrison. […]

If Egypt does not come off I shall perhaps consider the possibility of coming home for a month or five weeks – to give you a kiss and generally restore communications. I have to thank you for 12 volumes of Macaulay which I shall shortly begin to read. The eighth volume of Gibbon is still unread as I have been lured from its completion by *The Martyrdom of Man* & a fine translation of the *Republic* of Plato: both of which are fascinating. […] The former impressed me as being the crystallization of much that I have for some time reluctantly believed. […]

If the human race ever reaches a stage of development – when religion will cease to assist and comfort mankind – Christianity will be put aside as a crutch which is no longer needed, and man will stand erect on the firm legs of reason. […] One of these days – perhaps – the cold bright light of science & reason will shine through the cathedral windows & we shall go out into the fields to seek God for ourselves. The great laws of Nature will be understood – our destiny and our past will be clear. We shall then be able to dispense with the religious toys that have agreeably fostered the development of mankind. Till then – anyone who deprives us of our illusions – our pleasant hopeful illusions – is a wicked man & should – (I quote my Plato) – 'be refused a chorus'. [...]

I envy Jack – the liberal education of an University. I find my literary tastes growing day by day – and if I only knew Latin & Greek – I think I would leave the army and try and take my degree in History, Philosophy & Economics. But I cannot face parsing & Latin prose again. What a strange inversion of fortune – that I should be a soldier & Jack at college. [...]

Well my dearest Mamma, Good bye.
With best love, Ever your loving son
Winston S Churchill

— JSC to WSC —

5 February [1897]   35a Gt Cumberland Place

My darling Winston,

Both Jack & Warrender have written to you today & they will tell you more news than I can as I am in the throes of 24 to dinner tonight. My last flutter for some time, I wish you were here. I wonder what you will have thought of the Sirdar's letter? [...]

Arthur Balfour is too lazy about his big speeches, he doesn't take the trouble to work them up, hence mistakes, haltings etc. These last bye [sic] elections all going Radical[24] are a good thing as it will make them work up the constituencies & look to their laurels.

My next letter will be from Paris to you. Take care of yrself.

Ever yr loving Mother
JSC

---

24 JSC used the term Radical as a shorthand for Liberal (in 1859, the Radicals formed the Liberal party together with the Whigs and Tory supporters of Robert Peel). On 4 February 1897, the Liberals won a by-election at Walthamstow, defeating the Conservatives who had held the seat at the previous general election by 279 votes.

21 January 1897   Rajankunte Camp, Madras

My dearest Mamma,

Only a very short letter this. Here I am in camp at this arid place – bare as a plate & hot as an oven. All the skin is burnt off my face and my complexion has assumed a deep mulberry hue. [...]

I am deep in Macaulay and do not anticipate that being long in finishing. It is easier reading than Gibbon and in quite a different style. Macaulay crisp & forcible – Gibbon stately and impressive. Both are fascinating and show what a fine language English is – since it can be pleasing in styles so different.

We march tomorrow early and where I shall sleep is at present a mystery. I do not mind the life. My tent is a very comfortable pattern – far bigger than the English variety & the native servants are excellent at this nomadic sort of existence. [...]

Goodbye my dearest Mamma. Keep pegging away about Egypt. I do not mind waiting and you will never make me believe there is anything which you could not in time achieve.

Ever your loving son
Winston S. Churchill

PS I am sorry the Duchess was not cordial. Old age is sufficiently ugly and unpleasing without its too frequent accompaniments, capriciousness and malevolence.   *WSC*

12 February [1897]   Hôtel Bristol,[25] Paris

Dearest Winston,

Here we are in a wet muggy Paris. Jack goes to Versailles on Monday

---

25 Luxury hotel, then in Place Vendôme; now in rue du Faubourg Saint-Honoré.

& I return to London Tuesday. We dined with Cecil Rhodes[26] last night [...] . I cannot say that I was very much impressed with him, he does not give the idea of a clever man – a strong one if you like, determined & dogged, but intellectually weak. [...]

I hope the enclosed [notice of WSC's election to the Turf Club][27] will please you – 2 or 3 were blackballed that day. You must write and thank the Col [Brabazon] as he came up from the country expressly. I will pay your subscription but you must try & repay me as I am very hard up.

Warrender told me he had sent you the account of Cruikshank's trial – I do hope that we may get our money back. I ask for no more! What a scoundrel – & what a creature Cadogan is, just as bad. You were quite right about him. [...]

My dinner last week went off capitally a great success. That is my last flutter for some time. [...] Well my darling *à la semaine prochaine*. I'm afraid that I shall not be able to go abroad unless I win this case. I can't get any more money. Goodbye & bless you. Best love.

Yr loving Mother
JSC

— WSC to JSC —

4 February [1897]   Bangalore

My dearest Mamma,
The difficulty of finding energy, time and material for my weekly letters increases as the months progress. There are no longer new impressions to be recorded & the everyday life of a subaltern in India is

---

26 Born in Britain, Rhodes moved to southern Africa at the age of 17 and founded a business empire based on mining for diamonds. He was prime minister of the Cape Colony 1890–96.
27 Club in London, formed in 1861, noted for its aristocratic membership; originally to be called 'The Club' until members found the name was already taken; they chose 'the turf' to denote a shared interest in racing and gambling.

not marked by many incidents of interest. I have had a very busy week, as I am still doing duty as Adjutant and have written so many memos etc that to touch a pen is an effort.

Finally as time goes on one involuntarily becomes more centred in local surroundings & less conscious of the fact that such a place as "Home" exists. I no longer read *The Times*. The English mail which used to mark one half of my week with expectation and the other half with reflection – now comes in rather as a matter of course. Perhaps all this is just as well – as the last English mail brought me no letter from you – and had this occurred before I was settled down, I should have been very unhappy – instead of merely disappointed. [...]

After Meerut[28] with its hopes & fears, I shall try for 3 months leave & if I get it & if the quarantine is not so long as to stop me on the way – I think shall try a little visit to England. [...] I feel a great desire to get out of my peaceful groove before it becomes too deep – & before in philosophical contentment I cease to sigh for "England home and Beauty."[29]

I have been reading a great deal lately. Fifty pages of Macaulay & 25 of Gibbon every day. There are only 100 of the latter's 4000 odd left now. Will you send me Hallam's *Constitutional History*?[30] Also do you think you can find out for me – from some able politico or journalist – how & where I can find the detailed Parliamentary history (Debates, Divisions, Parties, cliques & caves[31]) of the last 100 years.

Goodbye my darling Mamma,

Every good wish & lots of kisses from, Your loving son
Winston

---

28 WSC hoped to visit Meerut (1,350 miles north of Bangalore) for an inter-regimental polo tournament.
29 From S. J. Arnold, *The Death of Nelson*, part of the lyrics of *The Americans*, an opera by John Braham, 1811.
30 Henry Hallam, *The Constitutional History of England*, published 1827.
31 As in 'capitulations' or 'surrenders'.

WINSTON HAD been away from England for only five months; yet this was his second letter to mention the possibility of a return home on leave. The idea exasperated his mother in the light of their financial difficulties.

– JSC to WSC –

26 February 1897   35a Gt Cumberland Place

Dearest Winston,

It is with very unusual feelings that I sit down to write to you my weekly letter. Generally it is a pleasure – but this time is quite the reverse. The enclosed letter will explain why. I went to Cox's this morning & find out that not only you have anticipated the whole of yr quarter's allowance due this month but £45 besides – & now this cheque for £50 – & that <u>you</u> <u>knew</u> you had nothing at the bank. The manager told me they had warned you that they would not let you overdraw & the next mail brought this cheque. I <u>must</u> say I think it is <u>too</u> bad of you – indeed it is hardly honourable knowing as you do that you are dependent on me & that I give you the biggest allowance I possibly can, more than I can afford.

I am very hard up & this has come at a very inopportune moment & puts me to much inconvenience. I found a £100 for you when you started for India in order that you shl^d not lose by the speculation we went into & I sent you £50 for yr birthday – all of which I cl^d ill afford. I understand that you wl^d get into trouble with yr regiment if this £50 which you got from the banker King[32] (& have probably spent) is not met, therefore I have paid it. But I have told them at Cox's not to apply to me in future as you must manage yr own affairs.

I am not responsible. If you cannot live on yr allowance from me & yr pay you will have to leave the 4th Hussars. I <u>cannot</u> increase yr allowance.

As for yr wild talk & scheme of coming home for a month, it is

32 Henry S. King & Co., bankers in India with whom WSC opened an account.

absolutely out of the question, not only on account of money, but for the sake of yr reputation. They will say & with some reason that you can't stick to anything. You have only been out 6 months & it is on the cards that you may be called to Egypt. There is plenty for you to do in India.

I confess I am quite disheartened about you. You seem to have no real purpose in life & won't realize at the age of 22 that for a man life means work, & hard work if you mean to succeed. Many men at yr age have to work for a living & support their mother. It is useless my saying more – we have been over this ground before – it is not a pleasant one. I will only repeat that I cannot help you any more & if you have any grit in you & are worth yr salt you will try & live within yr income & cut down yr expenses in order to do it. You cannot but feel ashamed of yrself under the present circumstances – I haven't the heart to write more.

Yr Mother
JSC

– WSC to JSC –

12 February [1897]   In camp, Bangalore

My dearest Mamma,

I was glad to get the Sirdar's answer. If anything happens in Egypt there will be vacancies & I shall get one. If not – I shall be well out of it. I forwarded my application to the A.G. Cairo. The colonel of his own accord added a most gushing recommendation saying I was a good rider, "a very smart cavalry officer" and knew my work in the field thoroughly. This ought to have a good effect. In any case however I hope to come home for a few weeks before going and if I can get leave I hope to be back about the twentieth of May. This plague quarantine may however spoil all. [...]

My face is blistered by the sun so badly that I have had to see a doctor. [...] I am consoled by the fact that I am doing "Brigade Major" a most important duty [...]. I am becoming my dear Mamma a very 'correct soldier'. Full of zeal etc. Even in homoeopathic doses

– Responsibility is an exhilarating drink. I am too tired to write more having been out all the morning.

With best love, Your own
Winston

J ENNIE CLAIMED to be too hard up to give Winston a higher allowance, although the estimate she gave of her annual income in her next letter turned out later to amount to only half of its true figure. Her sons would not discover the truth until 1914 when they became involved in the divorce negotiations to end her second marriage.

– JSC TO WSC –

5 March [1897]   35a Gt Cumberland Place

Dearest Winston,

    I was glad to get yr nice letter telling me of yr work as Brigade Major. What an extraordinary boy you are as regards yr business affairs. You never say a word about them, & then spring things upon one. If you only told me when you were hard up – & why – perhaps I shl^d not be so angry. But I don't believe you ever know how you stand with yr account at the Bank. I marvel at their allowing you to overdraw as you do. Neither the Westminster or the National Bank will let me overdraw £5 without telling me at once.

    Dearest this is the only subject on which we ever fall out. I do wish you wl^d try & reform – if you only realised how little I have, & how impossible it is for me to get any more. I have raised all I can, & I assure you unless something extraordinary turns up I see ruin staring me in the face.

    Out of £2,700 a year £800 of it goes to you 2 boys, £410 for house rent & stables, which leaves me £1,500 for everything – taxes, servants, stables, food, dress, travelling – & now I have to pay interest on money borrowed. I really fear for the future. I am telling you all this darling in order that you may see how impossible it is for me to help you – & how much you must in future depend on yrself. I make out that you get about

£200 pay, which makes yr income for the present £700 a year. Of course it is not <u>much</u> & I can quite understand that you will have to deny yrself many things if you mean to try & live within it. But the fact is, you have got to do more than try. Now when you receive this write me a sensible letter & tell me that I shall be able to count on you.

With best love, Yr loving Mother

JSC

8

ARMY OR POLITICS?

1897

'I am a Liberal in all but name'

W INSTON REMAINED uncertain whether he should stay with
the army in India or pursue a transfer to Egypt. Increasingly,
he judged these alternatives through the prism of their potential
impact on a future career in politics, which was now his ultimate
goal. Meanwhile, he continued to expand his reading.

— WSC TO JSC —

18 February 1897   Bangalore

My dearest Mamma,

I have had an awful disappointment. Sir Mansfield Clarke[1] who
commands the Madras Presidency has refused to allow the necessary

---

1   Commanded 6th Army Corps in the Boer War; governor of Malta 1903–7.

leave for the Polo team to go to Meerut for the Great Tournament. All our labours, practices, & expenditures are thrown away. [...]

The Lieutenant General imagines that in taking this course, he is vindicating his firmness. The great desire of obstinate people is to be considered firm. He is really only making himself very unpopular by depriving a hard working regiment of one of the few pleasures and of one of the most commendable pleasures which the Englishman in India can enjoy. [...]

Speaking generally – my soldiering prospects are at present very good. I complete today two years service. [...] I have every reason to believe that I shall be reported on in the Annual Confidential Report as one of the two most efficient officers in my rank.

Under all these circumstances – you will see that if I go to Egypt & if things there turn out well, it might be almost worth my while to stick to soldiering. At any rate I am certain of this that unless a good opportunity presents itself of my obtaining a seat in the House of Commons, I <u>should</u> continue in the army for two years more. Those two years could not be better spent than on active service. The question is 'where'? Egypt seems the only hope & therefore I beg you to leave no stone unturned in your endeavour to obtain a vacancy for me. [...] I hope to come home in May as this place offers few attractions during the leave season. I hope you will approve of the project. The distance seems so short. On my way I might pay my respects to the Sirdar. [...]

The garden is getting on well, though water is badly needed. I have 250 Rose trees & 70 different sorts so that every morning I can cut about 3 great basins full of the most beautiful flowers which nature produces. I am half way through Macaulay & you must find me something else as he is not half so solid as Gibbon & I have a good deal of time to read him in. I want Adam Smith's *Wealth of Nations*.[2] [...]

Best love my dearest Mamma, I am Your ever loving son
Winston

---

2   Published 1776; an exposition by the Scottish economist of the factors that built the wealth of a nation, such as labour, productivity and free markets.

JENNIE DISPATCHED the twenty-five most recent volumes of *The Annual Register* in response to Winston's request for 'the detailed Parliamentary history ... of the last 100 years'. Edited by Edmund Burke when it first appeared in 1758, the *Register* recorded each year's events, whether political or literary, in a format that remained largely unaltered throughout the nineteenth century. Winston explained to his mother in his letter of 31 March how he used the books to develop his political thinking.

Jennie mentioned another find that was to have a profound effect on her son's fortunes: Lord Randolph's bank had unearthed eight boxes of his personal papers in one of its vaults. Although Jennie thought that they should find a big name to write her husband's biography, Winston was keen to claim the mantle himself. Lord Randolph's two literary executors (his brother-in-law George Curzon[3] and a political friend, Ernest Beckett) would finally decide.

– JSC TO WSC –

11 March [1897]   35a Gt Cumberland Place

Dearest Winston,

I saw "Bimbash"[4] yesterday & he told me he had heard that Kitchener wanted to have you at the first vacancy – but you must take Bimbash's statements with a grain of salt! I hope you have received the books I have sent you & are duly grateful – for I find the *Annual Register* costs 14/- a time – & as you asked for a 100! you will not be surprised if I don't send

---

3   Richard George Curzon, married to Georgiana née Spencer Churchill, later Earl Howe, see People, p. 563. Because he was usually known as George Curzon, he is easily confused with George Nathaniel Curzon, a politician and future viceroy of India who first appears in the correspondence in WSC's letter of 25 February 1897 (see p. 572).

4   Harry Stewart transferred from the Gordon Highlanders to the Egyptian army, in which his rank of major was known as *bimbashi* – hence his nickname. His obituary in the *Evening Post* of 3 April 1907 painted him as 'a picturesque personality' whose 'habit of humorous exaggeration was well-known'.

them all – particularly as I have them in the library. However I have ordered from 1870 to be sent 2 vols at a time. [...]

I am finishing this letter in the train as I had no time this morning. I am on my way to Melton [Mowbray] to stop with Lady Gerard[5] & then go on to Brooksby[6] for the Sunday. If nothing happens to prevent me I hope to go to Monte Carlo next week for 10 days. I hate these east winds. [...]

Fancy my finding out the other day that there were 8 boxes at the Bank which had been overlooked. George Curzon & I have been through them & found all yr father's most private & interesting political letters. I'm afraid that few of them could be produced at present. I believe E. Beckett is slowly going through the papers – but I am rather unhappy at the thought that he & George Curzon are the custodians of the papers – for though they are most conscientious, they are both slow – & it will not be an easy thing to write a good biography, it wants a big man, & one with a name. [...]

I am so glad that you have work to do & are interested in it. Shl^d the Army turn out well for you, you cl^d not do better than to stick to it. After all it is what yr father wanted for you.

Goodbye my darling. Write & tell me about yr finances – tell me exactly how you stand. Cruikshank's case coming on the 28th – I am going to see Sir G.L. [George Lewis] on Saturday. I am afraid the Creature will bolt before then unless he has the money to pay.

Yr loving Mother
JSC

———

JENNIE AVOIDED the subject of Winston's possible return to England. Yet he had not given up on the idea; it was just that his plans now depended on a dispute that had flared up between

---

5 Mary, née Milner; wife of 2nd Baron Gerard, a soldier.
6 Brooksby Hall in Leicestershire, a hunting lodge purchased by a mining magnate, Joseph Williams 1891; leased by the dowager duchess of Marlborough for the 1894–5 hunting season.

Greeks and Ottomans in the Mediterranean island of Crete. Winston sensed this gave him an opportunity to repeat his success in Cuba, by reporting for a newspaper on the fighting while he journeyed home.

The population of Crete was mainly Greek-speaking, but since 1669 the island had belonged to the Ottoman empire. Two hundred years later it was allowed a degree of autonomy, until in 1891 the Ottomans reneged on their agreement. Open conflict over the issue had broken out between Greece and the Ottoman empire by 1895.

Britain's elite sided mostly with Greece, conditioned by its education in the country's history and language at school and by the popularity of writers sympathetic to the country like Lord Byron. Placing himself firmly in the Greek camp, Winston berated the pragmatic policy adopted by senior members of the Conservative government; his mother rebuked him for his political naivety (among other offences).

— WSC to JSC —

25 February 1897   Bangalore

My dearest Mamma,

I have had an answer to my first official applicant for Egypt, stating that my name has been added to the list of candidates and that though at present there are no vacancies, 'in the event of my services being needed, they will be called for.' I do not attach any importance to this official refusal [...].

I hope, if all goes well, to come home on April 1 instead of in May, as I formerly wrote. Out of the three months leave which I anticipate getting, I should have nearly 7 weeks in England and the voyage though long is not unpleasant. I suppress with difficulty an impulse to become sententious. Gibbon & Macaulay, however much they may improve one's composition of essays or reports, do not lend themselves to letter writing.

What an atrocious crime the Government have committed in Crete! That British warships should lead the way in protecting the blood bespattered Turkish soldiery from the struggles of their victims is horrible to contemplate. [...] When I think of all the principles which are bound up with this Government – the Union – the constitution – Imperialism – even Monarchy itself and when I think of those who have worked & toiled to make the party what it today is, the spectacle of great majorities frittered away – of staunch friends alienated – of splendid opportunities missed – becomes all the more mournful.

Among the leaders of the Tory party are two whom I despise and detest as politicians above all others – Mr Balfour & George Curzon.[7] The one – a languid, lazy lack-a-daisical cynic – the unmonumental figurehead of the Conservative party; the other the spoiled darling of politics – blown with conceit – insolent from undeserved success – the typification of the superior Oxford prig.

It is to that pair all the criminal muddles of the last 15 months should be ascribed. Lord Salisbury, an able and obstinate man, who joins the brain of a statesman to the delicate susceptibilities of a mule, has been encouraged to blunder tactlessly along till nearly every section of the Union party & nearly every cabinet in Europe has been irritated or offended.

[...] So much for politics. It is surprising how easily epithets and indignation rise in the mind, when the sun is hot has been hot & is daily getting hotter. Just as religion as it approaches the equator becomes more full of ceremony and superstition – so language & ideas here flourish with a florid fertility – which is unknown in more temperate climes. So you must take 50% off this letter when you read it. [...]

Best love my dearest Mamma and many kisses, from your loving son
Winston S. Churchill

– JSC TO WSC –

18 March 1897   Brooksby, Leicester

Dearest Winston,

I seem only to write disagreeable things, but will you attend to the enclosed & explain it to me. I am sending the man the £11 he asks, but

---

7   George Nathaniel Curzon, under-secretary of state for foreign affairs and later viceroy of India (see People, p. 572).

about yr dishonoured cheque I know nothing. My darling boy, you can't think how all this worries me. I have so many money troubles of my own I feel I cannot take on any others. You know how dearly I wl^d love to help you if I could – & also how much I wl^d like to have you come home – but quite apart [from] the advisability of such a step for such a short time, think of the expense. Every creditor you possess in England will be down upon you, & as far as I can make out you won't have a penny until May & I daresay that is forestalled – of course I can't coerce you & if you have made up yr mind to come, you must, but remember the consequences. [...]

I really think there is a good chance of yr getting to Egypt & in any case you are gaining much military experience in India & showing that you can work & do something. Darling I lay awake last night thinking about you & how much I wanted to help you – if only I had some money I wl^d do so. I am so proud of you & of all yr great & endearing qualities. I feel sure that if you live you will make a name for yrself but I know to do it you have to be made of stern stuff – & not mind sacrifice & self denial. I feel I am reading you a lecture & you will vote my letters a bore – but you know that I do not mean it in that way. [...]

I hope you have changed your mind about Crete – subsequent events must show you that the Concert of Europe[8] were <u>obliged</u> to act as they did altho' they were certainly slow to make up their minds.[9] I suppose after a bit the Cretans will settle down under a form of autonomy & afterwards will become annexed to Greece. I think things <u>are</u> looking more serious in the Transvaal.

Well my darling Winston you may have started for home for all I know but if this finds you still in India, as I hope, tell me in yr next all about yrself.

Post off. Best love. Yr loving Mother
JSC

---

8 System adopted by major European powers at the Congress of Vienna 1815 to resolve disputes amd maintain the continent's balance of power.

9 In February 1897, Austria-Hungary, Britain, France, Germany, Italy and Russia formed an international naval squadron to blockade Crete and deter a widening of the dispute between Greece and the Ottoman empire.

ACH OF Jennie's forecasts was to prove correct: Crete became autonomous in 1898 and was formally recognized as part of Greece by the international community in 1913. The difficulties in the Transvaal would lead to war between Britain and the Boers, the descendants of Dutch settlers in the eastern cape region of southern Africa, two years later, in 1899.

— WSC to JSC —

2 March 1897   Bangalore

My dearest Mamma,

I am very glad to have been elected to the Turf Club. It is of course a good thing to get in young as later on one is bound to make enemies, and mistakes of which the enemies take notice. [...] What delighted me as much as my election was your generous offer to pay my entrance subscription. I enclose you the necessary papers and remind you that it should be paid at once or I shall get into trouble. Please don't forget my dearest Mamma as it would look so bad to have one's election cancelled.

Now as to home. I anticipate obtaining 3 months leave on April first: getting home April 18th or thereabouts: & departing about June 10th. I should get Ascot and Epsom[10] and generally regain touch with civilization. I have no doubt you will not mind. The passage costs £80 return – but that includes 6 weeks board and lodging and if I went shooting in the jungle it would be just as expensive. [...]

Two years more will see this government ripe for a fall. A General Election now would probably bring the Radicals in. Certainly if they dropped Home Rule the country would vote for them. The swing of the pendulum has been accelerated by Ld Salisbury's obstinate boorishness, by Balfour's pusillanimous vacillations, by Lansdowne's ridiculous 'reforms' & by Curzon's conceit. In two years more they will not command a majority in the country. When that state of things arises any

---

10 Racecourses near London; each hosted a major race meeting in June, part of London's summer season.

accident might wreck them in the houses. At least that is how it seems to me – though perhaps I look through bilious-coloured glasses.

The sun is now increasing in heat & the mosquitos in number. I look forward eagerly to Park Lane & Piccadilly, to Willis's Rooms & the Gaiety[11] & last but really before all to Great Cumberland Place and its inmates. Salaam my dear Mamma and again salaam.

Ever your loving son
Winston

———

W INSTON'S ABILITY to forecast political developments proved less accurate than his mother's: the Conservative government lasted another eight years until 1905, rather than two.

Meanwhile, Jennie was visiting Monte Carlo for some sunshine and entertainment in the casino.

— JSC TO WSC —

25 March [1897]   Hôtel Métropole,[12] Monte Carlo

Dearest Winston,

For all I know you may have started for home by the time this reaches India. Of course if you have you can be sure of a warm welcome from me – you cl^d get no other – but I shall deprecate it – & I am sure that I am right.

Yr letter of the 2nd I received before I left London. I sent off yr letter to the Turf – with cheque enclosed for which I hope you will be duly grateful, as it came at a bad moment & found me more than usually hard up. The pony you are sending will I'm afraid be rather in the nature of a white elephant as I hear it takes them a long time to get acclimatized & sometimes they never do. [...]

---

11 London theatre; introduced a new style of musical comedy in the 1890s, featuring dancers known as the 'Gaiety Girls'.
12 Opened in 1889, built in the belle époque style.

The Duchess of Devonshire[13] is here & we breakfast & dine most days – up to now I have done no harm at the tables – but I am cautious. Ld Londonderry[14] told me he had heard from you & was very pleased with yr letter.

Goodbye for the present, take care of yrself darling.

With best love Yr loving Mother
JSC

— WSC TO JSC —

11 March [1897]   Government House, Guindy[15]

My dearest Mamma,

It is now almost certain that I shall be granted leave for three months beginning April 1. In this case I shall either – sail on the 3rd from Bombay & come round the whole way by sea thus avoiding quarantine & arriving about the 22nd April – or take train to Ceylon & wait at Colombo for a steamer which will not be liable to quarantine & will convey me to Brindisi or Marseilles. I think the latter route will be the one I shall probably adopt as it is more interesting and in view of the complications in Crete it might be worth turning aside at Suez and trying to see something of the impending war. I think probably England will draw me steadily homeward – but I wish to preserve the power to change in case things become serious at the last moment. [...]

I am impatient to get back into the reach of newspapers & letters. [...] Mr Balfour's contention that the Govt are bound to pursue their policy of acting with the [Great] Powers in the Eastern question is not one which can be admitted. He said in the House "We may be right, we may be wrong but right or wrong we have chosen our line, i.e. of co-operating with the Powers & must stick to it". But the moment

---

13 Louisa, widow of the 7th duke of Manchester, who had married the duke of Devonshire in 1892 when he was 59 and she was 60.
14 Charles Vane-Tempest-Stewart, 6th marquess of Londonderry; politician and a cousin of the Churchills (see People, p. 565).
15 Area in the city of Madras.

not infrequently arrives in private affairs, when an honourable man is compelled to separate himself from his associates. He has to say 'Up to the present we have been in agreement, now you go too far & as to that ground I cannot follow you'. And what is true of the honour of the individual applies all the more to that of the nation. [...]

Your ever loving son
Winston

— JSC ᴛᴏ WSC —

2 April 1897   Hotel du Rhin,[16] Paris

Dearest Winston,

In yr last letter from Guindy you seem to have made up yr mind to come home – therefore I suppose unless my letter deprecating yr return has stopped you, this will not find you. Under the circumstances I find it difficult to write at length. I have just arrived from Monte C. [Carlo] & am expecting Jack every moment. I was rather lucky at the tables & made enough to pay my expenses, which was very satisfactory.

The Prince [of Wales] came over from Nice & dined with me. I told him of yr wish to come home & he begged me to tell you that he was very much against it & thought you ought to take the opportunity you had now to go to the frontier & see something of the country. [...]

Goodbye darling boy, take care of yrself. It is snowing! Which is trying after the lovely weather of Monte C.

Ever your loving Mother
JSC

J ENNIE GAVE up writing to her son in India at this point, assuming that he would have set off for home before a letter arrived. His letters continued to arrive weekly.

16 In the 19th arrondissement, a less expensive hotel than those in which JSC had previously stayed.

– WSC to JSC –

17 March 1897   Bangalore

My dearest Mamma,

I have had to postpone coming home until May 1. We have so many officers sick that we were already short handed when [Hugo] Baring had the offer of a temporary appointment as ADC [aide-de-camp] to the Viceroy. He could not have accepted unless I had volunteered to stay & as May suits me equally well I of course did so. [...]

I set great store on going to Egypt if they go on this year. I long for excitement of some sort and the prospect of joining an English expedition attracts me immensely. I do hope you will not relax your efforts. [...]

From what I gather from Jack's letter you are opposed to my coming home. But what is there to do? Here is this place – very hot – very dusty – all the grass burned up on the polo ground – all the garden parched and withering – lots of fever and sickness: in fact a most unattractive spot. But I own my chief reason for desiring to move came from within. I am very restless. The time comes when books & roses prove insufficient interest. I shall not expect you to kill the fatted calf on my return. Indeed if the Sirdar will employ me I will remain in Egypt – though of course the perfect programme is Ascot first Dongola afterwards.

I was disappointed at not hearing from you this mail. I am sorry that stupid Cox refused my cheque. I was only £45 overdrawn. It was very kind of you to pay it. I enclose a cheque for £30 which is the best I can do towards payment at present. I must beg you to forgive the rest till 'my ship comes home'. I shall have to go into the question of finance when I come home myself. There are several bills in London unpaid that really will have to be paid soon. I shall have to borrow a certain sum on my life or effect a loan in some way or other. Of course it means so much less [income] per annum. But the other thing – i.e. not paying – means so much more worry.

I have completed Macaulay's *History* and very nearly finished his

Essays.[17] Many thanks for the books I received by this mail. The *Annual Registers* are just what I want. My darling Mamma do forgive the plain impatience with which this letter is written. This weather makes my temper so short I cannot control myself to form my letters.

I am very well and so far as I know in favour with God and man – but there are days when I feel I cannot sit still. [...]

> *Your ever loving son*
> *Winston*

———

I N HIS next two letters, Winston told his mother about the progress of his reading in India; set out how he used the set of *Annual Registers* to 'build up the scaffolding' of a 'logical and consistent mind'; and then, aged twenty-two, laid out the planks of the political platform that he was building for himself on top of this structure. As he acknowledged, most of them were distinctly liberal rather than conservative. Only the Liberal party's policy of Home Rule for Ireland prevented him from supporting it fully at this stage. Instead he chose the label of Tory Democracy, indelibly associated with the memory of his father.

— WSC TO JSC —

31 March 1897   Bangalore

My dearest Mamma,

Many thanks for your letter of the 11th [March] and for the two vols *Annual Register* & two *Wealth of Nations* – all of which have been safely received. [...]

I am reading a great deal. Since I have been in this country I have read or nearly finished reading (for I read three or four different books at a time to avoid tedium) all Macaulay (12 vols) all Gibbon (begun

---

17 T. Macaulay, *Critical and Historical Issues: Contributed to the Edinburgh Review*, published 1843.

in England 4000 pages) *The Martyrdom of Man – Modern Science and Modern Thought* (Laing)[18] the *Republic* of Plato (Jowett's Translation) *Rochefort's Memoirs*[19] Gibbon's *Life & Memoirs* & 1 Complete *Annual Register* on English Politics. I have hardly looked at a novel. Will you try and get me the *Memoirs of the Duc de Saint Simon*[20] & also Pascal's *Provincial Letters*[21] – I am very anxious to read both these as Macaulay recommends the one & Gibbon the other.

The method I pursue with the *Annual Register* is [not] to read the debate until I have recorded my own opinion on paper of the subject – having regard only to general principles. After reading I reconsider and finally write. I hope by a persevering continuance of this practice to build up a scaffolding of logical and consistent views which will perhaps tend to the creation of a logical and consistent mind.

Of course the *Annual Register* is valuable only for its facts. A good knowledge of these would arm me with a sharp sword. Macaulay, Gibbon, Plato etc must train the muscles to wield that sword to the greatest effect. This is indeed a nice subdivision of the term 'education'. The result of one kind of learning is valued by what you know: Of the other by what you are. The latter is far more important – but is useless in the total absence of the former. A judicious proportion should be observed. How many people forget this!

The education of the schoolboy – and of nearly all undergraduates – aims only at stocking the mind with facts. I have no ambition to "stifle my spark of intelligence under the weight of literary fuel" but I appreciate the power of facts. Hence my toil.

Ever your loving son
Winston S. Churchill

---

18 By S. Laing MP, published 1885.
19 By Coutilz de Sandras, published 1696.
20 By Louis de Rouvroy, duc de Saint-Simon, published 1820s; covered the life and court of King Louis XIV.
21 By Blaise Pascal (writing as Louis de Montalte) 1656–7; a satirical attack on Jesuitical casuistry.

— WSC to JSC —

6 April [1897]   Bangalore

My dearest Mamma,

[...] The mail this morning brought me your letter of the 18th March [p. 200]. I am indeed sorry that my cheque was dishonoured. When I left England as I could not pay this man, I gave him a post dated cheque. As the time approached when this cheque should have been presented, being still overdrawn – I wrote and suggested his waiting a little longer. This he does not appear to have done. [...]

All this worries me awfully. Indeed I don't know what will happen in the near future. I must raise a certain sum of money on a Life insurance or some other security & pay off these pressing liabilities lest I obtain a most unenviable reputation. This country is no economy. British Cavalry have to pay nearly double for servants, food, forage etc. Of course spending your capital means loss of income – already alas so small, but not to do so is to be almost dishonest in my case. On these, and all these matters we can consider when I return.

I anticipate leaving here on or about the 10 May and as quarantine is still enforced, I shall go direct to Brindisi: I shall pause a couple of days to visit Rome – the Imperial city around which my reading for so many months has centred. [...]

Our Machiavellian Government had better be careful lest they find themselves even outdone in vice. There are no lengths to which I would not go in opposing them were I in the House of Commons. I am a Liberal in all but name. My views excite the pious horror of the Mess. Were it not for Home Rule – to which I will never consent – I would enter Parliament as a Liberal.

As it is – Tory Democracy will have to be the standard under which I shall range myself.

1. Reform at home.

Extension of the Franchise to every male. Universal Education. Equal Establishment of all religions. Wide measures of local self-government. Eight hours. Payment of members [of Parliament] (on request). A progressive Income Tax. I will vote for them all.

2. Imperialism abroad.

East of Suez Democratic reins are impossible. India must be governed on old principles. The colonies must be federated and a system of Imperial Defence arranged. Also we must combine for Tariff & Commerce.

3. European Politics.

Non Intervention. Keep absolutely unembroiled – Isolated if you like.

4. Defence.

The Colonies must contribute and hence a council must be formed. A mighty navy must keep the seas. The army may be reduced to a training depot for India with one army corps for petty expeditions.

5. To maintain the present constitution of Queen – Lords – Commons – & the Legislative union as at present established.

There! That is the creed of Tory Democracy. Peace & Power abroad – Prosperity & Progress at home – will be the results.

Ever your loving son
Winston

— WSC to JSC —

14 April 1897   Bangalore

My dearest Mamma,

I am at last able to write positively of my plans. I sail from Bombay May 8 and hope to arrive in England by June 1 – via Brindisi and Paris. I shall spend two days in Rome and two in Paris, where I hope to see Jack and shall arrive in England for the Epsom meeting. You will I am sure be glad to see me and will extend me an amiable if not a hearty welcome. [...]

I am looking forward immensely to seeing civilization again after the barbarous squalor of this country. I do hope you will sympathise with my desire. Failing an advance up the Nile, I have every intention of returning to India on the expiration of my leave to complete my sentence. It is the story of Regulus & the Carthaginians[22] over again. The 8 months I have been in this country have as regards Indian information & knowledge been utterly barren. [...]

Poked away in a garrison town which resembles a 3rd rate watering place, out of season & without the sea, with lots of routine work and a hot and trying sun – without society or good sport – half my friends on leave and the other half ill – my life here would be intolerable were it not for the consolations of literature. The only valuable knowledge I take away from India (soldiering apart) could have been gathered equally well in Cumberland Place.

Notwithstanding all this I have not been unhappy, though occasionally very bored, and I contemplate without repugnance returning to my books my butterflies, & my roses. But I must have some holidays & you will be harsher than the Carthaginians if you refuse me them. [...]

Ever your loving son
Winston S. Churchill

———

SOON AFTER writing this letter, Winston changed his plans again, because the dispute over Crete between Greece and the Ottomans had flared up once more. A small force of irregular Greek troops had crossed into Ottoman-held Macedonia on 24 March; the Ottomans mobilized their army on 6 April; an official declaration of war followed on 18 April.

Winston expected his mother to find a newspaper for which he could report.

---

22 Marcus Atilius Regulus was one of two consuls who commanded Roman forces against Carthage in the first Punic War of 256 BC. Initially successful in sea and land battles, he was defeated and captured in 255 BC. After four years of imprisonment he returned on parole to Rome to deliver Carthage's punitive peace terms, which he advised the senate to reject. Having returned to Carthage with news of the rejection, he was put to death.

— WSC to JSC —

21 April 1897   Bangalore

My dearest Mamma,

I am afraid you will regard this letter somewhat in the aspect of a bombshell. The Declaration of war by Turkey on Greece has completely changed all my plans. By good fortune I am possessed of the necessary leave and I propose, with your approval, to go to the front as a special correspondent. [...]

Which side to go on. This my dearest Mamma must depend on you. Of course my sympathies are entirely with the Greeks, but on the other hand the Turks are bound to win – are in enormous strength & will be on the offensive the whole time. [...] You must decide. If you can get me good letters to the Turks – to the Turks I will go. If to the Greeks – to the Greeks. [...]

Special Correspondent. Of course nearly every paper has one there already, but I have no doubt that you will find one to avail themselves of my services. I would send telegrams and also write signed articles & if necessary crude sketches could be sent. I should expect to be paid £10 or £15 an article – customary rates for telegrams but would bear my own expenses. [...] These arrangements I leave to you and I hope when I arrive at Brindisi I shall find the whole thing cut and dried. [...] If you will do this for me you will be a dear – though if you won't you could be nothing else. [...]

Goodbye my dearest Mamma, Ever your loving son
Winston S. Churchill

A FORTNIGHT BEFORE he left India, Winston mentioned to his mother for the first time an ambition to transform himself into an author, rather than just a reader, of books.

— WSC to JSC —

28 April 1897   Bangalore

My dearest Mamma,

I terminate today the unbroken series of letters to you from India, which have amused my leisure every week. I sail next Saturday week in the *Ganges*[23] & changing to the *Ballarat*[24] at Aden hope to reach Brindisi by the 20th or 21st of May.

I hope I shall find the necessary letters awaiting me at the Poste Restante.[25] When you get this you will still have time to telegraph. If the war is not over I shall proceed at once to Constantinople & thence to the frontier. I shall be very grateful if you can place £50 to my credit at the Ottoman bank or at any other well-known house in that City.

If the war is of a short duration as is probable – or if I soon weary of its discomforts & vicissitudes I may have time & perhaps courage to pay a flying visit to Cumberland Place. If not the Prince may enjoy the pleasing delusion that I am engaged in a tour among the frontier fortresses of our Indian Empire.

I begin to think Egypt is a doubtful paradise. Three batteries of artillery for the Cape looks ominous.[26] Besides I hear the 9th Lancers are to remain there for the present. Is it feasible the Government contemplate an enterprise against the Boers? Well I shall not be far away. It will be a great thing to live once more after the peaceful slumbers of Bangalore. I have finished all the *History* and all the *Essays* & 6 *Annual Registers*, carefully annotated besides. On the voyage I shall begin the reading of the *Wealth of Nations*. [...]

---

23 Launched in 1882, owned by the Nourse Line; sold to Norwegian owners 1904, sunk in the Atlantic 1917.

24 Launched in 1882, owned by P&O; broken up 1904.

25 A service, available in most countries, by which post offices held mail until it was collected by the recipient.

26 Britain dispatched three batteries of artillery and one battalion of infantry to southern Africa in April 1897 as a precaution against the outbreak of hostilities with the Boer republic; *Military History Journal*, vol. 11, no. 3–4, October 1999.

When I come back from Turkey I hope to have material enough for a book – so indispensable nowadays to write a book. If you don't you expose yourself to dangerous notoriety. The man who has travelled and never written a book! Shocking! [...]

With very best love & many kisses, Ever your loving son
Winston

BEFORE WINSTON reached Brindisi, a ceasefire brought the conflict between Greece and Turkey to a close on 20 May.

— WSC to JSC —

26 May 1897   *SS Caledonia,*[27] off Brindisi

My dearest Mamma,
Here I am on the threshold of Europe. I have not yet received your letters which I expect to find at the Poste Restante – but I am anxious this should go by the train *de luxe*. I have reluctantly had to give up all hopes of Turkey as the war has fizzled out – like a damp firework. [...]

Alas I fear I shall have a bad welcome from you. Indeed at the last moment and on the receipt of your last letter [p. 205] I very nearly gave up the idea altogether. But there was nothing to do in India. [...] I hope this letter wh will precede me by two or three days will prepare my path as far as you are concerned – and that you will not be so unkind as to be angry with me for having decided to spend my leave in England. [...]

Your loving son
Winston S. Churchill

---

27 Launched in 1894, owned by P&O; troop carrier 1917–18; broken up 1925.

9

A SPLENDID EPISODE

1897

'I play for high stakes'

WINSTON ARRIVED home early in June 1897, aged twenty-two. He was in time for the Derby at Epsom. On 7 June his mother wrote to Jack: 'You can imagine what talks Winston and I have been having. [...] He looks very well, I think, and is more quiet.'[1]

Short of money and beset by the debts he owed to London tradesmen, Winston asked Theodore Lumley, the Churchill family solicitor, to help by arranging a loan from an insurance company, to be secured against his eventual inheritance on his mother's death. Lumley suggested that he might be able to raise £3,500 and was left to get on with the job.

Winston turned his mind instead to the first rungs of the political ladder. He registered his interest in becoming a parliamentary candidate with the secretary of the Conservative Party at its London

---

1   R. Martin *Lady Randolph Churchill*, vol. 2, p. 86.

headquarters and was advised to make a name by speaking to party audiences around the country. To this end the secretary put him in touch with organizers of a meeting of the Primrose League near Bath; there, on 22 July, he addressed his first political rally, following which Jennie gave a dinner party in his honour.

From Bath Winston travelled to the home of Aunt Lily and her husband, Captain Bill Beresford. Deepdene, near Dorking, provided a convenient base while he attended the 'Glorious Goodwood' race meeting on the South Downs, one of the last events of London's summer season. There, on the lawns of the racecourse, he heard news that Sir Bindon Blood, a fellow guest at Deepdene the previous year, had just taken charge of a campaign to suppress a rebellion on India's North West Frontier, in the Malakand district. When they met a year earlier, the general had promised Winston to take him onto his headquarters staff if he ever won such a command.

Winston headed straight for Brindisi to catch the next boat eastwards, leaving without the time either to complete Lumley's loan or to remember his dog, Peas.

— WSC to JSC —

7 August [1897]   Steamship *Rome*[2] near Aden

My dear Mamma,

We are just in the hottest part of the Red Sea. The temperature is something like over 100 degrees and as it is damp hot – it is equal to a great deal more. Several people who have been about 20 years in India tell me that they have never known such heat. It is like being in a vapour bath. The whole sea is steamy and there is not a breath of air – by night or day. Under these circumstances you will not mind my writing somewhat shortly. First:- I have heard nothing further from Sir Bindon Blood but expect a wire of sorts at Aden. Should I get one – I will add a P.S. to this.

---

2   Launched 1881, owned by P&O; used on its route between London and Australia; renamed SS *Vectis* 1904.

Second there are two or three things that I left undone in the hurry of leaving, and wh I beg you will do for me.

A. Walden[3] to write to James Bywater, 2 Ewald Road, Putney and tell him to send my polo sticks to Cumberland Place. After wh I want them sent out here as quickly as possible. [...]

E. I want Lord Beaconsfield's [the former Benjamin Disraeli] and Mr Gladstone's speeches. I told Bain [bookseller] but he did not send in time.

All this do my dearest Mamma and earn besides my affection – my gratitude. I have read a great deal on the voyage and had intended to give you my views on two books that impressed me – but the views have melted. [...]

> *With best love and – (no it is too hot)*
> *I remain your liquefied – evaporating but devoted son*
> *Winston S. Churchill*

P.S. Aden Aug 8 1897 9 a.m. No News yet. Alas   *WSC*

— WSC TO JSC —

17 August [1897]   Bangalore

Dearest Mamma,

I have heard nothing more from Sir Bindon Blood. I cannot think he would willingly disappoint me and can only conclude that someone at Headquarters has put a spoke in my wheel. [...]

Meanwhile we live in stirring times. 50,000 men are concentrated on the frontier besides the normal garrisons. Every stick of transport has been mobilised and preparations are being made for all eventualities. Down here we are forlornly deserted. [...] There is no chance of our being taken as so many cavalry regiments are nearer the scene of action. [...]

---

3 Lord Randolph's former valet, still in service to the Churchill family (see People, p. 578).

I am very much annoyed at forgetting to take 'Peas'. I had looked forward so much to bringing him out here & in the hurry and bustle of getting off – of course I forgot him. I have written to ask Mr Long, an officer in this regiment, who is coming to India on the 16th September – to bring him out. He is very kind to dogs and will take the greatest care of 'Peas'. [...]

Everybody here was, I think glad to see me again. I too was glad to get back for some reasons. I am arranging – if alive next year – to go tiger shooting with Barnes. (March & April). After that we can discuss; though I daresay I may hang on of my own free will for another year and in any case I shall of course be guided by you. [...]

Mamma – you are a dear. Do write long letters and believe me – every word will be appreciated. Perhaps you will think this letter pessimistic but I try in my letters to you to reflect my mind on to the paper – and honestly I am disgusted about Malakand.

I want some pictures of you in Theodora costume[4] – for my table. Also lots of letters. [...]

Goodbye, my dearest Mamma. Ever your loving son
Winston

P.S. I am counting on that money and have already written several cheques to pay the bills here. Hustle Lumley & wire if there is a hitch. [...]

A S BIDDEN, Jennie arranged for Peas to follow his master and found a newspaper that would take Winston's articles about the fighting. *The Times* had already recruited a correspondent, but she persuaded Sir Edward Levy-Lawson, the owner of the *Daily Telegraph*, to employ her son; they did not discuss a fee.

---

4   On 2 July, JSC had attended a fancy dress ball given by the duchess of Devonshire in London. All guests were photographed in their costumes: Jennie was dressed as the sixth-century Byzantine empress Theodora by the Paris couturier Worth.

Jennie as Empress Theodora at the Duchess of Devonshire's
fancy dress ball, July 1897.

9 September [1897]   [Blenheim]

My darling Winston,

Again I only write a line for I feel you cannot receive this for at least
5 or 6 weeks – & next week's letter will get to you just as soon. But by
the time you do get it – probably you will be on yr way back to join yr
regiment. Old Lawson answered a letter I wrote him by telegram saying
"Tell him to post picturesque forcible letters". I have no doubt if you
get a chance of sending any that they will be well paid – of course they
must be attractive.

As I said to you in my last I cannot say anything as to the merit of
yr going out to the frontier until I hear the circumstances of the case.
I received yr letter from Bangalore & felt for yr disappointment. The
loan will be all right as soon as they hear & know that you are in the
same state of health as you were when you left England.

Take care of yrself my darling – I am looking anxiously for a letter
from you. [...]

JSC

You shall have Peas & yr pony is all right.

———

WINSTON REACHED his regiment in Bangalore in the third
week of August, but there was still no word from Sir Bindon
or the Malakand Field Force.

He turned instead to his latest project – a novel that he provision-
ally called *Affairs of State*, although it would eventually be published
as *Savrola*. Set in the fictional Mediterranean republic of Laurania,
the hero of the tale, Savrola, was 'a man of culture and a very per-
suasive orator' who rebelled against Molaro, the country's despotic
ruler. Molaro sent his beautiful wife Lucile to distract the rebellious
Savrola, only for her to fall in love with him.

24 August [1897]   Bangalore

My dearest Mamma,

I hope this will catch the mail – but I have left it very late for two reasons. First because there is nothing to say and second because I have been writing my novel all day. I am still disgusted at my not being taken. Sir Bindon Blood has never replied to any of my wires since Brindisi. [...]

As to the Novel. I think you will be surprised when you get the MS [manuscript]. It is far and away the best thing that I have ever done. I have only written 80 MS pages – but I find a fertility of ideas that surprises me. Whether I publish my own name or an assumed one – depends on the finished result & ultimately on your opinion. It is called *Affairs of State*, a political romance. [...] All my philosophy is put into the mouth of the hero. But you must see for yourself. It is full of adventure.

> *Good night & goodbye till next week dearest Mamma.*
> *Ever your loving son*
> *Winston S. Churchill*

21 September [1897]   Langwell, Berriedale, R.S.O. Caithness[5]

My darling Winston,

I am surprised not to have had a wire from you from Nowshera[6] – I try to think that no news means good news, but I confess I wish what I cl^d hear from you. Lumley is still waiting for your wire to complete the loan – it is altogether very worrying. [...]

---

5   Langwell House, in Caithness; Scottish home of the dukes of Portland. R.S.O. denotes a 'regional sorting office' of the Royal Mail.
6   India's north-western railway and Grand Trunk Road passed through Nowshera (now part of Pakistan), which hosted a cantonment of British troops.

You may imagine how much I think of you. I only wish that I knew where you were. I received yr letter from Bangalore enclosing a cheque for £5. You had no idea of starting for the front then & I hope in yr next I shall hear all the particulars. Yr novel shall be taken care of when it arrives – meanwhile what has become of the "Scaffolding of Rhetoric"?[7] I wonder if you will have commenced any of yr letters to the *D.T.* [*Daily Telegraph*] – the "forcible picturesque" style old Lawson wanted. [...]

There are so many things I want to talk to you about, but I am so in the dark as to yr whereabouts or knowledge as to when this is likely to reach you that I find it difficult. [...]

Well! Darling I can only hope for the best & pray that all will come out well. I believe in yr lucky star as I do in mine. The enclosed will interest you – I don't believe that we can possibly get our money back – but it will be a satisfaction to know that the Creature will get a few years prison – also Cadogan. [...]

My money affairs worry me very much, I shall have to see Lumley & see what can be done. [...] Well goodbye for this week darling I pray that you are safe & well. That you are doing right I have no doubt of. God bless you.

Yr loving Mother
JSC

———·———

Winston telegraphed his mother on 28 September to say that he was on his way to the frontier, but the telegram had not yet caught up with her by the time of her next letter, dated 30 September, because she was 'visiting' in Scotland.

---

7   WSC later completed the article; its text survives (although it was never published).

30 September [1897]   Minto House, Hawick, N.B[8]

Dearest Winston,

I conclude you have been able to get on the staff – otherwise by now you wl^d be on yr way back to Bangalore. I do hope for yr sake darling that you have been able to get there. [...]

The enclosed may amuse you. I hope we shall get hold of Cadogan – I feel more angry with him than with Cruikshank, who is only a common swindler. I do hope that I shall not have to appear [in court] – the papers are so annoying & wl^d make sketches of one & rude remarks.

I wonder if you have answered Lumley yet? I wrote to him to go to Cox's at once & explain matters – in case yr cheques were presented. He is a vy tiresome man. My own affairs are in a dreadful state – & I hope to get him to put them right. How it is to be done Heaven knows. [...]

How I am looking forward to yr first letter from the front – to me – not the *D.T.* I go from here for another visit to Alloa, the Mar & Kellie's,[9] & then to London & Newmarket. I have a lot of visits Oct, Nov, & Dec & after that shall remain in London to try to economize. [...]

Goodbye my darling. When & where this will reach you Heaven knows.

Bless you & Good keep you from harm.
Yr loving Mother
JSC

————

W INSTON HAD written to his mother a full month earlier on his five-day journey northwards towards the frontier. His letter, which took five weeks to reach Jennie in Scotland, warned

---

8   N.B. denoted North Britain, a term sometimes used for Scotland after the union of the crowns of Scotland and England in 1603; South Britain comprised England and Wales. By 1900, use of 'N.B.' was largely confined to postal addresses.
9   Alloa Tower, near Stirling, seat of the earl of Mar and Kellie, head of the Erskine family.

India 1896–9 and the North West Frontier campaign, 1897

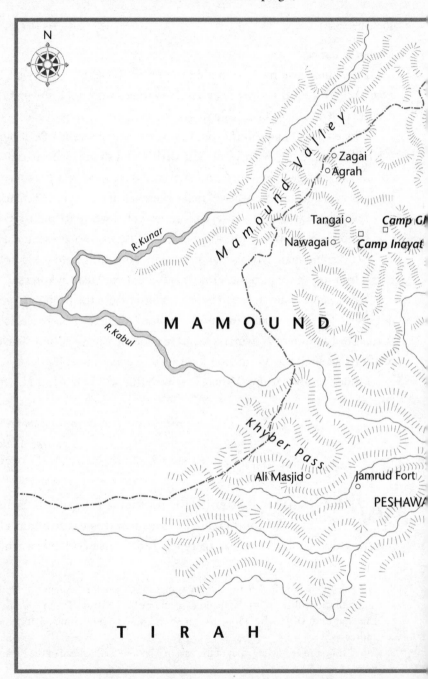

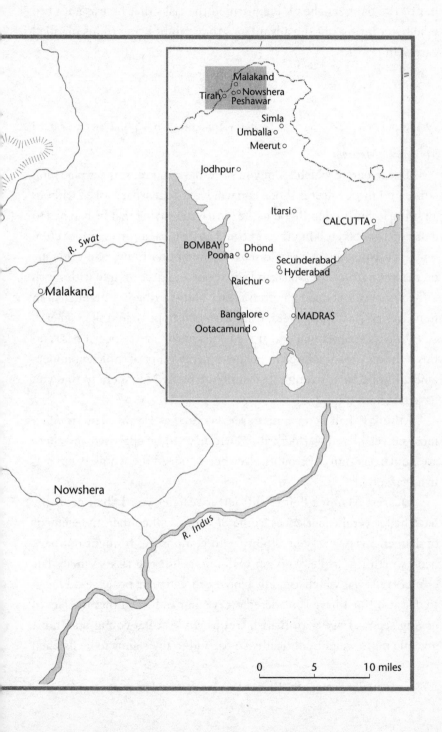

Malakand
Tirah
Nowshera
Peshawar
Simla
Umballa
Meerut
Jodhpur
Itarsi
CALCUTTA
BOMBAY
Dhond
Poona
Secunderabad
Hyderabad
Raichur
Bangalore
MADRAS
Ootacamund

R. Swat

Malakand

Nowshera

R. Indus

0   5   10 miles

her of the dangers ahead. He justified the risks that he was about to take by pointing out the advantages they might bring to his planned career in politics.

— WSC to JSC —

29 August [1897]   In the Train near Dhond, and later near Itarsi

My dearest Mamma,

The telegram which I sent you yesterday requires some explanation – though I most sincerely hope you will have done what I asked without awaiting it. Sir Bindon Blood wrote me a letter saying that he had had to make up his staff etc – but that if I could come up as a correspondent (the only excuse possible) he would seize the first opportunity of putting me on the strength of the Malakand Field Force. I accordingly with much difficulty have obtained a month's leave and starting last night shall in four days arrive at Nowshera, from whence I hope to join the General.

To go as correspondent, it is necessary to have a special pass and this is in some cases refused if the [news]paper is not of sufficient importance. I hope most strongly I shall not arrive at Nowshera to find you have taken no steps. [...]

I think I shall be in time to see as much as I want. The Afridi, a most powerful and warlike tribe,[10] will have to be chastised and there are numerous signs of trouble elsewhere. Indeed the whole frontier is in a blaze. [...]

Dearest Mamma before this letter reaches you I shall probably have had several experiences, some of which will contain the element of danger. I view every possibility with composure. It might not have been worth my while, who am really no soldier to risk so many fair chances on a war which can only help me directly in a profession I mean to discard. But I have considered everything and I feel that the fact of having seen service with British troops while still a young man must give me more weight politically – must add to my claims to be listened

---

10 A *pashtun* tribe living in the Khyber Pass and surrounding areas.

to and may perhaps improve my prospects of gaining popularity with the country.

Besides this – I think I am of an adventurous disposition and shall enjoy myself not so much in spite of as because of the risks I run. At any rate I have decided – and having taken a hand I shall do my best to play a good game. [...]

> *Ever your loving son*
> *Winston S. Churchill*

— WSC to JSC —

5 September [1897]   Malakand Camp

My dearest Mamma,

Your telegram received. Herewith 2 letters for the *D.T.* I do not know what terms you have made with them – but it should certainly not be less than £10 per letter. Having read please forward – and decide whether they should be signed or not. I am myself very much in favour of signing – as otherwise I get no credit for the letters. It may help me politically to come before the public in this way. [...]

[...] I live with Sir Bindon Blood – who is very kind to me. I am at present correspondent of the *Pioneer*[11] to which I have to telegraph 300 words a day. At the first opportunity I am to be put on the strength of this force – which will give me a medal if I come through.

As to fighting – we march tomorrow, and before a week is out, there will be a battle – probably the biggest yet fought on the frontier this year. By the time this reaches you everything will be over so that I do not mind writing about it. I have faith in my star – that is that I am intended to do something in the world. If I am mistaken – what does it matter? My life has been a pleasant one and though I should regret to leave it – it would be a regret that perhaps I should never know. [...]

In any case – I mean to play this game out and if I lose it is obvious

---

11 English-language newspaper in India, for which Rudyard Kipling had written 1887–9.

that I never could have won any other. The unpleasant contingency is of course a wound which would leave permanent effects and would while leaving me life – deprive me of all that makes life worth living. But all games have forfeits. Fortunately the odds are good.

The movement wh takes place tomorrow is a little romantic. For more than a week we shall disappear from the world. We let go our hold on Telegraphs and communications & plunge into an unknown country – with an uncounted & improved enemy. [...]

Goodbye my dearest Mamma – I will arrange to have your letters forwarded. Do not worry. A philosophical temperament should transcend all human weaknesses – fear or affection.

Ever your loving son
Winston S. Churchill

———

J ENNIE RECOMMENDED that Winston should combine his articles into a book about the campaign, suggesting as its title *The Second Afghan Risings*. Winston came up with the same idea, independently, in a letter written five days later. When the book appeared the following year, however, he called it *The Story of the Malakand Field Force*.

— JSC TO WSC —

7 October 1897   [Edinburgh]

Darling Winston,
I am writing in the hotel in Edinboro', on my way to Ld Wemyss[12] where I stay for a day or two & then go to London. You may imagine with what interest I received yr letters – & to know that you are safe. I suppose you will have seen some of the fighting & by the time you receive this will probably be thinking of returning to Bangalore.

———

12 The earl of Wemyss and March's home was Gosford House, East Lothian (see Places, p. 580).

I have little time to write today so will proceed to business at once. I hope you received my cable & were able to answer Lumley, at once – that beastly loan can't be completed until they know that you are all right. Meanwhile on Monday I will go to Cox's & explain.

I read yr letters for the *D.T.* to Ld Minto[13] who thought them excellent – but begged me not to sign yr name. He said it was very unusual & might get you into trouble. The 1st one appeared yesterday headed "Indian Frontier – by a young officer". The Editor[14] wired to say they wld give £5 a column – I'm afraid it is not as much as you had hoped – yr first letter was just one column. However I may try & arrange with Lawson for more.

I wrote to the Prince [of Wales] & told him to look out for yr letters. Also to lots of people. You will get plenty of kudos (can't spell it) I will see that you do darling boy. I have just bought a *D.T.* of today & see another letter which they seem to have cut in two – if they do that there will be more letters & you will get yr £10. I will send the cuttings to you by next mail [...].

You may imagine how much I think of you, & how in my heart I shall be glad that the war will be over soon, & that I shall know you safely back at Bangalore – & yet I am more than glad for yr sake that you managed to get up there – I hope you will be none the worse & will get yr medal. But I think of all the hardships you are going through & I feel for you darling.

Don't be worried about yr letters, you will be able to use them again in a pamphlet form – "The Second Afghan Risings" etc. They head the letter today "The War in the Indian Highlands", borrowing yr phrase which they evidently like. I hope you have not felt any ill effects of the rapid travelling and the sun. [...]

God bless you darling. I hope Sir B.B. [Bindon Blood] got my letter.

Yr loving Mother
JSC

---

13 Lord Minto had been a soldier until 1889; he succeeded to the earldom in 1891 (see People, p. 573).
14 John Le Sage edited the *Daily Telegraph* 1888–1923.

— WSC to JSC —

12 September [1897]   Nawagai

Temperature 110 degrees

Dearest Mamma,

Herewith 2 more letters for *D.T.* I do not like the 4th one. Use your own discretion in editing it – as I am too tired to write more now and then post it off. No fighting at present – but possibilities every moment. No ice – no soda – intense heat – but still a delightful experience.

Best of love my dearest Mamma. Please forgive this scribble – and believe

I love you

Your ever loving son

Winston S. Churchill

J ENNIE WROTE her next letter from Bridlemere Court, the Newmarket home of Sir Edward Levy-Lawson, the proprietor of the *Daily Telegraph* for whom Winston had been writing.

— JSC to WSC —

29 October 1897   Bridlemere, Newmarket

Darling Winston,

I am writing to you from here, where Bill & Marcus[15] Beresford dined last night – the former brought me yr 2 letters to him which he liked very much. You may imagine how relieved I am to think that you are safe back at Bangalore altho' I daresay it is a disappointment to you not to go on. However you can be well satisfied that you have done well & that you were <u>very lucky</u> to get there at all. [...]

I am going on a round of visits which would amuse me very much were I not worried & anxious about money. I felt so much for you being worried about that loan. I did the best I could for you. But you ought to

---

15 Lord Marcus Beresford, racing manager to the Prince of Wales.

have known my darling that I would have protected you in some way, & not let you get into trouble anew if I had begged the money for you. Oh! What a curse the want of it is.

Yr loving Mother
JSC

— WSC to JSC —

19 September [1897]   Camp Inayat Kila
Private

Dearest Mamma,

The enclosed 3 letters to the *Daily Telegraph* will tell you a good deal of what happened here. Please do whatever you think fit with them. I am tired of writing as these long letters take several hours.

But I must give you some account of my personal experiences on the 16th. I started with the Cavalry and saw the first shot fired. After half an hour's skirmishing I rode forward with the 35th Sikhs until firing got so hot that my grey pony was unsafe. I proceeded on foot. When the retirement began I remained till the last and here I was perhaps very near my end. If you read between the lines of my letter you will see that this retirement was an awful rout in which the wounded were left to be cut up horribly by these wild beasts.

I was close to both officers when they were hit almost simultaneously and fired my revolver at a man at 30 yards who tried to cut up poor Hughes' body. He dropped but came on again. A subaltern – Bethune by name and I carried a wounded Sepoy[16] for some distance and might perhaps, had there been any gallery, have received some notice. My pants are still stained with the man's blood. We also remained till the enemy came to within 40 yards firing our revolvers. They actually threw stones at us. It was a horrible business. For there was no help for the man that went down. I felt no excitement and very little fear. All the excitement went out when things became really deadly. […]

---

16 Indian soldier serving under British orders.

[...] In my novel I develop the idea that a "politician" very often possesses mere physical courage. Military opinion is of course contrary. But at any rate whatever I do afterwards, no one can say anything against me on this score. I rode on my grey pony all along the skirmish line where everyone else was lying down in cover. Foolish perhaps but I play for high stakes and given an audience there is no act too daring or too noble. Without the gallery things are different.

I will write again soon if all goes well, if not you know my life has been a pleasant one, quality not quantity is after all what we should strive for. Still I should like to come back and wear my medals at some big dinner or some other function. [...]

I do not look ahead more than a day – or further than the hills that surround the valley. I suppose other things have happened in the last week – but I did not realise it. Europe is infinitely remote – England infinitely small – Bangalore a speck on the map of India – but here everything is life size and flesh colour.

Ever your loving son
Winston

— JSC to WSC —

4 November 1897   Iwerne Minster House, Blandford

My darling Winston,

I have sent yr letters to the *D.T.* also the 5th one – altho' I still think it a mistake. You are not in a position to write in <u>a paper</u> on such matters <u>at present</u> – when you have left the Army it will be different. The letter is a good one & I daresay yr views are shared by many, but it is sure to put people's back up to be told the reasons why & wherefore, by one as young as you. However we won't argue about it.

You will be glad to hear that Col Brab sent me a letter from Sir Bindon B. in which he speaks of you in the highest praise & says he has mentioned you in despatches. You have done more than well my darling boy & I am as always proud of you. Forgive a piece of advice – which may not be needed – but be modest. All yr feats of valour are sure to come out & people will know. Let it be from others & not from yrself. One must be tempted to talk of oneself in such a case – but resist. Let them drag things out.

I will send you all the letters as they have come out, but there are no press criticisms as the general public do not know they are yours. The enclosed may be a little sop to yr vanity, legitimate I own![17] [...]

When you have time to go into them, let me know about yr finances. Have you paid yr bills? Let me know how you stand. [...]

My darling how I long to see you & how thankful I am that you are safe. Let me hear if you liked the books I sent. Send me the 1st part of yr novel & send back these scraps – & don't forget to let me know about yr finances. I will send you in my next a list of small bills here for which you can send me a cheque if you can!

Yr loving Mother
JSC

JENNIE MAY have thought that Winston's frontier adventure was almost over. He was, however, trying to arrange a transfer so that he could take part in a second episode. The Tirah was a mountainous section of India's North West Frontier between the Khanki valley and the Khyber Pass. For the previous sixteen years the British Raj had paid the Afridi tribe to guard the Khyber Pass and its approaches, while also maintaining its own regiment of Afridi soldiers for the same purpose.

Late in 1897, the Afridi tribesmen rose up against the arrangement, captured the mountain posts manned by their own countrymen and threatened the British army's forts closer to Peshawar. General Sir William Lockhart was ordered in September to raise a force to suppress the uprising, with the help of the Punjab Army Corps numbering 35,000 men. He would commence operations in what came to be known as the Tirah Expedition on 18 October.

---

17 The enclosure has not survived; it was presumably a piece in praise of the anonymous articles in the *Daily Telegraph*.

Sir Bindon Blood (standing, arms on the gun barrel) and staff,
Mamound Valley, 1897.

— WSC TO JSC —

27 September [1897]   Camp Ghosan

Dearest Mamma,

I was delighted to get your letter from Blenheim last night. I am
still alive and well after another exciting week. Since last writing we
fought the actions of Zagai & Tangai – both small engagements: the
former a sharp one. [...]

I am trying to get on this other expedition to Tirah – as that would
mean another clasp to my medal – but it is doubtful if I shall succeed. If
not – I shall be back at Bangalore Oct 15. If I should – then things may
run on until Christmas – or even later.

I am perplexed and worried by a telegram wh. arrived from England
and reached me two days ago saying "NO". Does this apply to the loan?
If so – I am indeed in a serious position. I have written £500 of cheques
in settlement of debts and if they are dishonoured, I really do not know
– or care to guess – what the consequences might be. [...] You can

understand that all this worries me much more than the dangers and discomforts of war. [...]

I have had some dangerous hours – but feel sure my luck is good enough to pull me through.

Your ever loving son
Winston

— WSC to JSC —

2 October [1897]   Inayat Kila
[in pencil]

My dearest Mamma,

Since I last wrote to you – we have had another severe action. Agrah – 30th September – I was under fire for five hours – but did not get into the hottest corners. Our loss was 60 killed and wounded – out of the poor 1,200 we can muster. Compare these figures with actions like Firket[18] in Egypt – wh are cracked up as great battles and wh are commemorated by clasps & medals etc etc. Here out of one brigade we have lost in a fortnight 245 killed and wounded and nearly 25 officers. I hope you will talk about this to the Prince and others – as if any fuss is made, they may give a special clasp for Mamound Valley. This has been the hardest fighting on the frontier for forty years. [...]

It is a war without quarter. They kill and mutilate everyone they catch and we do not hesitate to finish their wounded off. I have seen several things wh. have not been very pretty since I have been up here – but as you will believe I have not soiled my hands with any dirty work – though I recognize the necessity of some things. All this however you need not publish.

If I get through alright – and I have faith in my luck – I shall try and come home next year for a couple of months. Meanwhile the game amuses me – dangerous though it is – and I shall stay as long as I can.

18 7 June 1896. An estimated 20 Egyptian soldiers were killed; 800–1,000 of their opponents, the Mahdists.

It is a strange life. Here I am lying in a hole – dug two feet deep in the ground – to protect me against the night firing – on a mackintosh with an awful headache – and the tent & my temperature getting hotter every moment as the sun climbs higher and higher. But after all food and a philosophic temperament are man's only necessities.

I hope to heaven that money is alright. It seems like a bad dream from time to time.

Yr ever loving son
Winston

B Y T H E time Winston next wrote, ten days later, his involvement in the Malakand Field Force had almost come to an end; at this stage he had been unable to arrange a transfer to its Tirah counterpart. Instead he consoled himself by contemplating the writing of a book about his Malakand adventures, echoing his mother's suggestion of the same idea in her letter of 7 October (which had not yet reached him).

— WSC TO JSC —

12 October [1897]   Nowshera

My dearest Mamma,

One line to let you know that I am across the frontier and rejoining my regiment. I will telegraph you the day after tomorrow but as I am going to Jamrud[19] to see Hugo Baring and there is a probability of night fighting, I defer shouting until I am out of the wood.

Since last I wrote I have seen two [or] three sharp skirmishes and have now been 10 complete times under fire. Quite a foundation for a political life. I will write by next mail fully – but my letters to *D.T.* should give you some idea of my life. Please send me the copies and any criticism

---

19 Fort at the entrance to the Khyber Pass, site of a cantonment of the British army.

relating thereto. I intend or rather am seriously contemplating writing *The Story of the M.F.F.* [Malakand Field Force]. I know the ground, the men and the facts. It is a fine idea. But the novel would have to be shelved and the idea has filled my mind. I will let you know next time I write.

I hope you like the letters. I have earned my medal and clasp fully. [Sir Bindon] Blood says not one in a hundred have seen as much fighting as I have – and mind you – not from the staff or a distance but from the last company of the rearguard every time. A splendid episode. [...]

Yr loving son
Winston S. Churchill

BACK IN Bangalore, Winston conveyed to his mother some of the exhilaration of war, which he had now experienced twice. It was a feeling that never left him, yet which would attract criticism and admiration in almost equal measure.

— WSC TO JSC —

21 October [1897]   Bangalore

Dearest Mamma,

Once again I write to you from my old table and my own room here in Bangalore. It is only seven weeks since I left here – but what a lot of things have happened to me and how many more might have happened!

The period has been the most glorious and delightful that my life has yet contained. But the possibility was always in view that it might be abruptly terminated. I saw a great many people killed and wounded and heard many bullets strike all round or whistle by – so many that if I had counted them you would not perhaps believe me. But nothing came nearer me than a foot – in a former letter I said a yard – but since then the interval was decreased.

My luck was throughout extraordinarily good. Everything worked out just as in Cuba – mechanically. All arrangements fitted, no obstacles intervened – no unpleasant results occurred. I am immensely satisfied.

And now having had a fine experience and being entitled to a medal & I think two clasps – I am back at Bangalore to polo and my friends with a new stimulus to life. [...]

Poor Mamma you must have worried. I can quite understand it as frankly it was extremely dangerous. These sorts of things make life worth living however and I do not feel that my thirst for adventure is at all quenched. [...]

I think old Lawson will like my letters, as they are in all conscience "forcible and picturesque." I enclose you the last three. I have looked into the *D.T.* but do not see that they are published yet. I hope they are making a good impression. Politically they may do good.

Ever your loving son
Winston

— JSC ᴛᴏ WSC —

11 November [1897]   Highclere Castle[20]

My darling Winston,

Yr letter with three enclosed for the *D.T.* was forwarded to me here, & I have sent them off. I enclose a letter from the Editor which will please you. I rather hope that old Lawson will present you with a cheque over & above the payment of the letters. He ought to – but of course haggling about the price would not have done.

After all the letters have been given a prominent place (latterly on the 1ˢᵗ page), they have served their purpose by getting you to the front, & they have been much appreciated. I will send you the whole series when these last 3 have been published. I suppose you will now settle down & do some reading. I cannot tell you how grateful I am to Providence to think that you are safe at Bangalore. [...]

Speaking of finance, don't forget to let me know exactly the state of

---

20 Seat of the earl of Carnavon; the 'castle' was rebuilt by Sir Charles Barry in the Anglo-Italian style in 1878.

yr affairs. Lewis the Jeweller²¹ wants some money from you. Personally I am going through a very serious crisis. I will write to you the particulars as soon as I have come to some tangible plan. Lumley is trying to devise something. [...]

Yr loving Mother

JSC

I T WAS only when he reached Bangalore that Winston discovered his articles had appeared without his name attached to them in the *Daily Telegraph*; he was disappointed by what he saw as a lost political opportunity. His next set of letters suggests that his spell on theNorth West Frontier proved a turning point in his self-confidence and brought a new urgency to his ambition.

This was the period when Jennie and the Prince of Wales were at the height of their relationship. If hostesses of weekend parties in country houses wished to attract the Prince as a guest, they knew that Jennie's inclusion on the list of those invited could only help. Winston was aware of the state of play: for the first, but not the last time, he asked his mother to enlist the Prince's support for his transfer to Egypt.

— WSC TO JSC —

25 October [1897]   Bangalore

My dearest Mamma,

I saw in the week's papers that arrived yesterday the first three of my letters to the *D.T.* I will not conceal my disappointment at their not being signed. I had written them with the design, a design which took form as the correspondence advanced, of bringing my personality before the electorate. I had hoped that some political advantage might

---

21 H. C. Lewis (his pamphlet *Papers and notes on the genesis and matrix of the diamond*, was published by Longmans, 1897).

have accrued. This hope encouraged me to take the very greatest pains with the style and composition and also to avoid alluding to any of my own experiences. I do not think that I have ever written anything better, or to which I would more willingly have signed my name. On such a matter the advice of a soldier [Lord Minto] was of course worthless.

As to getting into trouble with the authorities, I am just as responsible now that they are not signed as if they have been. But in any case I have written nothing that could cause offence. However I left the decision in your hands and you have decided – not for the first time – upon a negative course. I will only add that if I am to avoid doing "unusual" things it is difficult to see what chance I have of being more than an average person. [...]

As I am deprived of all satisfaction on this account, I mean to solace myself financially. I will not accept less than £10 a letter and I shall return any cheque for a less sum. I particularly asked for that amount *au moins* and when I think of the circumstances under wh those letters were written, on the ground in a tent temperature 115 degrees or after a long days action or by a light which was dangerous to use lest it drew fire – when I was tired and hustled and amid other averse circumstances – I think they are cheap at the price.

The £75 which the *D.T.* propose to give me will hardly pay my ticket for self & horses. The *D. Chronicle* offered me ten pounds a letter to go to Crete and I will not be defrauded in this way. As Dr Johnson says, "No-one but a blockhead ever wrote except for money."[22]

[...] I am still thinking seriously of writing *The Story of the Malakand Field Force*. It would of course sell well and might do me good. I know all the people to get information from. The novel however interests me so much and is so full of promise that I am undecided & am loath to put it by for a time. [...]

I must now go to Egypt and you should endeavour to stimulate the

---

22 According to James Boswell's *Life of Samuel Johnson LL.D.*, Johnson said: 'No man but a blockhead ever wrote, except for money.'

Prince into writing to Kitchener on the subject. [...] Indeed my life here is not big enough to hold me. I want to be up and doing and cannot bear inaction or routine. Polo has lost half its charm and no longer satisfies me. I become more in need of serious occupation every day. [...]

I shall soldier for two years more, but they must be two busy years. You should be able to get me sent from one place to another. [...]

I write this letter for you alone, and I do not care if you smile at its contents. I feel plenty of confidence in myself now and am certain that I shall do something in the world – if physical injury does not befall me. Thank God finance is now settled. I am winding everything up and paying bills in all directions. [...] Now let me send you my love. I wish you could see the novel. It grows daily. 8 chapters now completed.

Ever your loving son
Winston S. Churchill

'FINANCE' WAS only 'settled' to the extent that the cheques Winston had written in the summer beforer he left England had been honoured by his bank. The respite was to prove short-lived and he had missed the significance of the reference by Jennie in her last letter to the 'very serious crisis' in her own finances and to her solicitor's attempt to devise a 'tangible plan' to overcome it.

– JSC TO WSC –

25 November 1897   Lambton Castle, Durham[23]

Dearest Winston,

This alas is going to be a short letter – as I have run it rather fine & the post is going shortly. I am here on a visit to Ld Durham[24] – the

---

23 Seat of the Lambton family, whose fortune was based on coal mining.
24 John Lambton, earl of Durham; his wife Ethel had been committed to a mental institution after they married in 1882.

Prince, Duchess of Manchester,[25] [...], Pembrokes,[26] Bertie Vane[27] etc. I return to London tomorrow. [...]

By the time you receive this you will have had a wire from me telling you to write an account of the fighting you saw – as I think it important to be first in the field. You might make quite a pretty penny of it. You will of course have to be discreet if you sign it & leave as much personal out of it as possible. I shl^d write an account as tho' I were an outsider. [...]

Write to the Prince, he will like it – I will tell him. [...]

I'm afraid I must stop. Cruikshank has pleaded guilty & has eight years penal servitude. This is lucky for Cadogan who is a knave. Next week I will write at length. Bless you my darling Boy – I think of you always.

Yr loving Mother
JSC

WINSTON'S NEW self-confidence brought with it a greater assertiveness towards his mother, whom he began to accuse of timidity – she had decided not to forward his fifth letter to the *Daily Telegraph* because it contained material that was critical of his military seniors. Jennie was unused to being accused of timidity. For the first time her son identified her own circle of friends as 'narrow' and unrepresentative of the society to which he aimed to appeal.

— WSC TO JSC —

[2 November] 1897   Bangalore

My dearest Mamma,

Yesterday's mail brought me your letter of Oct 14th [missing]. I wired at once to you to ask you to have the 5th Letter published. Far

---

25 Consuelo, duchess of Manchester, née Yznaga del Valle.
26 Sidney Herbert, MP 1877–85, 1886–92; succeeded as earl of Pembroke 1895.
27 Lord Herbert Vane-Tempest, third son of the 5th marquess of Londonderry.

from getting me into trouble it expresses what is essentially the military view. [...] It is decidedly – the best – the most valuable and the most interesting letter for the series. How you could think that it would be improper for me to publish such a letter is a mystery to me. The criticisms are extremely moderate and apposite. Of course if you will always be ruled by a syndicate of colonels – who though gallant and charming men – have a detestation of print – it is probable that you will see danger and impropriety in everything. [...]

I continue to feel disappointment at the letters being unsigned. Though I value the opinion of your friends in London, that narrow circle is not the audience to whom I had meant to appeal. Never was there such modesty as yours for me. If I am to do anything in the world, you will have to make up your mind to publicity and also to my doing unusual things. Of course a certain number of people will be offended. I am afraid some people like Brab will disapprove. For this I shall be sorry as I like and respect him very much.

But I recognize the fact that certain elements must always be hostile and I am determined not to allow them to interfere with my actions. I regard an excellent opportunity of bringing my name before the country in a correct and attractive light – by means of graphic & forcible letters, as lost. I have no doubt that I should make another one in the near future: but one cannot afford to throw away chances. [...]

The novel is getting on excellently. There are now nine chapters written and it reads excellently. [...] The hero, the great democratic leader, is a fine character. A man full [of] romance, sentiment & nerves, who can talk to anyone on their own pet subject, can electrify a public meeting, and by his charm win any heart, male or female. In strong contrast is the president – a pure materialist. [...] The struggle fought out in the book between the two is one between sentiment & materialism. The prize is not only political supremacy but as appears in the story "the most beautiful woman in Europe." [...] This occupation fills my mind and my time. [...]

Looking back on the whole picture of my experiences there I find that I was on seven distinct occasions under aimed fire for periods of from 4 to 13 hours at a time: and twelve nights of desultory shooting besides. In all these occasions I am glad to be able to tell you for <u>your personal and private information only</u> that I never found a better than myself as far as behaviour went. [...]

Goodbye my dearest Mamma. Respect my confidence and do not let the military element predominate too much in your counsels.

Your ever loving son
Winston

―――――

W INSTON WAS torn between trying to finish his novel *Savrola* and writing *The Story of the Malakand Field Force*. He made his decision early in November, a month after leaving the frontier.

― WSC TO JSC ―

10 November [1897]   Bangalore

My dearest Mamma,

I am disappointed at not receiving a letter from you this week, but I suppose I cannot complain as you could not have received one from me. [...] After a month's anxious consideration I have made up my mind to write an account of the whole campaign in a book form to be called *The Story of the Malakand Field Force.* [...]

It has been a great wrench shelving the novel wh had reached its 11th chapter and was progressing capitally, but I realise that this other should be published at once – Christmas – if possible. February at the latest.

[...] I hope you will approve of the project. I have been incited to it in some way as a means [of] repairing the non-signature of my letters. It is a great undertaking but if carried out will yield substantial results in every way, financially, politically, and even, though do I care a damn, militarily.

At any rate I am fully committed now as I have written to all the colonels and knowledgeable people I met up there for facts etc. and I do not doubt I shall receive volumes by return of post. Such is the modesty of the age. [...]

What I want you to send me by return post is:-

1. The Blue book relating to the retention of Chitral.[28]
2. Any information you can get hold of as to views, opinions and expression of prominent actors in the affair.

The first at all costs at once. The second if you can arrange should take the form of a private letter. [...] I shall of course apply my own judgment to the material I collect and having pronounced shall have to stick to it all my life. [...]

Goodbye dearest Mama, Ever your loving son
Winston

---

28 *The Relief of Chitral*, also known as the Blue Book, was written by two brothers, Major-General Sir George Younghusband and Lt.-Col. Sir Francis Young-husband. The book provided a first-hand description of events of 1895 in the Hindu Kush mountains, when a British expeditionary force lifted the siege of 400 fellow soldiers trapped within Chitral's fort. Local tribesmen had resisted the subjugation of Chitral, formerly independent, to the rule of the British Raj.

10

HOBSON'S CHOICE

1897–8

'My pen wanders recklessly'

PREOCCUPIED AS Winston had been by his military adventures and literary plans, he had missed his mother's references in her recent letters to her mounting financial problems. Now, nearing his twenty-third birthday, he acknowledged her difficulties for the first time, without yet appearing unduly concerned.

The partially complete *Savrola* had to wait in the wings while its author concentrated on *The Story of the Malakand Field Force*. The two projects prompted a thought in Winston's mind that he might be able to live off his earnings from writing while he climbed the lower rungs of the political ladder. (MPs remained unpaid until 1911, although cabinet ministers earned a salary of £5,000 a year.) After all, his two historical mentors, Edward Gibbon and Thomas Macaulay, had trodden the same path.

— WSC ᴛᴏ JSC —

17 November [1897]   Bangalore

Dearest Mamma,

Both your letters arrived this week [probably of 22 October — missing – and 29 October] and I was vy pleased to get them. The *D.T.* [*Daily Telegraph*] is most unsatisfactory. Two letters have either been mislaid or suppressed and for these letters I shall get nothing. Also they break the sequence of the series. [...]

Alas I am no longer on the scene. Life here seems very barren and insipid. I am working incessantly at the book on the operations and have made considerable progress both in collecting material of wh there is a volume, and in the actual composition. [...]

I am very sorry you are worried about money, I find that my original estimate of my liabilities was considerably below the actual amount. All borrowed money and a good number of the most pressing bills have been paid – but nearly £500 – to people like Bernau, Tautz, Sowter[1] etc. will remain. [...]

You must keep your eye on the political situation. Although I know & hear nothing out here, it is evident to me that a very marked reaction against the decision of the last general election has taken place. These numerous bye elections might, had I been in England, have given me my chance of getting in. [...] Of course should a vacancy occur in Paddington [his father's former constituency] – you must weigh in for me & I will come by the next ship. They would probably elect me even if I could not get back in time. I suppose Ld Salisbury's retirement is now only a matter of months.[2] There might be sweeping changes after that. [...]

Do not worry about money my dearest Mamma, if the worst comes to the worst you can let the house – and however annoying that might be

---

1   Bernau and Tautz were tailors in London, Sowter a saddle-maker; their bills remained unpaid until 1901.
2   Lord Salisbury in fact retired 55 months later, in July 1902.

you will always find lots of places glad to receive you while you remain the dearest & most beautiful woman in the world. Besides you must help me with the woman in the novel. She is my chief difficulty. I will bring both these books out before I come home and then we will see whether I may not perhaps supplement my income by writing.

Ever your loving son
Winston

———

A S A result of her many invitations to visit country houses whenever the Prince of Wales was heading the guest list, Jennie's reply was the first letter (to survive) that she had written from her own home for eight months. She was not due to stay there for long ...

— JSC TO WSC —

10 December 1897   35a Gt Cumberland Place

My darling Winston,

The weekly mail comes round & for once finds me at home. Yr letter of the 17th Nov interested me very much. [...] I am expecting Jack home the end of next week & then we proceed to Blenheim for Xmas – a large family party – they have got some theatricals in which we will all appear – Jack as a Chinaman & I as a female reporter. Personally I think it is a mistake, it is one thing acting a burlesque for friends & even tenants, but they are doing it for charity & the whole of Oxford may turn up, or any vulgarian from London who chooses to pay 10/- to see the Churchills playing the fool. I was not consulted –& of course it is no use giving advice now.

I go to Welbeck[3] on Monday for a large party, royalties etc – & after

---

3   Welbeck Abbey in Nottinghamshire, seat of the dukes of Portland (see Places, p. 581).

Blenheim, Chatsworth[4] & then I settle down here for some time. I met Lady Jeune[5] the other day, she was full of you & I told her about yr book of which she highly approves. I will see Sampson & Low [publishers] about it. I shall meet Arthur Balfour & Chamberlain next week & I think the former cl^d give me all the information I want as regards publishers etc. [...]

I will I hope give you some political news in my next – after seeing these politicians! I've been hotting up Fardell[6] but he is not prepared to resign as yet! I am expecting the financial paper you promised me. I am sorry you haven't enough to clear everything. Debt is so wearing. I will see what I can do for you out of this new arrangement I'm making. I will write to you fully on the subject when the papers are ready to go to you for signature.

Now au revoir *till next week Bless you my darling.*

Yr loving Mother

JSC

———·———

WINSTON'S EFFORT to produce a book on the frontier campaign had now turned into a race against his rival correspondent for *The Times*, Lord Fincastle, who had lent him his fez in Calcutta at the beginning of the year.

— WSC TO JSC —

24 November [1897]   Bangalore

My dear Mamma,

I was again disappointed by receiving no letter from you this week. I look forward v much to your letters and when they do not come the

---

4 Chatsworth House in Derbyshire, seat of the dukes of Devonshire (see Places, p. 579).
5 Later Lady St Helier, who reintroduced WSC to his future wife Clementine in 1908 (see People, p. 568).
6 Sir George Fardell remained MP for South Paddington until 1910.

mail is vy barren and unsatisfactory. I note that the *D. T.* have apparently received the letters that I thought were mislaid as it is in the paper – though out of proper sequence – this week. [...]

I am working very hard at the book and am daily receiving facts and letters from the frontier concerning it. I hear Ld Fincastle is also writing one and has received the pictures I had hoped to obtain. A great nuisance this as the subject is so small that there is not room for two books on it. [...]

As it is – I have got so far – and the book promises so well – that I do not mean to give in. It will of course make all the difference which comes out first. I want you therefore to approach the publishers on the subject and write to me. I hope to send the MS [manuscript] home in six weeks time at the latest. It need not be sent out later for corrections – as I am having it typewritten.

With best love I remain, Ever your loving son
Winston

J ENNIE PROMOTED her son's interests indefatigably while she toured the great country houses of England. A conversation at Welbeck Abbey with Arthur Balfour, who was himself a published author[7] as well as a politician, led her to the literary agent A. P. Watt,[8] who would help sell *The Story of the Malakand Field Force* to a publisher.

– JSC to WSC –

16 December 1897   Welbeck Abbey, Worksop

Dearest Winston,

I will not write to you at any length by this mail – as the hour is late

---

7   Balfour had published *A Defence of Philosophic Doubt* (1879), *Essays and Addresses* (1893) and *The Foundations of Belief* (1895).

8   Alexander Pollock Watt had started working as a literary agent in 1875 after earlier spells in bookselling and advertising. He incorporated the world's first literary agency in 1881 (see People, p. 577).

Welbeck Abbey.

& I have been standing on my hind legs all day & besides I must write to Sir B.B. [Bindon Blood]. We have an enormous party here – Prince & Princesses,[9] Chamberlains,[10] Devonshires,[11] Staals,[12] Chaplin,[13] Arthur Balfour, etc – the latter has been too nice about you.

I told him all about yr book (the Campaign) & he is going to put me in the way of a good publisher & everything. You need only send me the MS & I will have it all done for you. […] I think it is very tiresome about Ld Fincastle but I'm told he is a dull dog – you must be first in the field that is all.

A.B. [Arthur Balfour] said he had not read yr letters – but he had heard more than flattering things about them. The letters have been read & appreciated by the people who later on can be useful to you. […]

---

9   The prince's wife Princess Alexandra and their daughter Princess Victoria (aged 29); their other two daughters were already married.

10   Joseph Chamberlain and his wife Harriet, née Kenwick.

11   Spencer Cavendish, 8th duke of Devonshire, and his wife Louisa, née van Alten, former duchess of Manchester.

12   Georges de Staal, Russian diplomat, ambassador to the United Kingdom 1884–1902.

13   Henry Chaplin, landowner, racehorse owner, Conservative MP.

Have you received some of the books I've sent you? When you finish yr writing you must go through another course of reading. [...]

Goodbye my darling boy – don't be despondent, all is for the best. [...] Take care of yrself & keep well.

Yr loving Mother
JSC

LIKE ALL new authors, Winston was learning the difference between writing a short newspaper article and a full-length book. As he put it in this letter: 'Everything is worked out by hard labour and frequent polishing.'

– WSC to JSC –

2 December [1897]   Hyderabad

My dearest Mamma,

1. Both your letters of the 4th & 11th of the month [November] have reached me by the mail. I cannot tell you with what feelings of hope and satisfaction I receive your information that I have been mentioned in despatches by Sir Bindon Blood. If that is the case – and I daresay it may be – I shall feel compensated for any thing. I am more ambitious for a reputation for personal courage than anything else in the world. A young man should worship a young man's ideals. The despatches should be published soon and I shall know for certain. Meanwhile I live in hope. As to deserving such an honour – I feel that I took every chance and displayed myself with ostentation wherever there was danger – but I had no military command and could not expect to receive credit for what should after all be merely the behaviour of a philosopher – who is also a gentleman.

2. The novel is at present illegible and shelved. I will have it typewritten as soon as possible and send it to you – in part – for your opinion. But you must remember it is in the rough and must be expanded.

3. The article on [the Scaffolding of] Rhetoric must wait. I am dissatisfied with it and do not think as much of it as I did. Truth is there but not enough truth to make an article. It requires more working up. I must read Gladstone's speeches among others.

4. Your telegram is today received – forwarded from Bangalore. I knew you would remember my birthday – though these things lose significance when they pass beyond the cake and candle stage. Honestly I forgot it – till your wire arrived. [...]

5. The book on Malakand – absorbs my thoughts and occupies me for six hours every day. I believe – though others must decide – I am producing a fine piece of English and a considerable accumulation of valuable facts. It will reach you four mails from now and must be at once published. [...]

6. Finance. I cannot enter into this question until the Malakand account is worked off. I have shelved everything. In the meanwhile all debts are paid and only a few bills remain – nearly £500 however. I am living within my income at present. [...]

I cannot write any more Mamma – as I am weary of the pen – and quite a hole is worn in my second finger by it. I do not compose an account quickly. Everything is worked out by hard labour and frequent polishing. I confess delight at the cuttings you send me. As to boasting – I only unburden to my friends. They understand & forgive my vanity.

Ever your loving son
Winston

BEFORE WINSTON next wrote, the official news broke of his mention in a dispatch from Brigadier General Patrick Jefferys to his commanding officer, Sir Bindon Blood. It was dated 27 October 1897.

— WSC TO JSC —

9 December [1897]   Bangalore

Dearest Mamma,

I see by the publication of the Despatches that what I had hardly dared to hope had actually come off. I do not suppose any honour or dignity which it may be my fortune in life to deserve or receive will give me equal pleasure.

I am working night and day at this book. It is now almost complete – though fresh information and more interesting detail reaches me by each post. I have broken up the *D.T.* letters completely – you will only recognize parts of them. Most is entirely rewritten. I am ambitious – though of course the haste with which the book has been constructed militates against it – of something better than the Railway bookstalls. However I daresay I take inflated views of everything.

In the meantime I can write no more – and your letter must go begging – till this piece of work is over. I write at least 8 hours a day – and astonish myself by my industry and application. Two mails – or at the outside 3 should bring you the MS. I am still enamoured with living. It is a good & pleasant thing to do.

[...] I see officers are wanted for Egypt. Now is the time for you to make fresh application to the Sirdar. Strike while the iron is hot & the ink wet.

Your ever loving & devoted son
Winston

— WSC TO JSC —

15 December [1897]   Bangalore

My dearest Mamma,

Again only a line. The book is all but finished. [...] You shall have the first MS in a fortnight. This please take to the publishers and find out what they will give and let them generally look into the matter. A fortnight later – i.e. a month from now the finished MS will arrive &

must be printed word for word. I am weary of the pen. I will send full directions with the MS.

Altogether my dash across the frontier has been a good business. *De l'audace toujours de l'audace* – as Danton said.[14]

> *Dearest Mamma, Your ever loving son*
> *Winston*

– WSC to JSC –

22 December [1897]   Bangalore

My dearest Mamma,

A fortnight from today I shall, if the fates are propitious, send you *The Story of the Malakand Field Force, An Episode of Frontier War*, by Winston S. Churchill. I hope you will like it. I am pleased with it chiefly because I have discovered a great power of application which I did not think I possessed. [...] I will write you a covering letter with the MS explaining my views on the subject of its publication. But it should be worth a good deal of money. This we cannot afford to throw away.

I am very gratified to hear that my follies have not been altogether unnoticed. To ride a grey pony along a skirmish line is not a common experience.[15] But I had to play for high stakes and have been lucky to win. I did this three times, on the 18th, 23rd and 30th, but no one officially above me noticed it until the third time when poor Jeffreys – a nice man but a bad general – happened to see the white pony. Hence my good fortune.

Bullets – to a philosopher my dear Mamma – are not worth considering. Besides I am so conceited I do not believe the Gods would create so potent a being as myself for so prosaic an ending. [...]

---

14 Georges Danton, a leader of the French Revolution, said at the legislative assembly in Paris on 2 September 1792: *'De l'audace, encore de l'audace, toujours de l'audace, et la Patrie sera sauvée.'* ['Boldness, more boldness, always boldness and the Fatherland will be saved.']

15 WSC had observed the Spanish general Valdez riding the line on a grey horse when he travelled to Cuba in 1895.

'Fame' sneered at, melodramatized, degraded, is still the finest thing on earth. Nelson's Life should be a lesson to the youth of England. I shall devote my life to the preservation of this great Empire and to trying to maintain the progress of the English people. Nor shall anyone be able to say that vulgar consideration of personal safety ever influenced me. I know myself pretty well and am not blind to the tawdry and dismal side of my character but if there is one situation in which I do not feel ashamed of myself it is in the field. There I shall return at the first opportunity. [...]

You will see more of my views and philosophy when you read the novel. How glad I shall be to get back to it. Why should I vapourise like this. My pen wanders recklessly over the paper when I am writing to you for I feel you will read with a kindly eye. [...]

Now keep your eye on Egypt. It is much safer than the Frontier. At action of 16th we lost 150 out of 1000. We call it an <u>action</u>. At Firket [in northern Sudan] they lost 45 out of 10,000. They call it a battle. [...] Therefore try and get me there if only to be out of harm's way.

Dearest Mamma I end ere I weary you. You shall have some nice literary letters when the book is finished. For the present – Adieu.

Your ever loving son
Winston

— JSC to WSC —

13 January 1898   Chatsworth

Dearest Winston,

You see I am still here. The fact is the Duchess begged me to stay & [...] I had nothing to take me to London. However I go tomorrow & shall remain in London until I go to Cassels'[16] on the 20th & the week after Jack & I go to Sandringham. The Prince means to be very kind to both of you. By the way before I forget it – you ought to address him "Sir" & then go on "I hope Your Royal Highness will" etc, etc, ending

---

16 Ernest Cassel, JSC's friend and financial adviser to the Prince of Wales, had built a chalet in the Swiss Alps.

"Your faithful and devoted servant". It does not really matter how you began this time. But [it] is as well to know – in the course of the letter you bring in a few "Sirs" such as "You cannot imagine Sir what" etc. I am sure he will be very glad to get a letter from you. [...]

It is always a good thing to do what is right. Now as regards yr book, – I enclose letter from the man (A. Balfour's) who is negotiating the business. I hear he generally gets the best terms. You will be glad to get it off yr mind & be able to turn to something lighter – yr novel perhaps.

I wrote to the Sirdar – but I do not expect any result. I'm told you must have 4 years service to be taken. The advance on Khartoum[17] will not be until the Spring – May – & if they fight now it will be at once, before you could get there. [...]

I am finishing this in London – just arrived from Chatsworth. I am sending you a few cuttings about the parties – as you may not have seen them. I am off to see Lumley about business. He takes such a time to do anything. In time you will receive all the documents. If the arrangement I contemplate comes off I think it will be possible to find a few hundreds to settle those bills of yours. I will explain all to you later when the papers are ready. Goodbye darling for the moment. I hope you will make a lot of money out of yr book. Bless you.

Yr loving Mother
JSC

————

WHEN JENNIE arrived at Theodore Lumley's office, she discovered that her solicitor had already sent the papers for her financial reorganization to Winston in India, for him to sign. Neither of them had explained the background properly to him, although he was effectively being asked to sign away a portion of his inheritance.

The security for the large consolidated loan (from an insurance

17 Capital of the Sudan, formerly controlled by Egypt (in turn controlled by Britain), but stronghold of the rebel Mahdists since their successful siege of the city 1884–5.

company) that Lumley was arranging to replace Jennie's many smaller, expensive loans was to come from the capital of Lord Randolph's will trust (which Jennie called 'the property'). Unless she could repay the loan in her lifetime (which no one considered likely) or its investments grew in value by more than the amount of the loan, the result would be a cut in her sons' inheritance. Furthermore, because Jack was under the age of eighteen and could not therefore sign as a party to the scheme, its whole burden would fall on Winston's shoulders.

Jennie sent her son a hurried note to try to explain.

— JSC TO WSC —

14 January 1898   35a Gt Cumberland Place

Dearest Winston,

I have just returned from Lumley's & find that they have sent out the papers by this mail – their letter will explain the business part but I add a hasty note to explain in rough the situation. This £14,000 is in order to buy up all the loans I have made in different Insurance offices – with a margin enough to pay the interest for a couple of years & I think give you the few hundreds you require.

Of course in helping me to do this you understand that you reduce yr portion after my death – that is <u>if</u> the property is valued at not more than it is at present. I understand that a great deal more can be made out of that house in St J's [James's] Square[18] when it comes to me.

Anyhow it is Hobson's Choice. I can't give you an allowance or have anything to live on unless this is done. So sign the papers & send them back by return. I will explain in next, post off.

Yr loving Mother

JSC

---

18 No. 12 St James's Square, owned by the late 7th duke of Marlborough's will trust. His widow was entitled to its rental income during her lifetime. At her death, it would fall into Lord Randolph's will trust, of which JSC was the beneficiary. The property was leased to a club.

O N T H E last day of 1897 Winston triumphantly dispatched the manuscript of his first book to his mother from India.

— WSC TO JSC —

31 December [1897]   Bangalore

My dearest Mamma,

Herewith the book. It has by a great effort been finished a week earlier than I had expected. Maps & a photograph of Sir Bindon Blood for frontispiece, I hope by next mail, but do not delay publication on their account.

I have hurried vy much & it is possible there are still a few slips and errors of writing in the MS. I cannot have the proofs sent out here as that would take too much time. I want you therefore to ask Moreton Frewen if he will undertake the work of revising and correcting them for me. [...]

Now dearest Mamma I don't want anything modified or toned down in any way. I will stand or fall by what I have written. I only want bad sentences polished & any repetitions of phrase or fact weeded out. I have regarded time as the most important element. Do not I beg you – lose one single day – in taking the MS to some publisher. Fincastle's book may for all I know be ready now.

As to price, I have no idea what the book is worth but don't throw it away. A little money is always worth having. I should recommend Moreton's treating with the publishers, it is so much easier for a man. [...] I don't think I ought to get less than £300 for the first edition with some royalty on each copy – but if the book hits the mark I might get much more.

No more my dear Mamma. Believe me I am weary of the pen. [...]

Ever your loving son
Winston

ONCE HE had finished the book, Winston's thoughts turned to finding some military action in Egypt; his other option, less exciting but closer to hand, was to seek an attachment to the field force that had been operating in the Tirah region since October 1897.

— WSC to JSC —

5 January 1898   Bangalore

My dearest Mamma,

Both your letters of the 10th & 16th ult [December] arrived this morning. I send by this mail some Errata which have occurred to me. Not I fear the only ones the MS contains. As soon as it is printed send the proofs to me – but do not delay publication on that account. [...]

I agree with you about private theatricals. They are always stupid & undignified. I recall my own infatuation for them in my youth – with a blush – or at least a smile. I recd today from the *D.T.* a cheque for Rs 1,238 – about £80 at the current rate of exchange. I think they are most mean – and that the reward is altogether inadequate to the value or interest of the letters. The *Pall Mall*[19] would probably have paid 3 times as much. However I am in some measure soothed by their having been put on the front page. [...]

What I particularly want to write to you about – will have been explained by my telegram. You must make a tremendous effort to get me to Egypt. Get Bimbash Stewart to write and tell Kitchener – what you cannot vy well – that I have been mentioned in desp[atches] here & have seen much fighting on the frontier & also in Cuba. This may serve in lieu of age.

I shall run Tirah as a second string but the other is a better business – as Egypt is a more fashionable theatre of war. This is most important. It would mean another medal – perhaps two – and I have applied to wear my Cuban decoration so that with a little luck I might return quite ornamented.

---

19 A monthly illustrated literary magazine, founded in 1893.

Now do stir up all your influence. [...] Don't be afraid of trying every line of attack. So far I have done it all myself. You have so much more power. Write to me about the book.

Ever your loving son
Winston

— JSC to WSC —

20 January 1898   Gt. Dalby, Melton[20]

Dearest Winston,

[...] I received yr book & rushed off to Watt's with it. It appears Methuen[21] wl^d not undertake it as they already have one in hand by an officer on Sir B.B.'s staff — wl^d that be Fincastle? I don't think you need mind — as I hope yours will be out first. Longman [Longmans, Green & Co., publisher] has got it & I shall probably know tomorrow if they accept & on what terms.

Friday 21st.

I've received this morning Mr Watt's letter which I copy for you — I am awfully sleepy still as we danced till 3. Everything very well done. I have to finish before breakfast in order to get it off by today's mail.

Dear Madam,

As the result of my negotiations with Mr Longman I have the pleasure to inform you that he is willing to publish Mr Churchill's book The Story of the Malakand Field Force *on the following terms, which I have no hesitation in advising you are such as you may with entire confidence accept. They are —*

That Mr Longman will probably publish the book at 6/- at his own risk & expense, & will pay a royalty of 5% on his first three thousand copies of the English edition sold. [...]

---

20 Village in the hunting county of Leicestershire.
21 Methuen & Co., founded by Algernon Methuen 1889; it did publish Fincastle's account, *A Frontier Campaign*.

*On the day of publication he will pay in advance the sum of £50
on account of these royalties.* [...]

Well! I am going to show this to Mr Cassel & to Mr Lawson who is
here before wiring – but I have no doubt it is the best that can be done.
For Mr Balfour told me Watt was very good at making a bargain & it
is a great thing that yr first book shl^d be published by such a good firm
as Longman, also that it shl^d be done at their cost.

Now, shortly about Egypt. I wrote to the Sirdar 10 days ago. Lady
Jeune has written to Sir Evelyn [Wood][22] & Brab has been to the War
Office & they promised to "note" your name. There is to be no advance
until July or August so there is plenty of time. [...]

I can't write any more now, bless you my darling don't fuss – we'll
get you up there if it is possible. I may go to Cairo myself for a little,
if I do I can perhaps work the Sirdar at nearer quarters with more
chance of success. I will supplement business matters about loan in
my next.

Yr loving Mother
JSC

— WSC to JSC —

10 January 1898   Bangalore

My dearest Mamma,

I start for Calcutta tomorrow night, with the intention of asking
the A.G. [Adjutant-General] to give me an appointment with the Tirah
Field Force. My success is doubtful but I have some claims [...]

I beg you to redouble your exertions about Egypt – which would be
a much better business than Tirah, but it is as well to have two strings
to one's bow.

---

22 Adjutant-General of the forces, War Office; held the Victoria Cross (see People,
   p. 576).

I received a letter from the *D.T.* enclosing draft & stating that it was 'in accordance with the agreement made' with you v.i.z. £5 per column. I replied briefly acknowledging & remarked – "When I consider the trouble & labour of writing these letters, under varied circumstances, I cannot say I think the price is adequate. I am glad however that you liked them & was pleased to see they were latterly accorded a prominent place in your newspaper." All of wh ought to make them feel ashamed of themselves. Stingy pinchers. But you ought to have stuck out for a tenner, or sold them elsewhere. It is no good being too high and haughty over business matters. All men meet on equal terms and the labourer is worthy of his hire.

I shall try and write again to you in the train on my way to Calcutta. Fancy seven days in the train there and back & only three days there. Still I hope to come back via the Khyber Pass. You will at least commend my energy!

Oh how I wish I could work you up over Egypt! I know you could do it with all your influence – and all the people you know. It is a pushing age and we must shove with the best. After Tirah & Egypt – then I think I shall turn from war to peace & politics. If – that is – I get through all right.

I think myself I shall, but of course one only has to look at Nature and see how very little store she sets by life. Its sanctity is entirely a human idea. You may think of a beautiful butterfly – 12 million feathers on his wings, 16,000 lenses in his eye – a mouthful for a bird. Let us laugh at Fate. It might please her. [...]

Ever your loving son
Winston S. Churchill

– JSC to WSC –

27 January 1898 Sandringham

Dearest Winston,

If I am going to write you a short letter today it is because I have been busy on yr behalf. I have written to Buckle, Frank Harris – &

Norman[23] – asking them to review yr book favourably when it appears, which will be in a fortnight or so, so expeditious have Longman been.

I'm afraid after reading yr letter you will think the terms too moderate. [...] Arthur Balfour only got £200 down for his book I believe – & owing to the royalties he has made up to now £3,000. If your book sells you will make a good deal. A.B. [Arthur Balfour] told me I cl^d absolutely rely on Watt to get you the best terms. If the book is a success – & I am sure it will be – you can command yr own price next time. You must not be too greedy at first. [...]

I received the first batch of proofs this morning, about 3 chapters – & spent an hour reading them. [...] I think it is capital – most interesting & well written. It does you great credit & ought to be a gt success – but of course one cannot tell. I will "boom it" judiciously. [...] The Prince showed me yr letter. He was very pleased with it. It was quite rightly worded as regards formula – with the exception of the beginning – you might have added "sir" as I told you – but it really did not matter. [...]

I think you need not worry about Egypt. It is all quiet for the present – & there will be no fighting until July. India is much more likely to be the seat of war. I wonder that you want to miss yr chances there.

Goodbye for the present – I will wire when the book is out – & send you all cuttings. Bless you.

Yr loving Mother
JSC

– WSC TO JSC –

19 January 1898   Raichur

My dearest Mamma,

I am on my way back from Calcutta where I have had a pleasant, I hope, a useful visit. The trains do not connect well and I have to

---

23 George Buckle, editor *The Times*; Frank Harris, editor *The Fortnightly Review*; Henry Norman, editor *The London Chronicle*.

wait here six hours, which may be conveniently employed in writing my mail letters. At Calcutta I stayed at Government House with the Elgins. [...] My stay there was very short – but I met a lot of useful people, particularly military people. I dined one night with the C-in-C [Sir George White] and generally discoursed with generals. All were unanimous in advising me to employ every effort to get to Egypt. [...]

If Egypt fails or in any case when it is over – I think it will be time to turn to other things.

I am anxious not to completely sever my connection with the army – at any rate for the first few years and it might be advisable to exchange into some regiment in the Home establishment where I could await a [parliamentary] constituency. However that we can think of later. [...]

Now as to the book.

You must see that all efforts are made to launch it well. Reviews & editorial notes must be arranged & carefully looked to.

Write to me at great length about the book and be nice about it. Don't say what you think, but what you think I should like you to think.

Now goodbye my dearest Mamma, I don't expect you to write me as long letters as I write you till you are in as dull a country as I am. But write nevertheless. [...]

Ever your loving son
Winston S. Churchill

— WSC to JSC —

26 January 1898   Bangalore

My dearest Mamma,

[...] I read your wire about Egypt and the book. I am delighted to hear that the latter has arrived safely. All financial arrangements in connection with it – I shall leave entirely in your hands. But please have no false scruples or modesty about bargaining. [...]

The publication of the book will be certainly the most noteworthy act of my life. Up to date (of course). By its reception – I shall measure the chances of my possible success in the world. [...]

In Politics a man, I take it, gets on not so much by what he <u>does</u>, as by what he <u>is</u>. It is not so much a question of brains as of character & originality. It is for these reasons that I would not allow others to suggest ideas and that I am somewhat impatient of advice as to my beginning in politics. Introduction – connections – powerful friends – a name – good advice well followed – all these things count – but they lead only to a certain point. As it were they may ensure admission to the scales. Ultimately – every man has to be weighed – and if found wanting nothing can procure him the public confidence.

Nor would I desire it under such circumstances. If I am not good enough – others are welcome to take my place. I should never care to bolster up a sham reputation and hold my position by disguising my personality. Of course – as you have known for some time – I believe in myself. If I did not I might perhaps take other views. [...]

I shall send by next mail an Election address wh I have written. Captain Middleton[24] advised me to leave one in his hands – in case of Paddington falling vacant – or a General Election unexpectedly occurring. Having read it – please send it to the offices. Unless, that is, you violently disapprove. I am afraid it is very 'blood and thunder' – but that is the usual style for such literature.

I am still reading – though I should prefer to write. The novel lies still unfinished and I am longing to take up the threads. But the balance between Imports & Exports must be maintained. [...]

As to Egypt: I hope you are right – that the advance will not be made until next high Nile.[25] I [should] have thought that if Egypt were paying they would use the British troops at once – to save expense. Of course if they do not go till July – I can get up as a correspondent. But it is a poor way of doing it. All the risks – & none of the glory – or at least you have to take double chances to attract attention. [...]

I want:-

---

24 Richard Middleton, principal agent in the Conservative Party's central office.
25 The River Nile reached its lowest level each June, before rising sharply in July and August to reach its peak in September or October.

1. Proofs of book – but don't wait for corrections – Print at once.
2. 25 Copies.
3. Long letters from you.
4. To go to Egypt.

Goodbye my dearest Mamma, Ever your loving son
Winston S. Churchill

11

BOTH STONE BROKE

1898

'Relax not a volt of your energy'

WINSTON HAD been so absorbed by the effort of finishing *The Story of the Malakand Field Force* and by debating his future plans that he had not thought properly about the implications for him of any financial rescue scheme for his mother.

The documents that required his signature reached him in Bangalore at the end of January 1898 and it took time for their impact to sink in. The letter from his mother's solicitor, Theodore Lumley, mentioned a fresh loan of £17,000, whereas Jennie wrote of £14,000. Whichever the amount at stake, Winston worried that its impact on his future income – and, therefore, in the Victorian world, on his marriage prospects – could be doubled because Jack was too young legally to sign the papers and thus share the burden.

Until this point Winston had not appreciated how far beyond her means his mother had been living in the three years since his father's death. His initial reaction to her scheme was one of resignation, tinged by an undercurrent of mild admonition; after all, he and his mother had always shared a sense of entitlement to the best.

— WSC to JSC —

28 January 1898   Bangalore

Dearest Mamma,

I have written to you already this week – but the papers relating to the Insurance arrived today and tho – I do not think that they can be ready to catch the mail tomorrow – you will I expect be looking for an acknowledgement.

£17,000 is a great deal of money – about a quarter indeed of all we shall ever have in the world – under American settlement[1] – Duke's will[2] & Papa's property.[3] I suppose that when you have got this big loan all right – you will be able to pay off all the minor ones and that the £17,000 will mark the limit of our liabilities. If it does not then our position seems very serious indeed.

I do not quite understand how my signing the documents will affect my prospects. What I want to know – and that Lumley – if not a verbose fool – might easily have explained is – How much difference it will make. [...]

Lumley's letter is a mass of legal technicalities & stupidity – and it is possible that I am quite in error in my suppositions. But this I think you ought to engage to do – v.i.z. That if by signing these documents I lay any burden on my future income – you shall use your influence with Jack – that when he comes of age – it shall be equally shared between us. My tastes are more expensive and Jack will probably be the richer man – from other causes.

---

1   His mother's marriage settlement from the Jerome family, amounting to $250,000 [£50,000].

2   A reference to the 7th duke's will trust, due to fall into Lord Randolph's will trust when the dowager duchess died.

3   His father's marriage settlement from the Churchill family.

Speaking quite frankly on the subject – there is no doubt that we are both you & I equally thoughtless – spendthrift & extravagant. We both know what is good – and we both like to have it. Arrangements for paying are left to the future. My extravagances are on a smaller scale than yours. I take no credit to myself in this matter as you have kept up the house & have had to maintain a position in London. At the same time we shall vy soon come to the end of our tether – unless a considerable change comes over our fortunes and dispositions.

As long as I am dead sure & certain of an ultimate £1,000 a year – I do not much care – as I could always make money on the press [by writing] – and might marry. But at the same time there would be a limit. [...]

I hope you will not mind my writing in a candid manner. I sympathise with all your extravagances – even more than you do with mine – it seems just as suicidal to me when you spend £200 on a ball dress as it does to you when I purchase a new polo pony for £100. And yet I feel that you ought to have the dress & I the polo pony. The pinch of the whole matter is we are damned poor.

Forgive me dearest Mamma – for appearing to preach. I realise acutely my own follies & unbusinesslike habits. But I may at least urge in extenuation – that they are on a much smaller scale, that I am confident in my own powers to supplement my income, & that some excuse for improvidence is furnished by the hopes of an approaching campaign. [...]

Dearest Mamma – I send you my best love & do hope it will work out all right.

Ever your loving son
Winston S. Churchill

O VER THE next forty-eight hours, the impact of Lumley's proposals struck Winston more forcibly so far as his own position was concerned. He calculated that almost a half of his private income after his mother's death could be at risk. He decided to write to his mother again, this time in a stiffer and more formal tone.

– WSC to JSC –

30 January 1898   Bangalore

My dear Mamma,

I devote this letter entirely to business. I have received your short note of the 14ᵗʰ instant – and also several papers from Lumley. [...]

I have read all the papers very carefully and I understand that by signing, as you ask me to, I deprive myself for ever of an income equal to the sum of the Interest and Premium necessary to borrow £14,000 or perhaps £17,000 upon an Insurance policy. Neither you – nor Lumley, in whom it is inexcusable – have informed me what this amount will be.

[...] I learn that by signing I ultimately forego £700 per annum. As I understand that if Jack lives I shall only have £1,800 a year – you will recognise that this is a very serious matter for me. Nor do I think it ought to have been put before me in so sketchy and offhand a manner – as if it were a thing of no importance. I have written to Lumley on the subject.

I have thought the whole matter over and have considered all the different influences. I realise that my refusal would or might lead to your inability to continue my allowance. This of course I could meet by borrowing on my reversions[4] – probably with an economy. I do not intend to profit by this loan you are raising – or to confuse the matter by allowing you to think that I consent to deprive myself of half my property – for the sake of such a 'mess of pottage'[5] as a few hundreds of pounds to pay my bills.

I sign these papers – purely & solely out of affection for you. I write plainly that no other consideration would have induced me to sign them. As it is I sign them upon two conditions – which justice & prudence alike demand.

---

4 His inheritance expectations.
5 In Genesis 25, Esau sold his birthright to his younger brother Jacob for a 'mess of pottage' (a bowl of lentils); idiomatically the expression denotes the acceptance of an immediately attractive, yet ultimately trivial, reward in exchange for a more lasting benefit.

<u>First</u>. That you settle definitely upon me during your life the allowance of £500 per annum I now enjoy at your pleasure.

<u>Second</u>. That you obtain a written promise from Jack that on coming of age he will at once identify himself with this transaction, insure his life and divide with me the burden. And that you will engage to use all your influence and power – even to threatening to stop his allowances – to induce him to carry out this promise. [...]

I need not say how painful it is to me to have to write in so formal a strain – or to take such precautions. But I am bound to protect myself in the future – as I do not wish to be left – should I survive you – in poverty. In three years from my father's death you have spent a quarter of our entire fortune in the world. I have also been extravagant: but my extravagances are a very small matter besides yours. [...]

I hope you will write me a special answer to this letter – saying what you think about what I have said & requested. I write in full love and amity and you will do very wrong to be angry at the unpleasant things it is necessary to express. [...]

The mail does not go till Thursday [3 February] – and I will write to you another letter and tell you some of the news. [...]

Ever your loving son
Winston S. Churchill

WINSTON SENT a second letter by the same mail, reverting to the customary topics of his letters to his mother – the publication of his book and a transfer to the Egyptian army.

— WSC TO JSC —

2 February 1898   Bangalore

My dearest Mamma,

I have just got in here from camp – for a few hours to have the papers signed – so that they may be sent off by this mail. I hope they will be all right and will relieve your worries. Perhaps the future will bring us better fortunes – though I do not feel like marrying yet.

There is a great deal of work to do here – and as I am a better sketcher than most of the subalterns all the reconnaissance sketching falls on me. I have ridden nearly forty miles this day map making. A short letter therefore. First of all – the book: I am vy glad to hear Longmans are publishing – they are a good firm. [...]

As to Egypt: I beg you to continue to try from every side. My plans have crystallized since I knew the advance was not till the autumn. I shall take my 3 months leave June 15 to Sept 15 and go to Egypt as a Correspondent if they will allow – failing all other capacities – but I hope you will be able to get me attached – at any rate temporarily. [...]

With very best love, Your loving son
Winston

– WSC to JSC –

9 February 1898   Bangalore

My dearest Mamma,

[...] The terms which Longman offers for the book and wh I suppose you have accepted are very fair – and should I daresay mean about £300 eventually to me. I want vy much to hear from you whether Moreton Frewen will do the revising and proof correcting. As you will have realised from my letters I attach the vy greatest importance to this. [...]

I wrote a long letter to the old Duchess, also one to Brab[azon] by this mail. But have myself recd letters from nobody but you. I am still reading a good deal and the novel remains half finished. But there is no hurry about it. [...]

I cannot resist copying you out a quotation from Schopenhauer[6] which has seemed so true & applicable –

"We look upon the present as something to be put up with while it lasts and serving only as a way towards our goal. Hence

---

6   Arthur Schopenhauer, German philosopher, died 1860: WSC took this quote from his essay 'The Vanity of Existence'.

most people when they come to the end of life will find that all along they have been living *ad interim.*" [...]

Read – if you have not read it – *The Invisible Man* [by] H. G. Wells[7] – a most amusing tale.

Ever your loving son
Winston

———

BEFORE THIS letter reached Jennie, she had set off for Egypt, ostensibly to promote the cause of her son's transfer to the Egyptian army directly with its commander-in-chief, or *sirdar*, General Kitchener. Winston, meanwhile, was still trying to engineer a place on the staff of the Tirah Expeditionary Force, which remained in place, although it had regained control of the Khyber Pass by the middle of December 1897.

— WSC TO JSC —

16 February [1898]   Bangalore

My dearest Mamma,

I got your letter from Sandringham this morning and was delighted with all it contained. The mail also brought me a long & charming letter from the Prince – which I am Tory enough to regard as a great honour and which I have duly acknowledged. [...]

Your telegram reached me on Saturday – and I can assure you I feel vy grateful indeed to you for going to Egypt. It is an action which – if ever I have a biographer – will certainly be admired by others. I hope you may be successful. I feel almost certain you will. Your wit & tact & beauty – should overcome all obstacles.

[...] We are vy close together now you are in Egypt and I feel

———

7 An early work of science fiction published by the prolific English author in 1897.

almost inclined to suggest your wandering a little further afield. But the plague is now at its height in Bombay. [...]

Tomorrow I am off to Meerut to play in the gt polo Tournament and thence I hurry on to Peshawar[8] to try and induce them to take me on the Staff or the Transport of the Tirah force.

[...] Dearest Mamma – I hope you don't think me a beast over money matters. But I hated signing those papers more than you can imagine – & more than I should have thought. You left me very much in the dark about the whole affair, and after all it was a big business. After all I shall have to descend from my high horse – as I am still oppressed by bills & debts. I am selling all my ponies after the Tournament and when I go to Egypt the ties which bind me here will be very slender. [...]

With very best love, Your ever loving son
Winston

———·———

THERE WAS another, less official, reason for Jennie's journey to Cairo. She had for some time been conducting an intimate correspondence with a young officer of the Seaforth Highlanders, Major Caryl Ramsden, known as 'Beauty Ramsden'. She set off to visit him when his regiment transferred from service in Malta to Cairo.

There they stayed together in the Continental Hotel while Jennie corresponded with General Kitchener about Winston's transfer to the Egyptian army (on which subject the *sirdar* remained non-committal). The couple then shared a cruise up the Nile on a riverboat until Ramsden's regiment ordered his return to Cairo in preparation for a move to Wadi Halfa.

Jennie returned to Port Said to catch her ship home, but a delay in its departure gave her the chance to return to the Continental Hotel for a final goodbye with Ramsden. On reaching his room she found him in bed with Louise, the wife of Kitchener's military secretary, John Maxwell.

---

8   The distance between Meerut and Peshawar was approximately 500 miles.

News of the incident leaked to London, where the Prince of Wales took a dim view and started to turn elsewhere. Winston remained unaware of the complication.

— WSC TO JSC —

25 February [1898]   c/o Sir B. Blood KCB, Meerut

My dearest Mamma,

Owing to my journey up here, I have not yet received this week's mail. I do hope the book has been published by now and has had a favourable reception. [...]

I am enjoying my stay here – though as the house is small, I live in a tent which is chilly work. The general is of course charming and his wife is a vy pretty & amusing woman – many years younger than he is.[9] [...]

Meanwhile I hope you are making all things smooth in Egypt. As I have been attached to a Field Force I am entitled to three months leave on full pay and shall proceed to Egypt – subject to the approval of Providence – the last week in June. You should make certain of my being employed then. [...]

I have had a long and vy interesting letter from General Hamilton[10] – who has just assumed the command of the 3rd Brigade Tirah Expdy Force and who is a great friend of mine. [...] If he can find a higher post for his present orderly officer – (a major & too senior for such employ) he will wire for me. Indeed I have considerable hopes of getting in the field again – and in that expectation have brought with me tents, saddlery, uniform, etc. *Nous verrons.*

In the meantime the novel is forging slowly along, and I like it better every day. It is destitute of two elements which are rather popular

---

9   Sir Bindon's wife Charlotte, née Colvin, was probably born in 1863, so was at least 20 years younger than her husband.
10 Ian Hamilton, whom WSC befriended on a sea voyage to India; they remained lifelong friends (see People, p. 576).

in modern fiction – <u>squalor & animal emotions</u> – but for all that I have hopes that it may be attended with some success.

With best love, I remain, Ever your loving son
Winston S. Churchill

— WSC TO JSC —

7 March [1898]   Camp Ali Masjid,[11] Khyber Pass

My dearest Mamma,

But for my telegram the address might astonish you. I came on to Peshawar after the Polo Tournament as I told you I proposed to do. I went to see Sir Wm. Lockhart[12] in the hopes of being allowed to go and see General Hamilton – but without any expectation of employment. To my astonishment – I have been taken on his (Sir Wm's) staff as Orderly Officer. [...]

I have received a most remarkable assistance from Captain Haldane[13] – the general's ADC [aide-de-camp]. I have never met this man before and I am at a loss to know why he should have espoused my cause – with so strange an earnestness. Of this I shall learn more later. [...] My idea is that my reputation – for whatever it may be worth – has interested him. Of course you will destroy this letter and show it to no one. [...]

As to the future – the outlook is I fear pacific. The Tribes will probably submit and if so the General is off home on the 26th inst. Still they will probably find something for me & so I may be up here for some months – until Egypt in fact – on which point concentrate your efforts. [...]

Ever your loving son
Winston S. Churchill

---

11 British army camp situated on flat ground in the narrowest section of the Khyber Pass.
12 General since 1896, in charge of the Tirah expedition; served only in the Indian army (see People, p. 576).
13 Aylmer Haldane, later captured and imprisoned with WSC in the Boer War.

WINSTON STILL had not yet received a reply from his mother to his sharp letter of 30 January, which had imposed two conditions on his acceptance of her rescue scheme. Now it appeared to him that she had stopped the payment of his quarterly allowance into his London bank. His own financial difficulties dictated a retreat from the conditions that he had set down six weeks earlier.

— WSC to JSC —

18 March [1898]   Camp Peshawar

My dearest Mamma,

[...] I am worried by the news that my quarter's allowance has not been paid into Cox's bank. I have of course written cheques on it. These will be dishonoured and Messrs King & Co [WSC's local bankers in India] will be furious. However, what must be, must be. You will I hope negotiate the loan successfully and after all – much may happen in two years.

I still owe King, King & Co nearly £200 and I hope you will be able to spare me £500 for the settling up of the rest of my debts. These filthy money matters are the curse of my life and my only worry. As for Lumley, he is a fool. I enclose you a letter I have received in answer to mine. At last he puts things plainly. But if you had seen his first letter you would not have wondered at my doubt.

I shall next week send you a full account of my remaining liabilities. You will see my dearest Mamma that I have had to abdicate my proud position. Indeed I had counted somewhat on the book – but that will bring me more credit than cash. I am worried about the letter I wrote to you & the conditions I made. I hope you will not take either amiss. I do not think you ought to blame me for having done as I have done. I fear you think me a beast – ungrateful – what not.

But I shudder sometimes when I contemplate the abyss into which we are sinking. Personally I live simply – uncomfortable – squalidly. I eat bad food – I spend nothing on my clothes. There is no dissipation. Yet here are debts piling up and my allowance of £500 a year[14] is inadequate. And what I am doing on a small scale in this beastly country – you are doing in greater degree in England. We shall all finish up stone broke.

I am trying to sell my ponies, but in this country where there is no market – no place like Tattersalls [racehorse auctioneers in Newmarket] – it is a long and difficult job. I almost think I could live more cheaply in England. You see my mood – make allowances & believe that I love you very much. I shall always feel sorry for that letter. Yet I would write it over again. And when I look away from money matters all the rest of the horizon is unclouded. [...]

Meanwhile this last good fortune of mine – though I now fear fighting is all over – cannot be a bad business. I shall possibly get an extra clasp on my medal. It counts in my record of service and as an extra campaign. But the chief value lies elsewhere. I now know all the generals who are likely to have commands in the next few years. [...]

My vanity is also gratified in many small ways. But of these it is unnecessary to write. [...]

Well goodbye my dearest Mamma, With best love, ever your loving son
Winston

LONGMANS HAD published *The Story of the Malakand Field Force* in London on 14 March, four days before Winston wrote this letter. The day before it left in the mail, the proofs of his book caught up with him in Peshawar. He just had time to insert an anguished extra note to his mother.

— WSC to JSC —

22 March [1898]   Peshawar

My dear Mamma,

I add this letter to tell you that the 'revised proofs' reached me

------

14 Paid by his mother; WSC's salary as an army lieutenant was £200 pa.

yesterday and that I spent a very miserable afternoon in reading the gross & fearful blunders which I suppose have got into the finished copies. In the hope of stopping publication I have wired to Longmans, but I fear I am already too late. Still I may catch the Indian edition, in which the absurdities would be most laughed at.

I blame no one – but myself. I might have known that no one could or would take the pains that an author would bestow. The result, however, destroys all the pleasure I had hoped to get from the book and leaves only shame that such an impertinence should be presented to the public – a type of the careless slapdash spirit of the age and an example of what my father would have called my slovenly shiftless habits. [...]

Altogether there are about 200 misprints – blunders & mistakes, though some of these, perhaps 100 will only be apparent to me. [...] All this as I said reveals to the world my mind & nature as shallow – ill educated – slovenly etc. All this destroys my pleasure in the book and makes its very sight odious to me. [...]

God forbid that I should blame you my dearest Mamma. I blame myself – and myself alone for this act of folly & laziness which has made me ridiculous to all whose good opinion I would have hoped for.

I writhed all yesterday afternoon – but today I feel nothing but shame and disappointment. You could not be expected to know many of these things – but as far as Moreton is concerned, I now understand why his life has been a failure in the city and elsewhere.

For my own part unhappy as I feel and in spite of all the ridicule I shall have to face, I still have confidence in myself. My style is good – even in parts classic. [...] And I have learnt a lesson.

With best love, Your loving son
Winston

THE TIRAH Expeditionary Force disbanded in the last week of March. Winston prepared to return to Bangalore, but he still had not heard from his mother for weeks. He feared that he had deeply upset her.

— WSC to JSC —

27 March 1898   Peshawar

My dearest Mama,

[...] Am vy disappointed at not hearing from you this week. I had expected an answer to my letter on money matters – and I feel that your silence probably means that you have taken amiss what I then wrote. I think you will be wrong and unkind to do this. You must remember that you never put the case before me in any clear way – and that I had no other information as to it – than Lumley's involved letter. [...]

And although you may think me a beast and a money grubber yet in such a case I should like to be able to decide independently – and not to be given no choice but compelled by the force of circumstances. I hate these sordid considerations but they cannot be overlooked. I have also to reckon on the possibility of your marrying again – perhaps some man I did not like – or did not get on with – and of troubles springing up – which might lessen your affection for me.

Such things have been in other families – and though I feel you will hate and despise me for my distrust – yet I cannot be other than I am.

At any rate I may claim to have written candidly – and without reservations. I have no secrets from you – and what is in my nature must have its origin in yours.

I did not write without thinking and, much as I hated it at the time, much as I have hated it since, I do not desire to alter it – except as far as refusing to accept any of the money – which I am now unfortunately not in a position to do. [...]

I write you long and thoughtful letters and I look eagerly for replies. After all at present there are only us three in the whole world. A few years may – probably will – bring other interests into my life. It is a fact I believe that the ties that a man makes as he grows older more than compensate for those which drop out or become fainter. Such is life. But for the present I have no one that I care to turn to or to confide in. Do not, I beg you, disdain my letters. [...]

I cannot write you any more – because I have no more to write – and sometimes I feel that perhaps with all the long letters – the products of a nimble pen – I make our correspondence rather burdensome.

I should add to all this – tho – that I realise fully that you were so busy with writing to me about my book – that you did not have time or energy left for the discussion of those filthy money matters. Your letters are always the moment of the week to me – and when they don't arrive – you must ever expect & may perhaps excuse, a mournful answer from,

Your loving son
Winston S. Churchill

———

FOUR DAYS later, Winston received a letter that Jennie had written to him from Aswan while she was in Egypt. It does not survive, but it clearly asked him never to mention money in his letters to her again.

— WSC TO JSC —

31 March [1898]   Camp Peshawar

My dearest Mamma,

I have just received your letter from Assouan [Aswan]. I do not see any use in my trying to alter facts or disguise the truth. You ask me not to allude to the subject of money arrangements – and I agree with you that it is better not to prolong the affair. It has left a dirty taste in my mouth – and yet I would not be other than what I am or do other than I have done. The pain I feel in the matter is that it has brought a disagreeable element into our lives. I fear the effects may be permanent. Still you must remember this – I have made no reservations, adopted no disguise – I have exposed myself to you frankly for what I am – & that you must regard as a very great measure of my affection. I do not try to dress up for you.

It is no exaggeration for me to state that I care more for you at this present time than for any single human being.

You cannot think with what feelings of relief I received your letter. None came last mail and this morning when I went to see Sir William Lockhart at Headquarters where my letters are addressed I did not find yours. It arrived later. [...] I sat down and wrote several letters – furious – reproachful – bitter – what not – all of which I have destroyed with entire satisfaction.

I think there is a certain vein of cynicism about me which prevents my believing that anything is pure gold. I expect annihilation at death. I am a materialist – to the tips of my fingers.

As to the Biographer who may investigate another human wretch's life – I would say as Oliver Cromwell did to Sir Peter Lely – "Paint me as I am" and thereupon was painted wart and all.[15] [...]

Lady Jeune telegraphed to me yesterday "Soudan all right – writing" from which I gather that she has worked things for me. She is a clever woman and tho I believe you do not like her – she is worth knowing. [...]

If I hear by her letter that I am to be selected as a Special Service officer – and to be sent out "on duty" – then there will be no occasion for me to sacrifice my 3 month Privilege leave – and if the regiment can spare me I shall with your concurrence come home as soon as possible and try and have a month in England before the Nile.

My heart leaps towards such a prospect – in a way that you very likely do not realise. [...] But the desire to come home gives me a sore feeling in the front of my head – so that I could scream. When I think of 35A and my room – and the life of a great city – and amusing people – and comfort – and last of all of you – I feel like a school boy on the first Sunday in the Term.

[...] The book – well – I have seen a final copy. It is useless bewailing – but it is awful. Six or seven absolutely unpardonable errors. Twenty or thirty minor ones. And a great number of emendations which have made my blood boil. I will only observe – Never again. [...]

Good bye, my dearest Mamma, ever your loving son
Winston

---

15 Horace Walpole's *Anecdotes of Painting in England* (1762–71) quoted Cromwell as instructing the artist: ' Mr. Lely, I desire you would use all your skill to paint my picture truly like me, and not flatter me at all; but remark all these roughnesses, pimples, warts, and everything as you see me, otherwise I will never pay a farthing for it.'

WINSTON TRAVELLED from Peshawar to Bombay, a distance of more than a thousand miles. From the city that his mother had visited very briefly four years earlier while nursing her sick husband, he wrote to her from the comfort of Government House, on a headland at the westernmost edge of the city, where the sea surrounded it on three sides.

— WSC to JSC —

13 April [1898]   Government House, Bombay

My dearest Mamma,

I have just arrived here having had a long, tedious and terribly hot journey from Peshawar. [...] In spite of the gummy heat for which this place is famous it is the most comfortable and attractive spot I have seen in India. I daresay you have been here yourself, so I shall not attempt a description. My room opens out on to the sea front and it is quite a strange sound to hear the waves and see the water fading to the horizon once more. [...]

The sea also carried my thoughts to the other side – only 10 days to Cairo. [...] The Nile will not rise before it is ready, and I am quite easy in my mind that even July would be time enough. We shall see. If I am too late and all is over – I can only conclude that perhaps Fate intervened because Chance would have been malicious had I gone. Meanwhile relax not a volt of your energy. "The Importunate Widow" and the appropriate scriptural instances occur to me.[16] [...]

Do write to me my dearest Mamma. No letter arrived this week from you. That is only one I have received in three weeks, and you know I never forget, no matter what the circumstances may be. Do write, your letter is the central point of my week. If I thought mine gave you half as much pleasure, I should write all day. As it is I scribble most <u>damnably</u>.

Ever your loving son
Winston S. Churchill

---

16 The parable of the importunate (or persistent) widow appears in Luke 10.

ANOTHER WEEK passed without a letter from his mother, so Winston gave full vent to his feelings of neglect in his next letter to her. Just before the mail departed three days later, an explanation for her silence arrived by telegram. Winston was able to add a second letter, which caught the same mail.

— WSC TO JSC —

19 April [1898]   Bangalore

My dearest Mamma,

I am very unhappy at your silence. In the last five weeks I have received one single letter. It is really too unkind of you to leave me like this unnoticed and uncared for. [...] For my part I have hardly ever missed – and have always written at great length to you. [...] It is simply cruel. It makes me so irritable that I do not feel like writing, at length to you, letters which appear to be ill received and despised. I fear you are bored by my affairs and letters. Still a few things are necessary for me to say.

Egypt. Lady Jeune's letter arrived yesterday. Sir Evelyn will see that I get to the front if I get leave in August. This of course means that I must stay here till then – and broil out a hot weather – and also that I shall not see you or London until after Khartoum. The prospect of staying here till then is odious, but I must put up with it as every day's leave must be reserved for the Soudan. It is not rendered more inviting by the fact that you have apparently decided to leave me to stew in my own juice. I feel too unhappy. Why should you do this? I even sent you a telegram – but that failed to draw an answer. [...]

I am too sick at heart to write more. You have apparently no idea of what your letters mean to me. I cannot help thinking that if my luck should flicker in Egypt this autumn you might regret having disdained my weekly tributes. But this is a very commonplace sentiment – and may draw a smile of satire. [...]

With very best love and many kisses, I remain Ever your loving son
Winston

— WSC TO JSC —

22 April [1898]   Bangalore

Dearest Mamma,

I was so delighted to get your telegram, so that I have time to add this letter to the mail. Please cancel the other – though indeed it is a backhanded compliment. How unwise to have written to Peshawar! My plans are always so uncertain, and only two addresses in India are ever safe.

1.   c/o King, King & Co., Bombay
2.   4th Hussars, India

[…] I fear your letters will be lying [in] some Field Post Office. […]
Your ever loving son
Winston

———

JENNIE'S REPLY of 7 April to her son's complaints about her profligacy has not survived. Judging by Winston's summary of its contents, she was either profoundly mistaken about her income or she had already borrowed so much that the interest payments on these loans had swallowed up almost two-thirds of her income. For now, Winston accepted her version of events, increasingly hopeful that he would be able to earn his own living through his pen.

— WSC TO JSC —

25 April 1898   Bangalore

My dearest Mamma,

Your letter of the 7th [March] received [missing]. I am very sorry that things are so bad. I really don't quite understand how your income can be reduced to £900 – inclusive of my allowance and Jack's. I had always imagined that the £2,000 a year from America were absolutely unassailable. The situation as described by your letter is appalling. As you say it is of course impossible for you to live in London on such a pittance. I hate the idea of your marrying – but that of course would be a solution.[17] [...]

I have nearly finished my novel *Affairs of State*.[18] It is a wild and daring book tilting recklessly here and there and written with no purpose whatever, but to amuse. This I believe it will do. I have faith in my pen. I believe the thoughts I can put on paper will interest & be popular with the public. The reception accorded to my first book, in spite of its gross and damning errors proves to me that my literary talents do not exist in my imagination alone.

This literary sphere of action may enable me in a few years to largely supplement my income. Indeed I look forward to becoming sooner or later independent. We shall see. I have in my eye a long series of volumes which I am convinced I can write well. [...] I may perhaps make a classic. [...]

Now as to the future, I am entitled to 3 months' Privilege Leave on account of field service and shall go to Egypt in July. It is not perhaps wise to look beyond that, but should all work out agreeably I shall make – am already making – strenuous efforts to obtain employment at home. I have no present intention of leaving the army until I am sure of a seat in Parliament. Then I can be seconded, and at any rate draw £100 a year. Perhaps the Intelligence Branch might suit me or I them.

Meanwhile you send me no cuttings. Please do. My vanity is a very great source of pleasure to me.

Ever your loving son
Winston S. Churchill

---

17 JSC wrote to her friend Daisy, countess of Warwick: 'I am not going to marry anyone. If a perfect darling with at least £40,000 a year wants me very much I might consider it'; Frances, Countess of Warwick, *Life's Ebb and Flow*, p. 141.
18 Published as *Savrola*.

— WSC to JSC —

3 May 1898   Bangalore

My dearest Mamma,

I have again had no letter from you this week. I have said all I can on the subject and do not propose to allude to it again. But I shall content myself for the future with answering the letters you send me as it does not seem desirable that I should go on boring you with volumes of information for which apparently you have no interest. [...]

Ever your loving son
Winston S. Churchill

W INSTON'S ULTIMATUM was never put to the test: within the week a letter arrived from his mother, enclosing cuttings of the press reviews of his book.

With his reply Winston enclosed two letters: the first came from Colonel Ian Hamilton; the second from a small firm of publishers, Nisbet & Co. It invited Winston to write a biography either of his ancestor, the first duke of Marlborough, or of his father, Lord Randolph Churchill. (In due course Winston would write both books, although neither for Nisbet & Co.)

— WSC to JSC —

10 May 1898   Government House, Ootacamund[19]

My dearest Mamma,

[...] The second letter speaks for itself. I have replied that I would undertake to write a *Memoir of Marlborough* for the series, subject to your approval and have told them to communicate with you as to terms etc. I have also told them that the time has not yet come when Papa's

---

19 Summer residence of the governor of Madras, commissioned by the duke of Buckingham 1877.

Life can be written and that if ever I attempted it I should make it the labour of years.

I like the *Marlborough* idea. But you had better see Sunny [duke of Marlborough] on the subject and ask if he would have any objection. He might want to undertake it himself – and I will not do anything that will clash with his enterprises. At the same time I think it would produce something that would ring like a trumpet call. [...]

I find myself quite a "celebrity" here. All the South of India meets this week here for the races & Polo Tournament. I am paid many compliments, but I always had a good opinion of myself and plenty of ambition, and the book has done nothing to improve the one or stimulate the other.

With very best love and many kisses, Ever your loving son
Winston

———

ONCE BACK in Bangalore, Winston suggested to his mother that he might squeeze in another short period of leave in Britain before he joined the Egyptian army's advance in the Sudan.

Winston finished his letter with one of those passages of self-analysis that make his correspondence with his mother such a valuable source of insight into his character. In it he acknowledged that Cecil Rhodes had diagnosed his 'mental flaw', that he cared less about principle and more about his reputation and the impression that he created. It was a charge that would dog Winston for much of his political career.

— WSC TO JSC —

16 May 1898   Bangalore

My dearest Mamma,

Your letter (of the 27th April) [missing] was a great pleasure to me. It is not necessary for me to say that I do not mean what I write in the querulous letters you may have received. But when the mail comes in with no letter from you, I get in such a state of despondency & anger that I am not approachable by anyone and fly to my inkpot to let off steam.

I have many things to write to you about this week and therefore my letter may be less discursive than usual. First of all:- I send you The Preface, The Contents Table and the first six chapters of *Affairs of State*. You may show these to whoever you like and endeavour to get some opinion as to their value. [...]

As to the Publishing Agency: it is true that they take 10 per cent wh. is a bore. But I fancy from the large number of authors who avail themselves of them that they make it worth while using them. [...] However: it is entirely as you like and if you can add the 10 per cent to our worldly goods: *tant mieux.*

Now I pass to my plans. Here I am at Bangalore: very hot: lots of work: all my friends away on leave: polo ground deep in dust: indeed – life is very unpleasant. I have 3 months Privilege leave on full pay and allowances whenever I choose to take it. You may imagine how I long to come home and how your letter tempts me. [...]

Now what I should like to do would be this. To leave here on (say) 20th June. Come home, arriving (D.V.) [God willing] about 3rd or 4th July. Stay in England till 20th July and then to Egypt. It means 10 days more travelling [than going straight to Egypt] & would cost £40. But I should like to see England again very much and think it well worth it. [...]

I am trying to sell my ponies. I hope to get rid of them all soon. They eat. Unless you get a good offer, keep the Arab. I might take him to Egypt. A good-looking horse is half the battle from an ADC point of view. [...]

I am vy much impressed by C.J.R. [Cecil Rhodes] having at once detected my mental flaw. It is quite true. I do not care so much for the principles I advocate as for the impression which my words produce & the reputation they give me. This sounds vy terrible. But you must remember we do not live in the days of Great Causes.

Perhaps to put it a little strongly, I should say that I vy often yield to the temptation of adapting my facts to my phrases. But Macaulay is an arch offender in this respect. I think a keen sense of necessity or of burning wrong or injustice would make me sincere but I vy rarely detect genuine emotion in myself. [...]

So I believe that *au fond* I am genuine. But in most matters my head or my wits would direct and my heart would lend a little emotion whichever way was required. It is a Philosophic virtue not a human one.

Ever your loving son
Winston

B Y THE summer of 1898, Winston was a young man in a hurry, who held increasingly forceful and independent political views about the issues of the day that he liked to try out on his mother first. One of these was the policy to be adopted towards Russia's ambition to expand eastwards at the expense of either China or the Ottoman empire.

Lord Salisbury, who had kept the foreign affairs portfolio for much of his time as prime minister, had pursued a pragmatic policy of containing any European power that threatened essential British interests by reaching a limited accord at the time with countries similarly threatened. Joseph Chamberlain, the leader of the Unionist Liberals and therefore Salisbury's partner in government, mocked the policy by referring to it as 'splendid isolation'. In a speech to the Birmingham Liberal Unionists on 12 May, he argued that, to contain Russia, a more fundamental alliance was needed: history taught 'we must not reject the idea of an alliance with those powers whose interests most nearly approximate to our own'.

Winston's instinct that Joseph Chamberlain might eventually split the Conservative Party, just as he had the Liberal party, was to prove correct.[20]

---

20 13 May 1898, J. Chamberlain speech, Birmingham, *The Times*, 14 May, p. 12.

— WSC ᴛᴏ JSC —

22 May 1898   Bangalore

My dearest Mamma,

I have come to a decision. I sail from Bombay 18ᵗʰ June – hope to arrive in England 2ⁿᵈ July and start for Egypt presumably about 20ᵗʰ July. I trust you will approve of this. [...] Of course if I should find on arrival at Suez that an early advance is contemplated up the Nile, I should get out at once and start for the front. [...]

Now on several matters. (1) Sir B. Blood is also coming home by this ship and I want you to ask him to dinner and Lady B. (who is charming) and have some distinguished people – possibly the Prince – to meet him. [...]

(2) I want to have at least two good public meetings during my flying visit. Can you not arrange one at Bradford. [...] If not Bradford try some Metropolitan constituency. [...]

(3) I hope I shall be able to see a good deal of you and that you will try and accept few invitations during my flying visit.

(4) I am sending you by this week's mail 10 more chapters of *Affairs of State*. Next week expect the remaining six. I want these chapters to be in print (proof) by the time I come home so that I can correct them myself. [...]

(7) Egypt. Please redouble your efforts in this direction. My plans for the future will be much influenced by this. I am determined to go to Egypt and if I cannot get employment or at least sufficient leave, I will not remain in the army. There are other and better things ahead. But the additional campaign will be valuable as an educational experience – agreeable from the point of view of an adventure – and profitable as far as finance goes as I shall write a book about it. [...]

A long letter from Ivor [Guest]:[21] he is vy dissatisfied with the

---

21 WSC's cousin had just unsuccessfully contested a by-election in Plymouth.

Chinese policy or rather want of policy of the Government.[22] I have sent him a copy of my verses on the subject. Duplicate to you. I am very glad we have not allowed the busybody diplomatists to plunge us in a war which must mean – even in the event of victory – irreparable loss. [...]

It is the fault of all booms of sentiment that they carry men too far and lead to reactions. Militarism degenerates in brutality. Loyalty promotes tyranny and sycophancy. Humanitarianism becomes maudlin and ridiculous. Patriotism shades into cant. Imperialism sinks to Jingoism.

No one in the world is more proud of the British Empire than I am. I bow to none in my desire to see my country great and famous. For this reason I would avoid quarrels with Russia. Within [hours] of our declaration of war with Russia – France would request us to leave Egypt and the Transvaal would repudiate the convention and suzerainty. [...] I hold that civilized nations should not declare war upon each other until all the vast majority of their people have reached the conclusion that they can't live on friendly terms any more.

Enough of politics. Still if I make any speeches when I am home I shall most warmly defend Lord Salisbury's policy and I am not at all clear that Mr Chamberlain has not been very disloyal. "A political Vampire". He would not like the remark. Yet he has already broken the Radical and Liberal parties. Now perhaps he seeks to batten on Tory blood. But this naturally is between ourselves. I personally have great admiration for Mr C. He is a man.

Ever your loving son
Winston S. Churchill

---

22 Following China's defeat in the Sino-Japanese war of 1894–5, Russia and Germany forced China to concede parts of its territory; in June 1898 Britain signed a 99-year lease on territory of the Chinese mainland that allowed it to defend its island of Hong Kong.

— WSC to JSC —

1 June [1898]   Bangalore

My dearest Mamma,

[…] I start 18th June from Bombay & leaving native servant and campaigning kit in Egypt – tents saddles etc. [I] hope to arrive Victoria Station 2nd July. You cannot think with what joy I pen these words. […]

At any rate I cannot give up my fortnight in London. It is worth its minutes in sovereigns.[23] You will probably find that I shall not enjoy it actually vy much. Schopenhauer says that if you anticipate you only use up some of the pleasure of the moment in advance. And that therefore things which are greatly looked forward to usually disappoint – much of their pleasure having been prospectively enjoyed.[24] […]

I am trying to settle up my Indian affairs, but I am still encumbered with an incubus of horse flesh. I hope to sell much of it soon. I have taken a return ticket from which you may gather that the idea of leaving the army is not yet fixed in my mind. I am quite clear about the next election – but till then I see little opening and experience of war will always be valuable. […]

Ever your loving son
Winston S. Churchill

— WSC to JSC —

8 June [1898]   4th Hussars, India

My dearest Mamma,

This is the last letter I shall write you. I shall bring the next myself. The thought is very pleasant and I need not say how much I look forward to coming home, if only for a fortnight.

---

23 A gold coin with a face value of £1 (equivalent to more than £100 today).
24 In his essay 'On Women' (1851), Arthur Schopenhauer wrote: 'a man never is happy, but spends his whole life in striving after something which he thinks will make him so; he seldom attains his goal, and when he does, it is only to be disappointed.'

The mail brought me both your letters, that of the week before as well as the new one [both missing]. They were delightful to read and occupied me for a pleasant hour. The cuttings are very satisfactory and I was particularly pleased by that of the *Spectator*[25] – a very valuable criticism and strangely civil. The *Broad Arrow*[26] continue to be disagreeable over the Tirah Letters.[27] It is a despicable paper – but I enjoyed reading it vy much. Insensibility to Press criticism is one of the first things to acquire before embarking on a political career. [...]

I hope these meetings were arranged. Bradford particularly. I want a real big meeting at least two thousand men. Compel them to come in. I am sure I can hold them. I have got lots of good material for at least 3 speeches – all carefully written out and docketted.

You might arrange one or two dinners – and get me a few invitations. I want to see people and to get about. [...]

Au revoir, my dearest Mamma, I am looking forward above all things to seeing you. If possible let us dine alone together on the night I arrive – with Jack of course. [...]

Ever your loving son
Winston S. Churchill

---

25 Weekly political magazine, founded in 1828.
26 Naval and military newspaper.
27 Col. Henry Hutchinson had contributed letters to *The Times* on the Tirah campaign; Macmillan published these in book form in September 1898 as *The Campaign in Tirah, 1897–1898; an account of the expedition against the Orakzais and Afridis under General Sir William Lockhart.*

12

LANCES AND PISTOLS ON THE NILE

1898

'It passed like a dream'

WINSTON SPENT three weeks in England, in the middle of July. As requested, his mother arranged a political meeting in Bradford that took place on 14 July 1898. Its result convinced him to leave the army and commit his future to politics, confident now he could command an audience despite the speech impediment (or lisp) which he had mentioned to his mother two years earlier.

Winston sent his mother a written account of proceedings at Bradford on the following day, while still exhilarated by the experience.

— WSC TO JSC —

15 July [1898]   Bradford

My dearest Mamma,

The meeting was a complete success. The hall was not a vy large one – but it was closely packed. I was listened to with the greatest attention for 55 minutes at the end of which time there were loud & general cries of "Go on". Five or six times they applauded for about two minutes without stopping and at the end of the peroration – which the newspapers cut owing to necessities of printing – many people mounted their chairs and there was really a very great deal of enthusiasm. [...]

As to tangible results:- there was a supper afterwards at the Midland hotel[1] at which about 30 of the most important local men were present and in the numerous speeches that went on till midnight – the vy broadest hints were made to me to keep my eye on the Central Division. [...]

Personally – I was intensely pleased with the event. The keenness of the audience stirred my blood – and altho I stuck to my notes rigidly – I certainly succeeded in rousing & in amusing them. They burst out of the hall & pressed all round the carriage to shake hands and cheered till we had driven quite away.

The conclusions I form are these – with practice I shall obtain great power on a public platform. My impediment is no hindrance. My voice sufficiently powerful – and – this is vital – my ideas & modes of thought are pleasing to men.

It may be perhaps the hand of Fate – which by a strange coincidence closed one line of advance and aspiration in the morning – and in the evening pointed out another with an encouraging gesture. At any rate – my decision to resign my commission is definite.

With best love, Your ever loving son
Winston

A FEW DAYS later Winston left for the Nile, still unsure whether his regiment in India had officially sanctioned his temporary posting to the 21st Lancers; or whether his service in Egypt would be classified as time spent on leave or on active service.

---

1 Main hotel in Bradford, owned by the Midland Railway Company, completed 1890.

He briefed his mother on how to respond to any queries she received from the authorities.

— WSC TO JSC —

[late July 1898]   [no address]

Dearest Mamma

Arguments.

1. I have spent re the Egyptian business. Chargers 70. Telegrams 20. Ticket self 20 servant from India 20. Kit 30. Total so far 160.

   if forfeited, a heavy pecuniary price & poor.

2. Failing Egypt you are <u>afraid</u> I shall leave. I shall.

3. If my offence was sufficiently serious to deserve such severe treatment then surely I should have been recalled from leave.

4. My leave is still untouched. I have put down my money and am entitled to have a *veau*[2] for it.

At least let me join 21st [Lancers] & stay until my leave is up – enable me see country & write book.

Best love

Winston

W INSTON SAILED from Marseilles to Alexandria on the small French steamer *Le Sindh*, which had been launched in 1869 and was approaching the end of her life (she was decommissioned three years later).

---

2   Misspelling of the French by WSC, who intended to convey the meaning of '*vaut*' (translated as 'worth' or 'value'), and pronounced in the same way as '*veau*' (translated as 'veal').

— WSC to JSC —

28 July 1898   Paquebot *Sindh*

Dearest Mamma,

I am just off on this boat – a filthy tramp – manned by these detestable French sailors. However, I was glad not to have received a telegram
of recall so far. My having started makes my case much stronger. Perhaps
it is all right.

I anticipate an unpleasant voyage – but it is only 5 nights and four
days – so that I shall probably survive. [...] The journey hitherto has been
not uncomfortable though days of travel must in any case be reckoned
as wasted. The fact that I have seen no telegrams about the war or the
events of the world – reminds me that I am again slipping away from
the centre of civilization. I hope for the last time for some years. I am
tired of all this worry – and about all of the feeling of subordination
now vy heavily pressing upon me – even though you may not think it.

Your ever loving son
Winston

BRITAIN'S MILITARY presence in Egypt had turned the country
into a de facto British protectorate since the end of the Anglo-
Egyptian war of 1882. Egypt in turn largely controlled the Sudan
to its south, although the followers of a self-proclaimed saviour of
the Islamic nation (known as the Mahdi), Muhammad Ahmad, had
continued their resistance to Egyptian control sufficiently successfully
for William Gladstone's Liberal government to order a withdrawal
of British and Egyptian troops from the territory in 1884, to be led
by Major-General Charles Gordon.

Mahdist forces besieged Gordon's small force in the Sudan's capital,
Khartoum, until they attacked in January 1885 and killed General
Gordon. The Mahdi then declared a religious state under Shariah
law in most of the Sudan. British attempts to re-establish control
remained half-hearted until the new Conservative government

The Sudan campaign and the Battle of Omdurman, 1898

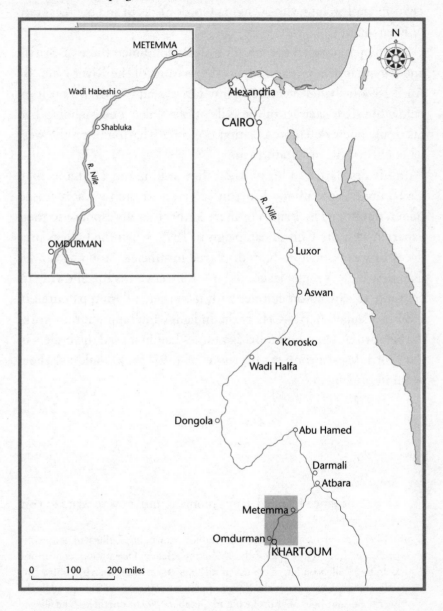

appointed General Kitchener to command the Egyptian army in 1896 and tasked him with avenging Gordon's death and the recapture of Khartoum.

Kitchener adjusted the advance of his combined force of British and Egyptian troops carefully to the seasons of the River Nile. By April 1898 he had driven the enemy forces southwards to a position below the sixth cataract of the Nile at Shabluka. The Mahdists had taken up a new defensive position opposite Khartoum, on the west bank of the Nile at Omdurman.

In his first letter to his mother after joining the 21st Lancers in Cairo on 2 September, Winston referred to the new soft-nosed bullet, developed by British military authorities in response to their experience in the Chitral campaign in 1895, when the bullet's predecessor was deemed to have displayed insufficient stopping power. The new bullet's metal jacket did not fully cover its tip, allowing its contents to expand on contact with its target, a design patented in 1897 by Captain Bertie-Clay of the Indian Army's ammunition works in the town of Dum Dum. British forces had first used the bullets in the North West Frontier campaigns of 1897; they would use them again in the Sudan.[3]

— WSC TO JSC —

5 August 1898   Luxor[4]

My dearest Mamma,

    I have not, since I landed, had a moment until now to write to you.

---

3 By 1899 Britain had distributed 66 million expanding bullets to its armies worldwide; however, on 29 July 1899, the Hague Declaration concerning Expanding Bullets outlawed the use of such bullets on ratification by contracting parties. Neither Britain nor the Boer Republic of South Africa had signed by the time the Second Boer War broke out in October 1899. Nonetheless the alleged use of such bullets by each side in the conflict became a matter of controversy and retribution between their soldiers. Britain ratified the declaration on 13 August 1907.

4 Ancient city of Thebes standing on the river Nile, 400 miles south of Cairo.

I have heard nothing definite about my leave being sanctioned by India – but as there has been no cancelling order & a fortnight has already passed I think I may now conclude with certainty that 'silence has given consent'. [...]

We are toiling slowly up the rising river – against a 6 knot current with only a balance of speed of 4 miles an hour. We do not therefore arrive at Assouan [Aswan] until 10th nor at the Atbara[5] until the 15th of this month. But that will be quite early enough as Sir E.W. [Evelyn Wood] said distinctly that he did not think that the attack on the Shabluka position would take place before the 15th of September. [...]

I will write to you under another cover on the subject of business and Lumley etc. I don't think the latter is more or less than a shark. Beware of him for we haven't got much for such a beast to bite at. He will soon swallow it all.

Meanwhile after the bustle and hurry – and not least the uncertainty – of my three weeks in London – this rest and quiet is vy refreshing and agreeable. The weather – tho' here called hot – is a vy different kind of heat to what we enjoyed this time last year with the M.F.F. [Malakand Field Force]. As far as I can see the campaign will be conducted in a luxurious manner. We are allowed 200lbs baggage in contrast to the vy strict Indian "80lb scale" [...].

It is a vy strange transformation scene that the last 8 days have worked. When I think of the London streets – dinners, balls, etc and then look at the Khaki soldiers[6] – the great lumbering barges full of horses – the muddy river and behind and beyond the palm trees and the sails of the Dahabiahs.[7]

And the change in my own mind is even more complete. The ideals & speculations of politics are gone. I no longer contemplate harangues. The anticipations of Parliament – of speeches – of political

---

5 Now in north-eastern Sudan, at the junction of the Rivers Nile and Atbara.
6 British troops first wore khaki-coloured uniforms in the Abyssinian campaign of 1867–8.
7 A shallow-bottomed passenger boat used on the River Nile, powered by sail.

life generally have faded before more vivid possibilities and prospects and my thoughts are more concerned with swords – lances – pistols – & soft-nosed bullets – than with Bills – Acts & bye elections.

[…] I will write on literary matters – in my next. Mind you boom the "Ethics of Frontier Policy".[8] Oliver B. [Borthwick][9] will put in a leader on it – for a little suggesting. He indeed shld do. It is the most thoughtful thing I have yet written – and contains the priceless gems of truth.

And now au revoir – With best love, I remain, Ever your loving son
Winston S. Churchill

W INSTON WROTE his next letter to his mother after his detachment of troops had passed Korosko, 120 miles south of Aswan. Their next stop would be seventy miles further up the Nile at Wadi Halfa where they would transfer to a newly built railway line, because the river became unnavigable while it negotiated its long Dongola bend. The railway took a short cut in a south-easterly direction, crossing the river at a bridge next to Abu Hamed before the track continued alongside the eastern bank as far as Atbara.

— WSC to JSC —

10 August 1898   On the Nile, between Korosko & Wadi Halfa

My dearest Mamma,

I enclose you herewith two letters to 'a friend' which I want published in the *Morning Post*. […] They will act as foundations and as scaffolding for my book. Before they are published I want you to tell Lady Jeune and perhaps show them to her. Tell her that I do not think I am bound by any promise not to write, as the promise she made me on my behalf to

---

8   Written by WSC in April 1898; published in the August 1898 edition of the *United Service Magazine*.

9   Younger son of Lord Glenesk, owner of the *Morning Post*; died aged 32 in 1905.

Kitchener was contingent on his allowing me to come to the Egyptian cavalry. He refused and therefore my undertaking also ends. [...]

Oliver [Borthwick] said he would pay me ten pounds a column – but you need not allude to money with him. I have written to him very clearly and fully in the private letter I enclose and which you should give him or send him with the two others. [...]

The advanced division of the Expedn Force is so close to Khartoum that everyone is anxious to get on as quickly as possible – lest we should be too late. I am impatient to finish with train & steamer of which I have had sixteen days on end and 32 days continuous travel out of the last 55. I do not think however that there is any danger of our missing the fighting. People talk vy airily about the Dervishes[10] making off in to the desert. I do not know much about the matter, but I feel sure there is hard & heavy fighting ahead. [...]

Dearest, do, do all my business for me at home. The first three letters to the *M.P.* [*Morning Post*] should pass in silence – so that it can be seen that they are quite harmless. Gradually, the authorship may leak out and you can give a para to Wyndham for the *Outlook*[11] – to the effect that "it is an open secret etc. that the letters" then you can tell your own friends "in strict confidence". [...]

I shall hope to be back in England in November and we will then have a couple of really big & well boomed meetings. One at Bradford and the other, I think, at Birmingham. You must consult with Marlborough. [...]

Life is very cheap my dearest Mamma. [...] I am not careless of the possible results for I want as you know to live and to accomplish much but I do not fear them nor shall I complain. Besides these fortifying, philosophic reflections I have a keen aboriginal desire to kill several

---

10 Members of the (Muslim) Sufi religious order who take vows of poverty and austerity; in the Sudan conflict, often used as an alternative name for the forces of the Mahdi.

11 Weekly review covering politics and the arts, founded in February 1898 by George Wyndham MP, after the demise of the *New Review* in which he was also involved.

of these odious dervishes & drive the rest of the pestiferous breed to Orcus[12] and I anticipate enjoying the exercise vy much. I should like to begin tomorrow.

That beastly man whistling again – a hymn – and out of tune. Surely the limit of endurance is reached.

Ever your loving son
Winston

––•––

THE RIVER Nile becomes navigable again all year round above Atbara. Kitchener's forces, however, planned to march the rest of their route southwards to Omdurman, a distance of just over 200 miles. First they would concentrate at Wad Habeshi, sixty miles short of their final objective.

— WSC TO JSC —

16 August 1898   Atbara Fort

My dearest Mamma,

I fear this must be a hurried scribble of uncertain length. We arrived here on the 14th crossed the river to the western side and there encamped – 2 squadrons of the 21st. Early this morning the squadrons marched south towards Wad Habeshi – 8 days march – at the end of which is war. I for the moment am left behind here to settle up several matters – sick horses, sick men, stores etc. But I am going to ride on alone after the troops and shall catch them up tonight or during the night. [...]

Things are approaching the conclusion. The opinion here is that by the 7th of next month Khartoum will be again under the Egyptian – and for Egyptian read British – flag. Myself I think there may be delays. But we are all to be concentrated – 25,000 men – at Wad Habeshi opposite

---

12 Like Hades, a god of the underworld.

the Shabluka position by the 25th. The advance thence to Kerreri[13] and Omdurman is only a matter of 10 or 12 days easy marching – provided the military part of the affair is satisfactory. [...]

I had hoped to send you another *M.P.* letter. Alas I have had no time – not a minute. Even now I must run [...].

[...] I foresee that I shall be able to do pretty much what I want if I stay much longer. Perhaps I may stay on after Khartoum in some other capacity! Who knows – I like this sort of life – there is vy little trouble or worry but that of the moment – and my philosophy works best in such scenes as these. [...]

Your ever loving son
Winston

––·––

WINSTON AND his detachment had completed almost half the distance towards Wad Habeshi when they stopped a passing steamer so that it could take on board some casualties of the march. It also took letters home written by the soldiers.

– WSC TO JSC –

19 August 1898   On Bank Nile, 20 Miles from Metemma[14]

Dearest Mamma,

Only a line. A steamer has just arrived – passing down with empty boxes to the Atbara. We signalled to it to stop from our bivouac here – in a shady palm grove. It will take down our sick – we have several bad cases of heat apoplexy and sunstroke – and it may also convey my best love to you.

We are making extraordinary marches 29 and 30 miles every day,

13 Seven miles north of Omdurman; Kerreri was to be the site of the battle known as Omdurman.
14 WSC's detachment was still 20 miles north of El Metemma, approximately one-third of the way from Atbara to Omdurman.

a gross piece of mismanagement and miscalculation on the part of the Sirdar. We kill 5 or 6 horses every day. It reveals an amount of folly and wicked waste of public money hardly credible.

I am well – never better. The 21st feed like pigs – we get nothing to eat but bully-beef, biscuits and warm beer. But my philosophic temperament enables me to enjoy life immensely. I am very happy and contented and eagerly look forward to the approaching actions. We should reach Metemma tomorrow and may get to Wad Habeshi 4 miles from Shabluka – three days later. [...] Needless to say this is all private.

Not a moment to put pen to paper for the *M.P.* Usually dead beat. [...] Flies awful. I missed my way the other night trying to catch up column and spent miserable night and day without food or water in desert. [...]

My dear Mamma, I will write again, perhaps from Metemma. In the meanwhile best love. We have passed skeletons etc which bear eloquent testimony to the Dervish work.

The steamer is off.

Your ever loving son
Winston

— WSC to JSC —

24 August 1898   Wad Habeshi, before Shabluka

Dearest Mamma,
        [...] We are but 60 miles from Khartoum and on the 27th we march 21 miles putting us in front of the infantry and in full contact. Within the next ten days there will be a general action – perhaps a vy severe one. I may be killed. I do not think so. But if I am you must avail yourself of the consolations of philosophy and reflect on the utter insignificance of all human beings. I want to come back and shall hope all will be well. But I can assure you I do not flinch – though I do not accept the Christian or any other form of religious belief. [...]

But I shall come back afterwards the wiser and the stronger for my gamble. And then we will think of other and wider spheres of action.

I have plenty of faith – in what I do not know – that I shall not be hurt. […] Au revoir, my dearest Mamma.

Ever your loving son
Winston

PS In case I am wounded or worse – I have asked F. Rhodes[15] – 'the silly old man of the Nile' as they call him up here – to wire vy fully to *The Times*. If a severe wound, you would do well to come out and help me back. *WSC*

— WSC ᴛᴏ JSC —

26 August 1898 N. of Shabluka

My dearest Mamma,

I had not thought to send you another letter. An opportunity however presents itself. We all move south tomorrow at daylight. Both your letters arrived by Molyneux[16] and the mail which the last squadron brought last night. 'Atbara' – 'Darmali' we are far south of these and tomorrow night will be within 30 miles of Omdurman. The whole matter is reaching its climax and I think a great battle is imminent. I am trying to get to the Egyptian cavalry as tho' more dangerous it is a much better business as far as chances of distinction go. […]

I wonder whether I shall keep out of harm's way. I assure [you] a mild curiosity is my only emotion on the subject. I am convinced however that there will be heavy losses. *Qui vivra verra.*[17]

Ever your loving son
Winston

---

15 Colonel 'Frank' Rhodes, brother of Cecil Rhodes; a correspondent of *The Times* at the Battle of Omdurman in which he was wounded.
16 Lt. the Hon. R. F. Molyneux, Royal Horse Guards, wounded at the Battle of Omdurman.
17 Idiomatically, 'Time will tell'.

BATTLE WAS joined on 2 September. Kitchener's force of some 25,000 British, Egyptian and Sudanese soldiers, equipped with rifles, machine guns and artillery, destroyed the 52,000-strong Mahdist army. Casualties were grotesquely one-sided: 12,000 Mahdists were killed and 13,000 wounded; British losses amounted to just fifty killed and around 400 wounded.

Winston rode with 300 men of the 21st Lancers, who responded to Kitchener's order to cut off the enemy's line of retreat by charging an estimated 700 Dervishes astride the path to Omdurman. They rode into a carefully prepared ambush: hidden in a dip in the ground a further force of some 1,500 Mahdists lay in waiting. Two minutes of hand-to-hand fighting ensued while the 21st Lancers forced their way through. The regiment lost twenty-one killed and fifty wounded, while three of its members earned the Victoria Cross that day.

Winston had armed himself with a Mauser pistol rather than the standard cavalryman's lance. As soon as the battle itself was over, after five hours of fighting, he sent Jennie a telegram which read: 'All right – Winston'. Two days later, he wrote more fully:

— WSC TO JSC —

4 September 1898   Khartoum
                                                    and be damned to it.

My dearest Mamma,

I hope that this letter will not long precede me – certainly not more than a fortnight. You will have been relieved by my telegram which I sent off at once. I was under fire all day and rode through the charge. You know my luck in these things.

I was about the only officer whose clothes, saddlery, or horse were uninjured. I fired 10 shots with my pistol – all necessary – and just got to the end of it as we cleared the crush. I never felt the slightest nervousness and felt as cool as I do now. I pulled up and reloaded within 340 yards of their mass and then trotted after my troop who were then

Wounded British officers in the aftermath of the Battle of Omdurman.

about 100 yards away. I am sorry to say I shot 5 men for certain and two doubtful. The pistol was the best thing in the world.

The charge was nothing like as alarming as the retirement on the 16th of Sept last year.[18] It passed like a dream and some part I cannot quite recall. The Dervishes showed no fear of cavalry and would not move unless you knocked them over with the horse. They tried to hamstring the horses, to cut the bridles – reins – slashed and stabbed in all directions and fired rifles at a few feet range. Nothing touched me. I destroyed those who molested me and so passed out without any disturbance of body or mind. [...]

I am just off with Lord Tullibardine[19] to ride over the field. It will smell I expect as there are 7,000 bodies lying there. I hope to get some spears etc. I shall write a history of this war. [...]

Your loving son
Winston

---

18 See WSC's letter of 19 September 1897, p. 230.
19 John Stewart-Murray, lieutenant, Royal Horse Guards; known by the courtesy title of marquess of Tullibardine; later brigadier-general and 8th duke of Atholl.

— WSC to JSC —

8 September 1898   Omdurman

My dearest Mamma,

I do not quite know when I shall be back in London. I have been detained here to take transport back by long slow marches to the Atbara and I do not expect to see Cairo for another month. [...]

I am not at all in favour here with the Sirdar and my being ordered to do such a long and tiresome job is an instance of petty spite and really quite ridiculous since time is of no consequence – and I have nothing more to win or lose out here. I am very well and do not mind this delay very much as I can write one or two things I have had in my mind for a long time. [...]

You may arrange me some meeting in the latter part of October. I am very doubtful now whether I shall return to India. After all I have seen a good deal of war.

Ever your loving son
Winston S. Churchill

— WSC to JSC —

17 September 1898   Wady Halfa

My dearest Mamma,

I shall follow this vy shortly. The telegraph will exactly fix the hour. Your telegram and letter of 1ˢᵗ instant have reached me – also 2 *Morning Posts*. Yes – you must have had an anxious time at the beginning of the month. I sent you my wire "All right" – the very night of the action and it may have got off before the press messages. There is no doubt the charge was an awful gamble and that no personal precautions were possible. The issue as far as I was concerned had to be left to Fortune or to God – or to whatever may decide these things. I am content and shall not complain. The steamer vibrates so I cannot write properly.

I am as usual annoyed about the letters in the *M.P.* [...] There need be no secret about my having written the letters and the allusions to Cuba & the Frontier were deliberate.

What really has annoyed me is the complete destruction of the "Private letter" farce. This was a most amusing conceit and from a literary point of view added to the elegance of the letters. [...] However – what are these matters compared to having one's head slashed in half. One of the uses of going to war is that one learns proportion in earthly things.

I thought about you a great deal my dearest Mamma – before the action – "battle" these Egyptian puffers call it. I fear it must have been with a beating heart that you read the telegrams and looked down the casualty list. I certainly thought when I looked at my watch at 9.30 a.m. after the charge that a very bloody day lay before us and as we had already lost 25% of our men & 35% of our horses it looked like really big proportions before night. However – the blood of our leaders was cooled and the regiment was handled with rare caution for the rest of the day. Quite wrong I think because there is no merit in making one charge. Three touches on the splendid. [...]

Your ever loving son
Winston

P.S. Think over my going out to India on G. Curzon's staff as ADC.[20] It is worth considering. £300 a year and no expense of any sort.

---

20 George Curzon's appointment as viceroy of India (which he took up in January 1899) was announced early in September 1898.

13

FINAL PASSAGE TO INDIA

1898–9

'Patriotism and art mix as little as oil and water'

W INSTON ARRIVED back in London early in October. He stayed in England for almost two months until he set off on 2 December for a final spell in India. He returned there only to settle his affairs and to play in the inter-regimental polo tournament before he resigned as an army officer and embarked on the second stage of his career. This, he planned, would mix politics and writing.

While in England he addressed three political gatherings. The first took place at Rotherhithe, in south-east London, before he wrote the following letter to his mother. The other two meetings were to take place in Dover and Southsea, near Portsmouth.

Winston understood that daily newspapers now played an expanded role in the political world. The parliamentary reform acts of the nineteenth century had enlarged the number of men entitled to a vote; the invention of the telegram now allowed reporters to file their stories more quickly to their head offices; and the new network of railways enabled the newspapers to be distributed more widely and cheaply. Winston therefore took care to cultivate good personal relationships with the senior figures of the industry.

Charles Moberley Bell had started with *The Times* as its Egyptian correspondent in 1875; now he was the newspaper's managing director. Alfred Harmsworth had acquired the *Evening News* with his brother Harold in 1894; then founded the *Daily Mail* in 1896.

— WSC TO JSC —

21 October 1898   35A Cumberland Place

My dear Mamma,

Both speeches are now made up and I think they are both good. I have been working vy hard at them. I dined last night with Mr [Ernest] Cassel – a most interesting dinner – 16 men – none of whom were wholly undistinguished for conversational powers.

I sat next to Moberly Bell – of *The Times* and we got on capitally. I must tell you more tomorrow. Tonight I am to dine at Marlborough House[1] and I suppose as there are vy few people I shall have some opportunity of talking to the Prince. [...]

Harmsworth is vy civil and will report the speech at Dover well.

Your ever loving son
Winston

— WSC TO JSC —

27 October 1898   35A Cumberland Place

Dearest Mamma,

I daresay you will have gathered from the papers that the Dover

---

1   London home of the Prince of Wales who wrote to WSC at this time, warning him against criticising his military seniors when writing about the Battle of Omdurman.

speech was successful. I think Wyndham was impressed. I had one moment when I lost my train of thought – but I remained silent until I found it again – and I don't think it mattered.

Perhaps I shall speak at Portsmouth on Monday night.[2] I am vy tired and will write no more.

Ever your loving son
Winston S. Churchill

WINSTON SAW little of his mother during this visit to England in the autumn of 1898: she was in the midst of her annual visits to the estates of her friends.

There was an added interest to her progress this year. Late in July, at the home of her friend Daisy, duchess of Warwick, she had met a young officer of the Scots Guards by the name of George Cornwallis-West. George was twenty-three years old, one of three children born to his mother Mary – more often known as 'Patsy' – by the time she was twenty. At the age of seventeen Patsy had married George Cornwallis-West, a landowner in Wales and Hampshire, to solve the problem caused by her affair with the young Prince of Wales, begun when she was sixteen. Any or all of her children may in fact have been the Prince's. Their arrival did little to deflect Patsy from a very active social life, in only part of which her husband joined her. The children were exceptionally good looking, so sometimes paraded before their mother's friends; but most of their time was spent in the care of an unsmiling nanny and then at boarding school – in George's case, Eton.

This complicated childhood may help to explain why George, only two weeks older than Winston, fell for a woman who was still lively, sophisticated and attentive, although old enough to be his missing mother. He was neither the first nor the last good-looking officer to fall for Jennie, but his initial interest grew into something of an infatuation.

---

2   He did – on Monday 31 October.

George Cornwallis-West at the Duchess of Devonshire's
fancy dress ball, July 1897.

By the middle of August Jennie had been invited to stay at his family's 2,000-acre estate in Hampshire. The Cornwallis-Wests owned another 5,000 acres in Wales, although they had recently given up their house in London on account of its cost. By September, close friends of Jennie were sufficiently aware of the romance between her and George to include him on their guest list if they were inviting her.

In the autumn of 1898, over dinner Jennie tried to persuade her friend George Curzon, newly appointed as viceroy of India, to take George with him as an aide-de-camp. The appointment would have provided an honourable way out of what many were bound to perceive as a scandalous match. Curzon declined to help, so George continued his pursuit and Jennie did not resist.

Meanwhile, Winston was left dealing with a domestic difficulty in London.

— WSC TO JSC —

14 November 1898   35A Cumberland Place

My dearest Mamma,

   I fear I am the writer of bad news. Your black pug dog escaped yesterday from the house and can nowhere be found. He is I am afraid lost – and I confess I do not feel hopeful about the prospects of getting him back. Walden[3] has however visited all Police stations – & goes this afternoon to Battersea.[4] I have offered £10 Ransom and have had 300 handbills printed and have inserted an advt in the *Morning Post*. More than that I do not think it is possible to do and you must resign yourself to the inevitable.

   I will send you a telegram should he be brought back.

Ever your loving son
Winston

---

3   Butler and valet in JSC's household; Mrs Walden cooked (see People, p. 578).
4   The Temporary Home for Lost and Starving Dogs; founded 1860, moved to Battersea 1871.

N THE course of her dinner with Curzon, Jennie had bemoaned her empty life as a single woman. Curzon consoled her up to point, according to an account that she later wrote in her volume of *Reminiscences*, but she decided that evening 'to do something, and cogitating for some time over what it should be, I decided finally to start a review'.[5]

By 'review' she meant a literary publication that would be transatlantic in outlook and sumptuous in quality – both in its production and in its content. It would appear once a quarter, extend to 250 pages in length and be bound as expensively as a book.

Winston was enthusiastic about his mother's project and volunteered to help with its business side. Just before he left for India, he met John Lane, a founder and partner of Bodley Head, an antiquarian bookselling and publishing business. Lane's credentials for partnering Jennie in founding the review was that he had published his own quarterly magazine, *The Yellow Book*, which had won high praise for its literary and artistic standards although it had closed after three years in the spring of 1897. It had suffered throughout its short life from the close connection with Oscar Wilde of its art editor, Aubrey Beardsley. Wilde was imprisoned for 'gross indecency' in 1895 and remained incarcerated when *The Yellow Book* closed.

— WSC TO JSC —

1 December 1898   35A Cumberland Place

My dearest Mamma,

Many thanks for your letters. Yesterday passed uneventfully but not unpleasantly. I went with Jack to the Gaiety [theatre] in the evening.

Now to business:- Mr John Lane called on me yesterday and after lunch we had a long talk. We agreed on nothing but I cannot help thinking you will find him vy satisfactory. This or something like this should be the scheme. You would have to guarantee say £1,000 for the

5   Mrs G. Cornwallis-West, *Reminiscences of Lady Randolph Churchill*, p. 121.

chance of loss on 4 numbers. £350 of this would be paid towards the first number. This would be your whole liability in the matter and should the magazine show a balance profit – this would of course not be wanted and you would not lose anything. [...]

[...] Should it become successful, you and he would divide profits. Lane thought these might amount to about £800 each. Harmsworth however said that it would not be worth your while unless you had at least £2,000 out of it. I dissent. I think that even £800 for a beginning will enable you to live in the house – apart from the pleasure of influencing thought and opinion and becoming generally known as literary and artistic. [...]

Your ever loving son
Winston

THE NEXT day Winston left for Brindisi, on the heel of Italy, where he boarded a ship bound for India. He used the journey to start writing *The River War*, a book about the Sudan campaign. He and his mother resumed their weekly correspondence, although sadly none of her letters from this period survive.

— WSC TO JSC —

4 December 1898   SS *Osiris*,[6] Brindisi

My dearest Mamma,

I have just arrived here after a peaceful journey. I hated the Channel passage worse than a flogging and was ill & wretched. However that is now over. I have received no news from India which looks either as if things were pacific or as if I had not much chance of getting to the Frontier. This will please you. [...]

Ever your loving son
Winston

---

6   New ship, delivered to P&O Express early in 1898 for service between Brindisi and Egypt; capable of 19 knots.

— WSC to JSC —

11 December 1898   SS *Shannon*,[7] off Aden

My dearest Mamma,

I daresay you will expect a letter – though in truth there is nothing to tell. We have had a vy rough passage down the Red Sea – of all places – and I have not enjoyed myself excessively. I have however made good progress with the book. Three vy long chapters are now almost entirely completed. The chapter describing the fall of Khartoum Gordon's death etc is I think quite the most lofty passage I have ever written. [...]

Ever your loving son
Winston

— WSC to JSC —

22 December 1898   Bangalore

Dearest Mamma,

I arrived here after a tempestuous voyage and have been received with open arms by everyone. I have got my Soudan medal[8] and hope to get the frontier one in a few days. I start for the big Polo Tournaments on the 20th of January – another month's leave after which I shall come back here for a fortnight to settle up my affairs and then home. [...]

I work all day & every day at the book and have done about a third. You must forgive my short letter on that account. Time is so precious and there is so much to do. [...]

Ever your loving son
Winston

---

7   Launched 1882; owned by P&O; capable of speeds up to 14.5 knots; broken up 1901.

8   Silver medal, the crowned figure of Queen Victoria on the obverse; a plinth supported by Nile lilies, carrying a figure of victory with a laurel wreath and palm branch on the reverse; the ribbon was yellow and blue, separated by a thin red line.

– WSC TO JSC –

29 December 1898   Bangalore

My dearest Mamma,

I was glad to get your letter – the first of the new correspondence. I have been working very hard and have done about half the book but I fear my progress will now be slower as I have to wait for material.

Please accept Macmillan's offer of £100 for the serial rights of the novel [*Savrola*].[9] [...] I do hope money matters can be held over till I come back. I fear very much for the future. It is appalling. In three years I can't think what will happen. God only knows. I detest business even more than you do. Years of trouble and squalor are before us. Poverty produced by thoughtlessness will rot your life of peace & happiness, mine of success. These little driblets I make by my pen only make one realise more bitterly.

I am rather low spirited today having worked all the morning and made no progress at all. [...] I do not feel as vigorous here as in England. A great stagnation of thought – a diminution of energy oppresses me. [...]

The book grows rather in bitterness about K. [Kitchener]. I feel that in spite of my intention it will be evident no friend has written it. [...] A vulgar common man – without much of the non-brutal elements in his composition. [...]

Your last letter was nearly as scrappy as mine. And you have less excuse having more news and less work.

Ever your loving son
Winston

———

J ENNIE WAS about to mark her forty-fifth birthday. Winston clearly felt that one of the chief advantages of her starting a literary magazine was that it would provide her with a cachet to keep her name

---

9 Serialized in *Macmillan's Magazine*, May–December 1899; published in book form by Longmans, Green & Co. 1900.

on the guest lists of London's society hostesses once the advances of age reduced her other attractions.

— WSC to JSC —

1 January 1899   Bangalore

My dearest Mamma,

Your letter has just arrived. I am vy glad that the project for the magazine is developing. I don't think you should allow all the money to be guaranteed by outsiders. It strengthens your position in every way if you could guarantee say £500. I have no doubt that the business will go on. If it does you will have an occupation and an interest in life which will make up for all the silly social amusements you will cease to shine in as time goes on and which will give you in the latter part of your life as fine a position in the world of taste & thought as formerly & now in that of elegance & beauty. It is wise & philosophic. It may also be profitable. If you could make a £1,000 a year out of it, I think that would be a little lift in the dark clouds. [...]

I must go on with my book now; I am very industrious. But the climate is enervating. Don't worry about the plague.

Ever your loving son
Winston

WINSTON QUOTED for his mother an excerpt from his draft of *The River War* that described the impact on the young Mahdi of the early loss of his father. As he acknowledged, the passage really concerned the effect on Winston of the loss of his own father.

On 17 December 1898, at the Constitutional Club, Lord Salisbury had defended his government against the charge that it had 'kept the country needlessly in the dark' in matters of foreign policy. He explained that he preferred reticence to 'a plain style of public speaking on diplomatic questions', a remark taken to refer to Joseph Chamberlain's style.

− WSC ᴛᴏ JSC −

11 January 1899   Bangalore

Dearest Mamma,

    I must again write shortly to you for the mail will go in a vy few minutes and had I more time I should write you no more for there is nothing to say. [...] I am going next week to Madras to play polo and shall stay at Government House. The week after that Jodhpore [now Johdpur] where we all stay practising for the Tournament with Sir Pertab Singh.[10] Then Meerut for the Inter Regimental Tournament, where I stay with Sir B.B. [Bindon Blood] & after that Umballa[11] for the Championship − a very pleasant six weeks. Then home and the more serious pleasures of life.

    Meanwhile I work continually at the book and progress slowly but still I think what is written is really good. Let me quote you one sentence − it is about the Mahdi who was left while still quite young an orphan.

> 'Solitary trees, if they grow at all, grow strong: and a boy deprived of a father's care often develops, if he escape the perils of youth, an independence and a vigour of thought which may restore in after life the heavy loss of early days.' [...]

    What a clever speech Lord S. [Salisbury] made at the Constitutional club. He is a wonderful man. Joe C. [Chamberlain] is losing ground a good deal. I feel it instinctively. I know I am right. I have got instinct in these things. Inherited probably. This life is vy pleasant and I pass the time quickly and worthily − but I have no right to dally in the pleasant valleys of amusement. What an awful thing it will be if I don't come off. It will break my heart for I have nothing else but ambition to cling to.

---

10 Also known as Sir Pratap Singh, officer in the British Indian army, maharaja of Idar (now Mujarat), chief minister of Jodhpur until 1895, regent 1895–8.

11 WSC had referred to the city (120 miles north of Delhi and containing a large cantonment of British troops) as Amballa in his letter of 17 December 1896; now Ambala, although the code for its railway station remains UMB.

All about myself – as usual. But what else can you expect & I flatter myself you are interested. I will write the old [Dowager] Duchess [of Marlborough] a letter & prepare her for my resignation of commission. She will protest but knows I think that I am a serious creature and don't only study pleasure.

Oh do be careful about money. […] Much money is worth nothing. A little is the breath of our nostrils. I think we might do worse than give up London altogether if the fates continue adverse and live in the country. The railway makes all places equally near nowadays.

Ever your loving son
Winston

———·———

JENNIE KEPT Winston abreast of the plans for her literary review, for which she had now entered into a formal partnership with John Lane. The two new partners jockeyed for position in the taking of important decisions, the most contentious of which turned out to be the title of the new review. Winston tried to influence the debate from afar.

His letter contains a first written reference to his mother's relationship with George Cornwallis-West, suggesting that she had touched on the continuing affair in her missing letters of this period to her son.

— WSC to JSC —

19 January 1899   Bangalore

My dearest Mamma,

I have not done vy much work this week as the information I expected from Egypt has not yet arrived and I have got nearly to the end of my own resources. So I have taken four days holiday. […] There is no news of any sort, but that everyone here is much excited by the approach of the big Tournament. […]

I shall be home before the Magazine comes out. No I don't like

The Arena – it is very commonplace. You want some name that expresses what the Magazine really is – something classical & opulent. It should be a literary Amphitryon.[12] There is probably some good Greek word which expresses this. Alas I am no scholar.

I will alter the article on Rhetoric when I come home & give it to Algernon West.[13] How is the other West? I shall look forward to seeing him when I come back from the East. Your letters are not vy long – and you have less excuse then me for I have such a lot of writing to do.

I was interested in the cutting about Papa's biography. You must use all your influence to get the papers for me. [Richard George] Curzon could not well refuse. The time has not come yet – but in six or seven years it will have arrived – and I shall insist on undertaking the work. G.C. [George Curzon] may edit if he likes. I have every right and can do it much better than any one else likely to get hold of the papers. Don't let them publish any rubbish now. I shall think you vy unwise if you allow it when in any way you can deter them. From a financial point of view alone – the biography would be worth £2,000.

Ever your loving son
Winston

THIS WAS the second occasion that Winston had laid a claim with his mother to write his father's biography in due course. On this occasion his sense of timing turned out to be prescient: his biography, *Lord Randolph Churchill*, would appear seven years later in January 1906. On the financial front, however, Winston's forecast proved uncharacteristically conservative: his publisher would pay an advance of £8,000 (see p. 422).

---

12 In Greek mythology Amphitryon was a Theban general, whose name had come to denote a generous host and entertainer.
13 Sir Algernon West had served as principal private secretary to William Gladstone 1861–94.

— WSC to JSC —

26 January 1899   Government House, Madras[14]

My dearest Mamma,

[...] I have had a very serious check in compiling my book, for Captain Watson[15] on whom I counted for a great deal of important information has been forbidden by the Sirdar to supply me with any. This will cause delay but it shall not prevent me from writing the account. [...]

In consequence of this hitch in my supply of information I must come home quicker and shall leave this country not later than 15th of March. I shall have to stop a week in Cairo on the way, but shall be in England the first week in April. I am sending in my [resignation] papers now so shall be out of the army before May. [...]

I am glad the Magazine is taking form. *The International Quarterly* is much better than *The Arena* – but very cumbrous and not at all original. You must try and find a title which expresses the character & special mission of the Magazine – something exquisite, rich, stately. [...]

Your ever loving son
Winston

— WSC to JSC —

2 February 1899   Bangalore

My dearest Mamma,

No letter from you this week, so only a vy short one from me – but not in revenge for I have nothing of any consequence to tell, and I shall be home so soon. I am working hard at the book, but it progresses

---

14 Purchased by the East india Company from a Portuguese merchant, Luis de Madeiros, 1753; expanded 1798–1803 by Lord Edward Clive, governor, to the designs of John Goldingham, architect and astronomer; another storey was added in 1860.
15 Captain James Watson of the King's Royal Rifle Corps, aide-de-camp to General Kitchener.

slowly as I am very short of information. I must stay in Egypt on my way home to collect some more. [...]

The more I think about the *International Quarterly* the less I like the name. There is no idea of elegance about it. It would suggest a very heavy ponderous publication. Not a literary epicure, feast which is what you want. [...]

I am settling up all my affairs in India. You will be glad to hear that the place will pay itself and even leave a small balance to take me home.

Your ever loving son
Winston S. Churchill

PS I had a long letter from George West. I fear he will be angry with a short answer. But I write so much now.   *WSC*

— WSC TO JSC —

9 February 1899   Jodhpore

Dearest Mamma,

I have had an abominable piece of ill luck. I had come here with the polo team and was practising for the Tournament next week, at Meerut. Everything smiled and our chances were good. Last night I fell downstairs & sprained both my ankles & dislocated my right shoulder. I am going to struggle down to polo this afternoon strapped up etc, but I am a shocking cripple and doubt vy much whether I shall be able to play in the tournament.

All these things are minor matters; merely pleasures – I don't overrate their importance, but I am too young not to feel bitterly disappointed. The regiment too are vy worried as their chances are weakened. It is better to have bad luck in the little things of life than in bigger undertakings. I trust the misfortune will propitiate the gods – offended perhaps at my success & luck elsewhere. [...]

Ever your loving son
Winston

TWO YEARS earlier, in his letter of 25 February 1897, Winston had called George Nathaniel Curzon 'the spoiled darling of politics – blown with conceit'. Now he was looking forward to staying with the new viceroy of India (who had taken over from Lord Elgin on 6 January) and hedged his bets.

— WSC TO JSC —

16 February 1899   Meerut

My dearest Mamma,

My shoulder is better and though still weak I shall play in the Tournament wh I think we may win. [...] After the tournament I go to Calcutta to stay with the Viceroy [Curzon] for a week. It will be interesting to see him in his new kingdom.

I beg you not to be in a hurry [about the magazine]. You will never get the advantage you now enjoy back for a second venture. All the prestige will be gone. A bad name will damn any magazine. I don't really like any that you suggest. Please don't begin till you are sure. A bad number doesn't matter. The next may be much better. A bad name sticks always. You can't change it without altering the whole Magazine. [...]

With my best love, Ever your loving son
Winston

———

JENNIE AND Lane scored a coup when they recruited Sidney Low as editor of their review; he had filled the same post at the well-regarded *St James's Gazette*.

A title for the new magazine remained elusive, however. A former soldier and diplomat, Sir Edgar Vincent (another of Jennie's reputed former lovers), was the first to suggest *The Anglo-Saxon*, which appealed to Jennie's transatlantic vision for the publication. It did not, however, impress her son.

— WSC to JSC —

23 February 1899   Meerut

My dear Mamma,

I was delighted to get your letter. The more I think about the Magazine, the more I wish you would not be in such a hurry. The title the *Anglo Saxon* is more unsuitable. It might do for a vy popular periodical meant to appeal to great masses on either side of the Atlantic. But it is very inappropriate to a Magazine de Luxe, meant only for the cultivated few and with a distinct suspicion [of] cosmopolitanism about it. [...] Mind you all your <u>prestige</u> will be destroyed if the first number is not a success. I do most earnestly advise you to wait a couple of months or another quarter. [...]

I am working incessantly at *The River War*, I think it will make a stir. It is not a bit venomous. Absolutely judicial. I propose to have it bound in blue & yellow [sketch included], the colour and pattern of the medal ribbon which as you perhaps know is meant to represent the blue Nile flowing through the desert and hence is not unsuited to *The River War*. [...]

Your ever loving son
Winston

————

W INSTON'S NEXT letter came from the Viceregal Lodge in Calcutta, where his views about Lord Curzon had undergone a change.

— WSC to JSC —

2 March 1899   Calcutta

My dearest Mamma,

Your letter of the 10th also Press Cuttings and some MS [manuscript] from Tullibardine. Many thanks. You will be glad to hear that we won the Inter Regimental polo Tournament – a very great triumph for it is perhaps the biggest sporting event in India. I hit three goals out of four in the winning match so that my journey to India was not futile as far as the regiment was concerned.

I have come on here for a week and am staying with the Curzons. Everything is vy pleasant and I have found him very delightful to talk to. His manners are wonderful. All the aggressiveness wh irritated me at home is gone. They have both won everybody's heart. But I fear he works too hard – nearly eleven hours every single day – so his secretary tells me. [...]

I must now turn to the Magazine. I am vy glad that you will not publish until June. I repeat all I wrote a fortnight ago about there being no hurry. But I think you have quite lost the original idea of a magazine de luxe. Your title *The Anglo Saxon* with its motto 'Blood is thicker than water' only needs the Union Jack & the Star Spangled Banner crossed on the cover to be suited to one of Harmsworth's cheap Imperialist productions.[16] I don't say that these have not done good and paid but they are produced for thousands of vulgar people at a popular price. People don't pay a guinea for such stuff. [...]

Of course as a title *Cosmopolis* would have done excellently. But it is taken already.[17] Literature is essentially cosmopolitan. Patriotism and art mix as little as oil and water. I don't want to be discouraging but I foresee so many difficulties and I am afraid that there is only one narrow road which will lead to success. [...]

Ever your loving son
Winston

———

AMONG THOSE whom Winston saw in Calcutta was Pamela Plowden, to whom he wrote afterwards: 'I have lived all my life

---

16 Alfred Harmsworth admired Cecil Rhodes; his newspapers reflected his own belief in an imperialist, 'Anglo-Saxon future'; Harmsworth stood unsuccessfully for Parliament as a Conservative candidate in 1895.

17 *Cosmopolis*, a literary review, appeared between January 1896 and November 1898. Although it was published in London, local editions appeared in Paris, Berlin and St Petersburg.

seeing the most beautiful women London produces. Never have I seen one for whom I could forgo the business of life. Then I met you [...]. Were I a dreamer of dreams, I would say "Marry me – and I will conquer the world and lay it at your feet".'

Marriage, however, needed 'money and the consent of both parties' to work and, in their case he sadly observed one of these requirements was 'certainly' missing (presumably money) and the other 'probably' (presumably Pamela's consent).[18]

Winston spared his mother the details of the latest state of play of his attempts to win Pamela. Instead, before leaving India he appealed to her again not to rush the first issue of her magazine. Finding that the name *The Anglo-Saxon* was already reserved, Jennie decided simply to add the word *Review* at its end. Winston remained doubtful of the choice. He was also sceptical of the business arrangement that she had negotiated with Lane and harboured his own hopes of finding himself an editorial position once he reached London, via Cairo.

— WSC TO JSC —

9 March 1899   Manwar Ry [Railway] Station[19]

My dearest Mamma,

I am afraid you may have thought my criticisms in my last letter unkind. I do hope you won't, because I keep on thinking of your money trouble, which I fear must be getting acute, and do not wish under any circumstances to do anything which would add to your worries, or discourage you from an effort to meet them. But I implore you to

---

18 March 1899, W. S. Churchill letter to P. Plowden, cited the *Observer*, 9 November 2003.

19 It is likely that WSC mistook the name of this station (where he changed trains and had time to post a letter) for Manmad. Manwar lies close to Nepal and would not have been on his route between Calcutta and Bangalore, whereas Manmad is a junction, north-east of Bombay, where India's east–west and north–south rail lines crossed.

wait till I come home before committing yourself with regard to the Magazine.

Believe me it is much easier for me to see Lane & such like people over money matters. Remember what I say about there being no second chances. Besides the actual loss – think of the ridicule wh would follow failure. Of course I am vy much in the dark as to the scheme and that is why I tremble. Yet what you have told me has not encouraged me.

I have had several delightful talks with the Viceroy. Really I misunderstood his manner entirely. [...]

Ever your loving son
Winston

W INSTON STOPPED at Cairo on his way home to research *The River War*. He stayed in the city's newest hotel, the Savoy, which had opened only five months previously. Overlooking the Rond Point Qasr Al-Nil, it boasted an electric lift, fireplaces in each bedroom and furniture newly imported from London.

His letter from the hotel was the first that he dictated to his mother. A shorthand writer (whom he called a stenographer and whom he had engaged to help his research for *The River* War) transcribed the letter by hand before Winston added a greeting and sign-off. It was a sign of things to come.

— WSC to JSC —

30 March 1899   Savoy Hotel, Cairo

My dear Mamma,

I arrived here four days ago, intending to go on by the next steamer to England, but I find so much valuable information and so many people willing to assist me in my book, that I have decided to stay until Sunday week – the 9th prox. This will bring me back to England on the 15th, in time for the Albert Hall meeting.

You must forgive me writing to you a dictated letter because my hand is quite tired with all the scribbling I have to do.

I got your letter with the [magazine] prospectus included and I think it very good. I want very much to go home and help you with it all. I begin to feel much more hopeful than I did although at the same time I cannot reconcile myself to your title. [...]

The book which, when I arrived here, might have been finished in a month, will now take a somewhat longer time. I have found a great many things which are of great interest and which rather alter the narrative as I have told it. A great many of my more acrid criticisms of the Sirdar I shall tone down or cut out. [...]

The future seems very full of plans and possibilities but for the present I shall confine myself entirely to my book and until I get this off my mind and properly in the hands of the publishers, I shall not think seriously about anything else. [...]

I wrote to the old Duchess to tell her I had sent in my papers [to resign his commission]. I do not expect she will be very pleased but after all her opinion is a matter of very great indifference to me.

I like to think of you working away at your Magazine. I do not really see why it should not become a great success but it will need the most unremitting labour and you will have to give up a great many social amusements. [...]

Ever your loving son
Winston S. Churchill

— WSC to JSC —

3 April 1899   Savoy Hotel Cairo

My dearest Mamma,

I got your telegram asking me to meet you in Paris on the 8th, but for the reasons which I gave you in my last it is quite impossible for me to leave Egypt before the 9th. I am getting hold of a great deal of very valuable information [...].

I have been very much flattered by the great kindness and attention which Lord Cromer[20] has shown me here. He has given me letters of introduction to everybody who is of importance in Cairo and has taken great trouble to explain all sorts of matters connected with Egyptian politics to me. [...]

I rather like these dictated letters. They are vy simple & natural and I think it is good practice in talking fluently. I gave this to the stenographer as fast as she could take it down and it runs quite smoothly.

Your ever loving son
Winston

---

20 Evelyn Baring, later Lord Cromer, British comptroller-general of Egypt 1878–9; finance member of the government of India 1880–83; consul-general of Egypt 1883–1907.

14

THE SINEWS OF WAR

1899–1900

'I understand you as no other woman ever will'

W INSTON REACHED London late in April 1899, just before his resignation from the army took effect. Now twenty-four years old, he set out on his new career in which he planned to combine writing and politics.

When he arrived, he found his mother in the throes of selling subscriptions to *The Anglo-Saxon Review*, the first edition of which was due to appear in June, two months later. In addition, Jennie was still preoccupied by the attentions of George Cornwallis-West, whose pursuit of her had intensified while Winston was away. The disapproving dowager duchess of Marlborough had died in April 1899, allowing the couple to be welcomed at Blenheim Palace, another small step in the acceptance of their relationship.

Winston wrote to his mother for the first time after his return on the day that *The London Gazette* officially confirmed his resignation from the army. The main topic of his letter was politics:

several Conservative constituency associations wished to explore the possibility of him standing as one of their candidates at the forthcoming general election.

— WSC ᴛᴏ JSC —

3 May 1899   35A Cumberland Place

Dearest Mamma,

[...] I have replied to Birmingham diplomatically, expressing my desire to accept, yet hesitating about my ability. I dined last night at the Rothschilds – a delightful dinner – Mr Balfour, Mr Asquith, Lord Acton,[1] self, Evelina[2] & Lord & Lady R [Rothschild].[3] A.J.B. was markedly civil to me – I thought – agreed with and paid great attention to everything I said. I talked well and not too much – in my opinion. [...]

The Macmillans cheque for £100 [for *Savrola*] arrived last night – Watt took £10 – but I don't begrudge it him. He took a lot of trouble. Take care of George.

Your ever loving son
Winston

[...] Do you see I am no more a soldier?

———

ONE OF those who approached Winston about standing for Parliament was Robert Ascroft, a Conservative MP for the two-member constituency of Oldham, in north-west Manchester. He contacted Winston because his fellow member had decided to retire

---

1 Former Liberal MP and historian, known for saying: 'Power tends to corrupt: and absolute power corrupts absolutely.'
2 Daughter of Lord and Lady Rothschild, aged 26; she married five months later.
3 Nathan ('Natty') and Emma; Lord Rothschild had served as a Liberal MP 1865–85 before his elevation to the House of Lords, which he was the first practising Jew to join.

due to ill health. Then, on 19 June, Ascroft himself suddenly died, triggering a by-election at which the Conservatives needed two new candidates in this working-class constituency, which they still held against the Liberals largely as a result of Ascroft's personal popularity.

Anticipating an uphill struggle, the local Conservative association selected first Winston, who had been Ascroft's favoured candidate, and then James Mawdsley, general secretary of the Cotton Spinners' Union, whom Winston described as 'Tory Labour'.[4]

'There is practically no local society,' Winston explained to his mother when asking her to join his campaigning, 'only multitudes of workers'. He was also keen for Pamela Plowden, now back from India, to join them.

— WSC to JSC —

25 June 1899   Birch House, Oldham

Mamma,

Everything is going capitally – when my shorthand writer arrives I will give you fuller details. Owing to the appearance of a Tory Labour Candidate it is quite possible we shall win. There is no meeting Monday but on Tuesday night I make my big opening address. I would like you to come down for that. [...]There is practically no local society – only multitudes of workers.

My speech last night at the club produced great enthusiasm and there is no doubt that if anyone can win this seat I can.

Find out if Pamela [Plowden] would like to come down – and wire me. Send me a box of good cigarettes – Jack knows the sort – and let me have all my letters to this address. Write every day.

Your ever loving son
Winston S. Churchill

---

4   The Labour party itself was founded the following year, 1900.

– WSC to JSC –

26 June 1899   Oldham

My dearest Mamma,

[...] I am glad you like the [election] address. Everything is going on very well here, but I am sorry to say that my left tonsil has become very much inflamed and I fear that the speaking may greatly irritate it. [Doctor] Robson Roose promised to send me down a special spray if I wanted it. Will you send round to him about it. I am writing to him and he will give it to you so that you can bring it down. The throat is the only thing that worries me but it would be no more extraordinary to win the Oldham Election with a sore throat, than it was to win the Polo Tournament with a dislocated shoulder. [...]

Looking forward to seeing you, Your loving son
Winston

THE NEXT day's headline in the *Oldham Daily Standard* read: 'TONIGHT'S MEETING – LADY RANDOLPH CHURCHILL – EXPECTED'.[5] Jennie had heeded her son's call, although Pamela stayed away. With Winston, Jennie visited the homes of constituents and attended a series of meetings, including a gathering of the Primrose League attended by 200 'dames'.

Jennie returned to Oldham in early July at Winston's request. When the result was declared on 6 July, the two Radical candidates captured both seats for the Liberal party by a margin of over 1,000 votes, although the *Manchester Courier* declared that Winston 'had not been disgraced'.[6] That was the verdict that Jennie took care to spread among her political contacts in high places.

Winston still leaned heavily on his mother for practical help with his early political steps. More broadly, however, the tenor of their

5   R. Martin, *Lady Randolph Churchill*, vol. 2, p. 144.
6   R. Churchill, *WSC*, 1:449.

relationship was beginning to shift. Jennie no longer delivered so many maternal strictures in her letters, while Winston began to deliver some lectures of his own to his mother as her affair with George moved to a new pitch.

— WSC to JSC —

23 July 1899   35a Cumberland Place

My dearest Mamma,

[…] Please keep my secrets and those of others and do not I beg you talk about my visit here or anything connected with it. I also beg you not to bet or play cards. You have so much to make life interesting that there is no excuse or sense or reason for taking refuge in the desperate forms of excitement which the brainless butterflies of the world long for. I feel a little worried about this because I know you played and gambled last year vy high at Goodwood [race meeting]: and it can if repeated only end in bringing the most terrible misery upon us all. Already we feel the sting sharply. Forgive my lecture. It is an appeal.

I want to have my little political dinner on Thursday, only 6 or 7. They will all be in town on account of parliament. I hope you will be able to arrange this for me. Leave me a line at C. [Cumberland] Place.

With best love, Ever your affectionate son
Winston

———

THE FIRST issue of *The Anglo-Saxon Review* had emerged in June to polite reviews, although the plaudits for its cover outnumbered those for its contents. The high price of one guinea per issue did not help its sales.

Nonetheless, its reception gave Jennie and George the confidence, after two nights spent together in Paris, to plan the formal announcement of their engagement at the end of the first week of August to coincide with the Cowes sailing regatta. On 4 August, however, the *New York Times* broke the story prematurely, giving time for the Prince of Wales, the Cornwallis-West family and George's commanding officer to warn him off taking the step. Winston, too, wrote to George, advising against any change in the couple's status.

They evidently took heed, because later the same day Winston asked the Associated Press to issue a statement denying his mother's 'reported engagement'. Jennie took herself off to France to stay in a hotel at Aix-les-Bains, from which she wrote to Winston. Her letter does not survive; the next to do so was not written until April 1900.

— WSC to JSC —

13 August 1899   Blenheim

My dearest Mamma,

I was delighted to get your letter this morning. I cannot, I am afraid write you much of an answer as I am struggling furiously with proofs [of *The River War*]. It is vy pleasant here and when P. [Pamela] comes on Wednesday it will be still more so. The duke beats me badly at chess, however, which annoys me.

I have seen several very spiteful cuttings about your projected alliance – one of which compared it to the marriage of Lobengula with a White woman. I tore it up – and I don't know why I waste my time in repeating such trash. [...]

Ever your loving son
Winston

———

WINSTON'S REFERENCE to Lobengula concerned the chief of the Northern Ndebele tribe, which dominated the area broadly corresponding to present-day Zimbabwe. Lobengula fulfilled the contemporary Briton's stereotype of an African ruler: he had at least twenty wives, weighed 19 stone and attracted the love of his people, yet showed no mercy to members of other tribes. In 1888 Britain had persuaded Lobengula to sign what he thought was a limited concession for mineral exploration; soon thereafter, however, it became clear that the British South African Company intended to annex his territory. Battle was joined in 1893 and British guns inflicted heavy losses on his tribe; the king died in 1894.

Winston's next letter described an author consumed by the labours of trying to complete a book. Pamela Plowden, who was visiting Blenheim at the time, may have expected a little more attention to be paid to her than the odd walk accompanied by the writer 'oppressed' with his task.

— WSC TO JSC —

16 August 1899   Blenheim

My darling Mamma,

I am still at Blenheim living vy quietly – working all day long & walking with Pamela in the intervals. The business of finishing up the book oppresses me. I am revising proofs all day and am utterly worn out by night. I hope however to be free by the end of the month. [...]

I am afraid this will not interest you vy much – as I talk of nothing but book; but it takes my whole energy and strength and now that the end is so near I am impatient to be done. Dearest forgive my writing you such bad letters. [...]

Your ever loving son
Winston

———

PAMELA REMAINED at Blenheim for nearly a fortnight. It is not clear how acute Winston was at reading her mind during this visit; Jennie had clearly passed on some gossip from John Baring (a merchant banker who had succeeded his father as Lord Revelstoke two years earlier) about one rival for Pamela's hand; Winston mentioned another, while remaining confident that he would prevail.

He also promised to support any decision his mother took about marrying George, although he warned her to think carefully about the practical consequences: Colonel Cornwallis-West had threatened to cut off George's inheritance if he married Jennie.

— WSC to JSC —

22 August 1899   Hartham Park,[7] Corsham, Wiltshire

My dearest,

Your long letter arrived this morning. I am interested to hear of your conversation with [Lord] Revelstoke. He talks nonsense when he says P. has spoilt his brother's career and I think it vy ill-natured of him to say so. Everard Baring[8] is exceedingly well advanced in the Service – far in front of the average of his age. She has been throughout his guiding star – respected his devotion and while not madly in love with him – would have married him. Now she loves me and this in no way alters her feelings towards him – although of course if there be any possibility of marrying she would marry me before him & either of us before Kenyon[9] who is most persistent. [...]

I received the enclosure [from Colonel William Cornwallis-West] three days ago, and have answered that I am not returning to London so that it would be well if he wrote to me upon the subject. I don't want to be dragged in to their family cabal.

Whatever you may do or wish to do, I shall support you in every way. But reflect most seriously on all the aspects of the question. Ivor Guest raised the subject one night at Blenheim and I was glad to hear Marlboro entirely endorse your point of view. He talked to me a good deal of the business aspect – on which, as you know I lay paramount stress. Fine sentiments & empty stomachs do not accord. [...]

Ever your loving & devoted son
Winston

---

7 Home of Sir John Poynder, MP for Chippenham.
8 Army officer, younger brother of Revelstoke; fought in the Sudan 1897–8. His army career was flourishing: he was promoted to major November 1898 and appointed military secretary to Lord Curzon, viceroy of India, December 1899.
9 Possibly L. P. Kenyon, who served in the army in India 1897–8.

— WSC TO JSC —

3 September 1899   Blenheim

My dearest Mamma,

I am vy sorry not to be in London to meet you, but I have already broken my visit here and missed the Saturday's shooting and Sunny is moreover alone tomorrow to shoot the partridges.

I have had a second letter from Colonel West, which since he has not marked it *Private* – I send you, but you must destroy it and not tell anyone that I showed it you, as I rather think he meant it to be looked on as private. [...] It is for George to settle with his family: for you to consult your own happiness. [...]

Pamela has gone off to Germany and I am lonely without her. The more I know of her, the more she astonishes me. No one would understand her as I do. Yet I am always seeing new sides to her character. Some are good & some weak – yet I like them all – indeed this is becoming quite an old story and I fear it shall provoke a smile.

[...] Please send me a telegram when you get this letter to say that you love me and will write the same sentiment at a greater length. [...]

Ever your loving son
Winston

After all I don't believe you will marry. My idea is that the family pressure will crush George.

———

AS JENNIE had foreseen two years earlier, tensions in southern Africa had continued to build between, on the one hand, the Boer descendants of early Dutch settlers in the Transvaal who declared an independent Republic of South Africa in that region; and, on the other, British settlers in the Cape district, who wished to expand their territory and exploit its deposits of gold and diamonds.

Since the spring of 1899 the British government had been sending out the men and machines that would be required for a military campaign to repulse the Boer forces. By the late summer, war was beginning to look more than likely.

Winston was already a seasoned war correspondent, having covered two campaigns for the *Morning Post* and one for the *Daily Telegraph*. On this occasion his friend Alfred Harmsworth joined the bidding for his services on behalf of the *Daily Mail*.

— WSC to JSC —

18 September 1899   35A Cumberland Place

My dearest Mamma,

Harmsworth telegraphed to me this morning asking if I would go as their correspondent to the Cape. I wired this to Oliver [Borthwick] and made definite offer to go for *M.P.* [*Morning Post*] for my expenses, copyright of work, and one thousand pounds – for four months from shore to shore – two hundred a month afterwards. He has accepted so that I am at their disposal. I think war is certain, but we shall know tomorrow. I return to London on Wednesday so write thither.

Ever your loving son
Winston

— WSC to JSC —

2 October 1899   35A Cumberland Place

Dearest Mamma,

It is definitely settled that I start on the 14th. I am glad that you will be back no later than the 7th as Oldham is on the 11th and 12th. I am not going to Germany. Pamela will be in England before the 14th. The book is finally finished, but my time is busy with preparations for departure. War is certain and I expect that there will be collision in a few hours.

Ever your loving son
Winston

— WSC to JSC —

17 October 1899   Madeira, *en route* South Africa

My dearest Mamma,

We have had a nasty rough passage & I have been grievously sick. The roll of the vessel still very pronounced prevents my writing much, and besides there is nothing to say. Sir R. Buller[10] is vy amiable and I do not doubt that he is well disposed towards me. [...]

I wonder what news we shall find at Madeira! Evidently the General expects that nothing of importance will happen until he gets there. But I rather think events will have taken the bit between their teeth. [...]

Ever your loving son
Winston

— WSC to JSC —

25 October 1899   RMS *Dunottar Castle*,[11] en route

My dearest Mamma,

We are having a cool & prosperous voyage, and although the ship is crowded and ill-found, I cannot say I hate it as much as I expected to. I am vy excited to know what will have happened when we land. Fourteen days is a long time in war, especially at the beginning. I expect George [Cornwallis-West] will be in SA within a fortnight of my getting there and I will go and see him.

The main campaign – as I learn on the best possible authority – for who can foresee such things – will begin about the 25th December and we should be at Pretoria via, Fourteen Streams and Bloemfontein[12] by the end of February. I may therefore be home in March:

---

10 General Sir Redvers Buller VC, general officer commanding Aldershot, while WSC was stationed there 1895 (see People, p. 575).
11 Launched in 1899, owned by the Castle Line for the Southampton–Cape Town route, a voyage which she reduced to 17 days, 20 hours; requisitioned by the government during the Boer War, carrying 1,500 troops at a time.
12 Capital of Orange Free State, captured by British forces 13 March 1900.

The Second Boer War, 1899–1900

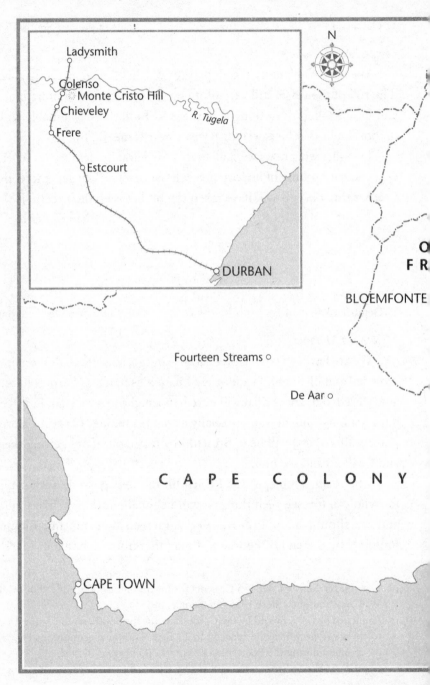

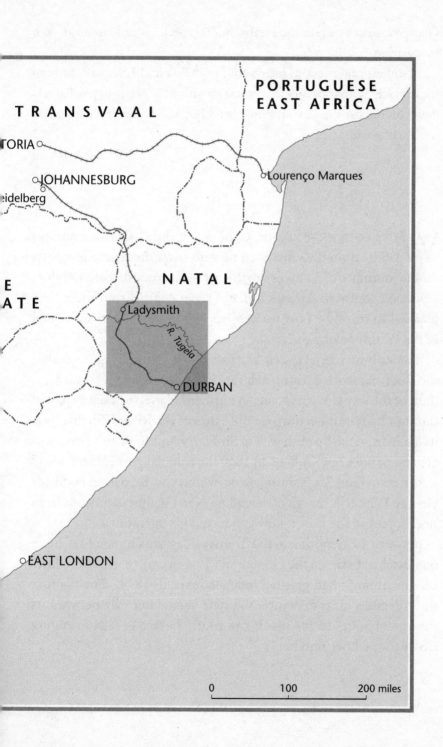

TRANSVAAL

PORTUGUESE
EAST AFRICA

ORIA

JOHANNESBURG

idelberg

Lourenço Marques

NATAL

E
ATE

Ladysmith

R. Tugela

DURBAN

EAST LONDON

0   100   200 miles

George I expect will see the Derby. But it is perhaps early to make such speculation.[13] [...]

I am all eagerness to hear about my book and I beg you to send me everything that occurs in connexion with it. I forgot to put Pamela down on the list I gave you. Please send her one of the first copies and write a line with it. [...]

Your ever loving son
Winston

———

W INSTON ARRIVED in Cape Town on 31 October and set off by train the same evening with two other correspondents on the journey of 550 miles north-eastwards towards East London, a port on southern Africa's Indian Ocean coast. From there they planned to travel by boat for another 300 miles to Durban, capital of the British colony of Natal.

The railway line between Durban and Johannesburg, capital of the Boer-controlled Transvaal, ran 370 miles north-westwards. A third of the way along its route, in northern Natal, the railway passed through Ladysmith, a town on the banks of the River Klip that took its name from the Spanish wife of Sir Harry Smith, British governor-general of the Cape Colony. In 1860 the colonial government added a fort to defend Ladysmith, from which the British general Sir George White, in charge of defending Natal against incursions from Boer forces to the north, now conducted his operations.

Between Ladysmith and the Transvaal lay the Orange Free State (sandwiched between the Orange and Vaal rivers), to which the British government had granted independence in 1854. For the first three decades of its existence, the state veered uneasily between its rival neighbours to the north and south, before gradually edging closer to the Boer republic.

———

13 WSC reached home four months later than he forecast, in July 1900.

— WSC TO JSC —

3 November 1899   In the train near East London

My dearest Mamma,

I write you a line – it can be no more to tell you my plans. The rest the *Morning Post* will inform you of as well as I can. We landed on the 31ˢᵗ and started the same night for Natal – train to E. London boat thence. [...]

I hope to reach Ladysmith tomorrow or the day after and I shall remain there until the preparations for the main advance are completed. This I may tell you privately is to be straight north through the Orange Free State. [...]

We have greatly underestimated the military strength and spirit of the Boers. I vy much doubt whether one army Corps will be enough to overcome their resistance – at any rate a fierce and bloody struggle is before us in which at least ten or twelve thousand lives will be sacrificed and from which the Boers are absolutely certain that they will emerge victorious.

Naturally I do not share that last opinion – but it is as well to bear it in mind. [...] We have had good luck so far, this being the last train to get through from de Aar,[14] and we have gained four days on all the other correspondents. I shall believe I am to be preserved for future things.

Your ever loving son
Winston

WHEN WINSTON wrote this letter, he was unaware that 21,000 Boer troops had already crossed southwards into Natal and reached the Tugela River which ran in an east–west direction, twelve miles to the south of Ladysmith. They had forced Sir George White to pull back 8,000 of his troops into Ladysmith, where they found themselves under siege from 3 November.

---

14 De Aar was the point between Cape Town and East London at which the railway line ran closest to the Orange Free State.

Boer forces had already cut the railway line well to the south of Ladysmith, so Winston and his colleagues had to halt their journey northwards at Estcourt, twenty-five miles short of the railway bridge over the Tugela at Colenso.

On 14 November Captain Aylmer Haldane, with whom Winston had served in the Malakand Field Force, invited him join a reconnaissance mission in an armoured train the next morning, up the line towards Colenso. They had travelled only six miles, just beyond Frere, when a group of fifty Boers ambushed Haldane's party, derailing part of the train. Winston offered his services to Haldane, who placed him on formal duty.

Winston helped the train driver to clear the line before leaving the engine to return to Estcourt with his belt and pistol. Meanwhile, he walked back up the line to help Haldane, but on the way he ran into the Boers who captured him, together with Haldane and fifty-four others (two men were killed and ten wounded).

Winston anticipated that his captors would read the letter to his mother that followed. To help secure his release, he carefully asserted in it that he had been unarmed and in possession of his credentials as a war correspondent.

— WSC to JSC —

18 November 1899   Pretoria

Dearest Mamma,

A line to explain that I was captured in the armoured train at Frere on the 15th, with some 50 officers and soldiers and some other noncombatants and platelayers and such like. As I was quite unarmed and in possession of my full credentials as a Press correspondent, I do not imagine they will keep me. They have always treated Press correspondents well and after Majuba Hill[15] the *Morning Post* corres-

---

15 The Battle of Majuba Hill, a decisive victory for the Boers, took place on 27 February 1881 in the first Anglo-Boer War.

Winston (right) as a prisoner of the Boers, November 1899.

pondent was released after a few days detention. You need not be anxious in any way but I trust you will do all in your power to procure my release. After all this is a new experience – as was the heavy shell fire.

Your loving son
Winston S. Churchill

W INSTON'S ESCAPE from the Boers, an adventure he would chronicle in his own words in *My Early Life*, took him from imprisonment in Pretoria – via two stowaway train journeys and a sea voyage from Portuguese East Africa (now Mozambique) – to safety in Durban, where Pamela greeted the news of his safe arrival on 23 December by sending a telegram to Jennie that read simply: 'Thank God – Pamela.'[16]

---

16 Cited R. Churchill, *WSC*, 1:506.

Unknown to Winston, Jennie was herself on the point of sailing for Cape Town. The first suggestion to her that Americans living in London should fund a hospital ship to treat British soldiers wounded in the war had come in late October. Jennie chaired an organising committee, helped to raise £45,000 by playing the piano at fund-raising concerts, charmed free medical supplies out of British companies and secured a suitable transport ship, the *Maine*, from a Baltimore millionaire who promised to keep paying the crew. Jennie then pulled strings with the secretary of state for war, the marquess of Lansdowne, and the first lord of the Admiralty, George Goschen,[17] who were both her friends, to secure the *Maine*'s official designation as a military hospital ship and to procure surgical staff.

By Christmas, the *Maine*'s conversion was complete and Jennie, together with a personal assistant, was ready to leave with her. There was some comment in the press that she might be anxious for a reunion in southern Africa with her lover, George Cornwallis-West, who was fighting there. If so, she was to be disappointed; just before she left, she heard that he was to be invalided home as a result of sunstroke. The more charitable explanation for her decision to accompany the *Maine* was that she had the force of personality to keep the peace between the *Maine*'s American crew and the British medical team. Tensions were already running high.

Following his escape, Winston made his way back up towards Ladysmith, which British forces were once again trying to relieve. Having heard of his mother's impending arrival in the *Maine*, he sent a letter to greet her when she reached Cape Town. In it he broke the news that, since her departure, he had made arrangements by telegram for Jack to leave his job as Sir Ernest Cassel's secretary in the City and to sail as a volunteer to join the war.

---

17 Former Liberal Unionist chancellor of the exchequer who had replaced Lord Randolph 1885–92; joined Conservative Party 1893; first lord of the Admiralty 1895–1900; created Viscount Goschen 1900.

— WSC to JSC —

6 January 1900 Camp before Colenso, Natal

My dearest Mamma,

All your letters have arrived in a bundle and I spent a delightful afternoon reading them. You must have had a very anxious time and what a surprise it will be to you to find me free again. Sir Redvers Buller has given me a lieutenancy in the S.A. [South African] Light Horse[18] without requiring me to abandon my status of correspondent so that I am evidently in very high favour. [...]

I have another piece of [news] that will surprise you. Jack sailed from England on the 5th and I have obtained him a lieutenancy in the S.A. Light Horse too. I feel the responsibility heavily but I knew he would be longing to come and I think everyone should do something for the country in these times of trouble & crisis. I particularly stipulated that Cassel should agree, and I hope you will not mind.

My dearest Mamma, I am so glad & proud to think of your enterprise & energy in coming out to manage the *Maine*. Your name will be long remembered with affection by many poor broken creatures. Besides it is the right thing to do, which is the great point. There is a great battle – the greatest yet fought – impending here. And of course I cannot run the risk of missing it although my military duties are purely nominal. After it is over, if I come through alive, I shall try to run down to Cape Town – or perhaps you will come to fetch the wounded from Durban.

These are anxious days, but when one is quite sure that one is filling one's proper place in the scheme of the world affairs, we may await events with entire composure. I should never care to go home to England, unless we are victorious here.

---

18 The unit comprised mainly settlers in southern Africa and was financed by local mining magnates.

The hospital ship *Maine* off Durban, 1900.

The reviews of the book seem satisfactory[19] – though there is an undercurrent of envy in some of them. One creates unknown enemies at every onward step.

Your second number [of *The Anglo-Saxon Review*] has just arrived. It looks splendid. I have not yet read it, but I think from what I have seen that it is every whit as good as its predecessor.

I think a great deal of Pamela; she loves me vy dearly.

Ever your loving son
Winston

PAMELA TRIED to persuade Winston to return home, without success: he was 'quite certain that I will not leave Africa til the

---

19 Longman, Green & Co. had published *The River War* (in two volumes) in London on 14 November 1899.

matter is settled. I should forfeit my self-respect for ever if I tried to shield myself like that behind an easily gained reputation for courage. No possible advantage politically could compensate.'[20]

Jennie and the *Maine* arrived at Cape Town on 23 January. She was not pleased to hear that Winston had persuaded Jack to fight; nor was she happy to be ordered by the authorities to sail straight back to Britain with a ship full of wounded soldiers. Insisting that the *Maine* had been fitted out as a hospital ship, she won her point. The *Maine* moved up the coast to Durban to be nearer to the main seat of fighting in northern Natal.

Early in February Winston cabled her to explain that Jack had been 'slightly wounded' just east of Chieveley, the campsite established by the British close to the spot where Winston had been captured three months earlier. Doctors at the camp extracted the bullet from Jack's leg the following morning, but Winston sent his brother down to the *Maine*.

— WSC to JSC —

13 February 1900   Chieveley Camp, Natal

My dearest Mamma,

It is a coincidence that one of the first patients on board the *Maine* should be your own son. Jack, who brings you this letter, will tell you all about the skirmish and the other action he took part in. He behaved very well and pluckily and the Adjutant, the Colonel and his squadron leader speak highly of his conduct. There was for ten minutes quite a hot fire. [...]

The '25 Brandy was a great source of satisfaction. I should like another bottle or even two. My own though '65[21] is not nearly so soft.

---

20 28 January 1900, W. S. Churchill letter to P. Plowden, cited R. Churchill, *WSC*, 1:510.

21 Six bottles of 'Very Old Eau de Vie landed in 1866' formed part of the consignment of alcohol from Randolph Payne & Sons that WSC took to southern Africa at the expense of the *Morning Post*, R.Churchill *WSC*, 1C2:1052.

I don't know when I shall be able to come down. Keep [me] informed of your movements and of those of the *Maine*.

Your loving son
Winston S. Churchill

———

G ENERAL BULLER had failed for three months to dislodge the Boer positions along the Tugela River, the key to relieving Ladysmith. He changed tactics in mid-February, attempting to outflank the Boers by seizing the high ground at Monte Cristo on the eastern edge of their positions on the river.

— WSC TO JSC —

18 February 1900   Monte Cristo Mountain, near Chieveley

My dearest Mamma,

Your letter has just reached me. We have made what seems to be a vy important and successful move here today & yesterday, reaching out round the enemy's right flank so that I really have hopes that we shall shoulder him away from Ladysmith altogether. […]

I have to see you before you go. […] Wire me exactly when you sail. You are quite right to travel with the ship – other things apart – I can easily arrange for you to come to Chieveley – if the fighting stops, but there is heavy firing going on all day long between our great guns and those of the Boers. I have now hopes that we shall relieve Ladysmith.

Yours ever
Winston

———

I N HIS next dispatch to the *Morning Post* Winston wrote that 'the victory of Monte Cristo has revolutionised the situation in Natal. It has laid open a practicable road to Ladysmith.'

— WSC to JSC —

26 February 1900   South Africa

My dearest Mamma,

[...] We are advancing slowly here and have captured a great part of the Boer position, camps, stores etc. Please telegraph to me freely. The brandy is vy welcome – I shall not give any of it to General Barton[22] – I want it myself. [...]

With Best Love, Your affectionate son
Winston

G ENERAL BULLER succeeded in relieving Ladysmith on the following day. Soon afterwards Jennie visited the general and her son, dining in a tent that overlooked the town.

Winston accompanied her back to Durban, where they spent two days with Jack before the *Maine* sailed home early in April with 175 wounded on board. She stopped briefly on the way at Madeira, from where Jennie posted a letter intended for the eyes of both her sons, who remained behind to fight and report.

— JSC to WSC —

15 April [1900]   Hospital ship *Maine*, off Madeira

My darling Winston

Here we are after an uneventful, smooth passage from St Helena.[23] I hope to get news here & indirectly gather a little where you 2 boys are – one more week & then home. I shall find all my work cut out for me there – between the [*Maine*] Committee & my [*Anglo-Saxon*] *Review*, & a 1000 things.

---

22 Major-General Geoffrey Barton, commander of 6th (Fusiliers) Brigade.
23 Island in the Atlantic Ocean approximately 2,000 miles north-west of Cape Town.

I have been vy busy drawing up an exhaustive record including everything – the work done on board since the ship left England, the financial situation & finally my reasons for bringing the ship home. I have taken great trouble with the report & intend to have it published & sent to each donator in America – as showing the work done. What the future of the ship will be I can't tell. Of course I will wire to you as soon as I know.

I have also been busy with my article for the *A.S.R.* [*Anglo-Saxon Review*] & have written more than half. The patients on ward are so well – 60 were discharged out of hospital yesterday. The officers are doing well [...] .

April 17th – Madeira

Darling Boys – We are about to depart & I am leaving this to be sent by the S.A. [South African] mail tomorrow. I have no idea where you are. [...]

I found lots of letters here – all interesting. The ship is coming out again within a week of arriving as we have plenty of money. I am much worried as Leonie is going to have an infant the 1st week of June & as she has not had one for 10 years it is always rather hard. I hate being away – she is everything to me. Yet I hate leaving the ship [...].

Bless you my darlings. G.W. [George West] writes that the papers have been criticizing some of your despatches – I am going to read everything I can get hold of.

Best love to you both – I will write by next mail.

Your loving Mother
JSC

WINSTON'S ESCAPE from Boer captivity had turned him into a household name at home. He had signed a contract with Longman for a book about the war before he left England; but now a letter from his former literary agent, A. P. Watt, arrived with a more valuable offer. Winston asked his mother to secure improved terms from Longman.

Jennie and the lightly-wounded Jack on board the *Maine*, February 1900.

— WSC to JSC —

21 March 1900   Ladysmith

My dearest Mamma,

Please see Watt's letter enclosed and also my agreement with Longman: but of course you will understand that the great scale of the war and my own extraordinary adventures, neither of which were foreseen at the time of the agreement, makes the book much more valuable than could have been expected. Therefore I want – and I don't think Longmans will refuse better terms. The book must be made worth at least £2000 to me.[24]

I trust you to try and get this for me & it is rather an important matter. Don't consult Watt unless Longman makes difficulties which I don't at all expect – for of course the situation is quite a new one. ...

Best Love
Winston

———

THE NEXT day Winston received an unexpected approach to tour America, making a series of paid lectures about his Boer War experiences. It came from the Lyceum Lecture Bureau, which was owned by a Major J. B. Pond. Winston instructed his mother to investigate.

— WSC to JSC —

22 March 1900   Ladysmith

My dearest Mamma,

Please see enclosed: which might be made into a really sound business. Now please don't let this thing be thrown away. First find

---

24 Longman's contract contained royalty rates of 15 per cent on the first 3,000 copies, 20 per cent on the next 7,000 and 25 per cent thereafter (see D. Lough, *No More Champagne: Churchill and His Money*, p. 447, fn. 28).

out whether <u>Pond</u> is the biggest man and if not who is. Then arrange terms. I would not go to the United States unless guaranteed <u>at least</u> a thousand pounds a month for three months and I should expect a great deal more. £5,000 is not too much for such a labour and for making oneself so cheap. I beg you to take the best advice on these matters. I have so much need of the money and we cannot afford to throw away a single shilling. [...]

Your ever loving son
Winston

———

THE *MAINE* docked at Southampton on 23 April. George was not there to greet Jennie, but he sent her a welcoming message. Friends who hoped that the couple's enforced separation of the previous six months would have cooled their ardour were soon disappointed; George renewed his protestations of love and proposed marriage again. For the moment, however, Jennie pleaded preoccupation with more immediate concerns, including fresh demands from Winston.

– JSC TO WSC –

12 May [1900]   Woodlands, Uxbridge[25]

My darling Winston,

It is ages since I heard from you – the African Mail came in bringing lots of letters this week but nothing from you. However I know you w[l]d write if you had time. Meanwhile I am doing all the things you want – I saw Longman yesterday & this is what he will do for you. It seems to me fair – considering that you had signed your agreement. He tells me you will make your £2000 if 25000 copies are sold – & this is pretty certain – altho' L. [Longman] tells me war books are not selling well[26] [...].

---

25 Inherited by Hugh and his sister Eleanor Warrender 1894.
26 *London to Ladysmith via Pretoria* sold only 14,000 copies in its first year, *idem*, p. 62.

Jennie writing in her cabin on board the *Maine*.

Pamela spoke to me about yr idea of a play – but I discourage it. Honestly it would not do. People won't stand any war play – you forget how it w^d harrow their feelings & it w^d be thought bad taste. Even a year after the A. [American] Civil War nothing c^d be given of that kind. [...] You will find plenty to write about without it. Meanwhile you have not given me your promised 'Ethics of Slaughter'.[27]

I am making all enquiries as to Pond – & I believe he is the man. You can make a fortune. But how long will it be before you can go? You will have to wait until the war is over. [...]

Do you send my letters on to Jack? I find so little time for writing. I am finishing my 'Hospital Letters'[28] & trying to settle a lot of bills & horrors. I am sorry to tell you the Nimrod Club[29] has gone smash –

27 Article that WSC had promised to write for *The Anglo-Saxon Review*.
28 Published in *The Anglo-Saxon Review*, June 1900.
29 London club for sportsmen, joined by WSC in 1895; it leased premises at No. 12 St James's Square that fell into Lord Randolph's will trust in 1899 after the death of the dowager duchess of Marlborough.

Lumley tells me that I can sell the property – of course the money wl^d have to be invested as trust money, which would bring in very little but it wl^d be a certainty. I shall talk to Cassel about it. He is too kind. He says he heard from you as to your financial aspirations[30] – more than I have! [...]

Your loving Mother
JSC

W HILE SIR Redvers Buller consolidated his position in Lady-smith and considered an advance northwards, Winston detached himself from the general and tried to transfer to forces of the commander-in-chief, Lord Roberts, whose troops were using a more easterly route to attack the Orange Free State.

The transfer was far from straightforward. Winston had written articles critical of Roberts' chief of staff, Lord Kitchener, for allowing British troops to kill wounded Dervishes after the Battle of Omdurman, a matter that had reached the floor of the House of Commons. As a former commander-in-chief in India, Roberts had known Winston's father well; he was not minded, however, to upset his chief of staff for the sake of accommodating a precocious twenty-five-year-old war correspondent.

– WSC to JSC –

1 May 1900   Bloemfontein

[no salutation]

I haven't had time to write to you since I came from Natal, because things have not been so satisfactory as I could have wished. I have been very uncomfortable, without any proper expedition and arrangements. [...] Lord Roberts made much difficulty about my coming as a

---

30 WSC asked Sir Ernest Cassel (as he now was) to invest his earnings as correspondent of the *Morning Post* in southern Africa.

correspondent with his army on the grounds that my presence here would probably be obnoxious to Lord Kitchener in consequence of *The River War*. [...]

I am so much looking forward to your letters from England, telling me about the feeling there regarding me, my writing and my affairs generally. I am rather in the dark concerning it here, but I think from the letters I receive from all sorts of strange correspondents that, although there is a considerable under-current of hostile and venomous criticism, upon the whole I have gained considerably by what has passed since I have been in South Africa. [...]

I have had several invitations to lecture in England and America, one of which I forwarded to you, and which has no doubt received your attention. Please see the enclosure[31] which I should like you to consider. [...] I do not relish lecturing in England, but you must remember how much money means to me, and how much I need it for political expense and other purposes, and, if I can make £3,000 by giving a score of lectures in the big towns throughout England on the purely military aspect of the war, it is very hard for me to refuse, but I should like you to ask Mr Balfour or Mr Chamberlain what they may think of such a course, and whether it would be likely to weaken my political position if I appeared as a paid lecturer on public platforms in this connection.

I do not know when this war will come to an end, and I have no intention of going Home until the Boers give in or Pretoria is taken: 'Here's to the friend that endureth to the end.' [...]

I should be so glad to get Home and occupy again a more dignified, if less powerful position than at present, and I have very nearly made up my mind to stand again for Oldham. They have implored me not to desert them. [...]

Mind you send me all the reviews on my new book on this war and I do hope you will realise the importance of making the very best

---

31 A letter from Gerald Christy's Lecture Agency, suggesting WSC undertake a lecture tour of Britain.

terms you can for me, both as a writer and lecturer. The sinews of war
are what I lack. [...]

Your ever loving son
Winston

J ENNIE WAS reaching her moment of decision as to whether
she would marry George. She worried not only about the social
and financial consequences of going ahead, but about the effect on
her relationship with her two sons, who still depended on her for
a home.

— JSC TO WSC —

26 May 1900   35a Cumberland Place

My dearest Winston

Your long letter from Bloemfontein dated May 1ˢᵗ has just reached
me, also one from Jack from the Biggarsberg Camp.[32] It was more than
welcome as you may imagine as I had heard nothing from either of you
since I've been home. I too have been, & am, more busy than I have ever
been, preparing for the 3ʳᵈ voyage of the *Maine*, finishing my "Hospital
Letters" which Longman is going to publish[33] & trying to cope with
bills & bores!

The *Maine* ought to arrive today at Capetown. The S.M.O. [Senior
Medical Officer] has been asked to fill her up as quickly as possible –
she is to return at once – & go out again. If this trip has not done well
without me, I shall probably go out [on] the 3ʳᵈ voyage.

But all my plans are vague. Sometimes I think I may marry G.W.
[George West]. I must not to you go over the old ground, but added to

---

32 Jack rejoined the South African Light Horse while Boer forces held a position
    on the ridge of the Biggarsberg range that ringed Ladysmith from the east to the
    north; Buller's forces did not breach these defences until mid-May.
33 Longman never published the 'Hospital Letters'.

the reasons in favour of it is his extraordinary devotion to me through all these trying times & my absence. Also the fact that it is possible for him to help me in a money way in the future if not at present.

There is no doubt that you will never settle down until you have a house of your own, & in the 4 years that I have had this house you have spent about 3 months in all in it. I mention this to show you why I do not feel that I would be breaking up our home if I do marry.

But there are so many things against my doing it that I doubt its ever coming off. At the same time do not be too astonished if I did – you know what you are to me & how you can now and always count on me. I am intensely proud of you, & apart from this, my heart goes out to you & I understand you as no other woman ever will.

Pamela is devoted to you & if yr love has grown as hers, I have no doubt it is only a question of time for you 2 to marry – what a comfort it will be to you to settle down in comparative comfort.

I am sure you are sick of the war & its horrors – you will be able to make a decent living out of your writings, & your political career will lead you to big things. Probably if you married an heiress you would not work half so well. But you may have a chance in America, tho' I do not urge you to try. You know I am not mercenary either for myself or you boys. More's the pity!

I long to see you & have a good talk. […]

[Incomplete]

———

BRITISH FORCES entered Johannesburg on 31 May, then took Pretoria, the capital of the South Africa Republic, on 5 June.

— WSC to JSC —

9 June 1900   Pretoria – again

Dearest Mamma,

As I thought, I have not found any opportunity to write you a letter since I left Bloemfontein, but I do hope that you will understand how rapid our movements have been, and how almost ceaseless the operations against the enemy. [...]

Now that Pretoria is taken I propose to come home, although as the line is at present cut by the Boers, and I may possibly go with General [Sir Ian] Hamilton to Heidelberg,[34] there may be some delay in starting. We shall, I think, fight an action tomorrow, which should have the effect of clearing the country east and north east of Pretoria, and should I come through all right I will seriously turn my face towards home [...].

I need not say how anxious I am to come back to England. Politics, Pamela, finances and books all need my attention. I do hope you will have been able to arrange good terms for me to lecture in the United States probably during December, January and February, and we can consider the desirability of my undertaking to lecture in England during the autumn when I come home. [...]

Best love, Ever your loving son
Winston

---

34 Fifty-five miles south of Pretoria; home of the Witwatersrand gold reef.

15

END OF AN ERA

1900–01

'Are all Mothers the same?'

JENNIE WAITED until Winston returned from Africa before she married George Cornwallis-West on 28 July 1900 at St Paul's Church in Knightsbridge. The Churchill family attended in force; the Cornwallis-Wests were absent.

Jennie was forty-six years old; George was twenty-five. The couple's age difference still offended much of Victorian society. Shortly before the ceremony, Jennie had torn up a letter from the Prince of Wales advising her not to proceed; the colonel of George's regiment told him he would have to resign if he went ahead. Defiantly, Jennie asked Winston to advertise in the papers that she wished in future to be known as Mrs George Cornwallis-West.

It was her younger son Jack's reaction, more than Winston's, which worried Jennie. Jack had not returned from southern Africa before the wedding and he was still only twenty years old. She realized that both boys would have to move out of her house in London once

George moved in as her husband. 'It seems hard, and it gives me a pang every time I think of it,' she admitted when breaking the news to Jack by letter.[1]

She wanted the boys to share a place in London that she would furnish and decorate, but Winston had other plans, thanks to an offer from his cousin Sunny, the young duke of Marlborough, with whom he had camped and travelled in southern Africa. The duke gifted his cousin the last two years of a lease on his set of bachelor rooms in Mount Street, Mayfair.

Winston had received offers to stand in several constituencies in the general election expected to be called for October 1900, but he had decided to keep faith with Oldham. He assured his mother he would move out of Cumberland Place before her honeymoon ended. He asked for a favour in return: that she would never show his letters to George.

Jennie's marriage to a man of his own age changed the relationship between Winston and his mother: he still depended on her for practicalities such as furnishing his rooms, but from this point onwards he seldom sought her approval for his plans or actions.

— WSC to JSC —

6 August 1900   35A Cumberland Place

My dearest Mamma,

Sunny has vy kindly offered me his rooms in London, unfurnished, for the unexpired portion of the lease – i.e. two years. I have of course accepted gladly and I shall move in there during the next few weeks. They are just what I wanted and will suit me capitally. I propose to take the furniture which you have offered me out of this room here – and I shall then be clear of the house before you return from abroad. [...] But all this can be left till you come back – I will just move in with bed, table & chest of drawers, and you shall settle everything else. [...]

---

1   23 July 1900, JSC letter to J. Churchill, CAC, PCHL 1/5.

I hope you will always understand that these letters are written for your eye alone and I could not write with any freedom if I felt they were ever to be read by any one else. Not that there is anything very intimate in this. [...]

> *Goodbye my dearest, Ever your loving son*
> *Winston*

— WSC TO JSC —

12 August 1900   Howick,[2] Lesbury, Northumberland

My dear Mamma,

[...] I cannot possibly concentrate my mind sufficiently to write you an article either worthy of your *Review* or of my literary reputation. I have got the material for the 'Ethics of Slaughter' in my head, and as soon as I have a week to myself, I will polish it off. Meanwhile since business is business I send you a cheque for the £50 you paid to the Oldham people. [...]

I am speaking at Oldham on Monday night & travel thither from here tomorrow morning early. After some days of wet and cold the sun is shining very brightly, and this pretty place with its beautiful flower garden is very pleasant to live in. It seems almost certain that the General Election will take place about the 15th of October. I have had an enormous number of invitations to speak for people about the country but have had, steadily, to refuse them, [...].

I must concentrate all my efforts upon Oldham. I am going to have a thorough campaign from the 20th to the 23rd of this month, speaking at 2 or 3 meetings every night upon the African question, and trotting through Cotton Mills and Iron works by day. Sunny is coming to help me. [...]

I sent a paragraph to the newspapers about your change of name, & I have seen it published in nearly all the principal Dailies. I hope

---

2   Howick Hall, home of Albert, Earl Grey, former MP, administrator of South Rhodesia 1896–8.

you are enjoying yourself in Paris, and that everything in the Garden is absolutely grand. [...]

Best love to George – I remain Ever your loving son
Winston

———

JENNIE HAD taken the proofs of the next edition of *The Anglo-Saxon Review* with her on her honeymoon, plus a sheaf of old bills for the attention of her new husband. Their long holiday took them through France, Belgium and then Scotland.

While they were still away, Winston wrote to his mother for the first time from his new address in Mount Street. He had cited Pamela as one of his three chief reasons for coming home, but it was politics, writing and his planned lecture tours that preoccupied him. Jennie mentioned to Jack that it was eight weeks since Pamela had received a letter from Winston – he did not after all appear ready to 'forgo the business of life' for her.

For his part Winston was more optimistic about the prospects for his lecture tours than about his chances at the general election. Oldham hosted the largest single concentration of cotton mills and spindles in Lancashire, which still accounted for half of the world's textile production. Yet employment had been falling steadily in the county throughout the 1890s as America, India and Japan each installed their own spinning and weaving capacities.[3]

Brokers on America's recently established cotton exchanges were also exploiting their new networks of information to the full, as they traded financial instruments such as commodity futures to influence (or manipulate, as many farmers and politicians saw it) the price of raw cotton. It was the era of cotton 'corners', the most notorious of which in 1903 would lead to a tripling of prices.

---

3   J. Robins, *Cotton and Race Across the Atlantic*, p. 30 *et seq.*

— WSC to JSC —

8 September 1900   105 Mount Street

My dear Mamma,

I am sorry not to be able to come until Wednesday morning, but I thought it better to attend the Annual Dinner of the Conference of the Institute of Journalists, at which I have been invited to reply for the war-correspondents. It is a good thing now and again to make a speech unconnected with politics and it is also a good thing, an opportunity not to be missed, to speak before an audience which represents practically the whole press, all the editors, all the writers of Great Britain. [...]

The arrangements for my lecturing tour are nearly finished; they include all the great towns of England and Scotland, and Belfast and Dublin in Ireland. They have taken the greatest halls in every place, The Free Trade Hall, Manchester, St George's Hall, Bradford, the St Andrews Hall in Glasgow, élite etc. [...]

Meanwhile I think the Election approaches, and the situation at Oldham will be much complicated by the great depression and struggle in the cotton trade, where the manufacturers of Lancashire have banded themselves together to try and break the necks of those odious American Corners which hold up cotton of a very inferior quality to a high price.

I am going to-night to see *Julius Caesar*[4] which I have looked forward to for a very long time, never having seen it given on the stage. I sail for America on December 1st, and I have perpetual engagements, political and otherwise, until then. [...]

Best love to George, Ever your loving son
Winston

---

4 William Shakespeare's tragedy, at Her Majesty's Theatre, Haymarket, owned by actor Herbert Beerbohm Tree.

Winston as the new member of parliament for Oldham, 1900.

– WSC to JSC –

20 September 1900   Crompton Hall,[5] Shaw, nr Oldham

Dear Miss Mamma,

I am too busy to write to you at any length but I hope that you and George will be able to come down here and stay at the Queen's Hotel, Manchester[6] for the last four or five days of the Election. It is thought that your presence here would do good, and if George takes any interest in electioneering, he will find plenty of opportunities of watching or of participating in it as much as he likes during the next fortnight.

Ever your loving son
Winston

---

5 Home of the Crompton family, cotton mill owners in Oldham.
6 Built in 1845 as the private home of textile merchant William Holsworth in Manchester's Piccadilly; converted by his nephew to an hotel; in 1898 *Manchester of Today* claimed 'its patrons compose the elite of all nationalities visiting the City'.

— WSC to JSC —

21 September 1900   Crompton Hall

My dear Mamma,

I write again to impress upon you how very useful your presence will be down here providing you really felt equal to coming down and doing some work. Mr Crisp[7] the other candidate has brought his wife down and she is indefatigable, going about trying to secure voters and generally keeping the thing going. I know how many calls there are on your time and from a point of view of pleasure I cannot recommend you to exchange the tranquil air of Scotland for the smoky tumult here, but I think it will be worth your while to see the close of the contest. [...]

I do not feel any great confidence in the result for although there is a great deal of enthusiasm everywhere and although things are better than last time I fear that in this constituency the organisation is still far from perfect as they will insist on managing it themselves, not allowing an expert or paid agent to do the work properly. [...] However I am not altogether without hope and I have been trying to get Mr Chamberlain to come down. I think perhaps a letter from you to Mr Balfour might have effect, he told me he might come down if there was a general election. [...].

Ever your loving son
Winston

J ENNIE ABANDONED the last stage of her honeymoon in Scotland where she left George while she helped Winston campaign in Oldham. The election was the first of several to be dubbed 'khaki elections' for its patriotic wartime backdrop and resulted in the Conservatives and Liberal Unionists defeating Campbell-Bannerman's Liberals by a margin of 130 seats. Winston was elected an MP in

7   Charles Crisp, the other Conservative candidate, came fourth in the poll.

Oldham on 1 October, defeating the second-placed Liberal candidate, Walter Runciman,[8] by a margin of 222 votes.

While Lord Salisbury embarked on the final leg of his third ministry, Parliament was not due to convene until February 1901. The delay provided Winston with a perfect window to carry out his programme of lectures in England and North America. Fortunately, he started with a trial run at his old school, Harrow.

— WSC TO JSC —

27 October 1900   105 Mount Street

Dearest Mamma,

[...] My lecture at Harrow last night was a success. But the lectures require much condensation. I only got a quarter through my notes in an hour and a half.

Your ever loving son
Winston

P.S. *Private* Sunny has given me £400 towards election expenses and has promised a £100 a year to keep up the registration.   WSC

———

THE BRITISH tour turned out to be a financial success: in just over a month Winston spoke at thirty venues, earning £3,782 from his share of the proceeds. When he reached the United States in December, however, his reception was rather different. Americans felt greater sympathy for the Boers, particularly in New York where many influential families shared their Dutch origins.

———

8   Runciman returned as an MP in 1902; he held office alongside WSC in Liberal governments before and during the First World War; he was still in office on 3 September 1939; created baron 1937. Father of Margaret Fairweather, the first woman to fly a Spitfire, and of historian Sir Stephen Runciman.

— WSC to JSC —

21 December 1900   Hotel Touraine,[9] Boston

[no salutation]

I encountered a great deal of difficulty in starting my tour properly. First of all the interest is not what Maj. Pond made out and secondly there is a strong pro Boer feeling, which has been fomented against me by the leaders of the Dutch, particularly in New York. However, all is now in train, but the profits are small compared to England [...].

I stayed with Bourke Cockran in New York, who worked indefatigably to make the lecture a success and who gave a large dinner party at the Waldorf before it. [...] In the end we had a very fine house in New York and Mark Twain,[10] who presided, made a most witty speech.

I get on very well with the audiences over here, although on several occasions I have had almost one-half of them strongly pro-Boer, and of course I do not have the great crowds that always came in England.

I stayed with Chauncey Depew[11] in Washington and he was very civil; showed me the Capitol, introduced me to a great many Senators of note and also presented me to the President,[12] with whom I was considerably impressed. [...]

I go to Canada tomorrow and shall spend Christmas with the Mintos,[13] both of whom have written me very charming letters. I hope my tour in Canada will be more congenial to me than this and I dislike the vulgar and offensive advertisements Pond has circulated

---

9   Opened in 1897, on the corner of Tremont and Boylston streets, near Boston Common.

10 Samuel Langhorne Clemens, who wrote *The Adventures of Tom Sawyer* (1876) and *The Adventures of Huckleberry Finn* (1885) under the pen name Mark Twain.

11 Elected United States senator from New York 1899; president, New York Central Railroad System; lawyer.

12 William McKinley, 25th president of the United States from 1897 until his assassination on 14 September 1901.

13 WSC had encountered Lord Minto, now governor-general of Canada, in India.

everywhere, but which I suppose are calculated to suit the temperament of the public. [...]

With best love, I remain, Your loving son
Winston

———

THE CROWDS at Winston's lectures were larger when the tour moved on to Canada at Christmas; but Major Pond had sub-contracted the events to Canadian promoters on terms that left his lecturer a smaller share of the takings than he was used to receiving in Britain.

Winston spent Christmas at Government House in Ottawa, where a familiar face from India, Lord Minto, had been governor-general since 1898. Another guest was Pamela Plowden, with whom Winston's romance had cooled since she had reportedly turned down a proposal from him in October.

— WSC TO JSC —

1 January 1901   Toronto

My dearest Mamma,

I was vy glad yesterday to get another letter from you. The lecture tour is by no means the success I had expected, although here in Canada there is a great deal more interest than in the States. Pond's terms are vy grasping compared to Christy's and he has been vy foolish in selling for fixed sums to local agents some of the best towns. For instance he sold Toronto for 500 dollars (£100) and the takings at the door amounted to near £450, out of which on his arrangement I got only £70. Naturally I protested against this sort of thing and we had a most unpleasant squabble. He is a vulgar Yankee impresario and poured a lot of very mendacious statements into the ears of the reporters and the whole business has been discussed in whole columns of all the papers. Peace has however, been patched up on my terms, and I propose to go through with the tour.

I had magnificent audiences in Montreal, Ottawa & Toronto and had great success with them, but did not benefit financially as I should have done, for the reason explained. Had I been able to foresee all this I would not have come but would have gone on with my tour in England which was more pleasant & far more profitable. [...]

I have spent 4 days at Ottawa with the Mintos which days were so pleasant that I shall go back again at the end of this week for 3 days more. Pamela was there – very pretty and apparently quite happy. We had no painful discussions, but there is no doubt in my mind that she is the only woman I could ever live happily with. [...]

I hope my dearest Mamma to be able to provide for myself in the future – at any rate until things are better with you. If you can arrange to relieve me of this loan,[14] with the interest of which I am heavily burdened – £300 per annum – I will not ask for any allowance whatever from you, until old Papa Wests [sic] decides to give you and G [George] more to live on. [...]

I am vy proud of the fact that there is not one person in a million who at my age could have earned £10,000 without any capital in less than two years. But sometimes it is vy unpleasant work. [...]

I am glad the article in the *Pall Mall* magazine[15] was well received. Of course writing articles is a considerable effort to me. I write vy rarely and when I do I like to get a vy wide circulation and to produce some little effect on the opinion of the country. But I will most certainly write something for your March number – though I wish we could join forces and work at some business-like publication – instead of your Pretty & Elegant *Anglo Saxon*; which will however win for you a place of your own in the history of 19ᵗʰ Century literature. [...]

> *Ever your loving son*
> *Winston S. Churchill*

---

14 Loan of £3,500, drawn by WSC in 1898 to fund his and Jack's living expenses for three years.
15 'The British Officer' appeared in the January 1901 issue of the *Pall Mall Magazine*, released December 1900.

WINSTON CLAIMED to have had 'no painful discussions' with Pamela, but he is thought to have tried to convince her to marry him one last time – without success. In a letter to Jennie, their host Lord Minto carefully described the atmosphere between the pair as 'very tolerably platonic'.[16]

By January 1901 *The Anglo-Saxon Review* had clearly failed commercially. Jennie's partner, John Lane, suggested that they should close it elegantly at the end of its second year of publication, with its eighth issue of March 1901. Jennie had demurred, so the December 1900 issue had appeared under her name alone. She considered Winston's suggestion of a merger with the rival publication, *St James's Gazette*, but nothing came of it.

On 22 January, while Winston was still lecturing in Canada, Queen Victoria died at home after sixty-three years on the British throne. Her son succeeded as Edward VII. Fifty-nine years old, jovial, portly and bearded, the new king was well known for his fondness of 'sweet women and dry champagne'. How he might change as king was the question that Winston put to his mother, who knew him better than most.

– WSC to JSC –

22 January 1901   Winnipeg

My dearest Mamma,

[…] So the Queen is dead. The news reached us at Winnipeg and this city far away among the snows – fourteen hundred miles from any British town of importance – began to hang its head and hoist half-masted flags.

A great and solemn event: but I am curious to know about the King. Will it entirely revolutionise his way of life? Will he sell his

---

16 R. Churchill, *WSC*, 1:544.

horses and scatter his Jews[17] or will Reuben Sassoon[18] be enshrined among the crown jewels and other regalia? Will he become desperately serious? Will he continue to be friendly to you? Will the Keppel[19] be appointed 1st Lady of the Bedchamber? Write to tell me all about this to Queenstown.[20] (SS *Etruria*[21] leaving New York on the 2nd prox).

[...] Edward the VIIth – gadzooks what a long way that seems to take one back![22] I am glad he has got his innings at last, and am most interested to watch how he plays it.

I have had a most successful meeting at Winnipeg. Fancy 20 years ago there were only a few mud huts – tents: and last night a magnificent audience of men in evening dress & ladies half out of it, filled a fine opera house and we took $1,150 at the doors. £230: more that is to say than in cities like Newcastle. Winnipeg has a wonderful future before it. ...

Always your loving son
Winston

PS I have been reading *An English Woman's Love Letters.*[23] Are all Mothers the same? *WSC*

---

17 The Prince of Wales enjoyed the company of rich friends, many of whom were Jewish, among them the Rothschilds and the Sassoons.
18 Director of a trading company founded by his father, David Sassoon, former treasurer of Baghdad; the Sassoons were sometimes known as the 'Rothschilds of the east'.
19 Alice Keppel, mistress of the Prince of Wales, now Edward VII, from 1898 (see People, p. 568).
20 On the south coast of Ireland, a common stop for transatlantic liners; originally known as Cove, since 1920 as Cobh (pronounced 'cove' in English).
21 Launched 1885; owned by Cunard Line; carried 550 1st class, 160 2nd class and 800 steerage class passengers.
22 The reign of Edward VI had ended on 6 July 1553.
23 Published in 1900, by an unknown author who later turned out to be a man, Laurence Housman.

16

BOTH HUNTED

1901–2

'Naturally we see little of each other'

W INSTON RETURNED to London in mid-February to start his new career as an MP. It was not the only aspect of his life that had changed so quickly. Two years earlier he had despaired at the prospect of his future finances; now he had saved £10,000. As he wrote later in *My Early Life*, 'I was entirely independent and had no need to worry about the future, or for many years to work at anything but politics.'[1]

On the day that he took his seat in Parliament, he made out a cheque to his perennially hard-up mother, in acknowledgement of her role in building his success.

---

1 W. Churchill, *My Early Life*, p. 358.

— WSC to JSC —

14 February 1901   [105 Mount Street]

My dearest Mama

I enclose a cheque for £300. In a certain sense it belongs to you; for I could never have earned it had not you transmitted to me the wit and energy which are necessary. […]

Your loving son
Winston

———

B Y T H E time he next wrote to his mother a month later, Winston had spoken in Parliament on four occasions. His new life was proving busier than he had expected, a problem that he compounded by agreeing to resume his lectures about the Boer War at the beginning of March, this time in a series of smaller English towns.

He asked his mother to help relieve the pressure by finding him 'a Secretary', by which he meant a male 'private secretary'.

— WSC to JSC —

13 March 1901   105 Mount Street

Dearest Mamma

As usual I am hunted to death. I have more than 100 letters unanswered. 30 or 40 I have not even had time to read. I am lecturing twice today at Hastings[2] and I shall be back here early tomorrow. It is quite evident to me that I cannot go on without a Secretary, and if you would try to get me one as a temporary measure, it would be an enormous help to me. […]

I wish I had a little time to live and it is quite clear to me that unless I get a Secretary, I shall be pressed into my grave with all sorts of ridiculous things – which I have no need whatever to do. After all

---

2   WSC lectured at 3 p.m. and 8 p.m., earning over £100 for the day.

if I were to spend the time I take answering invitations, letters from constituents, and doing all that little business myself in writing articles I could pay the salary of a Secretary twice over. What I want is a gentleman immediately, who will come for a month or six weeks while I can look around and make some definite arrangements.

Also please try to find me a box to put letters in, a large compendious cabinet, with all kinds of drawers and holes of every kind that I can put papers in. There is a pile on my table now which quite stifles me. [...]

[unsigned]

A FTER A few weeks in Parliament, Winston wrote to his mother of his disenchantment with the senior members of the Conservative and Liberal Unionist government that was still led by Lord Salisbury, now seventy-one years old.

— WSC TO JSC —

23 March 1901   105 Mount Street

My dear Mamma

[...] I polished off three more lectures at Bournemouth, Southampton and Portsmouth,[3] and cleared about £220 out of the three. I have decided definitely to play polo this year in a team which is being formed by young military friends, and I think if I get two days a week at Hurlingham or Ranelagh,[4] it will provide me with the physical exercise and mental countercurrent which these late hours and continual sittings of the house absolutely require. [...]

I have been looking through the speeches with a view to boiling them down, but I do not think I shall be able to do anything in this line

---

3 Bournemouth and Southampton on 20 March, Portsmouth on 21 March.
4 WSC joined the Ranelagh Club at Barn Elms, south-west of London, rather than the more expensive Hurlingham Club in Fulham; he paid an annual subscription of 15 guineas.

until the Autumn. Practically, one would miss the Spring Publication Season now, and while Parliament is sitting I have not much time or vital energy for bookmaking.[5]

There is a good deal of dissatisfaction in the Party, and a shocking lack of cohesion. The Government is not very strong. [...] and the whole Treasury Bench appear to me to be sleepy and exhausted and played out. As for Joe [Chamberlain][6] he devotes his attention exclusively to the Boer business, and I am not sure that things in this direction are not looking a little brighter.

Your loving son,
Winston

ON 13 May 1901, Winston spoke against the government's policy of increasing spending on the army rather than the navy, as proposed by the secretary of state for war, St John Brodrick. By the middle of the year, Winston was dining regularly with other young disaffected Conservative MPs, including Lord Hugh Cecil, who gave the small group its name of the Hughligans (or Hooligans). Several members of the Liberal Party were invited to join the Hughligans' dinners.

Winston did not write his next letter to his mother until nine months later, once Parliament had started its Christmas recess. Its text clearly suggests that he wrote it from Blenheim where he was to spend a week hunting and shooting, although he used stationery headed by the address of his home in Mount Street.

Jennie had commented on how little she now saw or heard of her son, who in the course of 1901 had spoken in Parliament nine times, given twenty lectures and addressed political gatherings in at least thirty towns and cities.

---

5   WSC later made a small book out of his early speeches about army reform, *Mr Brodrick's Army*, published 1903.
6   At the time secretary of state for the colonies, responsible for southern Africa (see People, p. 572).

During the parliamentary season Winston's diary shows a constant stream of lunches and dinners, including several with John Morley,[7] a senior Liberal and the biographer of William Gladstone. The Liberals had their eye on the new MP for Oldham: it was Morley who recommended that Winston read *Poverty: A Study of Town Life* by the social reformer Seebohm Rowntree. The book, a study of the urban poor in York, was to have a profound effect on Winston's political thinking.

— WSC to JSC —

13 December 1901   [Blenheim]

My dear Mamma,

[...] I had a wretched day yesterday. I started by the 10.15 train to open a bazaar at Oldham. I shd have arrived at 2.30. The bazaar was at 3. But when I got to Stafford[8] all the telegraph wires were broken by the gale and the poles in many cases lay across the railroad; so that it was 4 o'clock before I even reached Crewe.[9] Then I came back to London, it being useless to proceed further, and reached Euston at 10 o'clock after a most unprofitable day.

Today we have shot 500 rabbits in the park, wh was good fun as we were but three guns. Tomorrow I hunt; Sunday – Tring: and then if only the weather keeps open I shall get 6 days hunting next week, for I have my own 4 horses and some of Sunny's.

Two years ago I was in solitude with the vulture sixty miles from Pretoria and 250 from the frontier. It is strange to look back on these anniversaries from amid such peaceful surroundings.[10]

I dined with John Morley on Wedy night: most pleasant [...].

---

7 Former chief secretary for Ireland and a future secretary of state for India (see People, p. 574).
8 150 miles north-west of London.
9 30 miles beyond Stafford.
10 WSC escaped from his Boer captors on the evening of 12 December 1899.

Everybody so kind and caressing, particularly the host, who like so many of these Liberals commands my affection at once.

No my dear, I do not forget you. But we are both of us busy people, absorbed in our own affairs, and at present independent. Naturally we see little of each other. Naturally, that makes no difference to our feelings.

I remain always, Your loving son
Winston S.C.

———

I N ADDITION to pursuing field sports, Winston had travelled to Blenheim to broach the subject of his mother's finances with the duke of Marlborough. George Cornwallis-West's father still refused to make over any family money to his son after his marriage to Jennie. As a result the couple's finances remained severely stretched. For his part, Winston resented the interest that he was still paying on the loan he had taken out three years earlier so that he and his brother Jack could draw a monthly living allowance.

The duke did not give much away at first, except to criticize the extravagance of his cousin's hunting arrangements. Winston also tried to intercede on his mother's behalf with one of the trustees of his father's will trust, the former George Curzon who was now Earl Howe.

— WSC to JSC —

[December 1901]   105 Mount Street

Mamma,

I have just seen George Howe. He is vy sympathetic, but I do not think you can expect an immediate decision. He wants you to tell Lumley to make him a definite proposition by post on Monday. I do not think this can be accelerated. [...]

Your loving son
W

WINSTON NEXT wrote to his mother on 3 April 1902, the day that Pamela Plowden married the earl of Lytton. He had wished her 'all happiness and good fortune which wit and beauty deserve', assuring her that he would always be counted 'amongst your devoted friends'.[11]

Parliament was enjoying its Easter recess. Following the demise of *The Anglo-Saxon Review*, Jennie tried to boost her income by writing press articles and, in another sign of the reversal of their former roles, she now asked for Winston's help with one of her first efforts. (A collection of the articles that she wrote for *Pearson's Magazine* appeared in 1916 under the title of *Short Talks on Big Subjects*.)

— WSC TO JSC —

3 April 1902   105 Mount Street

My dear Mamma,

I am vy sorry to hear George has not been well; but I hope you and he wil be able to come to Blenheim on Sunday, for Sunny tells me he has asked you.

I have read through the article. There is a great deal of interesting matter in it; and I have nothing to say to the style; but I think there is a great lack of arrangement which makes it hard to follow and would militate against its success. It should I am sure be well worth your while to group your ideas again – making up your mind exactly what is the intention of each particular paragraph.

This would involve writing the article out again; but not comprising any new material. I enclose you a suggested skeleton which I have sketched out for you.

Yours always with best love
Winston S.C.

---

11 February 1902, WSC letter to P. Plowden, cited the *Guardian*, 9 November 2003.

B Y THE summer of 1902, Winston had secured permission from his father's literary executors to use Lord Randolph's papers to write a biography. He therefore spent much of the first part of Parliament's summer recess researching his subject in the Muniment Room of Blenheim Palace where the family archives were kept.

— WSC TO JSC —

15 August 1902   Blenheim

My dearest Mamma,

[...] I have been wading through two of the eighteen boxes of papers and they are certainly most full of valuable and interesting material. There are here all your early letters which are most carefully put away. [...]

There emerges from these dusty records a great and vivid drama, and I feel at each step a growing confidence that I shall be able to write what many will care to read. But I do not mean to put pen to paper until the whole of the evidence is before me, and as there are six times as many papers as those I have looked through you will understand that my days are very fully occupied. [...]

Will you send me a copy of the scrap-book you have of my Father's newspaper-cuttings, and please keep turning over in your mind any way you can help me in collecting material; all is grist that comes to my mill and the more saturated I am with the subject before I begin to write the better the work will be. [...]

Always your loving son,
Winston S. Churchill

I N SEPTEMBER 1902, Winston joined the ranks of politicians who were invited to stay for a few days at the royal family's private castle and estate at Balmoral in Scotland. Acquired by Queen Victoria in 1848 and later rebuilt by her husband Prince Albert in 1855, the castle had acquired a reputation among its visitors as a cold and draughty building. Yet no ambitious politician could afford to turn down an invitation a time when royal favour – or disfavour – could still affect his ministerial prospects.

– WSC to JSC –

27 September 1902   Balmoral

Dearest Mamma,

I have been vy kindly treated here by the King, who has gone out of his way to be nice to me. It has been most pleasant & easy going & today the stalking was excellent, tho I missed my stags.

You will see the King on Weds when he comes to Invercauld;[12] mind you gush to him about my having written to you saying how much etc etc I had enjoyed myself here.

I go to Dalmeny[13] with Lord R [Rosebery] tomorrow morning by car. Write me a line there & send me yr notes – if you have done them! I daresay other attractions have interrupted and delayed the task.

Ever your loving son
Winston S.C.

———

F ROM DALMENY Winston travelled to his aunt Cornelia's home at Canford Manor in Dorset, where he hoped to find more material for the biography of his father.

– WSC to JSC –

9 October 1902   Canford

Dearest Mamma,

I have now been here two days and find very valuable material indeed for my work. Cornelia had kept Scrap Books of almost every

---

12 Seat of the earl of Mar, adjoining Balmoral (see Places, p. 580).
13 On the Firth of Forth, near Edinburgh, home of the earl of Rosebery (see Places, p. 579).

The main staircase of Canford Manor, the home of Winston's
Aunt Cornelia and her husband Lord Wimborne.

incident of my Father's life, and with the letters which she also had, the material is now almost complete.

My secretary has gone away to India, (like a lot of other silly people)! so that I am very much stranded in regard to correspondence. Will you find out from Miss Anning[14] whether she could come to me, two days a week let us say, and she could make whatever arrangement would be suitable to her. It is essential that I should have someone that could answer the simple letters that I receive.

I come back for Parlt on 15th. Dinner?

Your ever loving son
Winston SC

EARLY IN December Winston travelled to Egypt for the ceremonial opening of the Aswan Dam across the River Nile. He was a guest of his mother's friend Sir Ernest Cassel, who had arranged the funding for the dam's construction. Sir Ernest's other guests included the king's younger brother, the duke of Connaught, his wife and Winston's aunt Leonie, who was particularly close to the duke.

This letter from Aswan evidenced Winston's distinctive attitude to industrial relations, which lay outside the mainstream of the Conservative Party and echoed his father's attempts, twenty years earlier, to build a new brand of 'Tory democracy'.

Trade unions had been legalized and given the right to strike in 1871. A decision of the House of Lords in July 1901, however, held that the Amalgamated Society of Railway Servants was liable for the financial losses suffered by the Taff Vale Railway Company as a result of a strike of its workforce. The Conservative government declined to change the law in 1902; an amendment had to await the Trade Disputes Act of 1906, an early piece of legislation enacted by the new Liberal government.

---

14 JSC's secretary at the time.

— WSC to JSC —

8 December 1902   Assouan

Dearest Mamma,

It was very pleasant to get your letter, and makes me realise that we may lose much by not writing more. But I have to use my pen so often & here I can find no shorthand writer.

I am not very well, having a touch of fever and – so the doctor asserts – of rheumatism, and today I am left alone on deck while everyone else is gone to see the dam. The Connaughts and Leonie arrive tomorrow & I still hope to attend the function. But after all that was not my only object in coming to Egypt. The trip so far has been vy comfortable & everything has moved on smoothly oiled wheels. The steamer is magnificent – the food good – too good I fear for me at present, and the company very kind and even-tempered. [...]

The Trade Union matter is as you suppose tiresome and difficult. There is much reason in their case: yet they make unreasonable demands. These demands the Conservatives meet with flat refusal. I want to see them grapple with the difficulties & remove the force from the demand by conceding all that is just in it. But middle courses are proverbially unpopular. [...]

I often think of you and Jack: and feel v anxious about him. Please concentrate your attention on him. He is rather untamed & forlorn.

Always your loving son
Winston

A GED TWENTY, Jack had returned from the Boer War in October 1900, reluctantly resuming his place at Sir Ernest Cassel's side in the City. His family's shortage of money had ruled out his becoming a full-time soldier or attending university. Jack did not find the work with Sir Ernest challenging, so spent as much time as he could either as a part-time soldier with the Oxfordshire Hussars (he had now reached the rank of captain) or helping his brother to sort through their father's papers at Blenheim.

— WSC to JSC —

19 December 1902   Savoy Hotel, Cairo

My dearest Mamma,

[...] Well here we are back in Cairo after what I would say has been a satisfactory and pleasant expedition. I have seen all the temples and sights and have pressed forward with my writing also to no inconsiderable extent.

Cassel is an excellent host — never exacting or touchy, always the same — and most anxious for everybody's comfort & contentment. Mrs Keppel is very good company & we have made other friends. Now there is a scheme — of which I have been given the arrangement — for a four days tour through the desert on camels to Fayoum, an oasis about 70 miles away from the Nile [south-west of Cairo]. We start on Monday so I shall not be able to catch my boat before the 29th via Brindisi or possibly even the 1st via Naples. I wonder whether we could meet in Paris. ...

This land is overflowing with agricultural prosperity and the people sprawl continuously on full bellies under a genial sun. I fear our poor folks at home are far from this happy state now that the winter threatens to be such a hard one. You will see in the near future what vindication my views of two years ago on economy and Army policy will remain and how much support they will get.

Always your loving son
Winston

17

THE PIG GOES TO MARKET

1903–5

'I cannot help admiring Chamberlain's courage'

J ENNIE AND Winston's correspondence broke off in the early part
of 1903 before resuming in August. The question that dominated
British politics after May of that year was 'free trade' versus 'tariff
reform', an issue that threatened to split the governing Conservative
Party.

Arthur Balfour had succeeded his uncle Lord Salisbury as the
party's leader and prime minister in July of the previous year. Balfour
sympathized with those who felt that greater prosperity would follow
the expansion of 'free trade' around the world; on the other side
of the argument, however, Joseph Chamberlain and his followers
favoured a policy of 'tariff reform', which would retain free trade
within the British empire, but erect a protective barrier around it.

A self-made businessman, Chamberlain hailed from the city of
Birmingham rather than from the Tory shires. Balfour accommo-
dated Chamberlain for as long as he could, by deploying his verbal

dexterity and professing that he leaned towards neither one side nor the other in the debate.

Winston's sympathies lay unequivocally with the 'free traders', even though his parliamentary constituency of Oldham was a natural breeding ground for 'tariff reform', because the town's textile industry depended on imports of raw cotton from inside the empire.

— WSC TO JSC —

12 August 1903   105 Mount Street
Private

Dearest Mamma,

[...] I have had eight small meetings in Oldham of 200 a piece, and have been extremely well received as you will see from the papers, and the Central Executive there have passed a unanimous vote of confidence in me although I have expressed myself unequivocally against the great man [Joseph Chamberlain].

There are of course a lot of Protectionist and Fair traders in the party there, and there is no doubt that everything will have to be handled very carefully; but they are all quite agreed in recognising that I am the only person that has got the slightest chance of winning the Election for the Tory party there, and in consequence, they are pleased to give me very wide liberty. [...]

All the evidence that I get here shows that Arthur Balfour is going to break with Chamberlain, and that Joe will leave the Government with a certain following and will drive on his own wild career as an independent person. This means his ruin. [...] I cannot help admiring Chamberlain's courage. I do not believe he means to give way an inch, and I think he is quite prepared to sacrifice his whole political position and [his brother] Austen's as well, for the cause in which he is so wrapped up. Of course the Unionist Free Traders will support Mr Balfour with great determination if Chamberlain should leave the Government.

I hope your cure has been satisfactory. I find myself in very good health but I shall be glad to lead a quiet, regular, temperate life, for a month. I shall do my exercises every day. [...]

I think you should write me a nice long letter in answer to this.

Ever your loving son
W

ON 9 September 1903, Chamberlain privately offered his resignation to Balfour, whose initial response was characteristically ambivalent.

— WSC TO JSC —

11 September 1903   Guisachan

Dearest Mamma,

You know I hate purposeless letters & will understand my silence hitherto. But I am really sorry not to be able to come to Lochmore.[1] It would however be an exhausting journey, merely for one or two days, & I am vy happy here working at my book. I got no answer to my telegram of two days ago and finally decided to abandon the project.

I have no news except that A. Balfour is believed to be about to issue a 'patching up' manifesto. I wonder what success it will have. J.C. [Joseph Chamberlain] is plainly beaten alike in scientific argument and popular opinion.

Please put everything straight for me with your host and hostess.[2]

Ever your loving son,
Winston

---

1 Estate in Sutherland, owned by the duke of Westminster.
2 The duke and duchess of Westminster, who was then Shelagh née Cornwallis-West, sister of JSC's husband George.

O N 14 September, Balfour forced the resignations of two of his 'free trade' ministers; a third resigned in protest the following day. On 18 September, just as Winston was writing to his mother from Scotland, Balfour announced all four departures, including that of Chamberlain, as a balanced package.

— WSC to JSC —

18 September 1903   Invercauld

Dearest Mamma,

I am indeed sorry to miss you here: but we shall see each other often in the autumn, & I may need your assistance in Oldham, if you have time & inclination.

The situation is most interesting & I fancy a smash must come in a few days. Mr Balfour is coming to Balmoral on Saturday. Is he going to resign or reconstruct? If he resigns will the King send for Spencer[3] or Devonshire?[4] If for either will he succeed in forming a govt & what kind of government? If he reconstructs – will it be a Protectionist reconstruction of a cabinet wh does not contain the Free Trade Ministers, or a Free Trade reconstruction of a Cabinet from which JC has resigned. All these things are possible.

I go to Dalmeny tomorrow. Write to me there. I have put my name down at Balmoral but I fear I am in disgrace.

Your loving son
Winston S.C.

———

W INSTON'S ASSUMPTION of royal disfavour will have arisen from the public position he had taken in favour of 'free trade' at a time when many senior Tories preferred to paper over the party's

---

3   Earl Spencer led the Liberal party in the House of Lords.
4   The duke of Devonshire, lord president of the council; he had first resigned, then withdrawn his resignation during this crisis.

cracks and the king was privately assumed to favour 'Imperial preference'. Winston, for example, had been one of the prime movers in July behind the formation of the Free Food League and had criticized both Balfour and Chamberlain in the House of Commons.

On 2 October 1903, Balfour finally showed a glimpse of his hand, implying in a speech at Sheffield that he was sympathetic towards changing his party's attachment to 'free trade', the policy it had espoused for fifty years. A number of Winston's friends were trying to use the issue to prise him away from the Conservative Party towards the Liberals: among them was his Aunt Cornelia, whose son Ivor Guest was a fellow member of Parliament. 'Of one thing I think there is no doubt,' she wrote to Winston in mid-October, '& that is that Balfour & Chamberlain are one, and that there is no future for Free Traders in the Conservative Party. Why tarry?'[5]

Winston arrived at her Dorset home at the end of November for a week's shooting. By this time he had made up his mind in the next session of Parliament to 'act consistently with the Liberal party'. As he put it privately in a letter to his close political colleague, Lord Hugh Cecil (drafted on 24 October but never sent): 'Free Trade is so essentially Liberal in its sympathies & tendencies that those who fight for it must become Liberals'.[6]

On Tuesday 1 December Winston travelled from Canford to Cardiff, where he spoke on the subject of 'Our Fiscal Policy – Dumping and Retaliation'.

— WSC TO JSC —

4 December 1903   Canford Manor, Wimborne

Dearest Mamma,

[...] We have had a very pleasant week here with good shooting

---

5   15 October 1903, Lady Wimborne letter to WSC, R.Churchill, *WSC* 2:69.
6   24 October 1903, WSC draft letter to Lord Hugh Cecil, R. Churchill, *WSC*, 2:71–2.

and all my friends. Much talk about Free Trade and politics, general conclusion in favour of much stronger and more detailed action. [...]

Cardiff was a great success, I spoke nearly an hour and a half listened to with the closest attention by an immense audience. Nothing could exceed the gush of the Cardiff papers, they say no meeting in Cardiff for many years has produced such an impression and speaking for myself, I have never had a more friendly welcome.

Chelsea Town Hall is fixed for Thursday, the 10th.[7] Do try to be there and make a supper party afterwards for friends. The meeting, I think, is going to be a very big one.

Best love

W

WINSTON KNEW that his stand for 'free trade' would cause him difficulties with his constituency association in Oldham. On 8 January 1904 a majority of its members resolved that their MP had lost their confidence and could no longer rely on their support at the next election. He therefore started to cast his eyes over alternative seats. At the same time he had to deal with his mother's renewed financial difficulties.

— WSC TO JSC —

26 March 1904   105 Mount Street

Dearest Mamma,

I am sorry not to be able to come down to Bournemouth; but I have had a deputation here this afternoon from B'ham [Birmingham], asking me to contest the Central Division, & I could hardly have reached you for dinner. [...]

I am sorry and startled to hear of these new financial difficulties.

---

7   WSC's 1903 diary confirms the engagement, without specifying the organiser of the meeting, CAC, CHAR 1/38/37.

I will not worry you by discussing these now: but I look with vy grave anxiety into the future. I don't care to think where we shall all finish up. I have told Jack to visit [Theodore] Lumley on Monday and ask him to draw up a scheme, which I will consider. But whether it will be practicable or not I cannot say.

I shall be in London on Monday night and will dine with you if you like at 35a [Great Cumberland St].

Your affectionate son
Winston

I N MID-FEBRUARY of 1904, Winston had made an outspoken speech at the Free Trade Hall in Manchester that included a passage taunting 'tariff reformers whose eloquence had been so much praised, whose rhetoric was so convincing ... that when they rose to address the House of Commons the members hurried out of the Chamber by the nearest way'.

On 29 March, Arthur Balfour gave Winston a taste of his own medicine by walking out of the Commons chamber as his young backbencher began a speech; the prime minister was soon followed by other ministers and the majority of Tory backbenchers.

On 3 April Winston wrote to his constituency party offering to resign as their MP, while carefully leaving open the possibility of standing again at the by-election that would follow. Taking the hint, his local association chose to live with him as their MP until the next general election, which was due in eighteen months.

On 31 May, the day after Parliament's Whitsun recess, Winston finally crossed the floor of the House of Commons to sit with the Liberal members. His parting of the way with the Conservative Party proved exhausting, so Winston relaxed in August by helping his mother and George Cornwallis-West to clear the weeds from the moat of the medieval home that they had leased outside London – as an economy measure. The downstairs rooms of Salisbury Hall, near St Albans, were oak-panelled; upstairs, in one of the eight bedrooms,

King Charles II was supposed to have entertained his mistress Nell Gwyn.

In this new setting Jennie and Winston talked at length about reining in her expenditure until the death of George's father, when they hoped that some of his family money might finally come their way (they were to be disappointed: Colonel William Cornwallis-West would not die until 1917, at the age of eighty-two).

Winston left in mid-August for the Alpine air of Switzerland where he was to spend three weeks as a guest of financier Sir Ernest Cassel in his newly built mountain chalet. He hoped to make some early inroads into the writing of his father's biography.

— WSC to JSC —

22 August 1904   [Villa Cassel, Mörel, Valais, Switzerland]

Dearest Mamma,

I have waited a week, so as to be able to write with certainty about the effect wh this place produces. It is wholly good. I sleep like a top & have not ever felt in better health. Really it is a wonderful situation. A large comfortable 4-storied house – complete with baths, a French cook & a private band & every luxury that would be expected in England – is perched on a gigantic mountain spur 9000 feet high, & is the centre of a circle of the most glorious snow encountered in Switzerland.

The air is buoyant & the weather has been delightful. Nearly every day is cool & bright, so that we can sleep with windows wide open & breakfast & dinner on the verandah. There are all kinds of beautiful walks & climbs, from the modest twenty minutes on the flat to very formidable scrambles & excursions. Far below in the valleys which drop on both sides of the house the clouds are drifting, & beneath & through these – green plains & tiny toy churches & towns. […]

The days pass pleasantly & vy rapidly. I am astonished to think I have been here a week. It seems three days since we cleared the duck weed from the Elizabethan moat. I divide them into three parts. The mornings when I read & write: the afternoons when I walk – real long walks & climbs about these hills or across the glacier: the evenings – of course 4 rubbers of bridge then bed. [...]

I thought a good deal over all you said to me about yourself & I feel sure you are right to concentrate on & take pains with the few people you really care about. But I have no doubt that when papa W[est] is at length gathered to Abraham you will be able to renew your youth like the eagle.[8] [...]

Ever your loving son
Winston

– WSC to JSC –

25 August 1904 [Villa Cassel]

Dearest Mamma,

[...] I have been working away at my book and am slowly getting into my stride. But the difficulty of the task impresses me as I proceed. What to leave out, how to work this in, what line to take in regard to a whole series of conflicting or contradictory letters? At present I am writing nearly everything. It will be easy to cut it down afterwards. [...]

Your affectionate son
Winston

– WSC to JSC –

1 September 1904 [Villa Cassel]

Dearest Mamma,

Your letter of 25ᵗʰ ult: seems to have wandered strangely on the road, through your using the telegraphic not the postal address – wh was not to say the last of it – clever.

I leave here Sunday 4ᵗʰ, spend Monday & perhaps Tuesday in Paris

---

8 Psalm 103, verse 5: 'Who satisfieth thy mouth with good things; so that thy youth is renewed like the eagle's.'

with Sunny, & will arrive at the ancient & moated mansion [Salisbury Hall] on Wed^y. [...]

I am now writing about your Russian expedition[9] wh makes an interesting episode.

Yours always

W

———

AT THE end of the first week of September Winston returned to Salisbury Hall, where he found that he could continue his writing with few interruptions. As a result he decided to stay put and to cancel the annual pilgrimage to Scotland on which his mother had already set off with George.

His first stop was to have been Guisachan, the home of his uncle by marriage Lord Tweedmouth,[10] a veteran Liberal politican whose wife Fanny (a Spencer-Churchill aunt) had just died of cancer.

— WSC TO JSC —

14 September 1904   Salisbury Hall

Private

Dearest Mamma,

I have been making such good progress here – alone all day – that I cannot bring myself to cart all my traps to Scotland tonight. In any case I shall stay here until Saturday. If you thought it possible for me to stay on in the absence of the Waldens[11] with Scrivings[12] & the kitchen maid – I would not leave at all. Here I can get my proofs day by day from the printers & all my material is at hand. This staying in one place – and

---

9 Lord Randolph Churchill and JSC travelled to Russia in the winter of 1887–8.
10 Chancellor of the duchy of Lancaster in the earl of Rosebery's cabinet (see People, p. 564).
11 Valet and cook to JSC and her husband (see People, p. 578).
12 Valet to WSC (see People, p. 578).

such a nice place – without continual disturbances has comforted me very much.

JM [John Morley] whom I saw yesterday begged me to press on with the work – of which he held most encouraging opinions. He seems to think I shall make a great deal of money, 8 or 10 thousand pounds perhaps. It is worth making a sustained effort.

I know how much time & energy is wasted moving about. Will you explain all this to T [Tweedmouth] or must I write him a separate letter. It would be a great relief to me not to go to Scotland at all. [...]

Your loving son

W

— WSC to JSC —

24 September 1904   Blenheim Palace

Dearest Mamma,

Jack departing for Blenheim on Saturday last, coupled with the flight of the Waldens, decided me to come too and I have moved a greater part of my tin boxes here and am now settled in the Arcade Rooms which are most comfortable.[13]

Consuelo[14] is quite alone here, and as you are not going to be at SH [Salisbury Hall] except for the Sunday, I don't think I will move until I go to Manchester which I do on 30th for two days on political and semi-political work. [...]

You will laugh when I tell you that I spent last Thursday night at Highbury[15] and had five or six hours most pleasant and interesting conversation with Joe [Chamberlain] about old letters and old politics. I suggested an interview in London and he replied by an invitation to dine and sleep. He is, of course, tremendously partisan in his views

---

13 Situated below Blenheim's Long Library, with a view over the water terraces towards the lake; now renamed.
14 Duchess of Marlborough, née Vanderbilt, American-born (see People , p. 565).
15 Highbury Hall, Birmingham; built by Joseph Chamberlain 1878; his home until his death in 1914.

both on me and things, but it was quite clear to me that we understand each other on lots of questions, and that my company was not at all unpleasant to him. [...]

I have done a quantity of work here – another whole chapter since I have been here and I am incubating the material for the Home Rule chapter which is one of the most important of the book. [...]

You see I am entirely bound up in the biography. Indeed I find it quite difficult now to turn my mind on to political speeches but it will be a change.

With best love, Your ever loving son
Winston S.C.

ON 10 November, Winston delivered a speech at St Andrew's Hall in Glasgow that criticized Balfour's government for increasing the power of the executive while reducing that of Parliament. He claimed that 'capitalistic interests had captured the government', illustrating his point by noting that two-thirds of all ministers held concurrent positions as company directors.

The chairman of the meeting, Mr Norman Lamont, had opened proceedings by claiming that Balfour's (temporary) illness had occurred 'in the nick of time' to save him from political disaster.[16]

– JSC to WSC –

12 November 1904   Sandringham

My dearest Winston

I read your speech at Glasgow with much interest. I did <u>not</u> discuss it with the King, you will be surprised to hear. I think it was rather a pity your chairman attacked A.B. [Arthur Balfour] the way he did. I see the audience resented it – at least so the papers make out. Henri de Breteuil tells me that in France, they look upon you as the coming man.

---

16 11 November 1904, *The Times.*

Here I am in a hotbed of protectionists. You have probably seen the party in the papers.[17] We have been asked to stay on till Monday. It has been most pleasant nice weather, pleasant people & excellent sport. George shot very well & we both seem in good favour – so <u>that</u> is all right.

Where shall you be next week? Salisbury Hall is at your disposal if you want to come. [...] We are thinking of going off to Paris for Xmas – why don't you come? The Breteuils would put you up. Now goodbye.

Yr loving
Mother

— WSC TO JSC —

15 November 1904   Dalmeny House

Dearest Mamma,

I shall be back in London either Thursday or Friday & am looking forward to spending a week at S.H. Your letter was vy pleasant to receive, & I am so glad that you have enjoyed yourself at Sandringham.

Glasgow was a very great success, & there is no doubt that I have made a very distinct impression on the city. They all declared that no such speech had been delivered in St. Andrew's Hall for many years. The whole audience stood up at the end, wh is vy rare in Scotland. Cock-a-doodle-doo!! [...]

Always your loving son
W.

————

D URING A week spent in Scotland, Winston's diary shows that he made four speeches, on 10, 11, 14 and 16 November.[18]

---

17 It included the marquis and marquise of Breteuil, Count Mensdorff (ambassador of Austria-Hungary), the marquis du Lau, the duke of Richmond, Lady Cadogan, Lady Maud Warrender, Mr and Mrs George Keppel and Henry Chaplin MP.

18 1904 WSC diary, CAC, CHAR 1/48/1.

— WSC to JSC —

17 November 1904   105 Mount Street

Dearest Mamma,

Scotland has been very successful, but I am glad it is over as I had to make so many speeches. I was quite wearied out.

I am going to hunt Friday and Saturday as I think I really deserve a holiday after my Scottish toils but I will come down Saturday night if possible – any way Sunday morning – and propose to stay with you – with the exception of Monday night – until I go to Panshanger on the 26th. [...]

Your loving son
W

———

WINSTON'S POLITICS and writing, in combination, had proved all-consuming during his thirtieth year. It took the head of the family, the duke of Marlborough, to point out that they had led him to neglect his mother's affairs, which were heading for yet another crisis.

— WSC to JSC —

21 January 1905   105 Mount Street

Dearest Mamma,

I have had this morning a long talk with Sunny about your affairs. He wants me to go into the whole matter with [Theodore] Lumley and to consider whether or not it would be desirable to transfer the business of looking after the property [Lord Randolph's will trust] to some other lawyer.

He tells me that both you and George have dwelt with emphasis upon my repeated refusal to take any interest in the matter. But you will allow me to say that I really have no right to interrogate Lumley without your authority. Will you therefore write me a letter authorising me to go into the whole matter and examine all the accounts. I will then endeavour to do that almost at once. […]

Ever your loving son

W

T HE NEW crisis in Jennie's affairs arose because the Norwich Union insurance company, which had loaned Lord Randolph's will trust a large sum of money six years earlier, was now insisting on examining a set of accounts to check whether the trust was being properly administered. Lumley could not compile these accounts because he had never succeeded in taming Jennie's spending or disciplining her to record it.

Characteristically, Jennie's response to her difficulties was to carry on travelling in the style to which she was accustomed.

— JSC TO WSC —

22 January 1905   Salisbury Hall

My dearest Winston

I enclose you a letter you can show Lumley if you like. It would be a very good thing if you could look into the whole thing. I am sure it will save you & Jack a lot of bother later on. It is really a very difficult estate to understand. Lumley is the only "puzzle" & I confess I am not equal to solving it. I sh^d like to know how much he has put in his pocket, in commissions etc – George will see the Norwich Union man in a week's time. If you write to me remember that I am at Eaton[19] this week.

Please let me know if I lent you your Father's watch. I have an idea I did. If not, I am afraid it has been stolen. […]

Bless you, Your loving Mother

J. C-W.

---

19 Eaton Hall, seat of the duke of Westminster in Cheshire (see Places, p. 579).

— WSC to JSC —

26 January 1905   105 Mount Street

Dearest Mamma,

Many thanks for your letter. I have appointed the 7th and 8th prox. as the days of the Inquisition & have written accordingly to Lumley.

I have proposed myself to Bend'or [the duke of Westminster] for Sunday and if he would like me to come, I could get to you for dinner Sat'y. Now do please read the *Manchester Guardian*.[20] You will find such good reports of anything I say in it. Things are going very well here. Lord Spencer[21] has bidden me for a few days! I have accepted. Keep this to yourself.

With best love I remain, Your loving son
W.

THERE IS no record of any conclusions from the sitting of the 'Inquisition'. They cannot have been fundamental, because Jennie continued to experience regular financial crises, while both she and her son continued to use Lumley's legal services for several years to come.

Winston was soon back to writing his biography of his father.

— WSC to JSC —

9 February 1905   105 Mount Street

Dearest Mamma,

Will you write me three or four sheets of recollections about your

---

20 Edited since 1872 by C. P. Scott, Liberal MP for Manchester, a stronghold of 'free trade'.
21 5th Earl Spencer, a senior figure in the Liberal Party, known as the 'red earl'; lord-lieutenant of Ireland 1868–74, lord president of the council 1880–83, 1886.

life in London and in Ireland with my father from 1874 to 1880?[22] You will remember how you first began in Charles Street I think – entertaining Mr Disraeli, hunting at Oakham [in Rutland], then the row [with the Prince of Wales], I suppose in 1877 [in fact, 1876], then Ireland. Do try and give me a few ideas about this. It does not matter how few they are as long as you really try and put me into possession of the personal aspect of his life in these days.

I have come to this part of the book now and I think I could very nearly write the chapter 'member for Woodstock'[23] if I had this blank filled in. I am counting upon coming down to you on Saturday the 18th and have marked it down in my book.

Your loving son
W

———

J ENNIE'S REPLY made only a passing reference (in a postscript) to Winston's request, even though she was staying at the time in Dublin Castle, as a guest of the lord-lieutenant of Ireland. The incumbent, William Ward, earl of Dudley (a conservative peer who had inherited estates covering large deposits of coal), had invited both mother and son, but Winston had cancelled late.

Like Jennie, Dudley was a personal friend of Edward VII, a frequent visitor to the earl's home at Witley Court in Wiltshire. Dudley's term of office in Dublin coincided with a long-running controversy over the devolution to Ireland of greater powers of self-government. As Jennie wrote, this had given birth to the so-called 'MacDonnell affair', which concerned the role of Sir Anthony MacDonnell, Britain's top civil servant in Dublin. Opponents of further devolution held that Sir Anthony had actively promoted the cause of Irish self-government, exceeding his brief as a civil servant.

---

22 Lord Randolph Churchill was private secretary to his father, the duke of Marlborough, while he was lord-lieutenant of Ireland (see Introduction, p. xxii).
23 Lord Randolph represented Woodstock in Parliament from 1874 until 1885.

— JSC to WSC —

28 February 1905   The Castle, Dublin

My dearest Winston

Dudley tells me he has received a nice letter from you – also the Hansard. I am glad you wrote – as I thought when I arrived yesterday that there was just a little frost in his manner. Poor thing he is very sick of the whole [MacDonnell] affair. His position is not an enviable one & he told me that he felt the whole back bone was taken out of everything – also that he w^d not be able to live at Witley [Court] for 2 or 3 years, when he leaves Ireland. I'm afraid he is very much in debt. [...]

I shall be back on Sat. Bless you darling

Your loving
Mother

[...] This old castle brings up many memories – what a thankless post! I hope Sunny will never accept it.

———————

B Y MARCH 1905 Winston felt that the biography of his father, to be called *Lord Randolph Churchill*, was sufficiently advanced for him to ask Longmans Green & Co, the publisher of his first three books, to make an offer for it. Longmans offered an advance of £4,000, half of the sum that John Morley had encouraged Winston to expect. He therefore delayed any decision about a publishing contract until the book was more complete.

As an MP holding the advantage of military experience, Winston took a close interest in the Conservative government's attempts to remedy the many failings of military strategy and organization which the Boer War had exposed in Britain's armed forces. Balfour had formed a new Committee of Imperial Defence on becoming prime minister in 1902 and subsequently established two Royal Commissions to report into the war's lessons. One commission, led by the earl of Elgin, reported in 1903 on the conduct of the war itself; the other, led by the duke of Norfolk, made recommendations on the future of the volunteer forces, which it adjudged 'unfit for service'.

In 1905 the Conservative secretary of state for war, Hugh Arnold-Foster,[24] brought measures before the House of Commons designed to introduce many of the reforms recommended. These encountered lively opposition both within the military and from Liberal Party backbenchers like Winston. His party chose him to open the House of Commons' debate on the measures on Monday 3 April, leading to a late change of plans for the Sunday before.

– WSC ᴛᴏ JSC –

2 April 1905   [105 Mount Street]

Dearest Mama,

I fear I cannot get down to you today [Sunday] at all. I have to open the debate tomorrow on the Army estimates & all my time is taken up. I am much better staying quietly here than travelling about. I am so sorry. But I have so much to do. I shall speak at 3 o'clock tomorrow quite a considerable affair.

Don't be vexed with me for chopping & changing. It would be a great struggle to come only for one night & I should be no company.

Your loving son
W.

W INSTON SPOKE for over an hour. Closely researched, his speech was well received. There was a growing sense at Westminster that the Conservative government was approaching the end of its days.

At a by-election in Brighton held on 5 April, the Liberal Party

---

24 Known as 'H.O.', Liberal Unionist MP 1892–1906, Unionist MP 1906–9; secretary of state for war 1903–5.

gained one of the constituency's two seats, both of which the Conservatives had held for the previous twenty years.

— WSC to JSC —

6 April 1905   105 Mount Street

Dearest Mamma,

I was delighted to get your telegram; for my conscience pricked me badly about Sunday. But my labour was well repaid.

Brighton is truly wonderful. Never has there been such a landslide. I do not think the govt will go on much longer.

I had a long talk with Lumley yesterday & am preparing a letter. [...] We shall be together either at Blenheim or Salisbury Hall the whole of the Easter holiday.

With best love, Your loving son
W

———

J ENNIE SPENT Easter (Sunday 23 April) at neither Blenheim nor Salisbury Hall. Despite her financial difficulties, she was enjoying herself in Paris.

— JSC to WSC —

19 April 1905   Paris

Dearest Winston

I am sorry not to have been able to write to you before – but I am so "hunted" here I haven't had <u>one</u> moment to myself. I am afraid you did not get to London on Sat: but never mind. When I return we will put that right! Prince Sagan[25] asked after you the other day.

---

25 Hélie de Talleyrand-Périgord (from 1910, 5th duke of Talleyrand and Herzog zu Sagan); in 1908, Prince Sagan married his cousin's ex-wife, the Countess of Castellane, formerly Anna Gould, daughter of an American railway entrepreneur, Jay Gould.

I am enjoying myself immensely – ride & skate, go to the races, dine out and then dance! It is unfortunate tho' that the weather which was rather divine is now rather wet.

Write me a line dear. I do hope that you are getting on well & that you are fit. Bless you. Do write.

Your loving Mother,
JSC

———

IN THE early hours of 21 July 1905, the combined forces of Liberal MPs and Irish MPs defeated the Conservative government by three votes at the end of a debate in the House of Commons about Ireland.

— WSC TO JSC —

21 July 1905   105 Mount Street

Dearest Mamma,

I expect the Govt will resign & that a dissolution will follow from last night's division. It was a great moment of satisfaction & excitement to all of us. [...]

Your loving son,
Winston.

———

THE GOVERNMENT did not resign for another five months. Meanwhile, Winston spent much of August 1905 first at Sir Ernest Cassel's villa in Switzerland, where he tried to complete *Lord Randolph Churchill*; and then at the Ashby St Ledgers estate, near Rugby. Owned by the Guest family it boasted its own polo ground.

A week before Winston wrote to his mother from there at the end of 31 August, Lord Curzon resigned as viceroy of India after a long turf war over military matters with the commander-in-chief of the army in India, Lord Kitchener. The government in London finally backed the general over the viceroy. Curzon was replaced by the earl of Minto, who had hosted Winston at Government House in Ottawa five years earlier.

— WSC to JSC —

31 August 1905   Ashby St Ledgers, Rugby

Dearest Mamma,

Your letter (which finds me here, where I have been for a week) makes me feel very guilty. It is very good of you to write, and I certainly do not deserve much consideration.

My only excuse is that I have toiled at my book almost incessantly since I left England. It is now very nearly done: another ten days will, I think, complete all the heavy work in connection with it. There will only remain a few checkings and revisings to be done before the pig may be taken to market. I can't tell you how delighted I am at the prospect of getting this off my hands; more than a thousand pages have really been a very serious undertaking, and nothing but a very vigorous and sustained effort during the last month would have enabled me to carry it forward so far. Really, in the meantime I have written to nobody. [...]

Switzerland was peaceful. We did exactly the same every day, namely, bridge, writing; bridge, walking; dinner, bridge, bed. But the monotony was pleasant, and as I took a great deal of exercise every day I certainly benefited by the change of scene. Cassel was most amicable, and we had many a long and pleasant talk. [...] I stayed three weeks all but two days, and returned here without stopping.

We play Polo here every day when the weather permits, and as I have just a small room to myself to write in, I labour undisturbed all of every morning. I am going to Blenheim for a night on Friday but shall return here the next day. [...]

Of course I am all for Curzon as against Kitchener, and for Constitutional against military power. I cannot believe a Liberal Government will allow a Commander-in-Chief in India to engross to himself so much power. I am thinking of breaking into print upon the subject in the course of the next few days. [...] I should be greatly disconcerted if

I thought the Liberal party were prepared to acquiesce in the handing over of the Indian Empire to an ambitious and indocile soldier. [...]

The appointment of Minto, poor dear thing, is another piece of *arthurism in excelsis*.[26] For equivocal disdain of public interests and contempt of public opinion, it exactly matches Brodrick's appointment to the India Office.[27] [...]

Always your loving son

W.

———

B Y EARLY October of 1905, Winston felt that *Lord Randolph Churchill* was ready for him to seek higher offers from publishers. He appointed Frank Harris[28] to act as his literary agent, on the basis that Harris would only earn a commission on any extra advance he secured above the £4,000 that Longmans had already offered in the spring.

— WSC TO JSC —

3 October 1905   Blenheim Palace

Dearest Mamma,

I shoot here this week except Friday, when I have to speak at Manchester. I daresay Sunny would be glad to have you here for Saturday. Shall I ask him?

All next week I have meetings at Manchester, culminating on Friday 13th in a Free Trade Hall Demonstration at which Lord Durham and Sir Edward Grey will speak.[29] Would you care to come? [...]

---

26 Reference to Arthur Balfour's reputed reluctance to take difficult decisions.
27 St John Brodrick, secretary of state for India 1903–5; created Viscount Midleton 1907, earl 1920.
28 Irish-born journalist, brought up in the USA; arrived in London aged 28; edited the *Evening News*, *The Fortnightly Review* and *The Saturday Review*.
29 John Lambton, earl of Durham, lord-lieutenant of the county of Durham; Sir Edward Grey, a senior member of the Liberal Party (see People, p. 573).

I am trying to get a great deal of money for my book. I want to tell you all about Touraine,[30] & learn in return of Germany.

Ever your loving son,

W.

————

WINSTON'S MEETING at Manchester's Free Trade Hall on Friday 13 October witnessed the beginning of the militant campaign by women to gain the vote: police arrested Annie Kenney and Christabel Pankhurst for disrupting the proceedings.

By the end of October, Winston's decision to employ Harris as his literary agent had been vindicated.

— WSC TO JSC —

30 October 1905   105 Mount Street

Dearest Mamma,

I am sorry we missed, but we shall meet at Newmarket on Wednesday. I go thither tomorrow with Cassel. His Majesty has been graciously pleased to signify his desire to meet me at dinner on Tuesday night and his determination to bring home to me the error of my ways.

I settled this morning with Messrs Macmillan that they shall publish my book on the following terms:-

£8000 to be paid as follows:

£1000 now

£1000 when the proofs are corrected and

£6000 on the day of publication

In addition to this after Macmillans have earned £4000 profit for themselves, we are to divide all further profits which may be realised during the period of legal copyright. I think you will agree that I was right to close with this. Tempting as it was to 'run' the book myself, I do not think anyone can say I have not sold it wisely and well. [...]

———————

30 A former province of France centred on Tours and the Loire valley.

Winston's favourite photograph of his mother, chosen by him to illustrate *Lord Randolph Churchill*.

It will be necessary now to push ahead with the business of publishing. Will you please bring with you to Newmarket any photographs which you may think suitable. [...] I think myself that the photograph of you with the star in your hair is the best and I have chosen that one but if you have any other choice, there may be within the next few days still be time to alter it. [...]

With best love, Yours always
W

18

TURNING THE TABLES

1905–6

'You evidently forgot you were writing to your Mother'

B Y LATE in 1905 the Conservative and Liberal Unionist government was approaching the end of a decade in power. The question was whether the opposition Liberal Party could overcome the internal divisions over its policy towards Home Rule for Ireland that had festered since the breakaway of the Unionist faction from the rest of the party in 1886.

The Liberal leader, Sir Henry Campbell-Bannerman,[1] had carefully crafted a policy of 'step by step' on Home Rule. This acknowledged that it would only be practical to implement modest measures of devolution in the course of the next parliament, yet it held on to the aspiration of full Home Rule for Ireland as the ultimate objective of party policy.

---

1   Known as 'C.B.', leader of the opposition Liberal Party since 1899 (see People, p. 572).

On 25 November 1905, Lord Rosebery, a former Liberal Party leader and prime minister, put this compromise at risk by suggesting in a speech at Bodmin that the party should drop Home Rule as its final objective.

— WSC to JSC —

28 November 1905   Canford

Dearest Mamma,
    I have cancelled all my meetings this week in order to have a good rest here. There is a wonderful rubber [masseuse] who has almost miraculous virtues & I am vy comfortable and peaceful. [...] I am practically restored, & am only resting to prepare myself for future labours.
    Rosebery has I regret to say greatly injured himself by his reckless speech. Parties do not forgive that kind of unnecessary quarrelsomeness at critical moments. Everyone knows there will be no Home Rule Bill in next Parliament.

Your loving son
Winston

W INSTON HAD known for more than a year that he would need to find a new constituency in which to stand as a Liberal at the next general election, which was due at the end of 1905. He chose the north-west division of Manchester, which he had already visited in June and October. Now he planned to return for the campaign in December. First, there was another priority.

— WSC to JSC —

1 December 1905   Canford

Dearest Mamma,
    I am vy sorry you will not come here next week. I am bound to stay here until next Thursday to finish my massage treatment, from wh

I have so greatly benefited; so that unless you come we shall not meet; for I go to Manchester on Thursday. Why don't you come? I have no doubt she could restore your circulation & digestion. She will say in a minute if she can't.

She also informs me I am tongue-tied. It is quite true. My tongue is restrained by a ligament which nobody else has. This is the true explanation of my speaking through my nose. I have made an appointment with [Sir Felix] Semon[2] in London for Monday to consider the matter.

I think it probable that the Government will resign today. CB [Campbell-Bannerman] if sent for will certainly accept the commission. The newspapers are quite ignorant & stupid about his intentions. I daresay the new Administration will be formed by this time next week. But we have had so many falls, it is rash to prophesy. […]

Your loving son
W

———

O N 4 December Arthur Balfour resigned as prime minister. Some Conservatives still hoped that divisions within the Liberal Party would prevent Sir Henry Campbell-Bannerman from forming a Liberal government when invited by the king to do so. Their hope proved unfounded. Winston waited to see whether the new prime minister would offer him a post.

— WSC TO JSC —

4 December 1905   105 Mount Street

Dearest Mamma,

I am much better. Sir Felix Semon refused to cut off my tongue, so that it is still 'tied'. I return to Canford tomorrow for two rubbings. Consuelo tells me she is going to bid you to Blenheim for Christmas.

———

2   Leading laryngologist of his generation, who practised in London from 1875 until his retirement in 1910.

Do come. I am arranging to have the rubber. All our tummies will be put straight.

I suppose the new Government will be formed during the next few days. It is rather exciting, especially as profound inactivity is the only course wh dignity & prudence alike enjoin.

The King wrote through Knollys[3] to enquire about my health! What a change! I will not allow myself to make any speculations or anticipations about the future. I think the hour is fortunate & the combination of circumstances most favourable. But confident in myself, I await with composure the best or worst that Fortune has in hand. [...]

Your loving son

W

ON 13 December Winston accepted a post in the new Liberal government, as under-secretary for the colonies. His secretary of state was the earl of Elgin, whom he had first met as viceroy of India when serving in the country as a young subaltern. Winston was attracted to the post because Elgin sat in the House of Lords, so would need his under-secretary to steer all the department's business through the House of Commons; Elgin had also reached the stage of his career when his Scottish estate beckoned more strongly than the palace of Westminster.

As soon as the new administration was installed, the general election campaign effectively began (although parliament was not formally dissolved until 8 January). Winston's constituency in North-West Manchester was one of the first to poll, on Saturday 13 January. He led his campaign on the issue of free trade, a cause with which Manchester had identified since its support for the repeal of the Corn Laws sixty years earlier. Winston defeated his Conservative opponent by a margin of 1,241 votes in an electorate of only 11,400 voters.

---

3 Francis Knollys, private secretary to Edward VII and George V; appointed Viscount Knollys 1902.

The Liberals won seven of Manchester's ten seats, having previously held only one. Nationally the Liberals won 377 seats, compared to 157 for the Conservative and Liberal Unionists combined. Backed by eighty-three Irish Nationalist and fifty-three Labour MPs, the Liberal government found itself in a position that led to a decade in power that defined the era. Yet its first majority government for twenty years was also to prove its last.

As Winston's ministerial career began, he moved into a larger home that Jennie helped him to find in Bolton Street, between Piccadilly and Curzon Street. He bought a short lease for £1,000. Since Pamela Plowden had married elsewhere, Winston had pursued at least two other women, the American actress Ethel Barrymore and British shipping heiress Muriel Wilson. At the age of thirty, however, he still depended on his mother to help him entertain important guests.

— WSC to JSC —

24 June 1906   12 Bolton St., W.[4]

Dearest Mamma,

Elgin is coming here to dine on the 6th & I want you so much to come too. He would not bring Lady E.

Our Manchester demonstration yesterday was a great success.[5] The suffragettes were ejected with almost incredible velocity!

Your loving son
W.

A UGUST 1906 brought a painful exchange of letters between mother and son that underlined the change in their relationship

---

4   Abbreviation of West, one of London's ten postal districts introduced in 1857 following the rapid expansion in the number of letters posted (see Introduction, p. xvii); numbers were not added to London's postcodes until 1917.

5   WSC spoke alongside David Lloyd George, president of the Board of Trade, at a Liberal demonstration in Manchester, in front of a crowd estimated at 30,000.

following Jennie's second marriage and Winston's elevation in public life.

On 12 August he left England for a month's holiday in Europe, starting first at Deauville on the north French coast where, he informed his private secretary, he gambled until five o'clock each morning at the casino. One of the later stops on his journey was to be Schloss Eichorn in Moravia, an estate owned by a fellow Liberal politician and friend, Maurice de Forest-Bischoffsheim – de Forrest, as Jennie wrote his name, or 'Tutz' to his friends.

Tutz's background was colourful, even by Edwardian standards. Born in Paris, he was initially presumed to be the son of a pair of circus performers, both of whom died of typhoid when he was three, leaving him and a young brother in an orphanage for five years. They were then suddenly adopted by one of Europe's richest couples, Baron Maurice Hirsch and his wife Clara Bischoffsheim, whose son and heir had just died. Only later did it emerge that Hirsch had fathered both 'orphans'.

Tutz's adoptive parents barely had time to educate him at Eton and Oxford before Baron Hirsch died in 1896 (and his wife in 1899). Their deaths left Tutz with a large fortune, including several estates spread across Europe (of which Schloss Eichorn was one).

The emperor of Austria-Hungary ennobled his new landowner, but Tutz settled in London and became a naturalized British citizen in 1900. The next year he married a wealthy French widow, Mme Menier, and converted from Judaism to Catholicism. This proved helpful when, shortly after the birth of a daughter, the pope agreed to annul his marriage in 1902.

Late in 1904 the word went around Tutz's circle that he planned to marry for a second time and his new wife was to be Ethel Gerard, daughter of a close friend of Jennie's, Lady (Mary) Gerard. Jennie had also known Tutz's father, Baron Hirsch, while she lived in Paris before 1870. To complicate matters, Winston was a friend of Tutz, with whom he shared a love of speed in cars – Tutz had held the world speed record for a car from 1903 until 1905.

Jennie stood accused by Tutz's circle (including Winston) of trying to foil the new match in 1904 by telling the bride's mother, her friend Lady Gerard, of scandalous skeletons in Tutz's past. The marriage had gone ahead,[6] but the couple had not spoken to Jennie since.

The first page of Winston's letter is missing; he finished it by offering to mediate when he visited Schloss Eichorn, but thought his mother should be prepared to apologize, or write an *amende* as he described it.

— WSC to JSC —

[20] August 1906   [Deauville, France]

[first part of letter missing]

[...] winks & shrugs. Do not do anything now; but let me know. I would like to put it right, & I think you might be quite ready to write an *amende*, if it is understood beforehand that it will be well received. But do whatever you like. There are some injuries wh are so serious and incurable that it is hardly worth while to plaster them over. [...]

Your ever loving son
Winston S.C.

P.S. I find I am to be the guest of the Emperor [of Germany] the whole time at the [army] manoeuvres, so that I may find some opportunity of flouting that ill-natured Pless possum.[7] In any case she is coming to Eichorn. The King sent me a gracious answer, desiring me to wear uniform & to write privately to him about S.A. [South Africa] I wrote a perfectly prodigious & "statesmanlike" epistle, the result of which I have not yet heard. It was pervaded by an air of dignified pandering wh ought to prove vy impressive to a royal aya.[8]   *WSC.*

---

6 It produced two children before it was dissolved in 1911.
7 Hans Heinrich XV, prince of Pless (see People , p. 569).
8 (In several languages) a female of creative or beautiful qualities.

J ENNIE'S REPLY touched first on Jack, who had recently joined the City stockbroking firm of Nelke, Phillips & Co. Jack had just complained in a letter to Winston that he was having to work in the office until eight o'clock every evening, throughout a hot August.

Jennie's husband George, now thirty-one, was also attempting to earn a living in the City as one of two principals in the firm of Wheater, Conwallis-West & Co. His duties were clearly less onerous than Jack's, because they did not prevent him from joining Jennie in a classic Edwardian progress that summer through some of the great estates of Scotland. Jennie summarized their itinerary to Winston before defending herself against his charges of loose gossip.

— JSC to WSC —

25 August 1906   Lowther,[9] Penrith

Dearest Winston

Your letter from Deauville finds me here where I have been passing a very pleasant week. It is a wonderful place & everything works like a small regulated clock. Of course I was pleased to get your letter & hear such a good account of yourself. I only wish poor Jack had half such a good time – he is in London working away & taking no holiday – altho' he has had some very nice invitations – to yacht with the Camdens[10] – to go to Doncaster[11] etc. What you say about him as regards his business capacity is I'm afraid true but you can't change him & his very qualities of steadiness & slowness probably stand in his way – still I think he will eventually make a decent living – & he is interested in his work & thinks that he is doing well which is all important as it must often be discouraging work.

George thinks that Nelke [Jack's firm] must have lost a lot of

---

9   Lowther Castle in Westmoreland (now Cumbria), seat of the earl of Lonsdale.
10 John Pratt, Marquess Camden, grandson of the 6th duke of Marlborough; first cousin (once removed) of WSC.
11 Doncaster racecourse, host of the St Leger race in mid-September each year.

money lately – but that does not affect Jack. [...] Meanwhile George & Wheater have done very well, they have made over £10,000 this last month – "Let the thing go on" I say!

We go from here on Monday to Gosford the Wemyss',[12] then the end of the week to Alloa the Mar & Kellies,[13] & on the 3rd of Sept: to Tulchan the Sassoons[14] for a week, Glenmuick for another week (the Neumann's),[15] then Dunrobin[16] & Rhifail Hugh Warrender's place near Thurso[17] – & then home on 1st of Oct: All these journeys by motor sending the servants by train – one really sees the country & we both enjoy it – now you know as much as I do about our plans.

I am delighted to hear that all is well with you in the Royal way – H.M. [His Majesty] only wants a little cossetting to be kept quite tame – I am truly glad that you are going to do the German manoeuvres in such a comfortable manner. George is also quite pleased to hear it, as he told me he had had a tiff with Daisy Pless [his sister] & told her she was ridiculous bringing in politics into her likes & dislikes – she knowing nothing whatever about them. I _hope_ her nose will feel much out of joint. Mind you are _very_ civil to old Hans Pless – as he had nothing to do with it – & probably is quite ignorant of the matter. [...]

Now about de Forrest – I know when you write your pen sometimes runs away with you & you evidently forgot you were writing to your Mother – why should you impute the meanest & lowest of motives to me over this business I fail to see. That I should deliberately take away a man's character on no other evidence but "sniffs winks & shrugs" for the only purpose of making myself important (?) – would indeed be as

---

12 Gosford House, East Lothian, owned by the earl of Wemyss and March (see Places, p. 580).
13 Alloa Tower, owned by the earl of Mar and Kellie.
14 Tulchan Lodge, shared by the earl of Seafield and the Sassoons (see Places, p. 581).
15 Glenmuick House, Deeside; owned by Sigismund Neumann (see People, p. 568, and Places, p. 580).
16 Dunrobin Castle, north of Inverness, seat of the earl of Sutherland (see Places, p. 579).
17 Rhifail Lodge near Thurso, standing on land owned by the earls of Sutherland.

you say a dreadful thing – & if you really think this you must have a very poor opinion of me – your Mother.

The real facts are these. When Ethel & de Forrest's engagement was on the *tapis* [idiomatically 'on the agenda'] – not quite settled – I arrived in London from Paris where I had been staying with Ferdinand Bischoffsheim, old Baroness Hirsch's brother, & I believe trustee & in some way guardian of Tutz & his brother. Bischoffsheim said to me "if you know the parents of the young lady they say Tutz is going to marry it is only fair that you should warn them that he is absolutely *un vaurien* ['good-for-nothing'] – those were his words – & then he went on to say that he had treated his first wife Mme Menier in almost inhuman and disgusting manner & that no one who knew the truth wl^d ever have anything to do with him. [...]

When I was in London, Hugh Warrender & Mason[18] had just returned from Morocco & speaking of this engagement they both told me under the promise of secrecy as regards their names – if I made use of their information to Ethel's family – that in Morocco they had come across traces of Tutz who had travelled there a little while before – & that there were some ugly stories about him. The dragoman[19] or guide who went with Mason & W., with his oriental ideas, gave the whole thing away, & thought it was quite natural that Tutz should have a young boy with him for a particular purpose.

The boy was afterwards sent back to his people with a large sum of money £50 or 60£. [...] A few days later I met Harry Milner[20] at Newmarket & he told me he hated the marriage, & then I told him what I had heard naturally withholding the names of W. [Warrender] and M. [Mason]. I also repeated to him what old Bischoffsheim had said. As regards the first story I said of course I did not vouch for the truth of the tale – but I thought it only fair form to tell him [...]. I believe they did

18 Alfred ['A.E.W.'] Mason, Liberal MP and author; his best-known book, *The Four Feathers*, was published in 1902.
19 Interpreter and guide in countries speaking Arabic, Turkish or Persian languages.
20 Widower of Newmarket figure Caroline, duchess of Montrose (who married Milner when she was 70, he 24).

make enquiries from the British Consul in Morocco – I <u>never</u> repeated that story to anyone but Mary [Gerard] who came to see me about it. There were no "hints or innuendos" I told it as it was told me. [...]

If the story or others like it got out – it was not my doing – I may have abused Tutz – but I did not spread this particular story. In Paris there were others of the same kind – which Mary herself told me with indignation.

There! I have written this at length because you abused me at length. I had no reason no <u>personal</u> motive to abuse Tutz. [...] I am quite ready to admit that I made a mistake in playing the part of the candid friend & am also prepared to say that I am glad to find that what I had heard is not true. I have no feeling of animosity towards the young couple & always thought that it was quite natural they should cut me. I should have done the same under the circumstances. If they like to forget I am quite ready to write. [...]

Now bless you & write to me – I am busy finishing my play – & writing an article for *Harper's* "Social London Past & Present"! Rather a wide range!

Sans rancune [idiomatically 'No hard feelings].

Your loving
Mother

——————

THE PLAY Jennie mentioned she was writing was *His Borrowed Plumes*, which would reach the stage in London three years later.

Jennie may have hoped that her son would let the matter of Tutz rest, because he was supposed to be relaxing at Sir Ernest Cassel's Alpine chalet. Winston declined to do so.

— WSC to JSC —

1 September 1906   Villa Cassel

Dearest Mamma

Many thanks for your letter. It lagged so long on the road that I had almost begun to think you had forgotten me. I am delighted to hear of George's good fortune. [...] I am still vy sad about my Unions.[21] It seems predestined that money is to avoid me except in such driblets that it cannot be enjoyed without feelings of uncertainty and anxiety.

I received a gracious reply to my long letter to HM [His Majesty] with a request for more. I sent another vy carefully considered screed, the result of which I have not yet learned. CB [Campbell-Bannerman] mentioned incidentally that the King had asked him to warn me not to be too frank with 'his nephew' [the emperor of Germany] at the manoeuvres. I expect I will have to mind my P's and Q's, so as to appear entirely candid & yet say nothing platitudinous or indiscreet. I go to Berlin from here on Tuesday. [...]

This place has been very pleasantly dull; & in spite of it being late in the year, the weather has been simply perfect. Not a cloud in the sky & delicious warm sun with glacier air. Cassel & I climbed the Eggishorn[22] yesterday. A vy long pull & I should never have got home without the aid of a mule. *Le vieillard* [Cassel] tramped it all out like a bird. Rather discreditable to me, I think. [...]

Now about Tutz. Of course there must be no *rancune* between us. I think we ought always to write quite frankly whatever we think. I do not quite see how I could have put my point more inoffensively. It was a disagreeable point & nothing would have made it pleasant.

I am bound to say that what you tell me of your authorities for the charge you made does not seem to constitute a very effective justification. You heard something from Warrender who also heard something from a Moorish dragoman. [...] The dragoman as evidence is not worth a rush light.[23] At the best it was only un-sustained and twice removed. Neither do I think that you could perfectly plead 'privilege'.

---

21 Shares of a South African mining company that WSC had sold before they rose strongly.

22 A mountain in the Valais, 2,927 metres (9,603 ft) high.

23 The most common candle before the advent of electricity: layers of fat were dripped over the surface of a rush, which – when lit – produced a light for some 20 minutes.

[...] An action for slander would certainly have cost you at least £5000 in the courts of England.

It is just as well to face these facts; & I put them seriously, because you argue the case seriously. You make out that you had a grave case & that you were bound in conscientious duty to your old friend to bring it to her notice. I say that such an explanation would not be accepted by the world or by the law upon the facts as they exist. It is better to say "I repeated gossip, like a good many others?" [...]

There – I would put this all a great deal stronger if I had the mood. – but please do not think I want to set myself up for a judge – least of all of you – for I know that I often say stupid & unaccountable things that were not true about people that I do not like. I am only glad to think that I have not – so far as I know – got into deep water. Mental resolve on my own part at any rate – to be more careful in future.

I think on the whole I will let this matter rest. I daresay that with time it will become quite natural for you both to bow to each other. [...] Now, my dearest Mamma, do not be vexed with me for writing frankly to you. It is the only style of intercourse between rational beings who know each well. [...]

With love to George & best love to yourself always & believe me

Your affectionate son

W

N OW IT was Jennie's turn to claim the last word; in the course of doing so, she acknowledged that her social position had lately become less prominent.

– JSC TO WSC –

4 September 1906   Tulchan Lodge

My dearest Winston

Your letter from Cassel's has just reached me – I wonder if you have thought of taking some [introduction] cards with you to Germany?

It is most important as you will have to return all those left to see you. If you have none – you can get some done in Berlin. [...]

I am most interested at what you say about Helle.[24] He is coming here on the 17th but I shall not see him – not being quite such a "Royal Pet" as I used to be. The younger generation have not only knocked at the door – but have come in!

If you like French novels – you must read Guy de Maupassant's.[25] You would like them – I am trying some 18 cent: Memoirs to get ideas for my article for *Harper*. I wish I had yr ready pen. [...]

The last word in respect to "Tutz". The Londonderrys said just as much as I said – C [Charles, marquess of Londonderry] to Mary Gerard that "he would rather his daughter dead than married to such a man". But it has all been forgotten. Mary G. was at Lowther & was most affectionate to me as she always is. [...] If Tutz had brought actions for libel against all the friends & relations of Ethel, who abused him before the marriage & had won them – he wl[d] have added a small fortune to his large one! But one will leave the subject – I will only say that altho' I shall never again play the part of the candid friend – had you been about to marry a girl who had we will say epileptic fits – & that Mary G. knew of it – & did not tell either you or me – I think I should have been very angry with her. No – I stick to my point, I did not repeat idle gossip. I really thought that I was doing right. [...]

I have revised & finished my play – & am going to send it to Marie Tempest[26] to show it to Frohman.[27] I am very doubtful about it. Poor

---

24 Familiar name for the German emperor, derived from *Tableau of Europe* (1553, part of the third book of *The Lusiads*) by Luís de Camões who recites the lands owned by 'their mighty Lord the German Emperor', referring in the next couplet to 'hapless Helle' who drowned in the Hellespont (now the Dardanelles).

25 Maupassant wrote some 300 short stories and six novels before he died aged 42 in 1893.

26 Famous soprano of Victorian light opera and Edwardian musical comedies; managed her own theatre company.

27 Charles Frohman, American producer who dominated US theatre for 20 years before turning to London 1904; first produced J. M. Barrie's *Peter Pan*; drowned in the sinking of RMS *Lusitania* 1915.

Pearl Craigie[28] was going to try to place it for me – I have her new book [*The Dream and the Business*], an advance copy she had ordered her publisher to send to me just before her death. I wonder why her boy is called John Churchill Craigie?[29]

She died an ideal death but 39 is too young. If I cl^d keep my faculties I sh^d like to live to 100! But that wl^d be keeping you out of yr patrimony rather too long!

Bless you my darling my thoughts are all with you. I shall be so interested to hear how you get on with the Kaiser. By the way Arthur Balfour came to lunch at Gosford the other day. He asked after you & was as usual nice. He seemed anxious to talk to me. He wondered if C.B. wl^d change his political life in any way on account of Lady C.B.'s death.[30] I said I thought not. [...]

Now goodbye.

Yr loving
Mother

————

A S JENNIE toured Scotland, she longed for news of her son and, hopeful that he might soon be promoted to the cabinet, passed on to him any political gossip that she heard. Her fellow guests at Glenmuick included Arthur Brand, a former Liberal MP who speculated that a reshuffle of ministers could follow the retirement of the marquess of Ripon, the government leader in the House of Lords, who was approaching his seventy-ninth birthday.

One disadvantage of promoting a new appointee to the cabinet at the time was that the law required him to seek re-election in his constituency. Winston's majority in North-West Manchester was already slim and he now risked the loss of support from Catholic

---

28 Anglo-American novelist and playwright, advised JSC on her literary ventures; died 13 August 1906 (see People, p. 567).
29 Born 1890, awarded the Military Cross for service with the Grenadier Guards in the First World War.
30 Lady Campbell-Bannerman died after a long illness in August 1906.

voters as a result of the Liberal government's policy on education. The party had vigorously opposed the Conservative government's Education Act of 1902 that authorized state funding for religious schools. Once in government, the Liberals had tried to reverse the measure, only to be blocked in the House of Lords.

— JSC to WSC —

16 September 1906   Glenmuick House, Ballater. N.B.

Dearest Winston

I have been following yr movements in the papers – but I hope you will find time to write & tell me of all yr doings. How did you get on with the Kaiser? Did you have an opportunity of talking to him & how did you like Fürstenstein?[31]

I haven't much to tell you. I had a letter from Marsh[32] who seems to have enjoyed himself. He was off to Italy today. We are staying with the Neumann's – Mr "Sigmund" still "grouses" about S. Africa & does not believe in a British majority. Mr Arthur Brand who was here told me he had heard that Ld Ripon wants to resign & that the govt. want you in the Cabinet but are afraid you might lose your seat owing to the Catholic vote which has been alienated on the education question. He also told us Mr Chamberlain had a fit in his bath some weeks ago. I see that he is about again.[33] [...]

I will write to you a line from Dunrobin where I go next week.

Bless you, Yr loving
Mother

---

31 Castle in Silesia, a wedding present to to the prince of Pless and his wife Daisy (sister-in-law of JSC).

32 Edward Marsh, private secretary to WSC at the Colonial Office (see People, p. 570).

33 On 13 July 1906, five days after his 70th birthday, Joseph Chamberlain suffered a stroke in his bathroom that paralysed his right-hand side. Although his mental faculties were unaffected, Chamberlain's limited physical recovery left him unable to return to active politics. He remained an MP until January 1914, dying later that year.

Kaiser Wilhelm II and his guest, Winston, at the German Army's
manoeuvres near Breslau, September 1906.

BOTH PARTIES had finally put the vexed topic of the Tutz affair to bed, yet Winston now had to raise another difficult subject with his mother – her husband George's finances.

Winston had received a letter in Vienna from his close friend, the duke of Westminster. It concerned the business affairs of George's firm, Wheater, Cornwallis-West & Co., whose early success in the City had given way to harder times in 1906. Its difficulties were compounded that summer when the firm was suddenly defrauded by a solicitor named Bloomer. George needed to find £8,000 to make up the loss and turned to Winston and Jack for help, when his bank would only lend him part of the sum.

The duke of Westminster, as George's brother-in-law and one of the richest men in Britain, heard of the affair while he was on holiday in Kenya. His letter offered to send Winston a cheque for £3,000 for him to pass on to George, so long as he disguised the duke as the original source of the funds.

First Winston sought to establish from Jennie the facts about George's position.

— WSC to JSC —

14 September 1906   Vienna

Dearest Mamma

I want you to tell me precisely how & on what terms George found the money necessary to pay that rascal who decamped; & secondly what is his financial position now? Is he in a great difficulty & very hard pressed? Has he made or lost a lot of money lately in his business.

You may be quite sure I do not ask this from motives of curiosity but with a serious reason, wh must however remain a secret for the present. Will you let me know this without talking to George upon the subject as soon as possible. I shall be at the Hotel Danieli,[34] Venice for

---

34 A luxury hotel in Venice – see letter of 29 September.

three or four days & an answer will reach me there. I will write to you thence about the German manoeuvres & all I saw & did.

I go on to Venice by the night train.

With best love, Believe me ever your loving son
Winston S. Churchill

P.S. I should add that my reason & motive in making these enquiries is entirely friendly to George & might in certain circumstances lead to results greatly to his advantage. But I must know the facts.   *WSC*

— JSC to WSC —

18 September 1906   Glenmuick House, Ballater, N.B.
Private

Dearest Winston

Your letter has reached me & I do hope this will still find you in Venice, tho' you say are only going to stay four days there.

George is out stalking therefore I cannot find out all the details you want to know. But this is as much as I know. Cox's [bank] advanced the £8,000 on George's reversion – to pay for the rascal Bloomer – & Arthur James[35] sent surety. The Bank made no difficulty & were sympathetic.

Things are a bit slack in the City just now – but in the last 2 or 3 months George & his partner Wheater have made from 10 to £12,000 – things are not going badly for them. I am not quite certain if they have not made more – perhaps it is £15,000.

I am sure if George had lost a lot of money, he would have told me – besides he is in very good spirits. He returns to work on this 30th & he & Wheater are going sometime in Oct: to Spain for a week to see the Cerro.[36] I can't think who has been alarming you with all sorts of

---

35 Wealthy racehorse owner, friend of Edward VII, ex-chairman of the Submerging Boat Company Ltd.

36 Disused copper and cobalt mines at Cerro Minado, Andalusia, originally operated by the Phoenicians and Romans; reactivated by English owners at the turn of the 20th century.

tales – you can be quite certain that if things had been very bad I would have told you.

I am off to Dunrobin tomorrow – our chauffeur Price has been ill which has upset our motoring plans. [...]

Bless you darling & thank you for your interest.

Yr loving
Mother

A FTER RECEIVING a cheque for £3,000 from the duke of Westminster, Winston sent the money to George on 18 October, hinting that Sir Ernest Cassel was its source. Before the end of the year, George had uncovered the true identity of his benefactor.

Meanwhile, Winston had been touring Italy in style, with Muriel Wilson among his party.

— WSC TO JSC —

29 September 1906   Siena

Dearest Mama,

Your letters all three reached me here yesterday after perfectly idiotic peregrinations in Colonial Office bags. Always write to Bolton Street when you have any doubt of my address.

I am glad to hear your account of George's affairs; & that he has weathered the storm. In certain circumstances I might have been able to help him to a limited extent. But I'm glad those circumstances have not arisen.

I must tell you about the German manoeuvres and my meetings with the German Emperor when I return. It would take too long to write. But everything I saw in Germany was most instructive & indeed my whole holiday has been full of varied interest. After Breslau I travelled with Bully Oliphant[37] to Vienna & so to Venice, where I luckily just missed

----

37 Major-General Laurence Oliphant, chief of Clan Oliphant.

Consuelo's yachting expedition. I then came on in Lionel Rothschild's motor car[38] with Lady Helen [Vincent][39] and Muriel [Wilson] on what has been a vy delightful tour. Forty miles an hour across Italy: Bologna, Ravenna, Rimini, Urbino, San Martino, Perugia, Siena. Such a lot of churches we have seen and saints and pictures 'galore'.

Today is the Atonement and our Jehu is fasting in solitude.[40] Tomorrow we return in one fell swoop of 330 kilometres to Venice, & I go on by the night train to Vienna and Eichorn. It has been vy pleasant. Nothing could exceed the tranquil *banalité* of my relations with M [Muriel]. But I am glad I came. [...]

Lord Elgin was very nearly in the Grantham Railway accident.[41] Poor old boy – what a Providential escape! He writes me most friendly letters & is doing all the work! While I remain

Your loving son
Winston SC

———

F AMILY PROBLEMS raised their head once again as the marriage between Winston's cousin Sunny, duke of Marlborough, and Consuelo Vanderbilt limped towards its end. Winston and his mother, whose sympathies lay primarily with Consuelo, tried to arrange a reconciliation.

---

38 Son of Leopold de Rothschild, Lionel, aged 24, enjoyed speed and was fined £5 for driving at 22.5 mph on the Great North Road in 1903. He established a new water speed record of 28.8 knots in 1906.

39 Wife of Sir Edgar Vincent, owner of a palazzo in Venice; painted by John Singer Sargent in 1904.

40 Yom Kippur, the day of atonement in the Jewish calendar; Jehu, a king of Israel, referred here to Lionel de Rothschild.

41 On 19 September 1906, the night express train from London King's Cross to Edinburgh derailed, killing 14 passengers.

— WSC to JSC —

13 October 1906   Blenheim
Secret

Dearest Mamma,

Sunny has definitely separated from Consuelo, who is in London at Sunderland House.[42] Her father returns to Paris on Monday. I have suggested to her that you would be vy willing to go and stay with her for a while, as I cannot bear to think of her being all alone during these dark days. If she should send for you, I hope you will put aside other things & go to her. I know how you always are a prop to lean on in bad times. We are vy miserable here. It is an awful business.

Your loving son
Winston SC

— JSC to WSC —

[October 1906]   Sunderland House, Mayfair

[No greeting]

Absolutely no use. I wash my hands of it.

Mr V. [Vanderbilt] says as a father he cannot add one word to the letter. He is to see his lawyer tomorrow morning. I did not hint that he might see you.

Your loving
Mother

— JSC to WSC —

26 December 1906 [postcard]   [35a Cumberland Place]

When are you going to warm your toes & burn yr hands again at this fireside – will you come this Sunday? – wire.   *JSC.*

---

42 London home, on Curzon Street, of the duke and duchess of Marlborough; completed in 1905 with Vanderbilt money.

19

SOLACE IN SCRIBBLINGS

1907–8

'Le Bon Dieu *has work for you yet*'

B Y 1907 Jennie's marriage to George Cornwallis-West was starting to creak and she was once again in financial trouble. Less than a decade earlier, Winston had depended on his mother for both emotional and practical help; now their roles were reversed. His ministerial duties, however, left him with little time to support her.

Jennie sent him her first letter of the year from a club in London's Dover Street that she had helped to found, the Ladies Athenaeum. It was one of five such clubs that appeared in the same street, catering for (as an article in 1899 put it) 'the modern professional woman, be she artist, journalist, clerk, doctor, teacher, or nurse, living as she often does in rooms in the suburbs, [who] needs some fairly central haven of refuge where she can drop in, when she has a spare hour, for a rest, a cup of tea, and a glance at the newspapers'.[1]

---

1   D. Jones, *The Ladies Clubs of London*, 1899.

Jennie occupied herself there by drafting her memoirs, which a London publisher, Edward Arnold, had undertaken to bring out the following year under the title *Lady Randolph Churchill's Reminiscences*. Arnold planned to hand her draft to a former soldier turned ghost-writer, Harry Graham. Graham, as aide-de-camp to the earl of Minto when he was in Canada, had just embarked on what was to prove a distinguished writing career.

— JSC ᴛᴏ WSC —

22 March 1907   Ladies Athenaeum Club, 31, Dover Street, W.

Dearest Winston

I am sorry that my visits sh^d always be tiresome ones – I have spoken to George, on the telephone & without going into particulars more than necessary, he will give me a cheque for £300 if you still advance £150.

With this sum I can wait for the completion of the book. I promise you this will not cost you anything. Try & come by this eve: I see so little of you – & it goes to my heart that I am so often a trouble when we do meet.

By the way I paid £35 interest in the autumn and out of my own pocket on that loan of Jack's.

Let me have an answer here.

Aurevoir, With love
Mother

JENNIE STOPPED in Paris on her way to stay with the former prime minister, Lord Salisbury, on the coast of the French Riviera, where he had built a house on a plot of twelve acres at Cap Ferrat, overlooking the sea.

— JSC to WSC —

[31 March 1907] Sunday   Hotel Ritz, Place Vendôme, Paris

My dearest Winston

I did not half thank you for that loan – but you <u>know</u> that I am grateful and even more for your sound and helpful advice.

I will not allow myself to be unhappy – but shall plunge into the book & in my scribblings find big solace & God bless you dearest. Never judge me harshly for with all my selfishness & faults I do love you.

. *Your*

Mother

W HILE HIS mother was in Paris, Winston stayed for a few days at Sir Ernest Cassel's chalet in the Alps, where one of his fellow guests was Alice Keppel, still Edward VII's mistress. Winston was relaxing for a few days before the start of a conference in London due to last for a month and to be attended by the prime ministers of all Britain's dominions and colonies.

— JSC to WSC —

17 April 1907   La Bastide, Beaulieu

My dearest Winston

I see by *The Times* that you are moving in Royal Circles![2] – I hope you are well & enjoying yrself. It is pleasant here. La Bastide is the villa built by Ld Salisbury, it has a most lovely view over the sea. [...]

I am very busy with my book – & have been able to write another chapter. I have no news – I see that things are a little better in the City. By the way, I met Consuelo [duchess of Marlborough] in Paris, who begged

---

2   The Court News in *The Times*, 16 April 1907, recorded WSC attending a dinner given by the Prince and Princess of Wales for the visiting prime ministers of Britain's colonies and dominions.

me to let bygones be bygones – of course I agreed – altho' I can never feel quite the same – she seemed very well & fairly happy. Her mother & the children were with her & we dined at the Ritz one night. […] The Parisians seemed rather surprised. The only thing she said about Sunny was "I hope he is happy now that he is free & rid of my presence" – I cannot but think, if they are both left alone – they will come together in time.

Bless you darling – give my love to the Cassels – & Alice K [Keppel] –

Yr loving
Mother

Arnold writes that he & his partners are "delighted" with the 4 chapters I sent him. He is agreeable to my keeping the American rights – but in that case he will only give me half of his original offer. £500 seems to me very little, as good or bad I think the book is bound to sell. […] You remember my telling you that he offered me £500 originally – but I was not to write it – only hand over material to Harry Graham. Surely the book might be worth more if I write it myself?

———

THE IMPERIAL Conference imposed many demands on Winston, one of its main hosts. His mother was clearly under strain at the same time.

— JSC TO WSC —

1 a.m., 7 May 1907   Ladies Athenaeum Club, 31, Dover Street. W.

Dearest Winston

I cannot sleep without telling you once more. I grieve that any disagreeable words sh^d have passed between us tonight – I was tired & hasty. You have always been a darling to me – & I love you my darling. Take care of yrself & take things a little easier.

If it suits you come to me on Sat. or Sunday.

Bless you, Yr loving
Mother

A S PARLIAMENT'S long summer session approached its end,
Lord Elgin was sufficiently concerned about his junior minister's
wellbeing to advise him to 'mind his health'. Unbeknownst to Elgin,
Winston had already consulted a doctor on twenty-two occasions in
the first half of 1907 and had undergone thirty-eight treatments with
a 'masseur and medical electrician'.[3]

Heeding this advice, Winston planned to take a month's holiday in Europe during August, followed by a semi-official tour of
several months around Britain's colonies in eastern Africa. He even
offered to pay his own way on the journey until his mother told him
that this would be a mistake; eventually he split its costs with the
various colonial governments along his route. He then recovered
his share by writing a series of articles about the journey for a
magazine, *The Strand*, later collecting them into a book, *My African
Journey*.

To help his deteriorating finances, Winston asked his mother to
find a temporary tenant for his home in Bolton Street. She engaged
a firm of local estate agents, Mabbett and Edge, before she set off
with George on the usual summer visit to Scotland, which began on
the north coast.

— JSC TO WSC —

12 August 1907   Rhifail Lodge, Thurso

Dearest Winston

It was vy good of you to read my trial chapter. I have noted what
you say about Blenheim. I only hope that my material will hold out
to the extent of 100,000 words! I have left three chapters with Eddie
Marsh and I <u>do</u> hope that you will be able to read them before you
leave. The 5th chapter is political and I daresay you will not like some
of the things I have said. In the 4th I have left some space for some Irish

---

3   F. Bisco, medical accounts, CAC, CHAR 1/69.

political notes – I do not know exactly where I can get my information. Perhaps you can help in this? Darling boy – I know I am asking a great deal – but I have such confidence in your judgement that I cannot do without it.

Now about yr house – I went to see Mabbett and Edge, who live in Mount St and made the man come with me and go over it. He is going to do his best to let it for you – for 6 months if possible. I went into all the particulars which I will not trouble you with. An inventory will be taken of everything including the books. This will not cost more than a few pounds. They charge a guinea a day. 2 days sh^d do the library. [...]

It is glorious here as regards air – one feels so fit, doubts on any subjects are impossible – I feel everything must succeed that I undertake. I hope it will turn out so. I can hardly realize that I shall not see you again for 6 months. Write to me before you go. Bless you darling I envy you your trip. Think of me sometimes. I love you very dearly.

Your
Mother

BEFORE HE could leave on his African journey, Winston had to pilot the second reading of the Transvaal Loan (Guarantee) Scheme through the House of Commons, a task that was complicated by the politics of the Cullinan diamond. Discovered in the Transvaal Colony in January of 1907, the diamond weighed in at 3106.75 carats in its rough state, the largest stone ever found.

The Transvaal government, headed by the former Boer leader Louis Botha, had bought the diamond and offered it as a present for the king's sixty-sixth birthday, due in November, as a token of the Colony's new loyalty (it had only become part of the British empire five years earlier in 1902). Boer members of the Colony's Parliament endorsed the gift, but many English settler members opposed it as an unduly extravagant gesture. The British prime minister, Sir Henry Campbell-Bannerman, therefore left the king with the final decision as to whether to accept the gift. He did so, as privately urged by Winston.[4]

On 19 August Winston spoke for more than an hour about the Transvaal Loan in the House of Commons. *The Times* reported his speech in full the next day.

— WSC to JSC —

21 August 1907   Colonial Office

My dearest Mamma,

I have not had a moment till now to answer your letter. You will see the reason in *The Times* of yesterday. That Transvaal loan took me a long time to prepare & consider & really I had no leisure to put pen to paper in other directions.

I am worried about the letting of the house. No Inventory has yet been taken & I wonder whether there is any real prospect of finding a satisfactory tenant. Also Miss Anning [Winston's secretary]. I wish you could manage to board her out for me during my absence. It is deplorable to think of all the expenses that will be mounting steadily up in my absence. I do rely upon you dear Mamma to help me in arranging these affairs; for wh I am not at all suited by disposition or knowledge. [...]

The [parliamentary] session drags on its belly to an end: not I fear before Thursday next. But these vy late sittings are making a great impression on Government business, & I think we shall have a very fair catch of fish to show for our pains in the end.

Nothing could be more poisonous than the behaviour of the Tories over the Transvaal Loan & the Diamond. Sneers and snarls of disappointed spite. I don't know why they wanted to drag these wretched Boers inside the British Empire, if they will not accept even their loyalty

---

4   The diamond was split into nine major stones and 96 smaller stones by Asscher Brothers of Amsterdam in 1908; two of the nine major stones form part of the Crown Jewels of the United Kingdom; the other seven are privately owned by Queen Elizabeth II.

so generously tendered. Late l[as]t night I replied again on the debate & walloped them well. [...]

Freddie [Guest] has chucked me for my journey. His wife began to fuss about her *accouchement* & he had vy little choice.[5] I expect he was wrong ever to contemplate going. Gordon Wilson[6] comes with me instead. This is in some ways an advantage as he is an older man, vy sensible, & high in the Army. He will be just the man to deal with the soldiers. Wingate[7] proposes to send me a special steamer to Gondo-koro,[8] as I wished.

With best love, Mamma, your ever loving son
W

I will read your chapter before I go.

J ENNIE ASKED for Winston's particular help in writing the section of her book that described Lord Randolph's sudden resignation as chancellor of the exchequer in 1886, when he had expected the prime minister to decline to accept his move, because there was no obvious successor among leading Conservatives (see p. 14). Lord Randolph had 'forgotten' to take into account George Goschen, who accepted the post, then held it for six years, while Lord Randolph never saw political office again.

There was a particular story about the incident that Jennie wanted Winston to relate. Given his grounds for declining to do so in his

---

5   Captain Frederick Guest, cousin of WSC, had married an American, Amy Phipps, in 1905; by August 1907 she was six months pregnant with their second child, Raymond, who was born in New York on 25 November (see People, p. 564).
6   Lt.-Col. Gordon Wilson, Royal Horse Guards, married to WSC's aunt Sarah, née Spencer-Churchill.
7   General Sir Reginald Wingate, commander-in-chief, Egyptian army, governor-general, the Sudan 1898–1916.
8   Island near the east bank of the White Nile, the point in northern Uganda where the Nile became navigable.

reply (of late August, see p. 458), it is safe to assume that the story had an anti-semitic edge, which was widespread among Jennie's generation, but not shared by Winston.

— JSC to WSC —

22 August 1907   Glenmuick House, Ballater, N.B.

Dearest Winston

The inventory of your house will only be taken when it is let. Don't worry about it – I shall be back the 28ᵗʰ Sept and if it is not let by then, I will do my best to find you a tenant. Sept is not a good month, as people are away – October wlᵈ be more likely. [...]

[...] I have been *au bout du monde* ['in the back of beyond'] at Rhifail, letters taking 3 or 4 days on the way, but I have followed the H of C [House of Commons] debates – and Eddie [Marsh] wrote me of your all-night sitting. [...] I liked your Transvaal speech and quite agree with you that the Conservatives are odious and rude about the diamond. Of course it is rather awkward for the King, if the gift is not unanimous.

Honestly I think Gordon Wilson is a good substitute for FG [Freddie Guest]. He is very resourceful and when 'on his own' a very pleasant companion. There is a fund of dry humour in him which few people know.

Do try and read my chapters at SH [Salisbury House]. The 3 will only take you an hour. – if as much – I want you to add to the 5ᵗʰ chapt[er] that story of yr father and Goschen and the Exchequer. If told at all it must be well told – and I feel diffident – also make a little note in the 4ᵗʰ as to where I can get some Irish data – that chap[ter] is too short. [...]

I hate to think of your going off for so long – and that I shall not see you again before your departure. But you will enjoy it, and it will be a great rest and change. I still think you need not have offered to pay for your journey – *c'est magnifique mais ce n'est pas la guerre*[9] – and no one

---

9 Said by French marshal Pierre Bosquet of the charge of the Light Brigade at the Battle of Balaclava in the Crimea, 1854.

will thank you for it. Mind you get Trevelyan's *Garibaldi*[10] to read en route – also *Memories and Impressions* of George Brodrick.[11] [...]

I told them at S.H. to send you a hamper of vegetables to London. I hope you get them. I miss my "wee doggins" very much. Did you play with them at S.H.? [...]

Goodbye my darling boy. I ramble on out of all bounds. Bless you. Do write again before you go. [...]

Your loving Mother
JCW[12]

George has been rather poorly & fainted the other night. The doctor said his heart was all right. He has been worrying about that beastly City. He is quite well again. [...]

ON SATURDAY 24 August, Winston spoke at a garden party in Cheadle for members of the North-West Manchester Liberal Association. After reviewing the achievements of the Liberal government in its first two parliamentary sessions, he then disparaged the opposition that it had often encountered from the Conservative-controlled House of Lords. In the section of his speech with which his mother's letter of 27 August was to take issue, he said: 'If there was one set of circumstances with which the House of Lords was more unfitted to deal than any other, it was that set connected with the transfer and tenure of land. Those good old gentlemen knew a good deal about the subject (laughter) ... as they had managed to get hold and keep a good deal of it.'

Before Winston left on his African journey, he and Jack had been

---

10 G. M. Trevelyan's trilogy, *Garibaldi's Defence of the Roman Republic*, vol. 1, published 1907; later volumes, 1909 and 1911.
11 George Brodrick, *Memories and Impressions 1831–1900*, published 1900.
12 Abbreviation of Jennie Cornwallis-West (a rare signature for JSC to use in her letters to WSC).

due to take over as the trustees of his father's will trust, because one of its original trustees, Earl Howe, was now refusing to sanction any changes in the trust until its lawyers produced a proper set of accounts. One of the trust's assets was the remaining seventeen years' lease of No. 12 St. James's Square, which had fallen into the trust on the death of the dowager duchess of Marlborough in 1899. Since then the building had housed the premises of the Nimrod Club, whose members shared a love of hunting. Backed by George, Jennie was keen for the trust to sell the lease and reinvest the proceeds so as to produce a higher income for her use. The building's sub-tenant, a Mr Long, had already agreed to pay £37,500 for the rest of the lease, more than the value assessed by independent surveyors.

– JSC TO WSC –

27 August 1907   Glenmuick House

Dearest Winston

I hear from Jack that perhaps you go off tomorrow to Paris. I read with interest your speech at Manchester. I liked it all but the part referring to the land – but perhaps I do not understand it. [...]

You had better let Jack settle with George in what the money of St James's Square is to be invested in. Jack is quite competent to look after it, & you had better lease him a power of attorney to act for you. We cannot afford to let the money lie idle in the bank – & it might be months not to say years before Lumley disgorges those accounts.

I hope you sent to SH for Sunday. I have no news. My book and golf take up most of the time. It is very comfortable here & one can please oneself. George has gone out stalking.

I'm afraid that poor Jack will be very dull without you or anyone – we do not return to SH until the end of next month. Write to me when you have a moment.

Bless you. I have written to Leonie about your house.

Your loving
Mother

THE FIRST part of Winston's reply has not survived, but he evidently refused to join the rush to sell the property in St James's Square. A new firm of lawyers, Nicholl Manisty, was due to take over the administration of the trust and they had warned Winston not to start as a trustee until a proper set of accounts had been prepared, in case he became liable for the trust's past maladministration. He thought in any case that the price for No. 12 should be higher.

Winston's more immediate concern was the cost of recent building work at his own home in Bolton Street which had been carried out by builders Turner & Lord. Jennie had tried to persuade him, through Jack, to borrow the money to pay their bill: 'It is <u>much</u> better to owe money to your bank than a tradesman,' she had advised.[13]

— WSC to JSC —

[Date, first section missing – late August 1907]   12 Bolton St., W.

[...] this house, and I don't suppose there was ever a tradesman who reaped such a rich profit from such a small job. This little room in which I write cost more than £1,000 to furnish, and odd bills from Maples[14] and others keep coming in. [...]

I have been much fussed and worried by a tiresome strike in my constituency which I laboured for a good many hours last week to settle, which I thought I <u>had</u> settled in fact when I left on Saturday evening; but they have all now gone off in different directions again which is too provoking. In the hopes of being useful, I have postponed my journey until Sunday night when I leave for Paris by train and not by motor as I had originally planned. [...]

The Session is at an end. Last week was the busiest of all for me. I had to make speeches every single day and two on some days – however all is well that ends well and although I live in the utmost private penury,

---

13 16 August 1907, JSC letter to Jack, CAC, PCHL 1/5.
14 Maple & Co., furniture maker, based in London's Tottenham Court Road.

I have succeeded in securing five million pounds for the Transvaal and two million for my Nigerian railways. [...]

I will not fail to read your chapter before I leave England and will send them to you from Crewe. I do not think the Goschen story would be suitable for publication. It would cause a great deal of offence not only to the Goschens but to Jews generally. Many good things are beyond the reach of respectable people and you must put it away from your finger tips.

With best love, Ever your loving son
Winston

— JSC to WSC —

30 August 1907   Glenmuick House

Dearest Winston,
I will not argue with you about George Howe or Turner & Lord. I daresay George & Jack can settle satisfactorily as to the investing of the money of St J's Square. You will certainly have to pay T. & L. [Turner & Lord] and it will be just as disagreeable later as now! The want of money is the clinch. [...] I daresay you are right about the Goschen story.

I am glad that you are going to have 4 months respite from all enemies. Make the most of it. You have done splendidly & I hope this next move in the Cabinet will be to take you in. [...]

I wonder if you will approve of the 3 chapters you have to read. I sometimes feel disheartened about the book & think it is not going to be good. [...] Bless you darling take care of yourself – & do write. Any scrawl however short. Send the chapters <u>here</u> – if you send them not later than Sat 31st. [...]

With best love yr loving
Mother

WINSTON MANAGED to read his mother's chapters before he left for France with his friend F. E. Smith.[15] His comments on them caught up with Jennie while she stayed with the duke and duchess of Westminster at their fishing lodge in Lairg.

— JSC TO WSC —

17 September 1907   Lochmore,[16] Lairg

My dearest Winston,

I wonder how you are getting on with the 'Froggies'. I hope you will find a moment to send me a line. Did F.E. Smith 'wear' as well as you expected?

We are still in Scotland as you see. It has been most pleasant here – Shelagh [duchess of Westminster] & Bend'or [duke] are enjoying life & sport. [...] George has killed as many stags as ever he cl^d desire. It is very mild up here, but I like the outdoor life, & have taken to fishing which I enjoy. I write all the mornings & have got on with the book. I received the chapters.

You were a bit scathing about Chap V but I did not mind as I ought to have told you that V was quite in the rough – merely a lot of notes put together which Miss Anning typed in order that you might see them. In any case I sh^d never have sent the chapter to the Century [American publisher] as you saw it. [...]

Bless you darling. Thank you so much for looking at my chapters & I forgive you for saying 'Fie!' to your loving

Mother

---

15 F. E. Smith, a close friend of WSC, a brilliant lawyer and Conservative MP, would die of cirrhosis of the liver (see People, p. 571).
16 Fishing lodge on the edge of Loch More, near Lairg in Sutherland, owned by the dukes of Westminster.

J ENNIE HAD already taken on the task of finding a placement while Winston was away for his secretary, Miss Anning. Now Jennie agreed to take on his cook, Mrs Scrivings, while her husband, George Scrivings, travelled with Winston to Africa as his manservant.

— WSC TO JSC —

26 September 1907   Eichhorn

Dearest Mamma,

You must not regard my criticisms as personal. Literary judgements are not worth much – but they are worth nothing unless they are at once impartial & impersonal. I am delighted to hear the political chapter was only in the rough. You have a great chance of making a charming woman's book about the last 30 years, & do I beg you lavish trouble upon it, & banish ruthlessly anything that will hurt other people's feelings. It is well worth while. [...]

Here it is vy pleasant. Sunny [duke of Marlborough], de Forest [Tutz], H. Farquhar,[17] & me – that's all – but lots of partridges & hares.

I start for Malta on Sunday night from Vienna via Syracuse [in Sicily]. It takes 3 days: & I meet the others there late on Wednesday night.

I have had a vy kind letter from the Prime Minister wh I think you will like to see. After reading it you might like to send it to Cassel [...].

I am in hopes that the house will have been let & the Anning in part at least provided for.

With best love, I remain Your affectionate son
Winston

---

17 Lord [Horace] Farquhar, former MP, master of the household to Edward VII.

— JSC to WSC —

25 September 1907   Strathconan, Muir of Ord[18]

My darling Winston,

One line to say goodbye. I hope when you are on board ship you will have time to write to me.

Jack will have written to you about yr house – 10 guineas is not much but no houses are letting in London – & £250 is better than nothing. I will try and find a place for Mrs Scrivings.

Post is just off –

Bless you darling, do take care of yourself – and let me hear from you.

Your loving

Mother

J ACK EVENTUALLY managed to let Winston's house at 12 Bolton Street, but to Bob Scrivier, a well-known 'character' who had recently been barred from the racing world. Winston was worried about the risk to his reputation of any link with Scrivier.

He arrived in Malta on 2 October. Speaking to the elected members of the island's executive council two days later, he warned them that they would have to make out a strong case if they were to win any greater devolution of powers which impinged on the interests of imperial security.

— JSC to WSC —

21 October 1907   The Warren House,[19] Stanmore

Dearest Winston,

I have no idea where this will find you, but I suppose it will reach you in time. I have been following your 'Royal Progress' with the

---

18 North-west of Inverness, historically owned by the Mackenzie family.
19 Owned by the Bischoffsheim family, just north of London.

keenest interest. I hear that Sir F. Hopwood[20] has spoken in high praise of your Malta speech – & said it had a very good effect. I have not seen F.E. Smith & therefore have never heard the account of your French manoeuvres – How I envy you your trip! but I could never undertake Uganda on my 10 toes – what will yours & Eddie's be like at the end of your promenade?

What can I tell you of things here? We had a very pleasant 6 weeks in Scotland. Lochmore with Bend'or & Shelagh was most enjoyable. Pamela & Victor [Lytton] were coming as we left. I am at home now for good. Jack & I keep each other company as George has been busy at the Potteries[21] and this week goes to his father for a shoot. I am happy to say he made £1,500 at Newmarket last week. Wheater put him on "Malure"[22] for the Czarewitch at 25 to 1. George hardly ever bets so it was rather lucky. [...]

I think that poor Austrian emperor will die although Mensdorff[23] says he is better.[24] It will make a great difference and probably Hungary will revolt. I hear Consuelo Marlboro' has gone to America. Jack who was at Blenheim last Sunday says Sunny wasn't best pleased. And he thinks it is a mistake her going. Meanwhile he sent up the children to see her off – which pleased her greatly.

I am going to lunch tomorrow with the Devonshires who start for Egypt Thursday. I believe she hates going poor old lady. [...] The book is progressing and the first chapter appears next month. I trust my material will hold out. I'm afraid this whole book will be light and frivolous. However many people prefer that sort of thing to the more serious. The

---

20 Sir Francis Hopwood, permanent under-secretary of state for the colonies.

21 At the time an area of Staffordshire that comprised six towns, well known for their pottery industry; in 1910 they 'federated' as Stoke-on-Trent.

22 A mistake by JSC: the winning horse in 1907 was 'Demure', ridden by Frank Wootton; its starting price was 4/1.

23 Count Albert von Mensdorff, Austro-Hungarian ambassador to the United Kingdom 1889–1914.

24 Franz Joseph I lived until 1916; he postponed the state visit to Vienna of the king and queen of Spain in October 1907 because he was suffering from bronchitis and pneumonia.

Queen's letters are making a stir – her style is to say the least of it, feeble![25]

I think Jack was quite right to let your house altho' I think the price rather low. Still you will be glad to have nothing to pay when you return. Someone told me that Scrivier took a house last year and was only [in] it about 3 weeks. He is always travelling about.

I saw the King at Newmarket, he was very amiable. He is shooting with Cassel this month – H.M. seems to have taken up Sarah[26] very much – she was at Newmarket looking very well.

Give my love to Gordon & to Eddie M. What do you think of the Ld Chancellor marrying Micky Hicky's daughter[27] [...]

Goodbye my darling boy, take care of yourself.

Your loving
Mother

Miss Anning is working for Ld Hugh Cecil.

———·———

THE ADMIRALTY supplied HMS *Venus*, an Eclipse class cruiser commanded by Captain Cuthbert Chapman, to carry Winston and his party from Malta to Mombasa on the coast of the British East African Protectorate.

— WSC to JSC —

19 October 1907   HMS *Venus*, at sea near Aden

Dearest Mamma,

You will think me a faithless correspondent, and I confess my

---

25 *The Letters of Queen Victoria*, vol. 1, 1837–43, edited by Reginald Esher and Arthur Benson, officially published by John Murray, 1 December 1907; vols 2 and 3 appeared in 1908. Critics concentrated on the cost of the publication, three guineas.

26 Probably Sarah Bernhardt, the French actress, with whom the king had long been linked.

27 Robert Reid, Earl Loreburn; married Violet, daughter of William Hicks-Beach 1907, after his first wife's death 1904.

Winston on board HMS *Venus*, en route to East Africa, October 1907.

shortcomings; but I trust Eddie will have given you some account of our pilgrimage, & in any case there seem to have been pretty full accounts in the newspapers.

Of course the Red Sea in October – especially when rough as well as sultry – is not an ideal condition. But it is nearly over now, and certainly, apart from nature, nothing could be more comfortable or more ceremonious, than this method of travel. I have two beautiful cabins to myself – one of which is quite a large room with a delightful balcony at the end overlooking the waves. The captain is unceasing in his efforts to promote our comfort, & all the officers are most civil & attentive. I spend a good deal of every day, and almost every dawn, on the bridge; & am becoming quite a mariner.

The Admiralty instructions are to the effect that the Captain is to study my wishes in respect to visiting any other ports than those originally mentioned; & I have availed myself of this to include Berbera, Somaliland, in my tour.[28] We shall reach Aden tonight & tomorrow we have to coal there. [...]

I have worked vy hard at Malta & Cyprus & have had to write several long reports upon things I want to have done. I expect I shall not get much shooting in East Africa. An Under-Secretary is a *rara avis* [rare bird] in these out of the way places & everyone wants to see him. [...]

Ever your loving son
Winston S. Churchill

———

BY THE time Jennie next wrote in November, her younger son Jack was engaged to the daughter of Lord and Lady Abingdon, Lady Gwendoline (known by the family as 'Goonie'); and the prime minister, Sir Henry Campbell-Bannerman (who weighed over twenty stone), had suffered a heart attack.

---

28 Berbera, the main port of the Somali seaboard, capital of the British Somali Protectorate 1884–1941.

— JSC to WSC —

21 November 1907   [no address]

My darling Winston,

I have not written to you for ages – but I understood from Jack that letters wl^d only have to wait for you. A 'Confidential pouch' is going tomorrow & probably will reach you sooner than the ordinary post. I was delighted with your one letter – but expected no more.

The Press has kept me *au fait* of your movements & speeches – I feel I have so much to say. I do not know where to begin. In the first place Jack will have told you his news – this will probably surprise you. I sometimes thought you had designs in that quarter – but not serious ones – & Goonie has always cared for Jack. They are both much in love but will have to wait a long time I'm afraid – ways & means are not brilliant – but there is no doubt a couple can do on little, if they have no aspirations to entertain or live in any style. […]

You will be sorry to hear that we have made up our minds to let SH [Salisbury Hall] for a year from January – & take a tiny flat in London. We intend only keeping the Waldens & my maid – George hasn't been able to draw one penny from his business this year – so we have no nest egg to fall back upon. Perhaps things will be better in a year. Anyhow it is the only thing to do. I am making the best of it – for it preys dreadfully on poor George who is getting quite ill over it all.

I wonder how CB really is? I hear they won't let him do any work for some time. I fancy there will be a change soon. He will probably go to the H of L's [House of Lords] & Sir E. Grey[29] will be Prime Minister & you will be in the Cabinet. Those are my views! How I envy you basking in the sun – & how interesting your journey has been.

I hear they say you are much missed here – they want you for speeches! Thank Goodness you are safely away from them! I have been

---

29 Sir Edward Grey, at the time foreign secretary (see People, p. 573); JSC was correct about Sir Henry Campbell-Bannerman's political longevity, but incorrect about his successor, who turned out to be Herbert Asquith.

opening an Exhibition of Books today in Bond Street. It has been got up by the *Daily Chronicle*. All the publishers & authors were there – & I made a speech & [publisher] Mr John Murray proposed a vote of thanks to me. He is very deaf & made a 'fuddly' speech – said 'Mrs Cornwallis – who is an authoress & the mother of an <u>authoress</u>!' Shrieks from the Audience – I will send you the report of the proceedings. We are going to stay with George Curzon of K [Kedlestone] next week. I will write to you from there & find out his news. [...].

Now Goodbye & good luck & Many happy returns of the day [30 November] – although it is a bit previous.

Your loving
Mother

————

WINSTON WROTE next as he journeyed along the Uganda Railway, construction of which had begun at Mombasa in 1896 and finished at Kisumu, the line's terminus on the eastern shore of Lake Victoria, in 1901.

— WSC to JSC —

6 November 1907   Camp Thika, (half way between Nairobi –
                                   Fort Hall) [now Muranga]

Dearest Mamma,

I wish I cld find time to write you full accounts of all this most interesting journey. But my days are occupied literally from sunrise till bed either in shooting & travelling or else in official work wh presses upon me – in state apt for decision – from every side. [...]

We left Mombasa after two days of functions & inspections & speeches, & proceeded up country by the Uganda railway. Everything moves on the smoothest of wheels for me – a special train with dining & sleeping cars was at my disposal all the way, wherever I wished to stop – it stopped. When it went on, we sat (Gordon & I) on a seat in front of the engine with our rifles & as soon as we saw anything to shoot at –

East African Journey, 1907

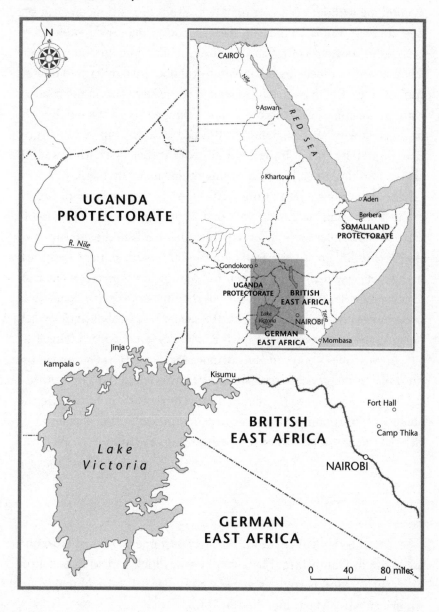

a wave of the hand brought the train to a standstill & sometimes we tried at antelope without even getting down. From the railway one can see literally every animal in the Zoo. Zebras, lions, rhinoceros, antelopes of every kind, ostriches, giraffes all end of the day. The lion hunting was nervous work – especially beforehand – till one had familiarised oneself with the idea. But of course I had several of the best shots in the country with me: & don't think there was much danger. I only saw one lion, & he escaped without being shot at. But he was a fine big yellow brute, plunging along through the high grass, & it was vy exciting wading along after him expecting to come upon him at any moment. [...]

I could only spend the night of the 6th & the morning of the 7th at the Thika camp, as I had to get on to Fort Hall, wh I did by motor-car – about 8 miles an hour over unmetalled roads in the afternoon of the 7th. The 8th, great Durbar of natives: 4000 – with all the chiefs stark naked in all essentials – and in their full war toggery – men & women all dancing together & chanting in curious rhythms from daybreak on. I was presented by the various chiefs with 108 sheep, 7 Bulls, about £100 worth of ivory, an ostrich egg, many fowls & some vy good leopard skins. [...]

Joyous times – you will say – & indeed it is true. The country across the Tana[30] is much richer than anything I have seen in India or S. Africa. It is no exaggeration to say that in beauty, in verdure, in fertility, in the abundance of running water, in the delicious coolness of the air, in its rich red soil, it will bear a fair comparison with the valley of the Po.[31] [...]

Your loving son

W

JENNIE SPENT Winston's birthday as a guest at Lord Curzon's estate in Hampshire, Hackwood Park, which he had leased after his return from his spell as viceroy of India in 1904 and where his American wife, Mary, had died in 1906.

---

30 Longest river in today's Kenya (620 miles).
31 Italy's Po valley runs from the western Alps to the Adriatic Sea.

Meanwhile the Churchill family's perilous finances continued to cast a long shadow. As an 'economy measure' Jennie and George planned to move out of Salisbury Hall into London's new Ritz Hotel; in the meantime, Goonie's father, Lord Abingdon, had rejected his daughter's engagement on account of Jack's poor financial prospects. Winston sent his brother a letter with a suggested line of attack.

— JSC to WSC —

5 December 1907   Salisbury Hall

My dearest Winston,

I wanted so much to send you a cable for yr birthday on the 30th. But in the first place I did not know where to address it – & in the 2nd – I thought it might be expensive. 'Strange fit of economy' you will say!

We spent last week with G.N. Curzon at Hackwood, the place he has taken near Basingstoke a very nice place & charmingly arranged – full of rich colour & comfort. But I thought it pathetic to think of him walking about with silk & velvet patterns under his arms, doing the work Mary C ought to have done. [...]

We have not had an offer for this place yet. We have cut down half the establishment – & have reduced expenditure by £1,000 a year. If we let it we intend to go to the Ritz – we find that we shall be able to live there cheaper than in any other decent manner. [...]

Jack's young lady has gone to Holland. There is nothing fresh about the situation which has to be kept dark until he can go to Lᵈ A [Abingdon] with your financial plan. I suppose you will be next to 'pop off'; it is always so in a family.

I hear Lloyd George was very much cut up about his daughter's death.[32] Poor man. [...] I wonder what you think of the Zulu rising.[33]

---

32 David Lloyd George, president of the Board of Trade (see People, p. 573); his daughter Mair, aged 17, died during an appendectomy.

33 Natal imposed a poll tax on white and black residents, leading to uprisings among the Zulu population early in December.

I suppose 3 or 4,000 natives will be killed – one white man will fall off his horse & so the rising will be quelled.

I have been to the dentist today who has hurt me so much that I feel a wreck, & must go to bed. Give my love to Gordon & the Eddie's altho' as he has never written he does not deserve it.

Bless you darling – I shall be very glad to get you back. You seem to have had a right royal tour. I expect to see you looking fit & twice your usual size!

Your loving Mother

— JSC to WSC —

13 December 1907   Ritz Hotel, London

My darling Winston,

I hope you are well & flourishing. I am here for a night & return to SH with Jack tomorrow. George has been so seedy these last 4 weeks with a cold that the doctors have ordered him off to St. Moritz [in Switzerland] to recover. Unfortunately owing to the expense I have not been able to go with him – which is depressing for both – as he feels ill & is lonely – & I hate being away from him as you know. However there it is!

I haven't much news to tell you. I dined with Cassel last night – who asked after you. I hear the German Emperor who met Leonie at Luncheon at Clarence House asked a great deal after me & said he remembered me in Berlin with R [Randolph].[34] He also spoke of you – he seems to have made himself very popular during his stay here. [...] I saw Consuelo in the distance yesterday looking very well & quite fat for her. She is going to take the children with her to Blagdon.[35] Where poor Sunny spends his Xmas I don't know. I'm told that he is trying to let Blenheim! Might as well let a white elephant! [...]

---

34 Lord Randolph and JSC spent five days in Berlin in early 1888 on their way back from Russia.

35 Blagdon Hall in Northumberland, home of the White Ridley family.

I hear of Pamela at Eaton & getting into her new house in North Audley Street but I have not seen her. I daresay you have heard from her. [...]

Bless you darling – love to Gordon & Eddie. Forgive the dull epistle.

Your loving
Mother

―――――

WINSTON CROSSED Lake Victoria by steamer to visit Kampala, the capital of today's Uganda, before he travelled back eastwards along the lake's northern shore to Jinja. Nearby lay the source of the White Nile river along which he was to trek by foot as far as Gondokoro where the river became navigable.

Sleeping sickness, a parasitic disease, had long been endemic in Africa. Since 1900, however, an epidemic along the shores and on the islands of Lake Victoria had killed an estimated 200,000 people by 1905. By the time of Winston's arrival, British medical experts were attempting to find the source of the disease and were homing in on the tsetse fly as its likely carrier, having noted the coincidence of the areas affected by the fly and by the disease.[36]

– WSC TO JSC –

23 November 1907   Jinja Victoria, Nyanza

Dearest Mamma,

Tomorrow we leave steam communications of all kinds and plunge on foot into this tremendous country, to emerge if all's well, at Gondokoro on the 15 December.

―――――――

36 In 1908 British administrators cleared the lake shore and islands of vegetation in order to deny the flies any breeding ground. While they had correctly diagnosed the tsetse fly as the carrier of the disease officially known as 'Human African trypanosomiasis', it persists today, although responsible for a much lower level of mortality.

Winston (seated, second left), with his private secretary,
Edward Marsh (behind), on their East African journey, 1907.

Everyone is extremely well & we have all enjoyed ourselves vy much
indeed. We are at this moment steaming along in the little steamer *Sir
William Mackinnon*[37] from Kampala the Capital of Uganda to Jinja,
the point where the Nile plunges out of the great lake & starts on its
journey of 3500 miles to the sea. Perfect weather, delicious cool breezes,
beautiful scenery, a cheery party – and islands absolutely depopulated
by sleeping sickness. A sinister contrast. [...]

We had long interviews with kings, chiefs & missionaries in Kampala & certainly the degree of civilisation to wh the natives of Uganda
have attained is vy wonderful. More than 200,000 can read & write, &
they seem a most peaceful & industrious people.

I am concerned to read of CB's illness. Such attacks however overcome are vy serious at 72. His removal from the scene would lead to
many changes; & I should be sorry to lose a good friend who has always

---

37 Named after the founder of the Imperial British East Africa Company (bought
by the British government in 1895) and of the British Steam Navigation
Company, owner of the steamers that plied across Lake Victoria after 1901.

shown me kindness. I expect political circles at home will have been busily buzzing. I am vy glad to be out of the way.

With best love, I remain, Your affectionate son

W

PS George ought not to gamble; but I am vy glad he won. [...]

———·———

JUST BEFORE Winston and his party reached Khartoum, on their journey back to Cairo, his manservant George Scrivings died within twenty-four hours of eating a food that caused what doctors at the time called choleraic diarrhoea. Winston telegraphed the news to his mother.

— JSC TO WSC —

30 December 1907   Blenheim

My darling Winston,

This may find you at Cairo. Sunny showed me yr wire from Assouan. I received your wire from Khartoum while I was at West Dean[38] where I was spending Xmas. I was greatly shocked at hearing of poor Scrivings' death. He was such a faithful devoted servant & a good fellow. You will miss him terribly. [...] I have heard of a very good man who might suit you – but we will discuss this on your return.

I suppose you saw the Devonshires at Assouan? I came here on Sat, Jack being here & George still abroad – F.E. Smith is here as pleasant as ever. He & Sunny talk of going out to meet you. What a delightful time you have had & I hope it has set you up in health for a long time. How I wish you cd have taken George with you. He needs an open air life. This City grind is very hard for him.

I hear old CB is at Biarritz eating & drinking far too much. I am

---

38 Near Chichester in Sussex, owned since 1891 by William James, whose wealth came from his American father.

told that HG [Herbert Gladstone][39] will be shunted & that you will be in the Cabinet. I hope so. We have not as yet let SH & if things get a little better we may not be obliged to. I see by today's papers that G. Curzon is going to return to active political life – if you can call the House of Lords "active"?[40] [...]

What can I tell you? When the German Emperor was here he went to see L^y Ampthill[41] & as he was going away he said to her son T. Russell "Sir E. Grey is a very nice gentleman". "And a great statesman" added Mr Marshall praising his chief. "So am I" exclaimed the Emperor in thunderous tones. [...]

I am longing to get you back – but it is cold & grey here. Stay away as long as you can is my advice.

Yr loving Mother

JSC

———

WINSTON REMAINED unsure whether his mother had received his telegram from Khartoum telling her of Scrivings' death and asking her to pass on the news to Mrs Scrivings.

— JSC TO WSC —

3 January 1908   The Ladies Automobile Club, Claridge's Hotel

Dearest Winston,

It was stupid of me not to mention in my New Year's telegram that I had received yours from Khartoum. Sir Frances Hopwood wired to me. I have seen Mrs Scrivings. I went to No. 12 [Bolton Street]. Poor thing she was very low and sad – but luckily she has a great deal to do. [...]

---

39 Youngest son of William Gladstone; home secretary until 1910.
40 Curzon chose to be elected as one of Ireland's 28 representative peers in the House of Lords, an appointment for life.
41 Emily, née Villiers, widow of Odo Russell, Baron Ampthill, Britain's first ambassador to the German empire who died *en poste*, aged 54, in 1884; their son Theophilus Russell, a diplomat who served in Berlin, was at the time seconded to Edward VII's court.

Rosie and Matt[42] offer you for 2 or 3 weeks 2 rooms at the top of their house in C [Carlton] Terrace. As there is a lift I think you should do very well there. Otherwise the Ritz is the best. I can make arrangements for you. George has returned from St Moritz a little better. He will probably have the operation to his nose the end of next week. Poor fellow he never seems to be out of hospital.

Stay away as long as you can. It is icy cold here & rather dreary. I am going to see a play of B. Shaw's tonight *Arms & the Man*[43] and then go to the Guests (A & I) [Alice & Ivor] who are entertaining frozen-out Mothers at supper. Bless you darling.

Yr loving
Mother

— JSC TO WSC —

7 January 1908 Salisbury Hall

My dearest Winston,

I am writing to send just one line from my bed as I have got a slight chill – I feel like a boiled gooseberry so do not expect a coherent letter – I wrote to you before that I had seen Mrs Scrivings.

This letter she had written before I had seen her. She told me she had a great deal to do which is a good thing. I am looking forward to your return & hope you will let us know the exact date. […]

Your loving
Mother

— WSC TO JSC —

3 January 1908 General's House, Cairo

Dearest Mamma,

I was surprised not to receive a telegram in answer to my wire about Scrivings' death, & I still hope for a letter from you about his wife.

---

42 Lord Ridley and his wife Rosamund, née Guest.
43 A comedy by George Bernard Shaw about the futility of war; first staged 1894.

I was most deeply grieved by this tragic end to our wanderings. It was as unexpected as a lightning flash. The doctors can only say 'choleraic diarrhoea' following the eating or drinking of something causing ptomaine poison.[44] I cannot understand how none of us were stricken too. For Scrivings ate our food always. It was a melancholy & startling event; & to me who have become so dependent upon this poor good man for all the little intimate comforts of my daily life, it has been a most keen & palpable loss. I cannot bear to think of his wife & children looking forward to his return – letters by every post – and then this horrible news to lay them low. [...]

I arrive in Marseilles – all being well – on the 12th; I propose to stay two days in Paris with Sunny, coming to London on the 16th. We might try to dine together that night. I shall stay at the Ritz till my house is free. I am quite glad not to reenter it till that unfortunate woman has got over her first grief. I must from ever-straitening resources make some provision for her future.

I thought as I walked after the coffin at Khartoum – I always follow funerals there – how easily it might have been, might then still be, me. Not nearly so much should I have minded, as you would think. I suppose there is some work for me to do. But if I had ended there, Jack could have married without any delay. Poor dear – we must manage to drive that through for him. 'Some gleams of sunshine, mid renewing storms'[45] precious, to be cherished. How happy he must be & how glad he must be & how glad I am he has not married some beastly woman for money. [...]

Always your loving son
Winston

---

44 A nitrogenous substance produced by bacteria during putrefaction of animal or plant protein.
45 Line from Robert Burns, 'Stanzas on the Same Occasion' (following 'In the Prospect of Death'), 1781.

— JSC to WSC —

12 January 1908   Salisbury Hall

My dearest Winston,

I received your letter of the 3rd from Cairo – last night. I am delighted to think that by now you are so near. First – in regard to my not
having wired about poor Scrivings, you will have had my excuse in a
former letter – it was stupid of me not doing so. And I also explained
about Mrs Scrivings. I think you need not dread seeing her. She is very
calm and as I said, has so much to do that she has no time to indulge
in her grief. […]

I have decided to accept for you the Ridleys' invitation – they themselves are hardly going to be in London at all […]. They give you a large
sitting room & a bedroom (lift to take you up) the library & dining room
being open downstairs. The house will be practically yours – servants &
cook, & they want you to stay until you get your house. You can lunch
and dine at the Ritz. It will save you a lot of money & you will be very
comfortable. I do hope you will be pleased with this arrangement. […]

The cold for the moment is intense, 22 degrees of frost. We have
been skating at Hatfield where I saw Lord Salisbury & Ld Hugh [Cecil]
– the latter very pale after his bad attack of influenza. He asked a great
deal after you.

I want you to come here next Sunday 19th. We are asking F.E.
Smith & I might get Ld Hugh to come over. […] I have heard of various
servants for you. One which sounds excellent. Unfortunately the man
is married and his wife is a very good cook. But of course you will not
part with Mrs Scrivings. I must try again. Thank God you escaped any
ill effects of those dangerous dishes. But indeed *le bon Dieu* has work &
happiness for you yet.

As for Jack he is very happy. Ld Abingdon is very ill at the moment
but when he recovers Jack will probably be able to go and make his
proposal *en règle* ['as it should be done']. What a lot we have to talk
about! I shall look forward to your articles which are sure to have a great
success. I plod on with the book. It is difficult to find material for all the

Chapters. One is full of vulgar twaddle about Sandringham – but I can't help it – on the whole it seems to go down. Bless you my darling boy – I am longing to see you – do telegraph to Gopsall[46] when you make up your mind the actual day & hour you arrive that your 'Mommer' may be there.

Yours lovingly
Mother

— WSC to JSC —

13 January 1908   Hotel Bristol, Paris

Dearest Mamma,

Very many thanks for all your letters, which relieve my anxiety about that poor woman & the effect upon her of the terrible news I had to ask you to convey. Certainly you did everything possible.

I arrived here this morning after a good & fast voyage in the new *Heliopolis* steamer 12,000 tons, & 20 knots,[47] in wh we were invited to travel as the guests of the company! A desirable economy. I stay here till midday 17th to meet Cassel. I will gladly go to Carlton House Terrace & it is vy kind of Rosie & Matt to put me up. I think I had better arrive at the Ritz in the first instance, so as not to upset them with an unexpected incursion & luggage etc. [...]

Masses of letters & papers have met me here: & there is a regular vista of speeches etc before me. There are rumours of changes wh reach me from rather authoritative quarters. But I do not see anything clearly. [...]

With my vy best love, always your affect son,
W

---

46 Gopsall Hall in Warwickshire, home of the Curzon-Howe family.
47 Launched 28 May 1907; operated by the British-owned Egyptian Mail Company between Alexandria and Marseilles; renamed SS *Royal George*, she became a Canadian troop carrier in 1914.

20

END OF A
MARRIAGE

1908–14

'Of what use to chain him to me?'

JENNIE WAS waiting at Charing Cross station to greet Winston
on his return to London on 17 January 1908. He dined with her
that evening, then he returned to the political fray on the following
day, speaking at a dinner to welcome him home given by the National
Liberal Club.

Jennie continued to follow the twists and turns of her son's fortunes at Westminster closely. As the under-secretary of state for the
colonies, he faced repeated questions in the House of Commons
about the working conditions of Chinese labourers imported to work
in the mines of South Africa and had to make a full speech on the
subject in the House on 23 March.

The following day, the Liberal government suffered an unexpected
loss at the hands of its Conservative opponents at a by-election in
Peckham, south-east London. The Liberal candidate had won the

seat easily in the general election of 1906; now, following the death of the sitting member, the Conservative candidate regained it with equal comfort.

— JSC TO WSC —

26 March 1908   Villa Périgord, Cannes

My dearest Winston

I have been reading with interest the debates – & yr speech of the Chinese labour – I hope you are not overworking yourself. What a fuss they made about Peckham. It will take a good many Peckhams to turn out the Govt.

I am annoyed with *The Times* in its obituary notice of the Duke of Devonshire – talks of L^d RC's [Lord Randolph's] revolt.[1] When one realizes that his resignation meant £5,000 less to him and that he resigned on high moral ground, it makes me feel indignant.

I am going to Paris on Monday – I shall be staying there a week and then home where I hope to see you soon. The weather is not very good – no sun. It is a bit early for the Riviera. I am staying with the Claytons[2] who have a nice villa. Cannes is too fashionable – dinners and dances. I prefer the lights of Monte Carlo. The Westminsters are out here. Bendor plays polo and dashes about generally.

I suppose you have done nothing about your house. The changes in the Cabinet are not likely to take place until Easter – so you will have to wait until then. […]

Don't overstrain yourself. Poulton[3] is here and a great friend of

---

1   The 8th duke died on 24 March 1908. *The Times*'s obituary of 25 March referred to Lord Randolph's 'freakish resignation'; the reference to his 'revolt' came in a leading article of the same day.
2   Col. Edward Gilbert Clayton and his wife Georgina; he was knighted in July 1908 after retiring as secretary to the Prison Commissioners.
3   Ronald Poulton, undergraduate friend of Herbert Asquith's son Raymond and an England rugby international.

Asquiths told him you could have what you liked – if you only asked. Bless you, love to Jack

Your loving
Mother

S IR HENRY Campbell-Bannerman's long-expected resignation as prime minister, on grounds of ill health, came at last on 3 April 1908. Less than three weeks later he would be dead. Following his resignation, the king summoned Herbert Asquith to Biarritz to ask him to form a new administration.

On 8 April Asquith asked the thirty-three-year-old Winston to serve in his cabinet as president of the Board of Trade. Like all new entrants to the cabinet, Winston had to resign his parliamentary seat and seek re-election. This time the Conservatives of North-West Manchester concentrated their fire on the Liberal government's record of raising taxes and restricting the role of religious groups in education. Winston lost by more than 400 votes and had to fight a new by-election in a constituency where the sitting Liberal member was elevated to the House of Lords: Dundee was a thriving industrial city, the centre of Scotland's jute trade.

Shortly after his promotion to the cabinet in April, Winston had attended a dinner party hosted by his mother's friend Lady St Helier,[4] who reintroduced him to her great-niece Clementine Hozier. The two had first met four years earlier, when Winston was almost thirty and she was only nineteen. The occasion was a dance, at which Winston asked for an introduction to Clementine, only then to stare at her for a prolonged period.

Clementine's parents had split up and had even less money than the Churchills. It was Lady St Helier who had sponsored her great-niece's presentation at court in 1904 and who was still trying to ease her path in London society four years later, now that she was

---

4   Former Lady Jeune (see People, p. 568).

twenty-three. Clementine's second encounter with Winston, unlike the first, lit a spark between them that ignited into a summer of courtship. For the next few weeks Winston often wrote to Clementine, but no letter to or from his mother survives.

He proposed to Clementine at Blenheim in August and they married on 12 September at St Margaret's Church, Westminster, in front of large crowds. The couple spent their first night together at Blenheim, from where Winston wrote to his mother, before he and Clementine set off the next day for a honeymoon in Italy.

— WSC to JSC —

13 September 1908   Blenheim

Dearest Mamma,

Everything is very comfortable & satisfactory down here in every way, & Clemmie vy happy & beautiful. The weather is a little austere with gleams of sunshine; we shall long for warm Italian suns. There was no need for any anxiety. She tells me she is writing you a letter.

Best of love my dearest Mamma. You were a great comfort & support to me at a critical time in my emotional development. We have never been so near together so often in a short time. God bless you.

What a relief to have got the ceremony over! & so happily.

Your loving son
W

P.S. I open this letter again to tell you that George said he could wish me no better wife or happier days than he had found in you.   *W*

———

A S REQUESTED by Winston (rather than Clementine), Jennie redecorated his bachelor quarters at 12 Bolton Street before the married couple returned from their honeymoon. Jennie was convinced, however, that her son should sell the remaining lease on his property at almost any price, so that he could find somewhere more suited to

Clementine, soon after her marriage to Winston in 1908.

married life. Winston felt that he could only afford to sell if someone would pay him a premium for the lease.

— WSC TO JSC —

20 September 1908   [Venice]

Dearest Mamma,

I send you another packet of letters, wh pray distribute. I am now quite determined not to sell Bolton Street without a premium. It is absolutely necessary to the furnishing of another house. Do try & find a rich bachelor. That is the line.

We have been happy here & Clemmie is vy well. She has written you of our doings so I will not repeat the tale. We have only loitered and loved – a good and serious occupation for which the histories furnish respectable precedents.

With all my affection, Your loving son
W

— JSC TO WSC —

29 September 1908   [12 Bolton Street]

My dearest Winston

I am writing from Bolton Street – where I have been working to get your house straight – no easy matter I can tell you! But I hope you will like it. I think you will be quite comfortable for the time being.

I was delighted to get yours & Clemmie's letters & to know that you were both so well & happy & enjoying yourselves. How I envied your going to Venice – it must have been too delicious for words. I have not written as I knew that you would be better occupied than reading my dull scrawls.

I spent a week after yr wedding at Ashby [St Ledgers] which was vy pleasant. Ld Hugh Cecil was there full of interest in the polo. He bought a hunter and is going to become a "horsey-doggie" man!

I suppose this will find you at Eichorn. Give my love to Ethel & Tutz. I hear that you will arrive here on the 5th – I shall try to come up and see you as we go to a shooting party the 6th.

Tomorrow I dine with [Edward] Arnold to meet Sir Ian Hamilton & a lot of publishers – I shall have to make a speech – only a few words but they are going to couple my name with "The publishing season of 1908!" I hate it!!

I was offered thirty guineas for a short article of 1500 [words] for the *New York World*[5] – something by way of an answer to an interview in 'American Society'[6] by Mrs W Astor[7] – I accepted and have just sent it off. I want very much to consult you about my American lecturing tour. I have received volumes about it – but have decided nothing.[8]

I never heard from yr solicitor about this house – and am still trying to place it for you – Trollope[9] has sent me lists of many suitable houses quite cheap – large – and under £300 & in some cases no premiums. I think you will have no difficulty in finding what you require. But first get rid of this – you will <u>never</u> get a large premium for it – better make up yr mind. [...]

> *Best love my darling old boy*
> *Your loving*
> *Mother*

---

5 Newspaper owned by Joseph Pulitzer, closely associated with the Democratic Party; closed 1931.
6 The *Saturday Evening Post*, a New York newspaper, carried a regular column called 'American Society'.
7 Née Nancy Langhorne, born in US 1879; married Waldorf Astor 1906; first female MP 1919–45.
8 JSC did not make an American lecture tour.
9 George Trollope & Sons Ltd, builders and estate agents in Belgravia.

WINSTON'S DAUGHTER, Mary Soames, wrote many years later in her book *Clementine Churchill* that her mother was 'greatly surprised' to find her bedroom redecorated on her return from Italy. 'In those early years of marriage,' Mary Soames continued, Clementine 'visited fairly severe judgement on her celebrated mother-in-law: she thought her vain and frivolous and, in her marriage to ... a man so much younger than herself, somewhat ridiculous'.[10] Another biographer of Jennie, Anne Sebba, has written of the irritation that Clementine and Goonie both felt when Jennie returned from trips to Paris with magnificent hats for herself from leading designers, yet cheap concoctions for them from the department store Au Bon Marché.[11]

Whether it was as a result of this coolness between Clementine and his mother, or simply because Winston saw Jennie frequently in London, no further letters between mother and son survive from the winter of 1908–9.

That autumn, Jennie's book *The Reminiscences of Lady Randolph Churchill* appeared to kind, if not overwhelming, reviews from critics. *The Spectator* thought that her writing showed her 'in her true character of a frank, indefatigable, and generous woman'.[12] The monthly magazine *Current Literature* described her in its December issue as 'The Most Influential Anglo-Saxon Woman in the World'.[13]

By May 1909, it was her first play that was on Jennie's mind: *His Borrowed Plumes* was almost complete. As so often was the case in her literary endeavours, she sought Winston's comments on the latest draft. Equally predictably, they were not encouraging.

---

10 M. Soames *Clementine Churchill*, p. 57.
11 A. Sebba, *Jennie Churchill, Winston's American Mother*, p. 289.
12 18 October 1908, *The Spectator*, p. 21.
13 Cited R. Martin, *Lady Randolph Churchill*, vol. 2, pp. 227–8.

— WSC to JSC —

14 May 1909   Board of Trade

Dearest Mama

I have read the play. The last half is the best. There are many criticisms I could make on detail or structure. But I will keep these until the
business of a production has actually been undertaken. Then I will give
you any assistance in my power.

I do not think that the work is sufficiently strong in originality of
plot, in situation, in dialogue, or in characterization to justify its public
production. If a professional manager were prepared to risk his money
upon it, I should gladly suspend my opinion in the face of such a practical
approach.

As it is I can only wish you success which I do in all affection.

Your loving son
W.

H IS BORROWED PLUMES started rehearsals in June, before opening
in front of a glittering audience at the Hicks' Theatre[14] in London's
Shaftesbury Avenue on 6 July. During its run of two weeks, Winston
and Clementine's first child, Diana, was born. The most lasting impact
of the play on Jennie's life, however, proved to be the introduction
that it gave her husband George to the actress Mrs Patrick Campbell,
who first visited the Cornwallis-Wests' temporary home in Cavendish
Square to discuss the possibility of her playing its leading part.

Thought to be forty-four years old at the time, 'Mrs Pat' was
probably eleven years younger than Jennie. She had made her reputation on the London stage before losing her first husband in the
course of the Boer War, and had then taken her two children with
her to New York where she met with as much acclaim as she had
received in London.

---

14 Now the Gielgud Theatre.

Jennie (seated centre) with the cast of *His Borrowed Plumes*,
including Mrs Patrick Campbell (seated, left), June 1909.

The difference between Jennie's and George's ages had gradually
taken its toll on their marriage. George, now thirty-five and unsuc-
cessful in the City, increasingly resented his fifty-five-year-old wife's
status in London's literary and social world. He had strayed before,
but now he began an affair with the leading lady of Jennie's play: Mrs
Pat's daytime attendance at Cavendish Square was soon followed by
nocturnal visits on George's part to her 'charming little house in
Kensington Square'.[15] When *His Borrowed Plumes* finished its brief
run, George began to spend more nights away from the marital
home than inside it.

Jennie was philosophical about the development: her approach
to life was to persevere. Recognising that the theatre was unlikely
to provide her with the financial independence she craved, she

---

15 G. Cornwallis-West, *Edwardian Hey-Days*, pp. 264–5.

found that the lease was for sale on the somewhat run-down house next to her own in Great Cumberland Place. It is unclear how Jennie managed to finance its purchase, but she evidently did so before redecorating and selling the property at a profit close to a cabinet minister's annual salary of £5,000. Winston applauded and encouraged her to try more of the same.

In his position as president of the Board of Trade, Winston had been trying to head off a strike by the Miners' Federation of Great Britain, one of the unions that had affiliated to the Labour Party in 1908 in order to pursue a more political strategy for its members. The other political controversy of the summer of 1909 concerned the Liberal government's 'People's Budget', introduced on 29 April by Winston's close political ally, the chancellor of the exchequer David Lloyd George. Winston enthusiastically supported its programme of social welfare and the taxes needed 'to wage implacable warfare against poverty and squalidness', as Lloyd George put it to the House of Commons. The budget required a general increase in the level of taxation and a decisive shift in its burden towards the land-owning classes.

The House of Commons passed the measures, but Conservative peers opposed them in the Lords, where they held a majority. Many Tory landowners particularly resented Winston's support for increased taxes on land; yet, although he had been born one of their number, Winston had not inherited a single acre.

— WSC to JSC —

4 August 1909   Board of Trade

My dear Mamma

I am so glad to hear of your excellent stroke of business. The utility of most things can be measured in terms of money. I do not believe in writing books which do not sell, or plays which do not pay. The only exceptions to the rule are productions which can really claim to be high art, appreciated only by the very few. Apart from that money value is a great test. And I think it is very creditable indeed that you should be able after two or three months work, which you greatly enjoyed, to turn so large a sum of money as a Cabinet Minister can earn in a year.

There is no reason why the experiment should not be repeated. There are lots of other houses in London, and you will have learned a great deal more than you knew before of the latest methods of furnishing. I really think it would be well worth your while looking about for another venture of the same kind. Your knowledge and taste are so good and your eye for elegance so well trained, that with a little capital you ought to be able to make a lot of money and if you sell a few more houses, you will be able, very nearly, to afford to produce another play. [...]

Has the unfortunate Walden gone under the hammer, or is he still your servant? Here I get on so well without a man, I do not think I shall ever have one again.

I had a great triumph over the Coal Strike.[16] We had 20 hours negotiations in the last two days; and I do not think a satisfactory result would have been obtained unless I had personally played my part effectually. I had a nice telegram from the King, and letters from Asquith and Grey all very eulogistic. It was a great coup, most useful and timely. [...]

I think it very unlikely that the Lords will throw out the Budget now. If it is done, it will be only because the Tariff Reform Peers take the bit between their teeth and bolt. And if they do so I firmly believe the consequences will be disastrous to them. I never saw people make such fools of themselves as all these Dukes and Duchesses are doing. One after another they come up threatening to cut down charities and pensions, sack old labourers and retainers, and howling and whining because they are asked to pay their share, as if they were being ruined. [...]

The German Emperor has invited me to the Manoeuvres as his

---

16 A reference to a dispute in Nottinghamshire where 15,000 miners stopped work between 1 and 15 July. The Coal Mines Regulation Act 1908 came into force on 1 July 1909, limiting the hours which miners were allowed to work underground each day to eight, compared to the ten or more that they had averaged beforehand. In response, many pit owners imposed a reduction of wages.

guest, and I am to be at Würzburg, in Franconia,[17] on the 24th September. Clemmie will come too, and I hope we shall have a good time.

Once more, let me tell you how wise you are to prefer a mind free from money troubles and petty vexations to the mere possession of a particular house; not being a snail you can get on quite well without it.

Your loving son
Winston S.C.

————

THE LIBERAL government faced a constitutional crisis during the winter of 1909–10, as the Lords continued to reject the budget (their stance was seen by many as a breach of the traditional primacy of the Commons). In an attempt to secure a renewed popular mandate, Asquith called for an election in January 1910; it produced a hung parliament, but he was able to continue in power with the support of the Irish Nationalist members.

Winston was comfortably returned by his constituency in Dundee and was invited by Asquith on 19 February 1910 to take on the post of home secretary, traditionally regarded as one of the four great offices of state. He was thirty-four years old.

— JSC TO WSC —

[February 1910] Tuesday 9.15   2 Norfolk Street, Park Lane

Darling

Many congratulations. I hope it is for long – George has gone out riding & intends going to see you. Be nice to him for my sake. I think it will do him a lot of good to go out to Mexico and I hope improve his health & his pocket.

Au revoir Yr loving
Mother

————————

17 Now in the state of Bavaria, straddling the River Main.

WINSTON SERVED in the post for two years, never wholly comfortable with its broad responsibilities for public order and justice, including the home secretary's lonely task of deciding in each case whether or not to reprieve those sentenced to death by the courts.

Clementine was seven months' pregnant with the couple's second child in March 1910, when she and Winston planned to travel after Easter (on 27 March) to join Jennie for a holiday in Biarritz, the French resort which was a favourite of Edward VII. The king had extended his usual spring visit because he was seriously ill, although his condition was not disclosed to the press in Britain. He returned home only shortly before dying on 6 May.

Winston and Clementine never reached Biarritz, because immediately after Easter Asquith scheduled a fresh attempt to break the budget deadlock in Parliament. It involved restricting the power of the House of Lords to veto any financial bills already passed by the elected chamber.

Winston wound up the case for the government on the second day of the debate, Thursday 31 March. He closed his speech with a passage that was especially controversial because it appeared to position the crown on the government's side of the dispute. The words in question were:

> Since the House of Lords … have used their veto to affront the prerogative of the Crown and to invade the rights of the House of Commons, it has now become necessary that the Crown and the Commons, acting together, should restore the balance of the constitution and restrict for ever the veto of the House of Lords.[18]

---

18 *Hansard*, House of Commons Debate, 31 March 1910, vol. 15.

— WSC to JSC —

9 April 1910   Home Office

Dearest Mamma

I am indeed sorry that your plans were upset through me. We could not get away until Saturday morning [2 April]; and when a very important Cabinet was fixed for Monday [4 April] at 12.45 it became clear that the jaunt, to which I had been looking forward so much, was beyond hope. [...]

I hope you have been rewarded for waiting longer at Biarritz by bright sunshine and regal smiles. My speech on the Veto fluttered the dovecote a good deal; but it has done no end of good, and I made it clear that I do not modify a word.

I am looking forward so much to seeing you. You can count absolutely on our coming. Do not be implacable to your prodigal and penitent son and daughter.

Yours ever

W

IN RETURN for the government dropping the most controversial measure of the People's Budget, a direct tax on land, the House of Lords finally passed the measure on 28 April 1910, a year to the day after its first introduction. The fundamental tension over the power of the Lords to reject legislation passed by the elected Commons remained unresolved for the time being.

Jennie did not write to Winston again until August, when she was staying with the Cunard family at their home in Leicestershire, Nevill Holt Hall. Winston and Clementine were about to leave for a cruise on Tutz's yacht in the Mediterranean; Jennie hoped Clementine, at least, would join her in September at Venice, where the duke of Marlborough had lent her his palazzo for the month.

In her letter, Jennie acknowledged that her marriage to George Cornwallis-West was crumbling, because he was leading his affair with Mrs Patrick Campbell increasingly in the open. To distract herself, Jennie worked on her second play, *The Bill*, a drama about women's efforts to gain the vote. It would eventually reach the stage, but not until July 1913.

— JSC ᴛᴏ WSC —

1 August 1910   Nevill Holt, Market Harborough

Dearest Winston

This is only a line to wish you a pleasant journey & to hope that I shall see you in Venice. Tell Clemmie I <u>count</u> on her & Goonie the 15ᵗʰ of Sept: I shall go out alone & chance finding some friends out there. I was sorry in a way that I told you the story of my encounter with Mrs P.C. [Patrick Campbell]. I laughed about it but I feel really very sore & broken over it – a little indignant that I should even have been put into such a position.

Bless you dear, be happy both of you. The thought of it is a great comfort to me. I am working hard at my play – I find it an interesting occupation – & a solace.

Best love
Mother

IN MID-AUGUST Jennie received a letter from George's mother, Patsy Cornwallis, apologising for her son's behaviour. Jennie drafted, but never sent, an anguished reply in which she wrote: 'He can have his freedom if he wants it – to marry Mrs Patrick Campbell or anybody else he thinks would make him happy – I have tried my best and have failed.'[19]

Neither Winston nor Clementine made it to Venice.

---

19 14 August 1910, JSC draft letter to Mrs P. Cornwallis-West, CAC, PCHL 1/5.

— JSC to WSC —

29 August 1910   Gopsall, Artherstone

My dearest Winston

You <u>have</u> been naughty about writing – not a line from either of you since you left. I have had 3 post cards and a letter from Jack and Goonie! Ah! Naughty!! I have found out from Eddie [Marsh] where to send this to. I hope it will reach you – it is hopeless writing to people who are yachting – here today & gone tomorrow.

I am going to London today & to Venice on Thursday. I am going to be quite alone there. But I shall find friends – & I have lots of writing to do. My play is nearly finished. I have been working very hard at it & am quite pleased with the 2 first acts. The 3rd will be more difficult & I have designs on you for a few spicy political arguments and sentences. I [think] the "good-gulling quack" ['deceiving doctor'] has come in very well. It may mean a lot of money to me so <u>really</u> you will have to help me – one hour of concentration on your part & the task is done!

I am sorry to tell you that George & I have made up our minds to part with the Waldens – & reduce our establishment generally. We have been living too long beyond our income. It's a great temptation to entertain when one has a very good cook. I shall only have a kitchen maid & a butler/valet & boy – Walden's book always came to at least £35 a month & Mrs Walden was getting every day more extravagant – But I have not complained to them and we are parting the best of friends all round.[20] [...]

I am glad to think you have all been enjoying yourselves so much & expect to see you looking like fighting cocks when I return at the end of Sept. I have been paying a round of visits & enjoying all the lovely gardens one never sees. George is in Scotland – he is much better & feeling in better spirits. I could have gone to Duart[21] where he goes this week – & he

---

20 It is doubtful that the Waldens ever left; he was certainly with JSC when war broke out in in 1914.

21 On the island of Mull, the old seat of the Maclean clan; repurchased for restoration by Sir Fitzroy Maclean, 26th chief of the clan, 1910.

wanted me to – but it was too late to change my plans without offending Sunny who has refused the Venice house to others on my account. [...]

Bless you all. I'm <u>so</u> sorry Clemmie can't come to Venice. It's a great disappointment. Give her my best love & to you.

Ever yr loving
Mother

————

NEITHER THE new king, George V, nor a Constitutional Conference of senior politicians that met twenty times during the summer of 1910, could forge a compromise over the future powers of the House of Lords. Armed with a secret promise from the king to create enough new peers to pass an amending bill if the Liberals won a fresh election, Asquith went to the country again in December.

The result was almost exactly the same as in January. The Liberals and Conservatives each won 272 seats, leaving the Irish Nationalist and Labour MPs with the balance of power. In Dundee Winston again topped the poll, although the Labour candidate came within some 300 of his total. Asquith and his government continued in office and the Lords backed down in the face of the threat to add many more members of a Liberal hue to their number. The Parliament Act 1911 exchanged their right to reject legislation passed by the Commons for rights of scrutiny and delay.

Jennie kept herself busy throughout the winter by campaigning to establish a national theatre in London. She formed an organizing committee, co-wrote a report called *The National Theatre, Scheme and Estimate*, then played a leading role in raising the £30,000 required for the first stage of the project. After her group merged with the similar Committee for a Shakespeare Memorial Theatre, she emerged as chairman of the combined organization. As part of its fund-raising programme, Jennie conceived the idea of mounting a gala ball at which all 600 guests would dress as a Shakespearean or Tudor character (she chose Olivia from *Twelfth Night*).

Meanwhile, her marriage to George reached breaking point in the spring of 1911, as he openly and repeatedly appeared in public with

Mrs Patrick Campbell. Without any money of her own, Jennie was reduced to wiring her two sons despondently on the afternoon of 4 April, asking for their help. Jack went straight to see Winston at the Home Office, where they each sent her £50 and tried to summon George, only to find that he was away. Winston was to give him a piece of their mind the next day.

'What he can hope to achieve by behaving as a blackguard I cannot understand,' Jack wrote that evening to his mother on behalf of them both. 'When all this is over, you will find yourself more settled and happier than you have been for some time, and you will come back again nearer to W [Winston] & me, whose love is always just the same.'[22]

Two days later, George offered to return to the marital home. Winston advised his mother against the move.

— WSC to JSC —

13 April 1911   Home Office

Dearest Mamma

I am quite sure it would not accord either with your dignity or happiness to seek by any promise of relations or circumstances to induce George to return to you. You would not wish to hold him in thralldom and such a condition could not last and would only be cruel to both of you. I agree with you that the immediate disentanglement & rearrangement of your affairs shd be effected before any avoidable publicity is given to your rupture. I have written George a letter.

Please prepare me with Jack the statement of your joint financial position from yr point of view. It is not necessary yet to consider what ultimate course should be taken, and it is important not to disclose in any way yr intentions. [...]

In the meanwhile please do not write to George. There is great strength in silence and that strength is often proportionate to the diffi-culty of preserving silence.

---

22 4 April 1911, Jack letter to JSC, CAC, PCHL 4/8.

I hope I was not rough in my manner last night. My heart bleeds for you and I am only trying to guide you upon the course which will secure the peace and honour of your life.

Do ponder over this. <u>You</u> cannot keep the smallest household under £1,000 a year. This will leave you almost nothing for all the things you want to do. On the other hand, if you can, at any rate for the present, abolish household expenses you will have more pocket money and more freedom than you have had for many years.

Ever your loving son
Winston

— JSC ᴛᴏ WSC —

14 April 1911   2 Norfolk Street, Park Lane

My dearest Winston

This is only a line to acknowledge your letter. I am about to go down to High Grove Pinner[23] to stay with Eleanor Warrender & her 2 sisters. Hugh [Warrender] is in Ireland. I shall return on Tuesday.

I quite agree with you about writing – I had the instinct <u>not</u> to do so from the beginning. And also I have never had any intention of asking George to return to me – what the future may bring I do not know. It is a terrible thing to break up a home but I feel the responsibility lies with George.

I am so tired after the misery and strain of the last fortnight – that I think I will not say any more on the subject at present.

I hope to have a financial account to give you. My papers are in fairly good order. Bless you darling – give my best love to Clemmy. Her flowers welcomed me & made me feel that I still have some who care for me besides you & Jack. Don't worry about me – I shall soon be all right.

Yr loving
Mother

Of course my intentions must be secret.

---

23 Shared by Hugh Warrender and his sister Eleanor, JSC's assistant in the hospital ship *Maine* at the time of the Boer War.

JENNIE CHANGED her mind a few days later and decided to try a reconciliation. Very few parties to a marriage sought a divorce (in the whole of the United Kingdom, only 580 parties petitioned in 1911),[24] because the process involved open hearings in the court and the presentation of evidence of adultery. Social humiliation was almost always the price paid for bringing a marriage to an end by divorce.[25]

On the evening of 18 April Jennie showed Winston a draft of the letter that she planned to send to George. Winston returned it the next day with two changes.

— WSC TO JSC —

19 April 1911   Home Office

Dearest Mamma,

I return the letter with pencilled amend'ts. "Freedom" has more meanings than one.

Dinner tonight 7.45. I am trying to get tickets for the Gaiety[26] wh I have not seen. Sir John Simon[27] is coming & perhaps Matthews![28]

If you want to talk privately come at 7.30. I was awfully tired last night: but have been rested by a good sleep.

Your loving son
W.

---

24 Office for National Statistics, Divorce Statistics for the United Kingdom, www. ons.gov.uk.
25 JSC was to write her third and final play on this theme in 1920. The text of *Between the Devil and the Deep Sea* was recently found amongst her papers at Churchill College, Cambridge, where the play received its first public reading in May 2018.
26 The musical *Peggy* opened at the Gaiety Theatre in London on 4 March, starring Phyllis Dare as Peggy.
27 Liberal MP since 1906, solicitor-general since October 1912 when he was knighted.
28 Henry Matthews, former home secretary, 1886–92; Viscount Llandaff.

Enclosed: JSC letter to George Cornwallis-West

19 April 1911   *2 Norfolk Street, Park Lane*

My dear George
Certainly come back to your own home – & with God's help we will start afresh. I see no reason why we should not be able to live in peace. I only want of you the respect & consideration *which is due to me as your wife. And on my side I will always try & help you in any way possible.*
In respect to our financial arrangements – these can be discussed amicably later – I accept your statement in respect to notice to servants, writing to people etc – I will only add that I want you thoroughly to understand that you return at your own wish & without any pressure or coercion from me. I do not wish later to be reproached [for not having given you your freedom] [excised by WSC].
Meanwhile your [room] [added by WSC] *is ready for you when you choose to occupy it –*

Yours affectionately
Jennie

FIVE MONTHS later Jennie embarked on her usual September round of visits to the Scottish estates of her friends, without her husband George, who had been hunting in Canada. On his way home, he had to undergo an emergency operation for appendicitis in New York on 29 August 1911.

Winston and Clementine travelled to Scotland, too, but they did not cross paths with Jennie. By now their family had grown, Clementine having given birth to their second child, a son, Randolph, on 28 May 1911.

— JSC TO WSC —

26 September 1911   Minto House, Hawick N.B.

Dearest Winston

I believe we just missed each other in Edinburgh on Sat. I was on the way here from Inverness – & the guard was rushing about looking for you as he had a telegram.

I am here quite alone with my old friends & it is very pleasant. I may go from here to Glenmuick for a few days tomorrow – or to London – if the Neumanns can't have me. I was taken to the Inverness gathering & balls last week. Lots of people there [...].

I hope you are enjoying yrself and are rested – you will have lots of golf at Balmoral. The war news looks better this morning[29] – George is going on all right but is still in hospital & until a few days ago was full of tubes. [...]

Bless you – love to Clemmie

Mother

— JSC TO WSC —

28 September 1911   Glenmuick House, Ballater N.B.

Dearest Winston

[...] I am sorry not to have seen you – but we shall soon meet in London. Meanwhile you have left a good "odour of sanctity" behind you at Balmoral. We went there for the dance last night, & everyone was charming about you – the King [George V] and Queen [Mary] sent for me to a private room before the dance began & he presented me with

---

29 At the request of Germany, the government of Italy had postponed for 48 hours the issue of an ultimatum demanding that the Ottoman empire cede its territory in North Africa (now Libya), on the grounds that Muslim fanatics in Tripoli were endangering Italian lives.

the Coronation medal[30] – making me a little speech about my "public hard work" etc. This I owe to you old Puss! Thank you very much.

I have let myself in to give a small farewell dinner to the Connaughts[31] next Thursday. I am sorry that you & Clemmie won't be in London. By the way I never heard such nonsense as the Duke repeated to you – I never said anything as to the war being a certainty or quoting an "authority". He is "gaga".

Well aurevoir. I go to London Monday night – George cables he has left the hospital & gone to the country. I think he will sail in a fortnight.

Love to Clemmie & much for yrself –
Yr loving
Mother

BEFORE LEAVING Scotland, Winston and Clementine visited the East Lothian home of Prime Minister Herbert Asquith and his wife Margot. While they were there, Asquith privately offered Winston the post that he had always coveted, first lord of the Admiralty. He could not resist dropping a hint of the move to his mother.

– JSC TO WSC –

1 October 1911   Glenmuick House, Ballater N.B.

Dearest Winston

You thrill me with curiosity – is it a change of Office? I hope a good one.

I shall look forward to seeing you in London the end of the week.

---

30 The coronation of George V took place on 22 June 1911; he presented a coronation medal to 5,000 people throughout the empire who did not attend the ceremony.
31 The duke of Connaught, seventh child of Queen Victoria, about to take up the post of governor-general of Canada, which he held until 1916.

My Connaught dinner is progressing – I so wish you & Clemmie were coming but you are *trop dans les grandeurs* already!

It is icy here. Such a cold house & snow on the hills. I leave tomorrow & go to Newmarket next week. I wonder what you think of Italy & Turkey.[32] I think the latter will give in – they are in a hopeless position. No navy & how can they get their troops to Tripoli? Would they be allowed to go through Egypt?

Well aurevoir. I am longing to see something of you & hear all yr news. Sly Puss! at Balmoral they thought you were leaving early in order to visit your "Mommer"!

How is the new car?[33] *Love to Clemmie –*

[no signature]

Oh! I played golf so well at Aboyne[34] –

———

I T WAS almost another year before Jennie and Winston exchanged a letter that survives. In the wake of Winston's onerous new duties at the Admiralty, in political charge of Britain's main fighting service, the Royal Navy, Jack took over the main responsibility for oversight of their mother's affairs.

Jennie busied herself for much of 1912 with a new scheme to help fund the building of a national theatre, even more ambitious than her last. She conceived the idea of mounting a pageant, *Shakespeare's England*, which was to run at the Earl's Court exhibition hall in London between May and October. The hall was to be converted into an Elizabethan town. Jennie demonstrated her continuing pulling

———

32 The Italian government presented its ultimatum on 26 September; its navy appeared off the port of Tripoli on 28 September, although it did not attack until 3 October. Italian forces won a comfortable victory, using aircraft for the first time, for aerial reconnaissance and to drop a bomb on Ottoman forces.

33 15 horsepower four-cylinder Napier Landaulette, bought for £610 from S. F. Edge Ltd of 14 New Burlington Street. The Churchills took delivery of the car at Balmoral on 25 September, CAC, CHAR 1/101/49,58.

34 Aboyne Golf Club in Deeside, founded 1883; moved to its current site in 1905.

power by recruiting the fashionable architect Edwin Lutyens to design its Tudor buildings and façades. The town's inhabitants would be dressed in period costumes, jousting tournaments would be held and Shakespeare's plays performed in a replica of the Globe Theatre.

To finance her scheme Jennie wheedled £40,000 out of the chairman of Winston's bank, Reginald Cox, plus another £15,000 from a family friend of George's. She was to keep 10 per cent of any profits; sadly, there were none. *Shakespeare's England* was deemed an artistic success, but a financial failure.

In September 1912, Winston asked his mother to join him and Clementine for a private holiday on board the HMS *Enchantress*, the Admiralty yacht which was put at the first lord's disposal. When telling her son that she could no longer join the voyage, Jennie broke the news of a final break from George.

Towards the end of her letter she referred to Winston's 'Federal Scheme' which he had outlined in a speech in Dundee on 12 September, when he emphasized that he was speaking personally, not on behalf of the government. The Irish Home Rule crisis, which was coming to a head, had stimulated him to think radically about a wider approach to devolution within the United Kingdom. His scheme, which he called 'Federal Home Rule', involved the devolution of powers to parliaments not only in Scotland and Ireland, but also in Lancashire and Yorkshire.

— JSC to WSC —

16 September 1912   2 Norfolk Street, Park Lane
Private

Dearest Winston

Jack & Goonie will give you news of me – I am sorry to say that the doctor who is looking after George says that there is no chance of his getting away for another fortnight or 3 weeks – therefore my little holiday is knocked on the head & I shall not be able to join you on the 19th as you asked me to.

George is anxious for me to go – but you know what a man feels like alone in a house – particularly when he is ill & depressed. I admit I need a change badly but I shall have plenty of time later when the [Shakespeare] Exhibition is over & this house is sold. We are doing our best to get rid of it. George & I have thrashed out the situation & intend to part when the financial position can be settled. We are very good friends & quite peaceful over it all.

But I feel that it is impossible for us to live together permanently. I could – but he will always hanker after the things he wants & imagine himself the most miserable of men. Of what use to chain him to me under those circumstances. If we made a mistake 12 years ago – & it seems a little hard that I should be the only one to suffer – but perhaps I shall suffer less in the long run if we part now – & it makes the sacrifice easier that if he gets what he wants & is happy – he will owe it all to me.

In saying this I don't want to pose as a heroine but after all I am very fond of him – & altho' I know – no one better – all his weaknesses, I want him to be happy. Lots of women have given up a man not to spoil his career or his life & if I did George an injustice in marrying him I can now put it right.

Now as to the practical part – he must do what he can to pay my debts & help towards my income. As to the procedure for the divorce it ought to be easy & without undue scandal. The Buck Barclay's who for years had gone their own ways divorced in a year without any trouble[35] but the preliminary step to all this is the selling of this house.

Now my dear old boy I have nothing more to tell you of myself. It is unfortunate for me that I can't have a change. I feel so stale – but I shall have it later. Tear this letter up & don't worry about me. I hope you are fit & well. I have read yr speeches with great interest. Your Federal Scheme is startling to say the least of it – but I see no reason in time why

---

35 I have been unable to identify the case to which JSC referred: Buck was usually an American name or nickname.

it shouldn't work. I read a poisonous speech of Londonderry's,[36] accusing you of leaving the Conservative party in order to get office. Considering the way they behaved to you the word "lie" is the only one applicable.

Well my darling I must stop. I shall be glad to see you again & have a talk. Tell me about Balmoral – did Clemmy like it? Give her my best love – I've not written as I felt stupid.

Bless you

Yr loving
Mother

– WSC to JSC –

19 September 1912 Admiralty Yacht

My dearest Mamma,

I have read your letter and feel so deeply for you in your troubles. I will write to you again in a few days, but substantially I agree with what you propose to do. Your affairs <u>must</u> be regulated first.

Clemmie tells me she has written to you. We both hope that at the end of the matter you may be able to come for a cruise. How would 26ᵗʰ or 27ᵗʰ suit you off the Welsh coast? [...]

With fondest love, always
Your loving son
W.

O N 13 January 1913 Jennie filed papers in court to start formal divorce proceedings against George. She hoped that she would not have to make a personal appearance in court.

Meanwhile, helped by a loan from Cox & Co., Jennie had acquired the business of the Nimrod Club, which still occupied No. 12 St. James's Square. She had redecorated the rooms – always her forte – and the club was trading well, a fact that she wished to hide from George while their divorce negotiations continued.

---

36 The marquess of Londonderry, a cousin of WSC, vigorously opposed Home Rule for Ireland.

- JSC то WSC -

15 February 1913   2 Norfolk Street, Park Lane

My dearest Winston

I went over the Club figures yesterday with my solicitor & took them to Mr Cox.[37] You will be glad to hear that as far as we can make out there will be between £1,400 & £1,500 profit yearly after everything is paid. Nearly £10,000 comes in in receipts – & an expenditure of £8,000 odd – Cox was very pleased. There is no reason why I shouldn't work up the Club to still better profits, if it could do so well with the filthy state it was in. How much more when it is nice and clean? Please don't mention anything about these figures for obvious reasons. [...]

Meanwhile I must [go] to see the solicitors about the divorce. They tell me that Russell [counsel for George] "put in an appearance" for G. which has the effect of retarding the proceedings a little, this in view of Russell <u>afterwards</u> suggesting that I sh^d sign an affidavit to the effect that I was not well and had to go abroad; looks as tho' he (Russell) had made a careless mistake but it appears that if I do get away, the Court sh^d accept my evidence in writing – which wl^d be splendid. In any case – the case will be put down as *West v. West*. I am writing against time to catch you – so forgive incoherence.

Russell in an interview with my man mentioned G's absolute poverty. If you see George – don't cut him – as you may later want to see him.

Bless you & best love to Clemmie – Enjoy yourselves & forgive my boring you with all this.

Yr loving
Mother

P.S. You may want to see George – if so (and it might [be] useful) Villa La Napoule, Napoule,[38] Cannes is his address.

---

37 Reginald Cox, chairman, Cox & Co., bankers.
38 Four miles west of Cannes, owned by George's sister, Daisy, countess of Pless.

O N 3 March Jennie did have to appear in court to obtain an order against George for the restitution of her 'conjugal rights'. A newspaper reported the next day on her brief appearance:

> There was something stately about her figure, dressed in black velvet, in exquisite taste. Magnificent sables dropped from her shoulders; a black toque crowned her rich black hair, and a large sable muff hid one hand, from which a dainty purse of chain-gold dangled.[39]

Once the hearing was over, Jennie travelled to Scotland to attend rehearsals of her second play, *The Bill*, in Glasgow. She stayed at the Marine Hotel next to the Royal Troon Golf Club on the Ayrshire coast.

— JSC TO WSC —

18 March 1913   Marine Hotel, Troon, Ayrshire

Dearest Winston

[...] This is quite a wild spot. I am practically alone at the hotel which is right on the links & on the sea. When I am not in Glasgow rehearsing *The Bill* I am playing golf with the hotel professional, a capital fellow. He gives me 2 strokes a hole & we have squared each match so far. I'm astonished at my fine play – quite good.

I am so tired at night that I have no time to be dull or lonely. I go to bed at 10 & have to catch a 9:00 train into Glasgow.

Poor Jack is kept busy with my rotten affairs – I wonder if they will ever be settled. You asked me the other day what I could count on in the way of money until the end of the year – £1500 from America[40]

---

39 R. Martin, *Lady Randolph Churchill*, vol. 2, p. 271.
40 The income produced by the marriage settlement contributed by her father.

£250 in May from Bristol[41] & £500 (minimum) from the Club. I may possibly get more.

I shall be back at the end of next week – the play is given for the first time on the <u>26</u>th – *priez pour elle!* It rehearses well & the actors like their parts – but I build up no hopes. It is in the hands of the Gods – & then pit!![42]

Love to Clemmie. Bless you

Yr loving

Mother

ONCE AGAIN, Winston invited his mother to join his party in May 1913 for a Mediterranean cruise in HMS *Enchantress.*

— WSC to JSC —

24 April 1913   Admiralty, Whitehall

Dearest Mamma,

It would do you a great deal of good to get away from England, worry & expense for three weeks & to bask a little in Mediterranean & Adriatic sunshine. Why will you not come with us on the 8th [May] & be delivered safely (D.V.) back on the 1st or 2nd of June. We start from Venice & go round by the Dalmatian coast to Malta, Sicily, Ajaccio, & Marseilles. (Perhaps Athens)

The Asquiths are coming; so that you wd have to make up your mind to get on with Margot & the P.M. But again why not? Otherwise we are only Admiralty and Admirable.

---

41 Almost certainly income from the Churchills' Marriage Settlement contributed by the English family; Bristol remains the headquarters of the trustee and executor services of National Westminster, the successor bank to those used by JSC.

42 Reference to the audience in the theatre; the play ran at the Glasgow Repertory theatre.

It would be so nice if you cd come, & Clemmie & I wd so greatly enjoy it. It will cost nothing or next to nothing. Answer please in the affirmative.

Always your loving son

W.

————

JENNIE DID join HMS *Enchantress* on this occasion, although she did not get on with Margot Asquith, according to Jennie's niece, Anita Leslie.[43]

On 15 July the divorce court heard the next stage of Jennie's petition. The judge refused a private hearing, so the witnesses gave their evidence in open session. First a Mr Drew, a private inquiry agent, testified that George Cornwallis-West 'stayed from March 28th to March 31st at the Great Western Railway Hotel at Paddington with "a woman unknown"'; then Louisa Mintern, a chambermaid, confirmed George's identity. It was a well-worn routine. Jennie received her decree, although it did not become absolute for another nine months.

For once she was not invited as a guest to the great Scottish estates that September. Instead she went to Munich and Paris. By contrast Winston did receive an invitation to Scotland, to stay between 1 and 7 September at Balmoral, where his fellow guests included Arthur Balfour, Andrew Bonar Law[44] and Lord Curzon.

— JSC TO WSC —

[undated, between 1–7 September 1913]   44 Rue Villejust, Paris

My dearest Winston

I am returning to London next Monday, & expect to go to the

———

43 A. Leslie, *Jennie*, p. 306.
44 Leader of the Conservative Party, later prime minister – the only one to be born outside the United Kingdom (see People, p. 571).

Speyers[45] at Cromer for a few days, & possibly return here in Oct:. My friend Mrs Marshall[46] with whom I have been staying has asked me to return. I had a perfect time in Munich & have thoroughly enjoyed myself, & am very fit & well.

I see by the papers you are at Balmoral – this may catch up with you there – anyhow they will forward it. I hope you are fit & have enjoyed the *Enchantress*. The talk here is the King of Greece's *faux pas* in Germany.[47] He arrives here Sat: & will not be very well received, but they say he will probably get the money he wants all the same. There is no doubt he is very stupid & is suffering greatly from a swelled head. [...]

Darling old boy I have no news & can only gush over my sight seeing & music which is dull. Alice van André[48] is at the Ritz – we travelled most peacefully together. But with all my faults I am a pleasant companion I know. [...]

I send you a naughty conundrum – don't be shocked – "Why was Rock savage?" "Because his pleasure was over Sassoon!"[49]

Bless you & best love, Yr loving
Mother

J ENNIE HAD switched her solicitors for her divorce from the traditional Churchill firm, Lumley & Lumley, to Messrs Woodhouse & Davidson of St James's Street. Following the financial failure of her Shakespeare pageant, which had just closed its doors, Jennie

------

45 Sir Edgar and Lady Speyer lived near Cromer; an immigrant from Germany, Sir Edgar chaired a merchant bank, Speyer Bros; after war broke out in 1914, he was accused of spying for Germany and left for the USA.

46 Possibly Nellie Marshall, née Ellen Pollard, second wife of British journalist and author Arthur 'Archibald' Primrose, who left the *Daily Mail* in 1911 to write in Europe.

47 On 24 August 1913, the new King Constantine of Greece travelled to Berlin to be awarded the baton of a German field marshal by Kaiser Wilhelm. The king publicly attributed the recent victories of the Greek army in the Balkans to his officers' German military training.

48 I have been unable to identify Alice van André.

49 On 6 August 1913, George Cholmondeley, known by the courtesy title 'the earl of Rocksavage', married Sybil Sassoon.

asked Herbert Woodhouse, the new firm's senior partner, whether he could design another scheme to raise for her some immediate cash, even at the expense of future income. She planned to open a new club in Paris.

No scheme would work, Jennie was told, unless she could find two guarantors for whatever sum she was able to borrow. Jennie sent Winston details of Woodhouse's scheme, because he had lent her £250 towards covering the losses of the pageant and she had him in mind as one of the guarantors.

— WSC to JSC —

29 November 1913   Admiralty Yacht

My dearest Mamma,

Woodhouse explained to me the plan you have in mind. Although there may be advantages in simplifying the control of your Insurance policies, the real effect of the transaction is to secure you about £2500 ready money, at the cost of permanently reducing your income by £300 a year. This is certainly not a good or wise arrangement, & only means a brief flutter followed by long deprivations.

Woodhouse tells me the [Nimrod] Club has realized a profit of almost £2000 this year. Surely with this you could manage to pay your way & preserve the income wh is already too small for your needs from further depredation.

Don't think about the £250 I paid for the Exhibition. It is never in my mind. I only wish your venture had had better success after all yr trouble.

Your loving son
W.

ON THE advice of his own lawyer (Theodore Lumley), Winston refused to guarantee his mother's new scheme. Jennie tried to change his mind face-to-face, then sent him an emotional letter.

— JSC to WSC —

3 December 1913   Ladies Athenaeum Club, 31 & 32 Dover Street
Private

Dearest Winston

Forgive me if I return to the "charge" & ask you to reconsider yr answer in respect to the Insurance Scheme.

The risk to you is infinitesimal & as far as any reduction to my income – I more than make it up in my Club & in the prospect of the new one – which you will be glad to hear is progressing well.

Please believe me that if it was not imperative I would not worry you. My position is an untenable one, & apart from anything else I must find a guarantor instead of George –

I had not received your letter when I saw you at Alice K's [Keppel's], & I want to thank you for it. I know you would do anything for me – & always have – but in this case you think it is best for me, to refuse.

If you do I shall have to try elsewhere – & I can't think of anyone. I don't think you realize what it means to me, the thought that I could pay you & Jack what I owe you. If I gave either of you an allowance, however small, I should not mind so much.

Now apart from the other benefits to me I have this one chance of settling this – of paying off the long-suffering Cox & of dropping out several unwilling and not well disposed guarantors. I think Mr Woodhouse can assure you. That there is very little risk – & he will have all the payments of interest & policies & only hands me over the surplus when all is paid (as Manisty[50] used to). He has been working 6 months at this Scheme for me & was much disappointed that you could only give him 10 mts the other day.

I hate having to write all this – as I know how overworked you are – but I can't very well help it. You will be glad to know that the

---

50 Solicitors appointed by Legal & General as 'receivers' to supervise the running of Lord Randolph's will trust, the main source of funds for the interest due on, or the repayment of, Legal & General's loan.

Paris Club is progressing & people are coming in. I am just getting my French circular out.

Bless you –
Mother

———————

WINSTON AND Jennie both spent Christmas at the duke of Westminster's hunting lodge in France. Already embroiled in delicate negotiations with David Lloyd George, the chancellor of the exchequer, over the number and the cost of battleships to be built for the Royal Navy, Winston decided against a simultaneous confrontation with his mother. He therefore acquiesced to her request.

On 9 January 1914 Jennie reached her sixtieth birthday; on the same day she told her sister Leonie: 'I shall never get used to not being the most beautiful woman in the room.'[51] By the end of the month, Winston had won his battle in the cabinet over the number of new battleships.

— JSC to WSC —

29 January 1914   Villa Isola Bella, Cannes

Dearest Winston

I am glad to see by the papers that the children are all right – & that you have your own way with L.G. [Lloyd George]. It was bound to be – I have no doubt however that you will have a *mouvementé* session!

I have been here since Monday – most lovely weather – roses & mimosas in full bloom & the "blue puddle" looking divine. There is no one staying here & very few people in Cannes – Juliet Duff[52] & Gwen Lowther[53] with whom I am going to play golf.

———————

51 A. Leslie, *Jennie*, p. 302.
52 Born Juliet Lowther, daughter of the 4th earl of Lonsdale, married Sir Robert Duff 1903.
53 Born Gwendoline Sheffield, married Lancelot Lowther, son of the 3rd earl of Lonsdale 1889.

I go to Rome next week & shall stay there till the end of Feb: when I return to London & the [Ladies Athenaeum] Club – I can't call it home!

I have heard from Woodhouse that he has seen you – & that the Insurance business is practically settled – for which I am <u>very grateful</u>. [...]

Everyone here rejoices at what they call your victory – in getting your own way. Monis's[54] revoking the Good Friday observance the French way has had a very bad effect. For the sake of pandering to a few socialist heathens he is despised.

Well bless you my darling boy, think of me sometimes. [...]

Ever your loving
Mother

— WSC to JSC —

10 February 1914   Admiralty, Whitehall

Dearest Mamma,

I think the naval estimates are now past the danger point & if so the position will be satisfactory. But it has been a long & wearing business wh has caused me at times vy gt perplexity.

I am so glad that you are enjoying yourself in Rome and the account you give certainly seems to represent a vy attractive life. I wrote to Sir E. [Edward] Grey about Hugh and his consulship.[55] It is not yet vacant, but I still think he wd stand a good chance if it were. [...]

I am going to attend to your affairs this week. I remain

Your loving son
W

---

54 Ernest Monis, French minister of the navy; formerly prime minister, minister of worship 1911. The main law separating French church and state passed in 1905; in France, Good Friday is only a public holiday in Alsace and Lorraine, where the law of 1905 has never applied because they then formed part of Germany.
55 I have not been able to trace WSC's letter to Sir Edward: 'Hugh' is probably Hugh Warrender, who remained in the army.

ON THE day after this letter was written, Lumley told Winston of the discovery that the wording of his father's will would almost certainly have allowed its trustees to appoint half the income from its trust to his sons when JSC remarried in 1900. It was a lawyer for the Legal & General Insurance Company who had made the discovery, while he was checking the paperwork for Jennie's new rescue scheme.

When Winston and Jack made more inquiries, they were shocked to find that their mother's income after Lord Randolph's death had been twice as high as she had claimed to them at the time. On 13 February they met Woodhouse and Lumley at the Admiralty to discuss the matter; it was clear that Jennie's rescue scheme could no longer go ahead, because the security to back it was now uncertain. The next day Jack wrote to Jennie for both himself and Winston. They did not wish to insist on demanding part of the trust's income, yet his message was clear:

> It makes a considerable difference finding that Papa's Will was not made – as we were always led to suppose – carelessly and without any consideration for us. We have begged you so often to live within your income – which is not a very severe demand. … Unless you are able to do so and if you start running up bills again – there is nothing that can save you from a crash and bankruptcy.[56]

Jennie did little to change her way of life. In March she travelled to Monte Carlo, from where Jack urged her to return to put her affairs in order. She replied:

> Who cares if I return or not? … Not that I do not know you and Winston love me, and are very good to me – but you lead busy

---

56 14 February 1914, Jack letter to JSC, CAC, CHAR 28/33/4-5.

Jennie, alone outside her home in Brook Street, London,
after her divorce in 1914.

lives, & have yr own families to be absorbed in. What am I? Only an old 5ᵗʰ wheel – I am not complaining, only stating facts.[57]

Jennie's divorce from George was declared absolute on 6 April. Later the same day he married Mrs Patrick Campbell. Jennie had already sent him her engagement and wedding rings, bidding him 'goodbye, a long goodbye'.[58]

Two months later, on 28 June 1914, the Archduke Franz Ferdinand of Austria and his wife were assassinated in Sarajevo, unleashing a sequence of events that would lead to the Great War. On 24 July, four days before Austria-Hungary declared war on Serbia, Jennie wrote to her sister Leonie:

> Every effort I make to get out of my natural selfishness meets with a rebuff. My sons love me from afar and give me no companionship even when it comes their way. The fault is undoubtedly with me. Every day I become more solitary and prone to introspection which is fatal.[59]

57 March 1914, JSC letter to Jack; J. & C. Lee. *Winston & Jack*, p. 245.
58 4 April 1914, JSC letter to G. Cornwalli-West, CAC, CHAR 28/39/19.
59 24 July 1914, JSC letter to L. Leslie; A. Leslie, *Jennie*, p. 307.

21

CODA AT THE FRONT

1915–18

'I am a great believer in your star'

NOT YET forty years old, Winston found himself at the heart of events in July and early August of 1914 which were to produce the European war that 'came from nowhere'. As first lord of the Admiralty he held the political responsibility for directing the Royal Navy, around which Britain's strategic defence had long been built.

Jennie's own records show that she still managed to lunch with him on 28 July and to see him again on 1 August, despite her claims of a few days earlier that her busy sons loved her only 'from afar'.

On 4 August, the day Britain declared war on Germany, she allowed her butler Thomas Walden to enlist in the army, replacing him with two parlourmaids whom she clothed in Tudor uniforms. Jack went off to war in the same month. On 30 August his wife Goonie wrote to him of a dinner party she had attended at Jennie's latest home, 72 Brook Street:

Needless to say we had a seven course dinner beautifully served, platters of luscious fruits etc, all in a lovely dining room the walls of which were decorated with lovely pictures – We afterwards sat in a 'pickled' oak room, beautifully lighted in the cornices by invisible electric lights, & filled with lovely bibelots, furniture rugs, flowers, in fact it looked very rich and opulent, comfortable & luxurious.[1]

Many in London expected the fighting to be over by Christmas, yet when that landmark passed there was no sign of a breakthrough on the Western Front by either German or Allied forces. Winston described the military situation privately to the prime minister, Herbert Asquith, as a stalemate; the government, he suggested, should consider a second front. Others to press for consideration of a move against the Ottoman empire included David Lloyd George (still chancellor of the exchequer), Lord Kitchener (now secretary of state for war) and Colonel Maurice Hankey (the influential secretary of the Committee of Imperial Defence and of the new War Council).

The scheme to force a way through the Dardanelles Strait to threaten Constantinople, the capital of the Ottoman empire, was not of Winston's invention. During its planning phase, however, it became an Admiralty-led operation of which he emerged as the leading advocate within government.

The navy's attempts to force the Dardanelles Strait began in earnest on 19 February, but by late in March it was clear that they had failed, due to poor planning and leadership on the spot. Military commanders decided to pursue their objective by adopting an alternative strategy of landing British and Anzac (Australia and New Zealand) troops at two points on the Gallipoli peninsula. Once again the plans went awry: by early May it was clear that substantial casualties had been suffered to little or no effect.

---

1 1 September 1914, G. Churchill letter to JSC, P. Churchill and J. Mitchell, *Jennie*, p. 250.

By the middle of May the succession of reverses in the Dardanelles had produced calls for a national government to be formed by leading figures from both the Liberal and the Conservative parties that Asquith could no longer resist. As the Conservatives' price for joining, their leaders demanded Winston's scalp as first lord of the Admiralty; they had never fully forgiven his desertion of the Tory cause in the previous decade. He resigned as first lord of the Admiralty on 22 May 1915, but remained a member of the government as chancellor of the duchy of Lancaster, a largely ceremonial post. He retained his seat on the cabinet's Dardanelles committee.

The next day, Jennie wrote to console her son. She was staying near the Channel ports at the East Sussex home of her friend Lady Warrender, who had been a fine soprano in her heyday. Jennie now accompanied her on the piano while they entertained wounded troops at nearby hospitals. It was a Sunday and Jennie had just read the *Observer*'s leading article, in which the newspaper's famous editor, J. L. Garvin[2] had written: '[Churchill] is young. He has lion-hearted courage. No number of enemies can fight down his ability and force. His hour of triumph will come.'

— JSC TO WSC —

23 May 1915   Leasam, Playden

Dearest Winston

I hope you liked the article in the *Observer.* It is just the right note.

Darling old boy I am thinking of you so much & this is only to tell you so. Aurevoir and best love to Clemmie and Goonie – I have no idea of the proper address. I hope this one will reach you –

Yr loving
Mother

---

2   J. L. Garvin, friend of both JSC and WSC; editor the *Observer* 1908–42 (see People p. 571).

Jennie, Winston, Jack and their families at Admiralty House, March 1915.
Back row: (left to right) Winston, Clementine (Sarah on her lap), Jennie,
Goonie, Jack; front row: Diana, Randolph, Peregrine, John.

W INSTON FOUND himself frustrated by his exclusion from effective decision-making. On 10 June he and his mother dined with the only war reporter who had witnessed the Dardanelles landings. Ellis Ashmead-Bartlett recorded that he 'looked years older, his face is pale, he seems very depressed'; towards the end of the evening, Winston 'suddenly burst forth into a tremendous discourse on the Expedition and what might have been, addressed directly across the table in the form of a lecture to his mother, who listened most attentively'.[3]

The news from both Flanders and the Dardanelles darkened further throughout 1915, prompting Asquith in November to replace the Dardanelles sub-committee by a smaller war cabinet of five men. Winston was not to be a member; on Saturday 11 November he resigned from the government, placing himself 'unreservedly at the disposal of the military authorities'.

---

3 A. Leslie, *Jennie*, p. 318.

Two days later *The Times* printed the full text of his letter of resignation to Asquith. In it Winston hinted publicly for the first time at what he felt were the reasons for failure: 'Even when decisions of principle are rightly taken, the speed and method of their execution are factors which determine the results.'[4]

On Wednesday 15 November, he divulged more in his speech of resignation to the House of Commons, where he was at pains to convince members that the Dardanelles campaign had not been his personal scheme. 'The naval attack on the Dardanelles was a naval plan,' he said, 'made by naval authorities on the spot, approved by naval experts in the Admiralty, assented to by the First Sea Lord and executed on the spot by Admirals who at every stage believed in the operations.' In its leading article of the following day *The Times* commented: 'The great revelation of Mr Churchill's speech was the extensive and wholly unpardonable gap which separated the naval from the military activities.'[5]

Three days later, on 18 November, Winston set off in the uniform of a major of the Oxfordshire Hussars to find his regiment in Flanders, leaving Clementine and the children to live with Jack's family at his house in Kensington, No. 41 Cromwell Road. Fortunately, it was large enough to hold everyone.

Turning the clock back twenty years to the time when Winston had gone off fighting in India, Jennie started writing to her son again every week, while campaigning for his political rehabilitation among her contacts at home. She passed on any political gossip that she heard: an early piece concerned Winston's old nemesis Lord Kitchener who had held onto his position as secretary of state for war, although Asquith and other members of the cabinet found him an impossible colleague. To help keep him out of the way, Asquith had dispatched Kitchener to the Dardanelles where he was to make recommendations on the future of the campaign.

---

4   *The Times*, 15 November 1916.
5   *Idem*, 16 November 1915.

Before Winston reached his regiment he was summoned to the headquarters of Sir John French,[6] the beleaguered commander-in-chief of the British Expeditionary Force and an old friend. Promising Winston a senior command in short order, Sir John dispatched him for a spell of acclimatization on the front line with the Grenadier Guards.

— JSC TO WSC —

21 November 1915   72 Brook Street, W.

My dearest Winston

You venturesome fellow. I might have known that 50 miles behind the line was not your particular style. I can understand that you want to study *sur place* this new phase of warfare. It is no use my saying "be careful". It is all in the hands of God. I can only pray & hope for the best.

I saw Sarah[7] who told me she had seen you at Boulogne. I have no doubt you have found plenty of friends & they are making a fuss over you – but that was a certainty. How I wish I knew what was the result of the Paris Conference.[8] Goonie dined with the P.M. [prime minister] last night – she gathered no news but the P.M. seemed very pleased that there were 6 "P.M.'s" besides himself at the Conference! – the "spotty one" [almost certainly Edwin Montagu][9] sat on her other side, but as I say, she heard nothing.

---

6   Already a field marshal, Sir John had first joined the navy 1866 (see People p. 575).

7   WSC's aunt Sarah Wilson, whose husband Gordon Wilson had been killed November 1914; she resumed front-line nursing, which she had also undertaken in the Boer War.

8   Anglo-French conference in Paris, 17 November; approved the formation of a Council of War to co-ordinate Allied action.

9   Edwin Montagu succeeded WSC as chancellor of the duchy of Lancaster in 1915 (initially without a seat in the cabinet); close to Asquith, Montagu was also the prime minister's rival for the love of Venetia Stanley, whom Montagu eventually married. The *Oxford Dictionary of National Biography* reports his complexion as 'faintly pock-marked'.

They tell a story of K. of K. [Kitchener of Khartoum] telegraphing that as his job was finished, he wl^d now return – but the whole Govt: frantically looked for something else to keep him out there.

Clemmie will have told you of our arrangements for the moment – I am trying to let the house for 6 months or a year – & have someone coming to see it tomorrow – but unless I let it for a certain sum it wl^d not repay me. Meanwhile until I do I propose to contribute toward the housekeeping at C. R^d. [Cromwell Road] as much as I can. I had tea there today with the children – great darlings.

While I have the house I mean now & then to have a dinner party. [J. L.] Garvin is coming on Thursday & I have asked Bonar Law[10] & George Curzon. I wish you were going to be here – it is like *Hamlet* without Hamlet. I will write to you how it all goes.

Ld Ribblesdale[11] came to see me today. I reproached him for making a rash speech in the H of L. on the evacuation of Gallipoli. He thought yr letter & speech splendid, & thought you were quite right to defend yrself as until yr speech, he, like many others, blamed you.

[…] I saw the Laverys[12] today – I haven't seen as yet your *chef d'oeuvre* of Goonie. She tells me that Jack is not at Salonika.[13] I can't imagine L^d. K. as a diplomat getting round Tino[14] – *quelle bagarre* [what a brawl] the whole thing.

Best love – write to me sometimes & let me know if you want anything – or want me to find out anything. Bless you.

Your loving
Mother

10 Andrew Bonar Law, secretary of state for the colonies (see People, p. 571).
11 Veteran Liberal peer whose only remaining son had died at Gallipoli.
12 Sir John Lavery and his wife Hazel; Sir John coached WSC when he started to paint in the summer of 1915 (see People, p. 570).
13 In October 1915 two British and French divisions landed in Salonika (now Thessaloniki) to help Serbia fight an invasion by Bulgaria.
14 Familiar name of King Constantine of Greece, who resisted his ministers' advice to allow Allied forces to land at Salonika. (Greece was officially neutral in the war.)

— WSC TO JSC —

24 November 1915   [No address given]

Dearest Mamma,

Clemmie will I am sure have shown you my letters to her, so that I only write a few lines by way of supplement. I am vy happy here and have made good friends with everybody now. I always get on with soldiers, & these are about the finest.

I do not certainly regret the step I took. I am sure it was right from every point of view. Also I know I am doing the right thing out here. Mind you write to me and tell me all your news and what plans you are making with Clemmie and Goonie. Keep in touch with people who can be useful and friendly.

With fondest love, Your loving son
Winston

P.S. Do you know I am quite young again.

— JSC TO WSC —

27 November 1915   Ladies Athenaeum Club

My darling Winston

I was very delighted to receive your little letter & to hear that you are well & happy. You may imagine what we all felt when we heard of you in the trenches, but I suppose it had to be in view of the future. By the way, Adèle Essex[15] dined with me the other night. She said she heard you had been offered a brigade, but had refused it. I told her she knew more than we did. Who gossips about these things?

Well! Garvin & George Curzon dined with me on Thursday. I tried to get Bonar Law & AJB [Balfour], but they were engaged. I shall ask the former again. George C. was full of you, he wants to write to you & I gave him yr address. […]

---

15 Adèle, countess of Essex, born in New York; president of the Soldiers and Sailors Families Association during the war.

I dined at C. R^d. last night. Goonie was not there as she had gone to see her parents for the weekend. Lady Helen Mitford[16] and Nellie[17] made our 4 up. I am trying hard to let the house but it is not easy – meanwhile I have arranged to pay £40 a month towards the house-keeping which I hope will be a help. Clemmie thinks it will make things easier. I am also giving Goonie £10 a month just for a little pocket money, as she has none – everything being swallowed up. <u>Don't say anything about this</u>. What a bore money is – or rather the want of it. It is lucky that I make my £50 a month with articles or I sh^d not be able to do anything.

I am sending you a pair of oil-silk stockings to be worn <u>sandwiched</u> between two wolley [sic] ones. They say they keep yr feet at the same temperature as when you put on the stockings – <u>not</u> very healthy but better than frostbites. Let me know how they do & I will send you some more.

I hope this will reach you in time for yr birthday – many <u>many</u> happy returns of it. Bless you, please be sensible. I think you ought to take the trenches in small doses after 10 years of a more or less sedentary life. But I am sure you would not "play the fool". Remember you are destined for greater things than men in the past. I am a great believer in your star, & I know that you are doing absolutely the right thing.

We shall all of us "hot up" your friends & keep the ball rolling. Rumours are awash that French is recalled[18] – & that the W.O. [War Office] has been swept & furnished thinking that K. wl^d not return – but here he is within 36 hrs!! with the Seals still in his pocket![19]

---

16 Lady Helen Freeman-Mitford, née Ogilvy, a cousin of Clementine.
17 Margaret Hozier, known as 'Nellie', sister of Clementine; due to marry Colonel Bertram Romilly ten days later.
18 Sir John French resigned as commander-in-chief of the British Expeditionary Force on 6 December 1915; no public announcement was made until 15 December.
19 Asquith relieved Lord Kitchener of his responsibility for war strategy in the government reorganization of November 1915. Kichener was in the Dardanelles at the time; the rumour was that Asquith had wanted to sack him completely, but the field marshal took the precaution of travelling with his seals of office.

Clemmie and the children are coming to luncheon & then she is going to play tennis with Jack Islington, & I am going to the Canteeen at London Bridge. I am getting up a big matinée in aid of it next Friday. [...] I am going to send you some of the thin paper *Times Literature*[20] – you can throw it away when read. Well once more "happy returns of the day" & much love from

Your devoted
Mother

[...] They say Gallipoli is shortly being evacuated but I disbelieve it.

———·———

H IS MOTHER'S concern that Winston should look after his feet stemmed from an outbreak on the Western Front of trench foot, a combination of fungal infection, frostbite and poor circulation. The *Soldier's Small Book*, distributed to British troops, made it clear that each soldier was responsible for looking after his own feet. Professor Sheridan Delépine, a Swiss-born pathologist and leading light in the promotion of public health in Britain, had advocated the use of silk impregnated with olive or whale oil to counter the threat.

The rumour of evacuation from the Gallipoli peninsula that Jennie had heard turned out to be well founded. After visiting the area, Kitchener had recommended the withdrawal of all Allied troops. On 7 December the cabinet approved their departure from Suvla and Anzac Cove; by 20 December they had left. The order to evacuate Helles was given on 28 December; the last troops left on 9 January 1916.

---

20 *The Times Literary Supplement* had started as a section of *The Times* in 1902; it became a separate publication in 1914.

— WSC TO JSC —

1 December 1915   [No address given]

Dearest Mama,

I think you have been vy generous & I trust you can spare the money. As long as you three stand together, all will be well. I do not expect the present state of things will last for more than a year at the outside.

I have now returned to G.H.Q. on a visit while the Grenadiers are 'resting' out of the line. I made good friends with them & they will be gladder to have me back than they were to have me. We had a little mild bickering wh cost some life & limb; & I found the time pass by agreeably. The cold & wet did not trouble me. An officer can change his boots & socks. Your new green waterproof socks will be an additional security.

The return of K delights me. What a world of shams it is! Well I am thank God only a spectator now, so I am much better situated to see the humour of the play.

You are quite right to keep in touch with our friends, also with our friends' friends. My attitude toward the government is independent not hostile, & yr tone should be salt not bitter.

Fondest love, Your loving son
W

J ENNIE NOW chaired the executive committee of the American Women's War Relief Fund, helping to organize buffets at London Bridge and other railway stations for troops who were setting off to, or returning from, the front.

She passed on discouraging news to her son about the course of the war in Eastern Europe and the Middle East. The British government called a conference in Calais with its French counterparts on 4 December, to recommend withdrawing Allied forces from Salonika in Greece. (French representatives reluctantly agreed, only to reverse their decision at another conference held two days later in Chantilly.) In Mesopotamia (modern Iraq), British troops were retreating southwards after the inconclusive Battle of Ctesiphon towards Kut-al-Amara, where Ottoman forces encircled them in December. (Successive attempts to relieve the siege failed and the British force would surrender on 29 April 1916.)

Jennie also visited General Sir Ian Hamilton, Winston's old friend, who had just returned to London from Gallipoli after being relieved of his command of the Mediterranean Expeditionary Force.

− JSC to WSC −

5 December 1915   72 Brook Street

Dearest Winston

I am relieved to hear that you are out of the trenches − you seem to have had a narrow escape. The enclosed relates more than you do on the subject!

I am afraid I have little news to tell you this week. I have been up to my eyes in organizing a matinée in aid of the London Bridge Buffet where we are now feeding 1200 a day! The matinée was a great success − Clemmie and Goonie sold programmes & looked their best. I went to the Asquith wedding[21] and of course to Nellie's[22] yesterday. [...]

I think the war news bad − Garvin points out the danger of the whole of Austria becoming under German rule. Last week we were 12 miles from Bagdad and now we are a 100! Yesterday (6th) I heard that K. had had a great row with Briand[23] & the Russians at the Calais Conference, as he wished to remove all the troops from Salonica & Gallipoli − to Egypt − but this probably is not true. The papers [know] little & everyone is at sea.

I went to see the Hamiltons − Ld[y] H. ill in bed, Sir Ian read me

---

21 On 30 November 1915 Violet Asquith (who had been 'almost engaged' to WSC in 1908) married Maurice Bonham Carter, her father's principal private secretary.

22 Now Nellie Romilly, having married 5 December 1914 (suggesting that JSC started her letter on 6 not 5 December 1915).

23 Aristide Briand, prime minister of France for the third time, October 1915– March 1917.

part of yr letter. They both looked so ill & wan & the poor thing seems quite in the dark as to what people say – talked of his being sent back – but was worried at Monro[24] being made C-in-C. "I'm afraid it means evacuation", Ian said.

I heard of someone who has just arrived from Berlin, an American woman whose husband is at the American Embassy & she says the Germans have lots of food & are quite confident. Well we certainly are in a nice mess! Thank God you have no responsibility for it.

I wonder if you have seen Hugh Warrender? He has been in Paris, but returns to the "mud and shells" shortly. I have a chance of going to Paris on the 17th for a few days. Could you get away?

Do write & give me your news. Would you like another pair of oilsilk stockings? And do you think they w^d be of any use to Jack? [...]

Bless you darling, I enclose latest *Times* war literature.

> *Your loving*
> *Mother*

— WSC TO JSC —

8 December 1915   General Headquarters, BEF

Dearest Mamma,

I expect to go into the line again tomorrow, as nothing is as yet definitely settled about my employment. Meanwhile it has been vy pleasant and peaceful here: & I have moved about & seen interesting things & soldier friends.

Yesterday I motored over & examined the trenches and positions at Nieuport and Westende[25] – on the extreme flank of the line. The day

---

24 Lt.-General Sir Charles Monro, appointed to supervise the evacuation of Allied troops from Gallipoli. He finished the war as commander-in-chief of the British army in India.

25 Nieuport lies on the River Yser, three kilometres inland from the Flanders coast; Westende one kilometre to its north-east along a canal. Belgian and British forces held the line of the Yser against the German advance in October 1914, preventing the loss of ports in north-eastern France by the Allies.

before I went to the 10th French Army to see the battlefields of Lorettte and Carency.[26] I am vy well treated wherever I go & everyone civil & unquestioning.

Your letter has just reached me and the broadsheets also. But I don't much care for these literary snippets. Indeed all reading is difficult except the reading of letters – ever welcome.

I am pretty well au fait with the situation now as I have received letters from England & also I hear the news here. All I hear confirms me in my satisfaction to be freed from any share in the present proceedings.

Mind you keep in good touch with all my friends. George Curzon is vy friendly. Garvin shd be cherished.

Best love my dear. Write often – all good luck attend you.

Your loving son

W

O N 9 December Sir John French told Winston that he was to be appointed brigadier-general of the 56th Brigade, which comprised four Lancashire battalions. In a letter the next day he shared the news with Clementine; his mother, however, had not heard of the appointment when she wrote on 12 December.

— JSC TO WSC —

12 December 1915   72 Brook Street, W.

My dearest Winston

I quite understand about the "literary snippets". Jack likes them – but of course he is out of the way, of books. I wish I knew more as to his

---

26 Lorette ridge, 165 metres (541 ft) above sea level at its highest, dominates the Douai plain and the town of Arras 12 kilometres to the south-east; the village of Carency lies close to the ridge. By December 1915 both ridge and village had witnessed four major engagements of the war.

movements.[27] Goonie tells me he is with Birdwood,[28] is he on the staff? I am told Birdwood is not luxurious & shares pretty much the same life as his men – what a muddle!

I tried to get Garvin to dinner but without luck. I mean to try again. I am going to concoct a dinner with the help of Clemmie & Goonie – of useful people. I spoke to Garvin on the telephone. He was concerned at yr having returned to the line. The enclosed from Shane Leslie[29] will interest you. You are a great hero in the U.S.A. & here too.

Vincent Caillard[30] and Eddie [Marsh] dined here 2 nights ago. They both said there was to be no compulsion [conscription] – I wonder if the Country will be very angry? It looks as tho' they had been got under false pretences, as many joined thinking that otherwise they would be taken. [...]

I wish I had some interesting news to tell you. We wondered reading of K's visit to Fontainebleau if he came away with a "bibelot"?[31]

Bless you

Love

Mother

ON 15 December, Winston took a telephone call from Sir John French in London. After passing on the news of his own dismissal, Sir John had to confess that Asquith had also vetoed Winston's promotion to command a brigade. 'Perhaps you might give him a battalion,' Asquith had ended his note.

---

27 Jack was camp commandant of the general headquarters of the Mediterranean Expeditionary Force (MEF), about to disband after the evacuation of Gallipoli.
28 Lt.-General Sir William Birdwood, interim commander-in-chief MEF (see People, p. 575).
29 WSC's first cousin, invalided out of the British Ambulance Corps; subsequently posted to Washington, DC (see People, p. 566).
30 Formerly financial representative of Britain, Belgium and the Netherlands in Constantinople; now finance director of the arms manufacturer, Vickers Ltd.
31 *Bibelot*, a small object of beauty. Kitchener visited Chantilly rather than Fontainebleau on 6 December.

By the time Jennie wrote on 19 December, she had heard part of the story of her son's treatment. She continued to work her contacts for him as vigorously as she could, yet it was hard to disguise the fact she was now often dealing with the 'B' list.

— JSC to WSC —

19 December 1915   72 Brook St, W.

Dearest Winston

You <u>are</u> giving us frights! – with G. McAlys killed near you,[32] & that horrid French warfare. Well! I suppose you know as much as we do about the attitude of the P.M. & the H. of C. in respect to your Brigade. I'm afraid that it is off for the moment. You will have seen Sir F. E. [Smith] who will have told you all there is to say.[33] It seemed to me the H. of C. was distinctly nice on the whole – it is only a question of time.

I dined with the Agha [sic] [Khan][34] last night & he put the Lovat Fraser[35] next to me – we got on very well. Towards the end of dinner he warmed up. He says there is much grumbling in the Navy against A.J.B. [Balfour] – they say he has gone to sleep & everything is left to slide. Fraser also said that K. was the stumbling block at the beginning, & still is so. He ended by saying that you must return at the first good opportunity. Altogether he was very friendly – & as he has not <u>always</u> been so to you, & that I know he writes nearly all the leaders in *The Times*, I thought he was a good person to "hot up".

George Warrender[36] dines with me tonight – Clemmie & a few others – I shall try & find out what they think in the navy. I believe he

---

32 British Forces records do not list anyone with this name dying in the First World War: it is possible that JSC misspelled the name: for example, soldiers named G. McAlees and G. McAleese both died in action in 1915.

33 WSC and 'F.E.' were unable to meet on this visit.

34 Sir Sultan Mohammed Shah, third Aga Khan, leader of the Nizairi Ismaili community.

35 Journalist, *The Times*, since 1907; editor, *Times of India*, 1902–6.

36 Vice-Admiral Sir George Warrender, commander of the navy's 2nd Battle Group.

can have [command of] Portsmouth if he wants it. I had hoped to have seen Gen: French but he left yesterday. [...]

I can't make out where Jack is, or whether Gallipoli is being evacuated. They say lots of troops are being sent to Mesopotamia – a foolish expedition Fraser says, as you can't hold an open town like Bagdad in any case.

I am going to the Warrender fortress & possibly to Paris for a week in the New Year. Any chance of yr getting away? This is only a scrawl. Do you know Haig? I remember him in the old days at Warwick, when he was devoted there.[37] A hard man – & a bit of a bounder – but I imagine a fine soldier.

You have never told me if you want another pair of oilskin stockings. Ld Esher[38] whom Clemmie & I met the other day says you are very well. Keep so! – & bless you, with fondest love

Mother

WHILE WINSTON waited for news about which battalion he was to command, he returned home briefly to London for Christmas. During his stay, Lloyd George gave him the impression that he was on the brink of leading a move to replace Asquith as prime minister, with Bonar Law; if they succeeded, Winston could expect to regain a leading ministerial position. Almost as soon as he returned to France on 27 December, however, the moment passed.

On 1 January 1916 Winston heard that he was to command an infantry battalion, the 6th Royal Scots Fusiliers. He joined its exhausted troops in the village of Moolenacker on 5 January.

---

37 Reference to an earlier affair between Sir Douglas Haig and Daisy, countess of Warwick.
38 Courtier, Liberal politician and an influential adviser to the War Office and on army reform; in wartime, Esher liaised unofficially between British and French generals.

— JSC to WSC —

6 January 1916   72 Brook Street

My dearest Winston,

It is late in the day to wish you a 'happier New year' – but my wish is nonetheless warm.

Your boots are going to you by K.M. [King's Messenger] & I trust they will be all right. I had a long & interesting letter from Jack dated 22 Dec: I gather he has gone to Egypt with his Chief [Birdwood] – or on the eve of doing so. He is looking forward to it, & hopes to get leave to come home for a week. Poor fellow he has not had any for 10 months – he says the P.M. and K of K ought to be very grateful to Birdwood for giving the Govt: a successful new lease of life over the successful evacuation. […] I hear the Govt. have kept back Sir Ian Hamilton's report to cut out a lot. They sent K. to him & Col. Repington[39] says he told him to go to h– [hell] – there was a scene – I believe the report comes out today.

Meanwhile the P.M. has weathered the storm, they will all accept the limited compulsion [conscription]. Of course there will be feeble rows in the H. of C. but the threat of the P.M. resigning will have a cooling effect on their ardour – I hear of L.G. [Lloyd George] looking worried – Goonie saw Lord E. Talbot[40] who talked pointedly of intrigue with L.G. to upset the Govt: I do not like to write too openly. I have not seen anyone of interest – my kitchen boiler is 'bust' so that I cannot arrange any dinners for the moment. […]

Since beginning this I have met Venetia James[41] who was in the House yesterday & says the P.M. was very badly received & that the Speaker told her he thought things wl^d not go well, notwithstanding

---

39 Col. Charles Repington, former soldier and influential war correspondent of *The Times* since 1904.
40 Lord Edmund Talbot, MP, chief whip of the Unionist Party; married to Goonie's aunt.
41 Née Cavendish-Bentinck, married to John James; friends of the late Edward VII.

the crowds of MP's brought back from the Front to vote with the Govt:.
Perhaps I am wrong [...].

Bless you – this is a disjointed letter but I will write again. My thoughts
are always with you – I hope you will have your battn: & that you like it.

With best love

Mother

— JSC ᴛᴏ WSC —

12 January 1916   72 Brook Street, W.

Dearest Winston

[...] I am sure that shams like McK.[42] [McKenna] and K of K. can't
stand the test of war for very long. [...]

I lunched with Bessie Bentinck[43] the other day & met the Carters
& Sir Francis Hopwood.[44] Violet [Asquith] told me that Lord Fisher[45]
came to lunch at D. Sᵗ. [Downing Street] last week & looked & talked
like a madman & that the P.M. buttered him up to put him in a good
temper, & then made for the door. Sir Francis asked much after you.

I have seen very few people. Commander Chilcote[46] spoke to me
at the play & told me that Admiral Brock[47] said the other day "We
shouldn't have one aircraft here were it not for Winston Churchill".
I see with the ascent of Mr Montagu[48] to the Cabinet that we shall soon

42 Reginald McKenna, chancellor of the exchequer; formerly first lord of the
Admiralty, home secretary.

43 Elizabeth, née Livingston; American widow of William Cavendish-Bentinck,
MP 1886–95.

44 I have been unable to identify the Carters; Sir Francis, previously under-
secretary of state for the colonies, was now a civil lord of the Admiralty.

45 Admiral, first sea lord 1904–10; recalled by WSC 1914–5 (resigned in the Dardanelles crisis).

46 Commander H. W. S. Chilcott (not Chilcote) who had written twice to WSC in
July 1915 about the Royal Naval Air Service.

47 Rear-Admiral Sir Osmond Brock, commander of the navy's 1st Battlecruiser
Squadron.

48 Edwin Montagu was promoted to the cabinet (still as chancellor of the duchy
of Lancaster) on 11 January 1916.

have a Jewish Govt:! They are undoubtedly clever, but have really no nationality. Probably you wouldn't agree.

Tell me what you think of *America Fallen*.[49] Clemmie says she has sent it to you. [...]

Bless you. Write when you can. I know how occupied you are.

Ever your loving
Mother

J ENNIE NEXT wrote on 23 January when morale at home was generally low. Early that morning a German Friedrichshafen FF 33b floatplane had dropped nine bombs above Dover, killing one man and damaging a brewery plus a pub.

— JSC to WSC —

23 January 1916   72 Brook Street, W.

My dearest Winston,

Your letter was a great delight – & I take some heart of your sayings. It is very difficult not to weary of the war & the long drawn misery of it all – we never seem to get even a glimpse of the silver lining of those black clouds. I am quite sure that you are right as regards your own line of conduct. There was nothing else to do – I wonder the Govt: did not ask us to illuminate our houses over [the successful retreat from] Gallipoli – that & Mons are our two victories! We are expecting Zeppelins tonight & the news is that there has been much damage done at Dover. I am meeting Garvin at dinner on Tuesday, & will write to you his news. I am going to ask Bonar Law to dine next week.

Goonie tells me that Birrell[50] told her he was giving up his motor car, as he did not expect the Govt: to be in long – & he did not want a

---

49 John B. Walker, *America Fallen: The Sequel to the European War*, published in New York 1915.

50 Augustine Birrell, chief secretary for Ireland until 3 May 1916.

"slump" in everything at once; Maudie Warrender told me today that the navy & Jellicoe[51] in particular are in despair about the blockade. 90 ships with cargoes have been released by order of the Govt: Germany is getting everything she wants. [...]

For what it counts I met Eustace Fiennes[52] the other day – he was full of your praises, he said he had had a charming letter from you. Goonie thinks that Birdwood is going to France, she hopes that Jack will be with him. How splendid that would be! She heard vaguely that this might be so. Perhaps you know?

I see in the *Observer* that 'Lt Col the Earl of Granard'[53] has been made Assistant Military Secretary to Haig! People are very critical of his appointments – The Duke of Teck[54] & P. Sassoon.[55]

Well, my darling boy I must now stop – I will write again in a couple of days – I may have some news for you unless the 'Zeps' have eaten me up. I enclose a photo: which you can tear up. I thought that the text wl^d amuse you. It is well that people shl^d think "Fortune's Favourite"! but I am lucky in having 2 such treasures – "the mother of the Magii" I have been calling myself – but now you are a Col:. By the way does Magii take 2 i's?[56]

Bless you my very dear. How time flies – tomorrow poor Randolph will have been dead 21 years. He was only 4 years older than you are now. Best love

Your loving
Mother

---

51 Admiral Sir John Jellicoe, commander of the Grand Fleet, which he led at the Battle of Jutland May 1916.

52 Soldier, Liberal MP, parliamentary private secretary to WSC 1912–14.

53 Bernard Forbes, earl of Granard; Liberal peer and formerly government whip in the House of Lords.

54 Younger brother of Queen Mary; military secretary to General Haig from December 1915.

55 Philip Sassoon, MP; private secretary to General Haig from December 1915.

56 *Magi* should have been the plural form; *magus* the singular.

GENERAL BIRDWOOD and his Anzac division, including Jack, did transfer to France. Meanwhile, Winston and his regiment moved up into the line at Ploegsteert just before dawn on 27 January. Their first spell in the trenches was limited to two days; later spells would last for six days.

— WSC to JSC —

29 January 1916   6th Royal Scots Fusiliers, in the Field

My dearest Mamma

[...] I brought my battalion out of the trenches this morning for a short rest. Certainly they work vy well and try vy hard to follow every risk or order. [...] We are in a vy good part of the line, & there are only the ordinary chances of war to risk. I am increasingly fatalistic in my mood about things & do not worry at all at the dangers when they come. I only fret when I think of the many things that ought to be done and my real powers lying unused at this time. But the temper of the country seems admirable; & remember we only have to persevere to conquer. In grt or in small station, in Cabinet or in the firing line, alive or dead my policy is 'Fight on'.

I am glad you are keeping in touch with some of my friends. I hope that FE & Ll George will pay me visits here during the next few days, & I shall thus learn how the big game goes. But this existence contents me & I am happy & at peace now that we are in the line or near it. Commanding a battalion is like being captain of a ship. It is a very searching test and a severe burden. Especially so when all the officers are young & only soldiers of a few months standing: & when a hundred yards away lies the line of a German army with all its devilments & dodges. [...]

A tiresome thing happened this afternoon. There is a battery in the fields behind our house wh the Germans try to hit; & this afternoon they put a dozen shells over us in search of it, wh burst with loud explosions at no gt distance. I had just had a splendid hot bath – the best for a month & was feeling deliciously clean, when suddenly a tremendous

Winston (seated fourth from left) in command of the
6th Royal Scots Fusiliers, Ploegsteert, 1916.

bang overhead, & I am covered with soot blown down the chimney
by the concussion of a shell these careless Bosch have & wh exploded
above our roof, smashing our windows & dirtying me! Well – it is an
odd world, & I have seen a gt deal of it. [...] I am sure I am doing right.

Your ever loving son

W

ON THE night of 31 January, nine German naval Zeppelins
attacked Liverpool, killing seventy civilians and injuring 113.
On 1 February Winston and his men went back into the trenches
for six days and nights.

− JSC to WSC −

3 February 1916   72 Brook Street, W.

My dearest Winston

Your letter gave me great pleasure altho' I had "creeps" when I read of the episode of the bomb on the roof! Dear boy I am sure that the *bon Dieu* has great use for you in the future, & you are right to be fatalistic.

I dined with Cassel last night − 16 of us − & who should take me in to dinner but the P.M.! He looked very dubious at first, but I exerted myself to put him at his ease, & we got on all right. No use being nasty − it does not help things − & so made friends with the mammon of unrighteousness!

Well! Of course he asked after you, & I told him you had just come out of the trenches, & repeated the story about the bath & the bomb. He got quite red with emotion. In the bottom of his heart I really think he is very fond of you, but he is so selfish he wl^d sacrifice anyone to his own conscience. I told him about your batt: & he said "Of course this is only the beginning & he will get the next step very soon" − those were his words.

We talked of the air raid [on Liverpool] over which he seemed quite calm − I avoided difficult topics − such as Navy, & even aircraft. But somehow we got on to K. of K. & I cl^d see that he is *très* [indecipherable], he chaffed about his "collecting" & then said − "I hear you won't have him at any price".

A certain Marshall, an American journalist is over here[57] − he talked of him as he wanted to interview the P.M. but he said the F.O. [Foreign Office] begged him not to. [...] He came to see me & was most interesting. He said that [President] Wilson[58] was very pro-Wilson and had but one idea − & that was *à tout prix* to get elected. For that reason he was certain Wilson intended to send a very drastic note to England [as] a bid for the German vote.

---

57 I have been unable to identify the journalist concerned.
58 Woodrow Wilson, US president since 1913 (see People, p. 574).

Marshall also said that the German propaganda over there was colossal – & that every attempt to get this Govt: or the Press to help to make a better entente between the U.S.A. & England was always snubbed & discouraged. He thought it a great pity. I think you won't agree.

Haldane[59] was at the dinner – he told me he had made a speech at Dundee in which he said that the Navy owed everything to you – & that your constituents cheered wildly. Haldane declared you were "all right" & would soon be back in the front line of politics. Everyone seems confident of that.

I sent the P.M. *America Fallen* today. Did you care about it? Clemmie sent it to you. What do you think about Jack getting the Légion d'Honneur?[60] He thinks it will do well for the Boulevardes later on. Goonie is in Ireland for the Viceregal – I hear Ivor & Alice are too pompous for words – & model everything on Buckingham Palace.[61] [...]

L.G. told me he had seen you & you were in g^t spirits & that yr men worshipped you. He was quite gushing, asking me to luncheon. He looked ill – pale – & his voice throaty. He was very well received but not enthusiastically.

The poor Aviation Dept:[62] seems to be faring badly, kicked from pillar to post. The latest news is that Fisher is to look after it – that is the new inventions & the building of any new aircraft. Ld Haldane amused me by saying that he had met Fisher who said in the course of

---

59 Richard, Viscount Haldane, lawyer and philosopher; MP 1885–1911; secretary of state for war 1905–12, responsible for army reforms; lord chancellor 1912–15; forced to resign for allegedly pro-German sympathies 1915.

60 Jack received the *Croix de guerre* and *Légion d'honneur*, 30 March 1916.

61 Lord Wimborne was installed as lord-lieutenant of Ireland on 17 February (shortly before the Easter Rising of April 1916).

62 An Air Committee was formed in 1912 to act as the intermediary between the Admiralty and the War Office in aviation matters. By February 1916 the lack of coordination between the army's Royal Flying Corps and the navy's Royal Naval Air Service persuaded the War Committee to establish a Joint War Air committee (on 15 February) to co-ordinate the design and the supply of materiel for both air services.

conversation – "I had hoped for big things but I am like Nebuchadnezzar – sent to grass".[63] […]

Bless you darling – & may God keep you from harm.

Your loving
Mother

CLEMENTINE WROTE to Winston on 4 February telling him of a visit that Lloyd George had paid the previous day to open one of her YMCA canteens; she wrote of him in unflattering terms. On 6 February Winston took over temporary control of the brigade to which his regiment belonged, in the absence of its brigadier-general.

— WSC TO JSC —

7 February 1916   6ᵗʰ Royal Scots Fusiliers in the Field

My dearest Mamma

Your vy interesting letter gave me great pleasure. I am vy glad you were tactful & did not show any irritation with Asquith. It is never any use. One cuts oneself off by giving way to one's personal feelings from connections wh may at any time become useful & wh are certainly harmless. My feeling agst him is due the fact that knowing my work, & having been a co-adventurer in my enterprises, (not merely an approver) he threw me over without the slightest effort even to state the true facts on my behalf; & still more that thereafter in all the plentitude of power he never found for me a useful sphere of acting wh wd have given scope to my energies & knowledge.

If I am killed at the humble duties I have found for myself he will no doubt be sorry & shocked. But the fact will remain that he has treated

---

63 Nebuchadnezzar II, king of Babylon 605–562 BC, suppressed his surrounding peoples; according to the book of Daniel, Nebuchadnezzar ignored God's warnings about his cruelty, given in a dream; consequently, he had to live in the wilderness for seven years and 'eat grass as the cattle do'.

me with injustice, & has wasted qualities wh might have been used in many ways to the public advantage in this time of war.

I am for the moment commanding the brigade, but the General returns to-night from sick-leave. I go back to the Fusiliers.

I had vy full accounts from Clemmie about her LG meeting. She is doing a gt deal of work, & doing it vy well. Mind you see people & write to me often.

Your ever loving son
W.

———

O N THE day before Winston was due to move back into the trenches, Jennie wrote again. She had just visited the family home at Cromwell Road, where she arrived as Clementine left to spend a weekend as the guest of the Asquiths at Walmer Castle on the Kent coast. (The castle normally housed the lord warden of the Cinque Ports; during the war, however, the incumbent, Earl Beauchamp, made it available to the prime minister as his weekend retreat, on account of its good communications with the front line in Flanders.)

— JSC TO WSC —

12 February 1916   72 Brook Street

My dearest Winston

I have just returned from C.R^d. where I saw Clemmie off to Walmer for the weekend. On returning home I find your letter. I send you the enclosed cuttings which it is possible you have not seen. No agitation will get Ld Fisher back, even this superannuated govt: would draw the line at 75![64] I do not suppose you wish for the Air Ministry – I hear it is to remain divided & inefficient.

---

64 Admiral Lord Fisher celebrated his 75th birthday on 25 January 1916.

Mr Montagu told Goonie that the govt: had taken more important decisions in the last month than in the whole duration of the war. We must wait & see the outcome of these great deliberations!

George Curzon dined with Anne Islington[65] the day he returned from France.[66] He gave me all your latest news & a description of your dug out. He seems very fond of you – between ourselves he was rather severe on F.E. [Smith] – but I know he does not like him. Of course F.E. has many enemies & people are down [on] him – but it will blow over. [...]

I dined at the Carlton [Club] last night – full of khaki. Ld Derby[67] had a large family party – Ferdy Stanley[68] had just arrived from the Front – very fat & quite bald. The Raymond Asquiths[69] lunched with me yesterday – he is here for a week. Hugh Warrender arrives on leave next Thursday – they give him 8 days in the trenches, 4 days out. He has like you been acting as a brigadier. [...]

I am trying to sell the house and get a smaller & cheaper one. It is best to liquidate if I can – Income dwindling, taxes higher and everything more expensive. The making up my mind was most unpleasant, but now that I have I am anxious to carry it out. I know of a doll's house which will just suit me – now for the buyer!

Bless you my dearest. In a letter to Goonie Jack says he hopes for K. of K.'s reputation that he would be found out. But that is too late – *c'est fait*. Again bless you.

With best love
Mother

---

65 Anne, Lady Islington, wife of Baron Islington, under-secretary of state for India, governor of New Zealand 1910–12.

66 Lord Curzon met WSC on 6 February and visited the front line with him.

67 Director-general of recruiting in the War Office.

68 Son of the earl of Derby; at the time serving in France with the Guards as temporary captain.

69 Son of Herbert Asquith; married to Katharine, née Horner; killed in action 15 September 1916.

S.L. [Shane Leslie] had a talk with one of Col. House's syce[70] who said Col. H. was most impressed with the efficiency of everything on Germany. Meanwhile 8 big banks have failed & the [Deutche] mark was never lower.

— JSC ᴛᴏ WSC —

20 February 1916   Warwick Castle

My dearest Winston

I am spending a Sunday here with my old friends – I have been looking through the visitors book – & it takes me back a long way!

I met L.G. the other day & he told me to tell you that if you issue a fresh report[71] not to forget to send it to the C.&C. I understand from L.G. that it was rather a grievance that you had not sent him the 1st paper. […]

What a place this is! We have been walking about all day, & not withstanding a dull misty atmosphere it has been delightful. I am one of the few "yanks" who like the country. Before I die I hope to have a small "Hoe Farm"[72] where the children can come to & which I can leave to you 2 boys.

These castles in Spain[73] are very well but to come down to the prosaic – I am rather bored at the idea of turning out again. I had hoped that I might have kept the last house – it suits me so well. There are one or two people after it & probably this week I may come to terms. I must not let it go at a disadvantage for it is my only asset.

---

70 Edward House, chief adviser to President Wilson on European affairs; his syce (literally a groom) was an assistant.

71 WSC circulated a paper about improving front-line defences through deeper trenches, stronger dugouts and more sandbagging.

72 Country property near Godalming in Surrey, jointly rented by WSC and Jack in 1915 for the summer use of their families.

73 'Building castles in Spain' referred to nurturing hopes or dreams that have very little chance of succeeding.

I met Arthur Balfour the other night listening to music at Maud Cunard's![74] He asked after you & said "I hear he is enjoying himself". [...] I hope to hear from you soon. Bless you

Your loving
Mother

— WSC to JSC —

23 February[75] 1916   6ᵗʰ Royal Scots Fusiliers, in the Field

My dearest Mamma,

If you mean C.in C. or Commander in Chief, I sent him a copy before I showed it to anyone else. Who do you mean?

I am looking forward to coming home for a week on Mar. 2 and I shall then review the situation as it affects me. I hope Clemmie keeps you informed of my affairs & fortunes.

We go into the trenches tomorrow for six days at the end of wh I shall be vy glad of a bed, bath & a good dinner. It is freezing hard and the ground is white. It will be interesting to see how this affects our patrolling & other trench work. The artillery seems to be hampered by the haze & have fired little for the last 2 days. We manage to keep ourselves warm; but it will be hard on the men.

Always your loving son
W

You are quite right to part with the little house – charming though it is. The pinch will steadily increase at all points as the year advances.

————

WINSTON AND Clementine carefully planned his week in England, due to start on 2 March, so that they could entertain

---

74 American-born society hostess, also known as Emerald; married Sir Bache Cunard 1895.

75 Incorrectly dated by WSC in the original as 23 January 1916.

as many political friends as possible. Winston wished to assess his prospects for a successful political comeback at Westminster.

On his arrival in England he heard that the House of Commons was due to discuss the naval estimates on 7 March and he determined to take part in the debate. On the evening he reached London, Jennie gave a dinner party at which Winston rehearsed his planned speech in front of close friends from both the world of politics and the press. He criticized the government's conduct of the war, but made no reference in this rehearsal to Admiral Fisher.

At the debate itself, however, he wound up a serious speech by recommending Fisher's return to the Admiralty as first sea lord. By doing so, he attracted ridicule and destroyed the impact of the rest of his intervention. The next day Balfour, his successor at the Admiralty, completed Winston's humiliation in the House. While sanctioning an extension to his leave on 9 March, Asquith advised him to save his political career by returning to France, however briefly.

Winston took the prime minister's counsel, returning to Flanders on 13 March. Nevertheless, he felt that his rightful position was back in the House of Commons. It was now merely a question of when, not if, he should return. His decision was confirmed when he heard six days later that he was not to be given command of his brigade; instead that was to go to Colonel Gerald Trotter.

— JSC to WSC —

28 March 1916   72 Brook Street

My dearest Winston

I wonder why I have not written to you [before] this time? Perhaps it is that I hate writing dull letters, & Clemmie tells you all the news. You know for all that – my thoughts are ever with you & I hear all there is to hear as to your plans.

As you have made up your mind (& I think wisely) to come back at the first opportunity, I do not suppose that you mind Col: Trotter getting the brigade. Of course you know him & I do, from South Africa. All the same it was promised you – & the P.M. as usual failed you. Isn't he a weasel!! Sooner than face the House when things are difficult for him, he has a convenient illness, & then goes to France – & on to Rome.[76] [...]

I haven't seen anyone of interest. [...] I still haven't sold my house. Such a bore when one has made up one's mind to sell – not to do so. However I may find a purchaser any day. The income tax is "orrid"![77]

Archie Sinclair[78] is dining with me tonight – we had a long talk about you the other day. It is very difficult to advise which is the best course for you. The Govt: is getting very disliked & is to say the least shaky. The press is unanimous in abuse. The first disaster cl^d turn them out. It is a great thing to be on the spot. Write me a line & tell me if there is anything I can do – or anyone I can see for you!

Bless you – with much love
Mother

W INSTON CONTINUED to debate the timing of his return almost daily by letter with Clementine, who advised delay. Late in March he wrote to several of his political friends at home asking them for their views.

— WSC TO JSC —

3 April 1916   6th Royal Scots Fusiliers, in the Field

My dearest Mama,

It was very nice hearing from you. I am simply living here from

---

76 Asquith was ill until he left Britain on 25 March to attend an Inter-allied war conference in Paris, 26–28 March; on 30 March he travelled to Rome, arriving on 31 March and staying until 2 April.

77 The standard rate of income tax was 6 per cent in 1914; in 1916 it increased to 25 per cent.

78 Sir Archibald Sinclair, WSC's second-in-command in the 6th Royal Scots Fusiliers. WSC and Sir Archibald, who became lifelong friends, each had an American-born mother.

day to day pending the result of some enquiries I am making. My mind is unchanged about returning. It is only a question of how & when. I expect to decide vy soon now. But I like the life out here & linger on vy pleasantly. The time passes quickly & easily both in & out of the trenches. Few days pass without shells or bullets; but so far they have been vy kind, & also we have been lucky in finding a quiet sector of the line. [...]

I will let you know when I come to any decision. Meanwhile try to get hold of Donald[79] of the *Daily Chronicle* & without telling him my plans try to make him friendly & well-disposed. After all he is a Fisherite – so he ought to be pleased.

Your ever loving son

W

— JSC to WSC —

7 April 1916   72 Brook Street, W.

My darling Winston

I am writing to you from my bed – not that there is anything very much the matter. For years I have suffered from an inflamed toe – & incipient varicose veins. Owing to canteen work I have aggravated this to such an extent that [Dr] Feiff[80] advised me to have one off; & the others out – which I have done. I have had days of pains & then gas but am all right now – stitches to be taken out next week – & in a few days I shall be about. People are awfully kind, my room is like a flower shop.

Fancy my having burglars here – they carried off the whole of the contents of one of those glass vitrines in the drawing room – unfortunately the one which contained all my most precious little *objets d'art* including all my royal gifts 7 or 8 in no: They wl^d have taken more but Rivers's[81] door banged & they made off.

---

79 Robert Donald, editor of the *Daily Chronicle* since 1904.
80 I have been unable to trace a Dr Feiff (possibly a misspelling by JSC: Pfeiff is more common).
81 JSC's servant at 72 Brook Street; an Emily Rivers wrote to WSC after JSC's death in 1921.

I was so interested in your letter – oddly enough I have occasion to see Donald about some munition work I want him to puff up and I shall take the opportunity to find out what he thinks of the situation. I am told that Bonar Law has the government in the hollow of his hand, but he does not want to precipitate things. The government are cautious over Carson[82] failing at the last moment or that his health should fail. It looks to me as tho' he was missing the opportunity.

Meanwhile Moreton [Frewen] had a cable from Washington to say that [Theodore] Roosevelt[83] & Elihu Root[84] had joined hands after 5 years estrangement & that Root will probably stand for the presidency & Wilson is certain to be beaten.[85]

I can't write any more. Bless you & God bless you.

Your loving Mother

The P.M.'s portrait was hissed at the Coliseum[86] last week!

O N 19 April Winston returned to London to speak at a closed session of the House of Commons on the subject of conscription, due to be held on 25 April. He asked the military authorities for permission to remain a further two weeks in London while a new crisis in the life of the coalition government resolved itself, but

---

82 Sir Edward Carson, lawyer, MP, leader of Ulster Unionist Party 1910–21; resigned from the coalition cabinet in October 1915; his support was widely seen as essential if any move to unseat Asquith as prime minister was to be successful.

83 Former president, United States 1901–9; strongly critical of President Wilson's wartime policies, yet he refused his nomination by the Progressive Party for the 1916 presidential election.

84 US secretary of war 1899–1904; secretary of state 1905–9; winner, Nobel Peace Prize 1912; senator from New York 1909–15.

85 Woodrow Wilson narrowly defeated his Republican opponent Charles Hughes in the 1916 presidential election (see People. p. 574).

86 The London Coliseum, St Martin's Lane opened 1904; after 1914 it held gala performances to raise funds for war relief.

was recalled to Ploegsteert on 27 April when his battalion rejoined the line.

It was to be his last spell in the trenches because the 6th and 7th battalions of the Royal Scots Fusiliers had both become so depleted over the course of the war that the military authorities decided to merge them under the command of the colonel of the 7th Battalion, who was a regular soldier. Winston took the opportunity to return to his parliamentary life, leaving Flanders on 7 May.

From this point onwards, Jennie and Winston saw a good deal of each other, so had no need to write. They were together at Herstmonceux Castle in June and at Blenheim in August. No further correspondence between them survives for the remainder of the war.

The poisonous legacy of the failure at Gallipoli dogged Winston's attempts to return to front-line politics for the remainder of 1916, even when Lloyd George unseated Asquith as prime minister in December. A turning point was reached in March 1917 when the official Dardanelles Commission delivered a first report, which made it clear that blame for the failure should be widely shared. By July 1917 Lloyd George felt himself in a strong enough position to restore Winston to ministerial office (if not to the inner war cabinet), as minister of munitions.

In March 1918, at the age of sixty-four, Jennie visited her sister Leonie in Ireland in the company of Montagu Porch, who was forty-one years old and taking three weeks' leave from war service at the front. Jennie had first met Porch in 1914, just before the beginning of the war, at a family wedding in Rome. A quiet, courteous man, he came from a landed family in Glastonbury.

On 1 June 1918 Porch became Jennie's third husband. This time she set two conditions in advance: she would not be joining her husband in Nigeria when he resumed his role there in the country's civil service after the war; and she would not be changing her name from Lady Randolph Churchill.

22

LAST WORDS

1920–21

'*You are tired out and a little disheartened*'

O N 9 January 1919, his mother's sixty-fifth birthday, Winston became secretary of state for war and air, part of a post-war reconstruction of the cabinet by David Lloyd George, who remained prime minister. The newly remarried Jennie remained as vivacious as ever, redecorating a new home near Hyde Park, entertaining friends, learning new dances, flying in an aircraft for the first time and promoting the revival of theatre and opera in post-war London.

In July 1920 she asked Winston to give up ten minutes of his time at the War Office to the visiting president of the council of the European Association of India, Mr G. Morgan, who had publicly approved of the actions of General Dyer. In July 1919, the British general had ordered his troops to fire on unarmed protesters at Amritsar; they killed at least 379 Indians, possibly as many as 1,000.

Opinion was split over the general's actions at home and in India. The British government, led on the issue by Edwin Montagu as secretary of state for India, had censured Dyer; Winston, too, criticized the general strongly in the House of Commons.

— JSC TO WSC —

16 July 1920   8 Westbourne Street, Hyde Park

Dearest Winston

It is too angelic & generous of you & Clemmie to offer me your house for August. I can't tell you how sweet I think it is of you both – I am writing to Clemmie about it.

Meanwhile I want to know if you can give 10 mts: of your time at the W.O. [War Office] to Mr Morgan President of the European Association of India, who returns to India tomorrow, & is very anxious to have a few words with you – he is a charming man, & very influential in India. He has been seeing a lot of E. Montagu. Do see him. It would be a pity not to hear his views as he knows more of conditions etc in India than anyone. He has no axe to grind with you – just telephone & I will pass on yr message.

Love
Mother

— JSC TO WSC —

5 August 1920   18 Portman Street

My dearest Winston

I was much touched by your letter [missing]. I am glad that you felt yourselves in an atmosphere of love & sympathy – you are tired out & a little disheartened. We are all feeling like that – for one reason or another. I know it will come right. Bless you & let me know when you will come again. You are always more than welcome.

Your loving
Mother

Love to Clemmie

O N 1 January 1921 David Lloyd George asked Winston to move from the War Office, where he had clashed with the prime minister over Britain's response to the Bolshevik revolution in Russia, to the Colonial Office. The department was to take on the extra responsibility, at Winston's suggestion, for supervising a new post-war settlement of the Middle East in accordance with Britain's mandate from the new League of Nations.

News of his appointment was not made public until 13 February.

– JSC to WSC –

14 February 1921   16 Berkeley Square

Winston dearest – DO look in here tomorrow night (Tuesday) after your Burns dinner – F.E.[1] & his wife to come, Jack & Goonie – rows of nice people you love. I want you to see Goonie's picture – & I must have a frame for yours. Can you lend me one also *au easel* [on the easel]? They shall all go back to you – "honest Injun"!

Your loving
Mother

Come early!

O N THE evening of 1 March 1921, Winston was due to leave London for Marseilles, where Clementine, who had been playing in a tennis tournament in the South of France, would join him. They were then to travel together to Cairo, where Winston was to preside over a conference to reshape the borders of the Middle East.

---

1   The former F. E. Smith, now lord chancellor and known as Lord Birkenhead (see People, p. 571).

- JSC TO WSC -

1 March 1921   16 Berkeley Square

Dearest Winston

This is only a line to wish you *bon voyage* – & a speedy return. Give my love to Clemmie – I hope you will find her none the worse for her 'prowesses'. I will look after the children & give you news of them. They are great darlings & do you both great credit!

Bless you

Your loving
Mother

I N APRIL, on her way to Rome, Jennie stayed with the Laverys at their house on Cap d'Ail on the French Riviera. Winston and Clementine joined the house party on their way back from Cairo.

Once Jennie reached the Italian capital, her friend the duchess of Sermonetta helped her to celebrate her recent coup in the London property market by escorting her on a shopping trip. (With the help of her new husband's money, Jennie had bought and done up a property in London's Berkeley Square, making a profit of £15,000 on its sale.) Rome was 'very gay, races, dances, *antiquaries*', she told her sister Leonie.

Back in London, Jennie wrote her last surviving letter to Winston. It concerned her niece Clare Sheridan, who had turned to sculpture after her husband Wilfred had been killed in 1915. Winston had encouraged his cousin's move, appreciating her artistic temperament, until she sculpted two members of a visiting Soviet Russian delegation to London in September 1920 – a delegation officially shunned by the government. To make matters worse, Clare had accepted an invitation from the delegation to visit Moscow to sculpt Lenin and Trotsky themselves.

— JSC TO WSC —

[27 April 1921] Wed: 16 Berkeley Square

Dearest Winston

I received the enclosed from Clare this morning. She begs me to see that it gets to you <u>direct</u>. It is rather pathetic how she hankers after your goodwill. Don't be hard on her.

Bless you – you know I am expecting you tomorrow to dinner, only Jack & the Laverys. I will try & turn up tomorrow morning – 10.15 – but may miss you.

Love
Mother

I N ROME, Jennie had bought a pair of fashionably high-heeled shoes. She put them on early in June, while staying at the Somerset home of her friend Frances, Lady Horner.[2] Hurrying downstairs when the gong sounded, she slipped, fell down the stairs and broke her ankle badly.

Jennie was taken back to London, where she was bedbound for several days in great pain. The wound became infected, then turned gangrenous and surgeons had to amputate her lower leg. Jennie seemed to be recovering well until the morning of 29 June, when she suddenly suffered a haemorrhage and died. Winston arrived at her home just too late to witness his mother's end.

Jennie's funeral took place three days later in the small village church at Bladon, on the edge of the Blenheim estate, where Lord Randolph was buried. Her husband Montagu Porch was still in

---

2   Lady Horner married the barrister Sir John Horner in 1883; they had four children, one of them by now the widow of Raymond Asquith. Frances's father John Graham had been a leading patron of Edward Burne-Jones and other Pre-Raphaelite artists.

Winston (left), Jack and family follow Jennie's coffin,
Bladon churchyard, 2 July 1921.

Nigeria,[3] so her sons walked behind her coffin into the churchyard where their cousin Oswald Frewen recorded in his diary 'a
sympathetic parson, boys' and womens' voices in the choir, the grave
lined with white roses and pale mauve orchids'.[4]

Winston kept copies of the obituaries that more than 200 newspapers around the world published about his mother. They ranged
in Britain from the *Aberdeen Free Press* to the *Yorkshire Evening Post*;
and in America from the *Boston Globe* to the *St. Louis Star*.

Letters of sympathy poured in to her sons. To one from David
Lloyd George, Winston replied simply: 'My mother had the gift of
eternal youth of spirit.'[5]

---

3   Porch remarried an Italian in 1926 and lived in Italy until her death in 1938; he
    died in Somerset in 1964, aged 87.
4   A. Leslie, *Jennie*, p. 355.
5   P. Churchill and J. Mitchell, *Jennie*, p. 267.

APPENDIX

PEOPLE

IN THE Churchill and Jerome family sections below, the relationships (shown in brackets after each entry) are those between the person described and Jennie, then Winston respectively.

CHURCHILL FAMILY

Curzon, Richard George later Earl Howe (1861–1929) (brother-in-law, uncle by marriage).
Viscount 1876; married Georgiana, née Spencer-Churchill, sister of Lord Randolph Churchill 1883; Conservative MP, treasurer of the household 1885–1900; executor and trustee of Lord Randolph's estate 1895–1908; succeeded as earl 1900; lord chamberlain to Queen Alexandra 1903–25.

Guest, Ivor, 1st Baron Wimborne (1835–1914) (brother-in-law, uncle by marriage).
Son of ironmaster Sir Joshua Guest, owner of the Dowlais iron foundry

in Wales; inherited baronetcy and the business 1852; several failed attempts to become a Conservative MP; created baron 1880; left the Conservative Party after tariff reform to become a Liberal peer.

Guest, Lady Cornelia (1848–1927)
(sister-in-law, aunt).
Née Spencer-Churchill; married Sir Ivor Guest (later Baron Wimborne) 1868, five children; active philanthropist.

Guest, Ivor later 1st Viscount Wimborne (1873–1939)
(nephew by marriage, first cousin).
MP 1900–10 (Conservative 1900–4, Liberal 1904–10); appointed Baron Ashby St Ledgers 1910; paymaster-general 1910–12; succeeded as Baron Wimborne 1914; lord-lieutenant of Ireland 1915–18; created viscount 1918.

Guest, Frederick ('Freddie') (1875–1937)
(nephew by marriage, first cousin).
Third son of Lord and Lady Wimborne; joined the army 1894–1907, serving in Egypt, southern Africa; married Amy Phipps 1895, three children; private secretary to WSC 1906; Liberal MP 1910–22, 1923–4; returned to the army 1914–17; chief whip, coalition Liberal MPs 1917; secretary of state for air 1921–2; represented Britain at Olympics polo 1924; Conservative MP 1931–7.

Majoribanks, Edward, 2nd Baron Tweedmouth (1849–1909)
(brother-in-law, uncle by marriage).
Married Lady Fanny Spencer-Churchill 1873, one son; Liberal MP 1880–94; baron 1894; lord privy seal, chancellor of the duchy of Lancaster 1894–5; first lord of the Admiralty 1905–8; lord president of the council 1908; sold estate at Guisachan following his wife's death 1904.

Spencer-Churchill, Frances, 7th duchess of Marlborough
(1822–99) (mother-in-law, grandmother).
Née Vane, dowager duchess and widow of 7th duke of Marlborough,
with whom she had eleven children; a domineering figure within the
family and the Blenheim estate, which she did much to rejuvenate.

Spencer-Churchill, Lilian, 8th duchess of Marlborough
('Lily') (1854–1909) (sister-in-law, aunt by marriage).
Née Price, in Troy, New York; married (first) Louis Hammersley, a
New York property magnate (died 1883); (second) the 8th duke of
Marlborough 1888 (died 1892); (third) Lord William Beresford 1895,
following which she was known as Lady William Beresford (died 1900).

Spencer-Churchill, Charles, 9th duke of Marlborough ('Sunny')
(1871–1934) (nephew by marriage, first cousin).
Succeeded as 9th duke aged 21 in 1892; Conservative peer; paymaster-
general 1899–1902; under-secretary of state for the colonies 1903–5;
married American heiress Consuelo Vanderbilt 1895, separated 1906,
divorced 1921; remarried Gladys Deacon 1921.

Spencer-Churchill, Consuelo, 9th duchess of Marlborough
(1877–1964).
Née Vanderbilt, daughter of US millionaire William Vanderbilt and
his wife Alva; at the insistence of her mother, married 9th duke of
Marlborough, bringing a substantial dowry 1895, two sons; remarried
Jacques Balsan 1921; author *The Glitter and the Gold* (1921).

Vane-Tempest-Stewart, Charles, 6th marquess of Londonderry
(1852–1915) (none, first cousin once removed).
Landowner in Ireland and England, Conservative politician; MP 1878–
84; married Lady Theresa Chetwynd-Talbot 1875, three children;
lord-lieutenant of India 1886–9; postmaster general 1900–2; president
of the Board of Education 1902–5; lord president of the council 1903–5.

JEROME FAMILY

Frewen, Clarita ('Clara') (1851–1935) (sister, aunt).
Eldest of the Jerome sisters; married to Moreton Frewen with whom she had four children.

Frewen, Moreton (1853–1924) (brother-in-law, uncle).
Married Clarita Jerome; acquired a ranch in Wyoming; serial entrepreneur (largely failed); writer on economic affairs, including bi-metallism, tariff reform.

Jerome, Clara (1825–95) (mother, grandmother).
Née Hall; married Leonard Jerome in New York 1849, four daughters (Camille died aged eight); moved with her daughters to Europe 1867.

Jerome, Leonard (1817–91) (father, grandfather).
Studied at the College of New Jersey and Union College; lawyer in Rochester, New York State; moved to the city of New York as entrepreneur in newspaper and financial industry; built Jerome Mansion, corner of Madison Avenue and 26th Street; opera lover; founder of American Jockey Club and Jerome Park Racetrack, New York.

Leslie, John 'Shane' (1885–1971) (nephew, first cousin).
Son of Leonie; married Marjorie Ide 1912; joined British Ambulance Corps 1914–15; assistant to British ambassador, USA 1916–18; writer; succeeded to baronetcy 1944; remarried Carola Laing 1958.

Leslie, Leonie (1859–1943) (sister, aunt).
Youngest of the Jerome sisters; married John Leslie, soldier and heir to an estate of 70,000 acres in Northern Ireland, five children.

FRIENDS OF JSC

Albert Edward ('Bertie') Prince of Wales (1841–1910), second child and eldest son of Queen Victoria and Prince Albert; married Princess Alexandra of Denmark 1863, six children; earned a reputation for numerous affairs; acceded as King Edward VII 1901.

Breteuil, Henri (1847–1916) marquis de; joined army 1870–7; MP 1877–92; friend of the Prince of Wales, the Russian royal family and JSC; married first Constance, second (1891) the American Marcellite Garner, whose fortune allowed the restoration of the château de Breteuil and the purchase of a large residence in Paris; friend of Marcel Proust who based the character of Hannibal de Bréauté in *À la Recherche du Temps Perdu* (1913–27) on Henri Breteuil.

Cassel, Ernest (1852–1921), born to a Jewish family in Germany; arrived in Liverpool 1869; started his own banking business in London 1870; a leading investor in railroad companies, sugar, diamond and gold mines; knighted 1899; financial adviser to the Prince of Wales (later Edward VII); retired following the king's death 1910.

Cockran, William 'Bourke' (1854–1923), born in Co. Sligo, Ireland; educated in France; emigrated to United States 1871; teacher; qualified as barrister 1876; member of the US House of Representatives 1887–9, 1891–5, 1904–9, 1921–3.

Craigie, Pearl (1867–1906), née Richards in Boston, moved to London soon after birth; married 1886, one son, divorced 1895; wrote novels (including *Some Emotions and a Moral*, 1891) and five plays (including *The Ambassador*, 1898) under the pseudonym John Oliver Hobbes; writer for *The Anglo-Saxon Review*; adviser to JSC on her literary ventures.

Edward VII, *see* **Albert Edward ('Bertie'), Prince of Wales.**

Hindlip, Lady (1846–1939), née Georgiana Millicent, married 1868 Samuel Allsopp, brewer and MP until he succeeded as Baron Hindlip in 1887; main home at Hindlip Hall in Worcestershire.

Hirsch, Moritz 'Maurice' (1831–96), baron, German Jewish financier; educated in Brussels; married Clara Bischoffsheim, banking heiress 1855; entered family banking business, Bischoffsheim & Goldschmidt; homes in Paris, London, Hungary; philanthropist, supporting Jewish education (as did his wife who died 1899); adopted Maurice de Forest.

Jeune, Susan (1845–1931), née Stewart-Mackenzie in Germany; married Colonel John Stewart 1871–8, two daughters; married Francis Jeune, later Baron St Helier, 1881, one son; hostess, essayist, philanthropist; alderman, London County Council 1910–27; appointed dame 1925.

Keppel, Alice (1868–1947) née Edmonstone; married George Keppel 1891, two daughters; society hostess, mistress of the Prince of Wales, later Edward VII, from 1898 until his death in 1910; lived in Italy 1925–40.

Kinsky, Karl 'Charles' (1858–1919), son of Austro-Hungarian prince; horseman, diplomat; conducted a longstanding affair with JSC; married Countess Elisabeth Wolff-Metternich zur Gracht 1895; lived in London until the outbreak of war in 1914; refused to fight against Britain in the war, so served on the Eastern Front.

Neumann, Sigismund (1815–1916), born in Bavaria; financier of mining in southern Africa; racehorse owner; married Alva, a keen sportswoman; owner, S. Neumann & Co., London; director, London Joint Stock Ltd, African Banking Corporation and other companies; fortune founded on the diamond mines of South Africa; created baronet 1912.

Pless, Hans von Hochberg (1861–1938), joined German army 1881–2; prince 1882; world hunting trip 1883–5; diplomat 1885, posted to London 1890; married Mary Cornwallis-West 1891, four children, divorced 1923; succeeded as prince of Pless 1907; colonel, German army 1914–18; retained estates in Poland, Polish citizen 1922; remarried Clotilde de Candamo 1925, divorced 1934.

Warrender, Hugh (1868–1926), youngest son of Sir George Warrender, 6th baronet; joined the army in the Grenadier Guards, later captain; brother-in-law of JSC's friend Lady Maud Warrender; died unmarried.

Wilton, Lady Elizabeth (1836–1919), née Craven; widow of 3rd earl of Wilton, who died 1885; remarried Arthur Pryor 1886; hosted hunting parties at Egerton Lodge, near Melton Mowbray in Leicestershire, well placed for the leading Belvoir, Cottesmore or Quorn hunts; childless, she styled herself in letters to WSC as 'your deputy mother'.

Wolverton, Frederick ('Freddie') (1864–1932), member of the Glyn banking family; married Edith Ward 1895; succeeded to baronry, 1888; author *Five Months' Sport in Somali Land* 1894; served in Imperial Yeomanry 1900 Boer War; Conservative peer; vice-chamberlain of the household 1902–5.

FRIENDS OF WSC

Barnes, Reginald (1871–1946), joined army reserves 1881, regular army 1890; accompanied WSC to Cuba 1895 and India 1895–9; served in southern Africa (Boer War) 1899–1901, India 1904–6,

Malta 1909–11; lieutenant-colonel 1911; war service in France, 1914–18, brigadier-general 1915, major-general 1918; knighted 1919; married Gunhilla Wijk 1921, one son.

Garvin, James 'J.L.' (1868–1947), journalist 1891; leader writer *Daily Telegraph* 1899; editor, *The Outlook* 1904–6; editor, *Observer* 1908–42; editor, *Encyclopaedia Britannica* 1926–32; author *The Life of Joseph Chamberlain* (1932).

Harmsworth, Alfred, 1st Viscount Northcliffe (1865–1922), freelance reporter 1870; founded a magazine business, later Amalgamated Press (with his brother Harold) 1887; purchased the *Evening News* 1894; founded the *Daily Mail* 1896; purchased the *Observer* 1905 (sold 1912), *The Times* 1908; knighted 1904; Baron Northcliffe 1905; viscount 1917.

Lavery, John (1856–1941), born in Ireland; studied painting in Glasgow, Paris; married Kathleen MacDermott 1889, who died 1891, one daughter; married Hazel Martyn 1909; official artist 1914–18; knighted 1918; elected to the Royal Academy 1921.

Marsh, Edward (1872–1953), joined civil service, private secretary to Joseph Chamberlain, secretary of state for the colonies 1896; then private secretary to WSC at each ministerial post in which he served between 1905 and 1915, 1917 and 1922, 1924 and 1929; assistant private secretary to the prime minister 1915–6, private secretary to secretaries of state for the colonies, 1929–37; knighted on retirement 1937; collected the paintings of British watercolourists; edited anthologies of *Georgian Poetry* 1912–22; literary executor to Rupert Brooke.

Plowden, Pamela (1874–1971), daughter of the British Resident (senior civilian official) in Hyderabad; declined marriage proposals from WSC 1899–1900; married the earl of Lytton, with whom she had four children, 1902.

Smith, Frederick, 1st Viscount Birkenhead, 'F.E.' (1872–1930), taught law Oxford University 1896–9; married Margaret Furneaux 1891, three children; appointed king's counsel 1908; Conservative MP 1906–18; served in army 1914–15; solicitor-general 1915, attorney-general 1915–19; lord chancellor 1919–22; secretary of state for India 1924–8; created Baron Birkenhead 1919, viscount 1921; died of complications caused by cirrhosis of the liver.

POLITICIANS

Asquith, Herbert (1852–1928), fellow of Balliol College, Oxford 1874–82; journalist, *The Spectator*, *The Economist* 1876–88; barrister, QC 1890; MP 1886–1918, 1920–4; home secretary 1892–5; barrister 1895–1905; chancellor of the exchequer 1905–8; leader of the Liberal Party and prime minister 1908–16; created earl of Oxford and Asquith 1924.

Balfour, Arthur, 1st earl of Balfour (1848–1930), nephew of former prime minister Lord Salisbury; leader of the Conservative Party 1892–1905; former secretary for Scotland 1886–7; chief secretary for Ireland 1887–91; prime minister 1902–5; first lord of the Admiralty 1915–16; foreign secretary 1916–19; created earl 1922.

Bonar Law, Andrew (1858–1923), born in colony of New Brunswick (now part of Canada), moved to Scotland 1870; entered iron industry 1874; MP 1890–1923; married Annie Robley 1891, six children; parliamentary secretary, Board of Trade 1902–5; leader of the Conservative Party 1911; secretary of state for the colonies 1915–16; chancellor of the exchequer 1916–19; lord privy seal 1919–21; prime minister (for 221 days) 1922–3.

Bruce, Victor, 9th earl of Elgin (1849–1917), grandson of Thomas

Bruce, 7th earl who shipped the sculptures from the Parthenon in Athens, known as the Elgin Marbles, to Britain; succeeded to earldom 1863; married Lady Constance Carnegie 1876, eleven children; entered politics as a Liberal; treasurer of the household 1886; governor-general and viceroy of India 1894–9; chairman, Elgin Commission into the Boer War 1902–3; secretary of state for the colonies 1905–8.

Campbell-Bannerman, Henry (1836–1908), joined family drapery business in Glasgow 1858, partner 1860; married Sarah Bruce 1860, no children; Liberal MP 1868–1908; financial secretary to war office 1871–4, 1880–2; chief secretary for Ireland 1882–3; secretary of state for war 1886, 1892–5; knighted 1895; leader of the opposition 1899–1905; prime minister 1905–8.

Chamberlain, Joseph (1836–1914), business owner, mayor of Birmingham; became a Liberal MP aged 39; president of the board of trade 1880–85; split the Liberal Party after resigning over the issue of Home Rule for Ireland 1886; led breakaway Liberal Unionists, eventually into coalition with the Conservatives 1895; secretary of state for the colonies 1895–1903; resigned over the issue of tariff reform, splitting the Unionist Party.

Curzon, George Nathaniel, 1st Marquess Curzon (1859–1925), MP 1886–98; under-secretary of state for India 1891–2, for foreign affairs 1895–8; viceroy of India 1899–1905; minister, coalition government 1915; leader of the House of Lords 1916; foreign secretary 1919–24; lord president of the council 1924–5; earl 1911, marquess 1921.

Disraeli, Benjamin, 1st earl of Beaconsfield (1804–81), born a Jew, converted to Anglicanism aged 12; solicitor 1821–4; investor and newspaperman, incurring large debts 1824–5; author (his novels include *Vivian Grey, Coningsby* and *Sybil*) and European travel

1826–37; Conservative MP 1837–76; married Mary Anne Lewis 1839, no children; chancellor of the exchequer 1852, 1858–9, 1866–8; leader of the opposition 1868–74, 1880–81; prime minister 1868, 1874–80; earl 1876; last novel *Endymion* published 1880.

Elliot-Murray-Kynynmound, Gilbert, 4th earl of Minto (1845–1914), joined the army in 1867, serving in India, southern Africa, Egypt and Canada, resigned 1889; married Lady Mary Grey 1883, five children; succeeded to earldom 1891; governor-general of Canada 1898–1904; viceroy of India 1905–10.

Gascoyne-Cecil, Robert, 3rd marquess of Salisbury (1830–1903), fellow of All Souls College, Oxford 1853; MP 1853–66; chairman, Great Eastern Railway Company 1868–72; succeeded as marquess 1868; secretary of state for India 1874–8; leader of the Conservative Party 1881–1902; prime minister, foreign secretary 1885–January 1886, July 1886–92, 1895–1902.

Gladstone, William (1809–98), Conservative MP 1833–45; married Catherine Glynne 1839, eight children; under-secretary of state for war and the colonies 1835; president of the board of trade 1843–5; colonial secretary 1845–6; Liberal MP 1847–95; chancellor of the exchequer 1852–5, 1859–66, 1873–4, 1880–2; prime minister 1868–74, 1880–5, 1886, 1892–4.

Grey, Edward, 1st Viscount Grey (1862–1933), baronet 1882; Liberal MP 1885–1916; married Dorothy Widdrington 1885, no children; under-secretary of state for foreign affairs 1892–5; secretary of state for foreign affairs 1905–16; created viscount 1916; ambassador to US 1919–20; married Pamela, Lady Glenconner 1922.

Lloyd George, David, 1st Earl Lloyd-George (1863–1945), solicitor 1884–1905; married Margaret Owen 1888, five children;

Liberal MP 1890–1945; president of the Board of Trade 1905–8; chancellor of the exchequer 1908–15; minister of munitions 1915–16; secretary of state for war 1916; prime minister 1916–22; leader, Liberal Party 1926–31; following the death of Margaret in 1941, remarried Frances Stevenson (his secretary and mistress since 1913) 1943; created earl 1945.

Morley, John, 1st Viscount Morley (1838–1923), married Rose Ayling 1870, no children; barrister 1873; journalist, editor *The Fortnightly Review* 1867–82, *Pall Mall Gazette* 1880–83; Gladstonian Liberal MP 1883–1908; chief secretary for Ireland 1886, 1892–5; author *Life of Gladstone* 1903; secretary of state for India 1905–10; created viscount 1908; lord president of the council 1910–14; other literary works include biographies of Oliver Cromwell, Richard Cobden, Robert Walpole.

Primrose, Archibald, 5th earl of Rosebery (1847–1929), later Lord Dalmeny; succeeded as earl 1868; Liberal secretary of state for foreign affairs 1886; prime minister 1894–5; leader of the opposition 1895–6; sportsman and historian, who wrote biographies of Lord Chatham (Pitt the Elder), Pitt the Younger, Napoleon and Lord Randolph Churchill.

Wilson, Woodrow (1856–1924), scholar and professor; married Ellen Axson 1885; president of Princeton University 1902–10; governor of New Jersey 1911–3; twenty-eighth president of the United States 1913–21.

Wyndham, George (1863–1913), joined the army 1883; private secretary to Arthur Balfour 1887; Conservative MP 1889–1913; founded *The Outlook* magazine 1898; under-secretary of state for war 1898–1900; chief secretary for Ireland 1900–5; author of several works on poetry and of biography, including *Walter Scott* (1908).

SOLDIERS

Beresford, Lord William (1847–1900), joined the army 1867, initially in India; won the Victoria Cross in the Zulu War 1879; returned to India, winning the Viceroy's Cup at the Calcutta Turf Club four times; married Lilian, dowager duchess of Marlborough, 1895; one son.

Birdwood, William, 1st Baron Birdwood (1865–1951), joined army in 1883, serving in India, southern Africa (Boer War); assistant military secretary, commander-in-chief India 1902; quartermaster-general India, 1911; lieutenant-general, commander ANZAC forces, 1914 (led Gallipoli landing April 1915); interim commander-in-chief (c-in-c), Mediterranean Expeditionary Force (MEF) December 1915; commander 1 ANZAC Corps, British 5th Army, France 1916–18, general 1917; baronet 1919; field marshal, c-in-c, India 1925; baron 1938.

Brabazon, James Palmer (1843–1922), joined the army 1863, resigned as captain to manage his Irish estates 1870; rejoined as lieutenant 1873, serving in India and the Sudan; colonel of 4th Hussars 1892–7; commanded Imperial Yeomanry 1899, temporary major-general.

Buller, Redvers (1839–1938), joined the army 1858, serving in China and Africa, awarded Victoria Cross, Anglo-Zulu War 1879; chief of staff, First Boer War 1881; head of intelligence, Egypt and knighted 1882; the Sudan 1883–6; major-general 1886; quartermaster-general 1887–90; adjutant-general 1890–98 (lieutenant-general 1891, general 1896); commander, Natal Field Force 1899–1900, superseded as c-in-c by Lord Roberts; dismissed 1901.

French, John, 1st earl of Ypres (1852–1925), joined the navy 1866, army 1870; major-general, southern Africa 1899–1902; knighted 1900; general, inspector-general of the Forces 1907–12; chief of the imperial general staff 1912–14; field marshal 1913; c-in-c British Expeditionary Force (BEF) 1914–15; viscount, c-in-c Home Forces 1915–18; lord-lieutenant, Ireland 1918–21; created earl 1922.

Haig, Douglas, 1st Earl Haig (1861–1928), joined the army 1884, serving in the Sudan, southern Africa 1898–1902; inspector-general of cavalry, India 1903–6; staff duties, London 1906–9; knighted, chief of staff, India 1909–11; general, commander Aldershot 1911–14; commander 1st Army, BEF 1914–15; c-in-c BEF, 1915–18; c-in-c, Home Forces 1918–21; earl 1918.

Hamilton, Ian (1853–1947), joined the army 1870, serving in India, Egypt and Burma; brigade commander, Tirah expedition 1897–8; major-general, knighted, Boer War 1899–1901; lieutenant-general, chief of staff South Africa 1901–2; military attaché, Manchuria 1904–5; adjutant-general 1909–10; c-in-c, MEF 1915.

Kitchener, Herbert, 1st Earl Kitchener (1850–1916), joined the Royal Engineers; governor of British Red Sea territories 1886; adjutant-general, Egyptian army, *sirdar* (c-in-c) 1892–8; chief of staff 1899–1900, c-in-c British Forces, Boer War 1900–2; viscount 1902; c-in-c India 1902–7; field marshal 1909; created earl 1914; secretary of state for war 1914–16; drowned travelling to Russia 1916.

Lockhart, William (1841–1900), joined the Indian army 1858; brigade commander, knighted, Third Burmese War 1886–7; c-in-c Punjab 1890–95; commander Tirak expedition 1897–8; c-in-c India 1898–1900.

Wood, Evelyn (1838–1919), joined the navy 1852, army 1855, serving in Crimea, India (Victoria Cross 1858), Africa (Ashanti War 1873–4, Zulu War 1878–9, First Boer War 1881); knighted 1879;

sirdar, Egyptian army 1882–5; officer commanding, Aldershot 1889–93; quartermaster-general 1893–7; adjutant-general 1897–1901; field marshal 1903.

OTHERS

Lewis, George (1833–1911), articled to the family firm of solicitors, Lewis & Lewis 1850, subsequently partner; first specialized as a lawyer in financial cases; after 1875 noted for handling prominent criminal cases including 'the royal baccarat scandal' 1891; married Victorine Kann, died 1865; remarried Elizabeth Eberstadt, three children; knighted 1893, baronet 1902.

Lumley, Theodore, partner with his brother Walter Lumley in the firm of Lumley & Lumley, solicitors, of Bond Stret, London, with other offices in Old Jewry, London, and Paris; the firm handled the legal affairs of the Churchill family.

Roose, Robson Dr (1848–1905), physician, practising in London and Brighton, where he lived; Churchill family doctor.

Watt, Alexander A. P. (1834–1914), bookseller and advertising agent, Edinburgh 1870s; originated role of literary agent 1875, incorporating his 'literary agency' 1881; represented Thomas Hardy, Arthur Conan Doyle, Rudyard Kipling.

Welldon, Revd James (1854–1937), headmaster of Dulwich College 1883–5; Harrow School 1885–98; bishop of Calcutta 1888–1902; canon of Westminster Abbey 1902–6; dean of Manchester Cathedral 1906–18; dean of Durham Cathedral 1918–33.

SERVANTS

Everest, Elizabeth 'Oom', 'Woom', 'Woomany' (*c*.1832–95), born in Chatham, Kent; joined the Churchill family as a nanny to WSC in 1875; remained with the family until 1893; died of peritonitis in 1895.

.

Scrivings, George (d.1907) **and Mrs**, George was manservant to WSC, Mrs Scrivings cook from 1900; George died of choleraic diarrhoea while accompanying WSC on a visit to Africa 1907; Mrs Scrivings continued in service until resettling in Canada.

Walden, Thomas (d.1921) **and Mrs**, Thomas started service with the Churchills as valet to Lord Randolph Churchill; accompanied on expedition to southern Africa 1891, world voyage 1894; accompanied WSC to southern Africa 1899–1900; the Waldens continued in service with JSC until 1914.

PLACES

Banstead Manor, near Newmarket, Suffolk; rented by the Churchills from the owners, the Cotton family, with the financial help of the dowager duchess of Marlborough; used during the summer while WSC and Jack were young.

Blenheim Palace, near Woodstock, Oxfordshire; home of the dukes of Marlborough, where WSC was born; built in the early eighteenth century, largely funded by grants of land from the crown and money from Parliament as a reward to the first duke for his victories in battle against France, including those at Blenheim (1704), Ramillies (1706), Oudenarde (1708) and Malplaquet (1709).

Canford Manor, Wimborne, Dorset; estate of 17,000 acres owned by Lord Wimborne (formerly Sir Ivor Guest), who married Lady Cornelia Spencer-Churchill, a sister of Lord Randolph Churchill; the Guest family fortune was based on iron.

Chatsworth House, near Bakewell, Derbyshire; home of the Cavendish family, now dukes of Devonshire, since 1549; largely rebuilt by the 4th earl of Devonshire, who became the 1st duke, late in the seventeenth century; the gardens were redesigned by Launcelot 'Capability' Brown in the eighteenth century under the 4th duke.

Dalmeny House, near Edinburgh; home of the earls of Rosebery; designed in Gothic Revival style on the exterior, but with Regency interiors, to replace the former family seat, the nearby Barnbougle Castle; the interiors were enriched with paintings from the Rothschild family collection following the 5th earl's marriage in 1878 to Hannah Rothschild.

Deepdene estate, on the south-east edge of Dorking, Surrey; originally owned by the Howard family (dukes of Norfolk), who built a large house and ornamental gardens in the seventeenth century; this was replaced by a Palladian mansion in the 1760s. The estate was acquired by the Hope family in 1808 and its house further enlarged in the style of a Renaissance palazzo; leased by the Hopes to Lily, dowager duchess of Marlborough.

Dunrobin Castle, near Golspie, north of Inverness; seat of the earls of Sutherland since the thirteenth century; remodelled by architect Sir Charles Barry from fort to house in Scottish Baronial style 1845; destroyed by fire 1915; rebuilt to the design of Sir Robert Lorimer in Scottish Renaissance style.

Eaton Hall, near Eccleston, Cheshire; home of the dukes of Westminster; owned by the Grosvenor family since the fifteenth century; two former houses on the site were replaced by a larger Victorian building, designed by Alfred Waterhouse, completed in 1882; surrounded by an estate of 11,000 acres.

Glenmuick House, near Ballater, Deeside; formerly Braichlie House, now demolished; house and estate of 14,000 acres acquired in the mid-nineteenth century by Sir James Thompson MacKenzie, friend of the Prince of Wales; subsequently acquired by Sir Sigismund Neumann, South African-born financier.

Gosford House, near Longniddry, East Lothian; home of the Charteris family, earls of Wemyss and March; built between 1890 and 1900 to the designs of Robert Adam.

Guisachan, near Inverness; the Guisachan estate, a deer forest, was acquired by Dudley Majoribanks, later Lord Tweedmouth, who built Guisachan House; his wealth came from his father, a partner in bankers Coutts Co.; Tweedmouth, a Liberal politician, married WSC's aunt, Lady Fanny Spencer-Churchill.

Invercauld, Braemar, in Deeside, Aberdeenshire; centred on Braemar Castle, seat of the earls of Mar, head of the Farquharson clan; the family sold the adjoining Balmoral estate to Queen Victoria in 1848.

Invermark Lodge, near Brechin Castle, Angus; home of the earl of Dalhousie whose estates stretched to approximately 150,000 acres across the Scottish counties of Angus and Midlothian.

Iwerne Minster House, near Blandford, Dorset; originally built by the Bowyer Bower family 1796; bought by George Glyn, Lord Wolverton 1876; rebuilt to a design by Alfred Waterhouse 1878; sold by the Glyn family 1908.

Minto House, near Hawick in the Scottish borders; home of the 4th earl of Minto who had succeeded to the title in 1891; the original house on the site was remodelled in the eighteenth century to plans by William Adam; Victorian alterations by William Playfair resulted in a four-storey structure.

Panshanger House, near Hertford; the home of 7th Earl Cowper; the house had been completed in 1806 in Regency-Gothic style; the park had been landscaped at the end of the eighteenth century under advice from Humphry Repton.

Sandringham House, Norfolk; estate bought by Queen Victoria in 1862 for the Prince of Wales and his new Danish wife, Princess Alexandra; originally a Georgian house built in 1771, but remodelled after its royal purchase by the Victorian architect A. J. Humbert 1865–70; part of the house had been destroyed by fire 1891.

Tulchan, Dalchroy House, near Inverness; a shooting and fishing lodge on the River Spey; its land was owned by the 7th earl of Seafield; the sporting rights were let to Sir Philip Sassoon who rebuilt the lodge following a fire in 1906.

Welbeck Abbey, in north Nottinghamshire; site of a monastery until its dissolution after which it was bought in 1607 by Sir Charles Cavendish whose son William became 1st duke of Newcastle; seat of the dukes of Newcastle, who converted it to a country house, until it passed in the eighteenth century to the Bentinck family, to become the English seat of the dukes of Portland.

Wynyard Park, in County Durham; English seat of the Vane-Tempest-Stewart family, marquess of Londonderry (cousins of the Churchills); the original house had been destroyed by fire in 1841 and rebuilt to the design of Ignatius Bonomi.

ACKNOWLEDGEMENTS

I am grateful to Curtis Brown, London on behalf of the Master, Fellows and Scholars of Churchill College, Cambridge (© The Master, Fellows and Scholars of Churchill College, Cambridge) for permission to quote from the unpublished letters of Jennie, Lady Randolph Churchill; and to Curtis Brown, London on behalf of the Estate of Winston S. Churchill (© The Estate of Winston S. Churchill) for permission to quote from the speeches, works, writings and letters of Winston S. Churchill. I also thank the trustees of the Sir Winston Churchill Archive Trust for permission to use the documents and images in their possession.

I appreciate the encouragement given to me in this undertaking by Randolph Churchill, Winston's great-grandson, and am particularly grateful to him for writing a foreword. I would also like to mention the inspiration which I found in the late Lady Soames's collection of the letters between Clementine and Winston. Anyone who has enjoyed *Darling Winston* but not yet read *Speaking for Themselves* should get hold of a copy.

All writers tackling the life of the Churchill family have reason to be grateful for the official biography *Winston Spencer Churchill*, written by his son Randolph Churchill and by Martin Gilbert.

I have constantly referred to Volumes I–IV and their companion books of documents, which span the forty years covered by this correspondence.

My chief thanks for help during my research for this book go to the teams at the Churchill Archives Centre of Churchill College in Cambridge and at Bloomsbury Publishing in London, which publishes the digital version of the Churchill Archive.

I have been able to find images of most of the letters between Jennie and Winston through the digital archive and am most grateful to Bloomsbury Publishing (particularly Frances Arnold, Elizabeth Cameron and Emily Drew) for allowing this. It is a wonderful resource for historians and students around the world. The days of having to operate a reluctant microfiche reading machine in Cambridge are now over and for the most part unlamented.

On the other hand it is still a great joy to climb the stairs at Churchill College and find such a warm greeting from the unfailingly helpful and knowledgeable team of the Churchill Archives Centre. I was lucky, therefore, that some of the letters between Jennie and Winston have so far escaped the scanner's eye. Another good reason to visit Cambridge was to consult Natalie Adams on the deciphering of Jennie's handwriting, which bears all the flamboyant flourishes of a veteran Victorian letter-writer. Natalie has kindly pored with me over troublesome words or names and I am hugely grateful for her help in cracking all but one conundrum, where I have reluctantly entered the word [indecipherable]! Dr Allen Packwood, the director of the Archives centre, as always sets the pace for his whole team and I am hugely grateful to him once again, not only for his encouragement and for help with copyright matters, but for his time and expertise in looking over my text.

My thanks also go to Elizabeth Harford and James Harte at the National Library of Ireland, which houses some letters between Winston and Jennie that ended up in the Leslie Papers; to Tace Fox, the archivist at Harrow School; and to the London Library, a haven for readers and writers in the heart of London at No. 14 St James's

Square (next door to No. 12, St James's Square which features several times in the letters, as it was owned by Lord Randolph's estate and housed Jennie's Nimrod Club for a while, as alert readers may have spotted!).

Closer to home, may I thank Margaret Atkins for typing most of the text of the letters with admirable accuracy; and Carol Turner, who used to assist me in my business days and who has returned to check my work and find at least as many authorial slips as she found different types of errors in banking days of old.

My thanks for his guidance and wise handling go to my literary agent, Andrew Lownie. It has been a delight to work again with my publishing team at Head of Zeus in London, particularly Richard Milbank, who expertly acted as my editor; Georgina Blackwell who has helped with the illustrations; Clémence Jacquinet and Adrian McLaughlin who have had to meet the unusual challenges of presenting letters attractively on the written page; and to Jessie Price who designed the cover. I am grateful to Richard and Holly Collins for their help as copyeditors. I am delighted to be working in the US on this occasion with Pegasus Publishers in New York and would like to thank in particular Claiborne Hancock and Jessica Case. Any mistakes that have survived all this help and scrutiny are entirely my responsibility.

Finally, I always appreciate the wonderful support of my family, particularly of my daughter Rosie, who has again helped with proof-reading and advice, and of my long-suffering wife Felicity. I have dedicated this book to her because she has provided much of its inspiration. At its root it is surely an homage to motherhood and I have been lucky enough to observe at very close range Felicity's brilliance as a mother to our children.

DAVID LOUGH
Penshurst
March 2018

IMAGE PERMISSIONS

SOURCES AND LETTER REFERENCES

SOURCES

United Kingdom

The Churchill Archives Centre, Churchill College, University of
   Cambridge
Winston S. Churchill papers – Chartwell Collection
Lord Randolph Churchill Papers
Lady Randolph Churchill Papers
John S. Churchill Papers
Henry Winston 'Peregrine' Churchill Papers
The British Library, London
The Blenheim Papers
Rothschild Archives, London
Lord Randolph Churchill bank accounts and correspondence

Ireland

The National Library of Ireland
The Leslie Papers

United States

Yale University, Connecticut (Beinecke Rare Book & Manuscript Library)
Lady St Helier Papers
Library of Congress, Washington, DC
Moreton Frewen Papers
New York Public Library, New York
Sir Edward Marsh Papers
A.P. Watt Papers

LETTER REFERENCES

Almost all the letters are sourced from the Churchill Archive Centre (CAC) and its Chartwell series of papers. The following listing therefore omits the CHAR prefix that usually precedes the reference in the CAC's catalogue reference.

Some letters are lodged in two other collections of papers at the CAC, which are abbreviated in CAC catalogue and below as follows:
Henry Winston ('Peregrine') Churchill Papers: PCHL
Winston Churchill Additional Materials: WHCL

References to volumes of the official biography, *Winston S. Churchill*, by Randolph Churchill or Martin Gilbert, or its companion volumes of documents are shown in the following format:
WSC 1:123   denoting volume one of the biography, page 123;
WSC 2C3:456   denoting companion volume three to volume two of the biography, page 456.

[1881]	Private collection	[25 January 1890] Saturday	1/8/7
[1881]	28/13/2	7 February 1890	1/8/8
1 April [1882]	28/13/6-7	12 March 1890	Leslie Papers
[3 December 1882]	28/13/15	12 June 1890	1/8/9-11
[17 June 1883]	28/13/17	[19 June 1890]	28/18/38-40
[November 1883]	28/13/23	[September 1890] Friday 19	1/8/12-3
16 March 1884	28/13/34	[21 September 1890] Sunday	28/16/14
8 June 1884	28/13/36-7	[13 October 1890]	28/16/14
28 October 1884	28/13/45	[November 1890]	28/16/15-6
21 January 1885	28/13/48	[21 January 1891]	28/18/53-5
9 May 1885	28/13/62	[22 January 1891] Thursday	1/8/12-3
9 June 1885	28/13/67	[late February/early	
2 September [1885]	28/13/76	March 1891]	28/17/57
14 February 1886	28/13/86	[April 1891]	28/16/23
5 October 1886	28/13/95	[29 April 1891] Wednesday	1/8/17
14 December [1886]	28/13/104-5	[10 May 1891] Sunday	1/8/18
17 May 1887	28/14/11	[19 May 1891]	28/16/25
11 June 1887	28/14/17	[13 June 1891]	28/16/27
[? 12 June 1887]	28/14/18-9	[18 June 1891] Thursday	1/8/19
[15 June 1887]	28/14/20	[19 June 1891]	28/16/28
[19 June 1887]	28/13/109	[21 June 1891]	28/16/29
[24 June 1887]	28/14/20	[25 June 1891]	28/16/30
[July 1887]	28/17/1-2	[28 June 1891] Sunday	1/8/20
[late July 1887]	28/17/3	[29 June 1891]	28/16/31
[14 July 1887]	28/14/26	3 July 1891	28/16/32-3
22 October 1887	28/14/44-5	[5 July 1891] Sunday	1/8/21
14 December 1887	28/14/52	[6 July 1891] Monday	1/8/22
12 January [1888]	28/14/56	[14 July] 1891	28/16/34-5
7 February 1888	28/15/2-3	[July 1891]	1/8/24
16 March 1888	28/15/9-11	[24 July 1891]	28/17/60-2
[20 April 1888]	28/15/14-5	[July 1891]	1/8/23
[14 May 1888]	28/17/4	[19 September 1891]	28/6/38-9
[27 June 1888]	28/17/4	[22 September 1891]	28/16/40
[October 1888]	28/17/20	[27 September 1891]	28/16/23
7 November 1888	28/15/29	[28 September 1891]	28/17/65-6
[March 1889]	28/17/27	[29 September 1891]	1/8/25
[15 May 1889]	28/17/31	28 October 1891	1/8/27
[21 June 1889]	28/17/36	[early November 1891]	28/16/45
[28 September 1889]	28/18/13-4	[10 November 1891]	1/8/28
[5 October 1889]	28/16/8-9	15 November [1891]	1/8/29
[November 1889] Monday	1/8/6	[mid-November 1891]	28/16/47
[November 1889]	28/17/41	[22 November 1891]	28/16/49
[November 1889]	28/18/24	[6 December 1891]	28/16/50

[8 December 1891] Tuesday	1/8/30-1	16 March [1894]	28/20/11
[9 December 1891]	28/16/51	[17 March 1894] Saturday	1/8/54
[15 December 1891] Tuesday	1/8/32	[22 April 1894] Sunday	1/8/55
[16 December 1891]	28/16/53-4	24 April [1894]	28/20/16
[December 1891]	28/16/56	30 April [1894]	1/8/56
[22 December 1891]	28/19/1-2	1 May [1894]	28/20/18-9
[27 December 1891]	1/8/32	10 May [1894]	28/20/22
Sunday 10 January 1892	1/8/33	13 May [1894]	28/20/23
[14 January 1892]	8/16/63	17 May [1894]	1/8/57
[January 1892]	28/16/64	19 May 1894	28/20/25
[7 February 1892]	28/16/64	24 May [1894]	1/8/58-9
[February 1892]	28/16/65	25 May 1894	28/20/26
[16 March 1892]	28/16/67	10 July [1894]	28/20/28-9
[24 March 1892]	28/17/68	17 July [1894]	28/19/28-9
[28 March 1892] Monday	1/8/35	22 July [1894]	28/19/30-2
[27 March 1892]	28/17/69	31 July 1894	28/20/30-1
[3 April 1892] Sunday	1/8/36	3 August [1894]	28/19/33-4
[May 1892] Monday	1/8/37	26 August [1894]	28/19/35-6
[24 September 1892]	1/8/39	11 October 1894	PCHL/1/6
[September 1892]	28/16/70	4 September 1894	28/209/34-6
[21 November 1892]	28/16/75-6	15 September 1894	28/20/37-8
[7 February 1893]	1/8/41	19 September 1894	28/20/39-40
[February 1893]	1/8/40	4 November [1894]	PCHL/1/6
[March 1893]	1/8/42	21 October [1894]	28/20/42
2 April 1893	28/19/4	2 November 1894	28/20/45-6
[7 April 1893] Friday	1/8/43	8 November 1894	28/20/47-8
19 April [1893]	1C1:375	25 November 1894	28/20/50
14 June 1893	28/19/5	9 December 1894	28/20/53
[18 June 1893] Sunday	1/8/44	17 December 1894	28/20/55-6
7 August 1893	1/8/45-6	11 January [1895]	28/21/1-2
14 August 1893	28/19/8-9	19 February 1895	28/21/3-4
19 August 1893	1/8/47-8	20 February 1895	28/21/5-6
23 August 1893	28/19/10	24 February 1895	28/21/9-10
30 August 1893	28/19/11	2 March 1895	28/21/11-3
17 September [1893]	28/19/13-5	23 March 1895	28/21/19-21
20 September [1893]	28/19/16-7	27 April 1895	28/21/25-30
13 October [1893]	28/19/20-1	2 May [1895]	28/21/31-3
21 October [1893]	28/19/22-3	8 May [1895]	28/21/34
10 December [1893]	28/20/54	16 May [1895]	28/21/35
25 December [1893]	28/20/57-8	23 May [1895]	28/21/37-9
11 February [1894]	1/8/49	6 June [1895]	28/21/40-2
13 February [1894]	28/20/3	17 June [1895]	28/21/43-6
[20 February 1894] Tuesday	1/8/50	23 June [1895]	28/21/47-8

3 July [1895]	28/21/49-50	7 January 1897	28/23/8-9
6 July [1895]	28/21/51-3	29 January 1897	1/8/86-7
16 August [1895]	28/21/59-61	14 January 1897	28/23/10-1
24 August [1895]	28/21/62-4	5 February [1897]	1/8/88
31 August [1895]	28/21/65-6	21 January 1897	28/23/12-3
4 October [1895]	28/21/71-2	12 February [1897]	1/8/89-90
11 October [1895]	1/50/60-1	4 February [1897]	28/23/15
21 October [1895]	28/21/74-5	26 February 1897	1/8/91-3
8 November [1895]	28/21/78-81	12 February [1897]	28/23/16-17
10 November [1895]	28/21/82-4	5 March [1897]	1/8/94-95
20 November 1895	20 November 1895	18 February 1897	28/23/18-9
6 December 1895	28/21/92-4	11 March [1897]	1/8/96-8
26 January 1896	28/21/82-84	25 February 1897	28/23/20-1
1 May 1896	28/22/4-6	18 March 1897	1/8/99-101
4 August 1896	28/21/96-9	2 March 1897	28/23/22-3
23 September 1896	1/8/62-63	25 March [1897]	1/8/102-103
18 September 1896	28/22/7-8	11 March [1897]	28/23/24-26
1 October [1896]	1/8/64-5	2 April 1897	1/8/104-105
21 September 1896	28/22/9	17 March 1897	28/23/27-8
8 October 1896	1/8/66-7	31 March 1897	28/33/29-30
30 September 1896	28/22/10	6 April [1897]	28/23/31-3
22 October [1896] Friday	1/8/68	14 April 1897	28/23/34-5
4 October [1896]	28/23/1-3	21 April 1897	28/23/36-8
14 October [1896]	28/22/11-3	28 April 1897	28/23/39-41
5 November [1896]	1/8/70-1	26 May 1897	28/23/41A-B
21 October 1896	28/22/15	7 August [1897]	28/23/42-43
13 November 1896	1/8/72	17 August [1897]	28/23/44-46
26 October [1896]	28/22/16-7	9 September [1897]	1/8/106
19 November [1896]	1/8/73-4	24 August [1897]	28/23/47-8
4 November [1896]	28/22/18-23	21 September [1897]	1/8/106
27 November [1896]	1/8/75-6	30 September 189	1/8/109-110
12 November [1896]	28/22/24-5	29 August [1897]	28/23/49-50
18 November [1896]	28/22/26-7	5 September [1897]	28/23/52
11 December [1896]	1/8/77-78	7 October 1897	1/8/111-2
24 November [1896]	28/22/28-9	12 September [1897]	25/23/53-4
17 December 1896	1/8/79-80	29 October 1897	1/8/113-4
2 December [1896]	28/22/32-3	19 September [1897]	28/23/57
24 December [1896]	1/8/81-2	4 November 1897	1/8/115-6
8 December 1896	28/22/34-5	27 September [1897]	28/23/58
16 December 1896	28/22/36	2 October [1897]	28/23/59
23 December 1896	28/22/37	12 October [1897]	28/23/63
15 January 1897	1/8/85	21 October [1897]	28/23/64-6
1 January 1897	28/23/4-5	11 November [1897]	1/8/117

25 October [1897]	28/23/67-68	[late July 1898]	28/25/57
25 November 1897	1/8/118	28 July 1898	28/25/27
[2 November] 1897	28/23/71-3	5 August 1898	28/25/28-9
10 November [1897]	28/23/76-8	10 August 1898	28/25/31
17 November [1897]	28/23/79-81	16 August 1898	28/25/32
10 December 1897	1/8/119	19 August 1898	28/25/33-5
24 November [1897]	28/23/82-83	24 August 1898	28/25/32
16 December 1897	1/8/120-1	26 August 1898	28/25/38
2 December [1897]	28/23/84-5	4 September 1898	1C2:973
9 December [1897]	28/23/86-7	8 September 1898	28/25/42
15 December [1897]	28/23/88-9	17 September 1898	28/25/43-5
22 December [1897]	28/23/90-2	21 October 1898	28/25/46
13 January 1898	1/8/122-3	27 October 1898	28/25/47
14 January 1898	1/8/124	14 November 1898	28/25/49
31 December [1897]	28/23/93-5	1 December 1898	28/25/51-52
5 January 1898	28/24/2-10	4 December 1898	28/25/53
20 January 1898	1/8/125-6	11 December 1898	28/25/54
10 January 1898	28/24/13-16	22 December 1898	28/25/55
27 January 1898	1/8/127-8	29 December 1898	28/25/56
19 January 1898	28/24/20-5	1 January 1899	28/26/1
26 January 1898	28/24/26-9	11 January 1899	28/26/2
28 January 1898	28/24/30-2	19 January 1899	28/24/93
30 January 1898	28/24/33-5	26 January 1899	28/26/3
2 February 1898	28/24/36	2 February 1899	28/26/4
9 February 1898	28/24/37-9	9 February 1899	28/26/5
16 February [1898]	28/24/40-41	16 February 1899	28/26/6-7
25 February [1898]	28/24/42-3	23 February 1899	28/26/9-10
7 March [1898]	28/24/45-6	2 March 1899	28/26/11-12
18 March [1898]	28/24/49-53	9 March 1899	28/26/13
22 March [1898]	28/24/54-7	30 March 1899	28/26/14-7
27 March 1898	28/24/65-7	3 April 1899	28/26/18-20
31 March [1898]	28/24/74-77	3 May 1899	28/26/21
13 April [1898]	28/24/78-84	25 June 1899	28/26/22
19 April [1898]	28/24/85-6	26 June 1899	28/26/23
22 April [1898]	28/24/87-9	23 July 1899	28/26/27
25 April 1898	28/24/90-2	13 August 1899	28/26/28
3 May 1898	28/25/1-2	16 August 1899	28/26/29
10 May 1898	28/25/3-5	22 August 1899	28/26/30-31
16 May 1898	28/25/6-8	3 September 1899	28/26/32-33
22 May 1898	28/25/10-13	18 September 1899	28/26/34
1 June [1898]	28/25/14-16	2 October 1899	28/26/35-6
8 June [1898]	28/25/21-23	17 October 1899	28/26/39
15 July [1898]	28/25/25-6	25 October 1899	28/26/40

3 November 1899	28/26/43	12 November 1904	2/18/67–8
18 November 1899	28/26/44-45	15 November 1904	28/27/31
6 January 1900	28/26/46	17 November 1904	28/27/32
13 February 1900	28/26/47	21 January 1905	28/27/33
18 February 1900	28/26/48-49	22 January 1905	1/50/7
26 February 1900	28/26/50-51	26 January 1905	28/27/34
15 April [1900]	PCHL/1/6	9 February 1905	28/27/35
21 March 1900	28/26/52	28 February 1905	1/50/17–18
22 March 1900	28/26/53	2 April 1905	28/27/38
12 May [1900]	PCHL/ 1/6	6 April 1905	28/27/39
1 May 1900	28/26/54-8	19 April 1905	1/50/19
26 May 1900	PCHL/1/6	21 July 1905	28/27/40
9 June 1900	28/26/59-60	31 August 1905	28/27/42-3
6 August 1900	28/26/61	3 October 1905	28/27/44–45
12 August 1900	28/26/62-64	30 October 1905	28/27/46-47
8 September 1900	28/26/66-8	28 November 1905	28/27/48
20 September 1900	28/26/69	1 December 1905	28/27/49
21 September 1900	28/26/70-1	4 December 1905	28/27/50-51
27 October 1900	28/26/74	24 June 1906	28/27/52-3
21 December 1900	28/26/77-9	[20] August 1906	28/27/57
1 January 1901	28/26/80-82	25 August 1906	1/56/34-38
22 January 1901	28/26/88-93	1 September 1906	28/27/54–6
14 February 1901	28/26/94	4 September 1906	1/56/42-45
13 March 1901	28/26/96–7	16 September 1906	1/56/46
23 March 1901	28/26/98–100	14 September 1906	28/27/58-9
13 December 1901	28/26/103	18 September 1906	1/56/49–50
[December 1901]	28/26/104	29 September 1906	28/27/60–2
3 April 1902	28/27/1	13 October 1906	28/27/63
15 August 1902	28/27/2–3	[October 1906]	1/57/31
27 September 1902	28/27/5	26 December 1906 [postcard]	1/57/58
9 October 1902	28/27/5	22 March 1907	1/65/27
8 December 1902	28/27/10	[31 March 1907] Sunday	1/65/28
19 December 1902	28/27/8–9	17 April 1907	1/65/29–30
12 August 1903	28/27/11-7	1 a.m., 7 May 1907	1/65/27
11 September 1903	28/27/18	12 August 1907	1/66/4–5
18 September 1903	28/27/20	21 August 1907	28/27/67–68
4 December 1903	28/27/21–2	22 August 1907	1/66/10–12
26 March 1904	28/27/23	27 August 1907	1/66/14
22 August 1904	28/27/24	[Date, first section missing –	
25 August 1904	28/27/25	late August 1907]	28/27/64–6
1 September 1904	28/27/26	30 August 1907	1/66/20
14 September 1904	28/27/27	17 September 1907	1/66/28–9
24 September 1904	28/27/28–30	26 September 1907	28/27/72-73

25 September 1907	1/66/31	18 March 1913		1/392/9-10	
21 October 1907	1/66/39-40	24 April 1913		28/28/9-10	
19 October 1907	28/27/69-70	[undated, between			
21 November 1907	1/66/54-55	1–7 September 1913]	WCHL 14/1/20		
6 November 1907	28/27/75-79	29 November 1913		28/28/11	
5 December 1907	1/66/63–4	3 December 1913		1/392/17-18	
13 December 1907	1/66/66–8	29 January 1914		1/392/11-12	
23 November 1907	28/27/80-81	10 February 1914		28/28/14-15	
30 December 1907	1/66/77-8	23 May 1915		1/117/63	
3 January 1908	1/72/7	21 November 1915	WCHL 14/1/1-2		
7 January 1908	1/72/10	24 November 1915		28/120/1–2	
3 January 1908	28/27/82-3	27 November 1915	WCHL 14/1/9-10		
12 January 1908	1/72/13-14	1 December 1915		28/120/3–4	
26 March 1908	1/72/47	5 December 1915	WCHL 14/1/12-13		
13 September 1908	28/27/86	8 December 1915		28/120/5–6	
20 September 1908	28/27/86A	12 December 1915	WCHL 14/1/15		
29 September 1908	1/72/95	19 December 1915	WCHL 14/1/17-18		
14 May 1909	28/27/87	6 January 1916	WCHL/14/1/22-4		
4 August 1909	28/27/88-91	12 January 1916	WCHL 14/1/26-7		
[February 1910] Tuesday 9.15	1/95/80	23 January 1916	WCHL 14/1/26-7		
9 April 1910	28/28/3	29 January 1916	Leslie papers		
1 August 1910	WCHL 14/1/7	3 February 1916	WCHL 14/1/28-30		
29 August 1910	1/95/48-9	7 February 1916		28/120/7–8	
13 April 1911	Leslie Papers	12 February 1916		1/392/13–14	
14 April 1911	1/39/2	20 February 1916		1/392/15	
19 April 1911	28/28/4-5	23 February75 1916		28/120/9–10	
JSC letter to George		28 March 1916	WCHL 14/1/31-32		
Cornwallis-West	28/28/6	3 April 1916		28/120/11-2	
26 September 1911	1/392/1	7 April 1916		1/392/16	
28 September 1911	1/392/3	16 July 1920		1/135/9	
1 October 1911	1/99/42	5 August 1920		1/135/10	
16 September 1912	1/392/4-6	14 February 1921		1/138/15	
19 September 1912	28/28/7	1 March 1921		1/138/18	
15 February 1913	1/392/7-8	[27 April 1921] Wed		1/138/22	

BIBLIOGRAPHY

Balsan, Consuelo Vanderbilt, *The Glitter and the Gold* (George Mann, 1973)

Birkenhead, Earl of, *F. E.: The Life of F. E. Smith, First Earl of Birkenhead* (Eyre & Spottiswoode, 1959)

Blow, Michael, 'Churchill in Cuba', *Quarterly Journal of Military History*, 3:1, autumn 1990

Cannadine, David, *The Decline and Fall of the British Aristocracy* (Yale University Press, 1990)

Churchill, Peregrine, and Mitchell, Julian, *Jennie: Lady Randolph Churchill, A Portrait with Letters* (Collins, 1974)

Churchill, Randolph S., *Youth: Winston S. Churchill 1874–1900* (Heinemann, 1966)

—, *Young Statesman: Winston S. Churchill 1901–1914* (Heinemann, 1967)

—, *Companion* Volume I, parts 1, 2 *1874–1900* (Heinemann, 1967)

—, *Companion* Volume II, parts 1, 2, 3 *1901–1914* (Heinemann, 1969)

Churchill, Winston S., *The Story of the Malakand Field Force* (Longmans Green & Co., 1899)

—, *Lord Randolph Churchill* (Macmillan & Co., 1906)

—, *My African Journey* (Hodder & Stoughton, 1908)

—, *Liberalism and the Social Problem* (Hodder & Stoughton, 1909)

Cornwallis-West, George, *Edwardian Hey-Days* (Putnam, 1930)

Cornwallis-West, Mrs George, *The Reminiscences of Lady Randolph Churchill* (Edward Arnold, 1908)

Corsini, Carlo, and Viazzo, Pier Paolo, eds, *The Decline of Infant Mortality in Europe, 1800–1950* (UNICEF, 1993)

Egremont, Max, *Balfour: A Life of Arthur James Balfour* (William Collins, 1980)

Fass, Paula, *The End of American Childhood: A History of Parenting from Life on the Frontier to the Managed Child* (Princeton University Press, 2016)

Field, Leslie, *Bendor: The Golden Duke of Westminster* (Weidenfeld & Nicholson, 1983)

Foster, R. F., *Lord Randolph Churchill* (Oxford University Press, 1981)

Gathorne-Hardy, Jonathan, *The Rise and Fall of the British Nanny* (Hodder & Stoughton, 1972)

Gilbert, Martin, *Companion* Volume II, parts 1, 2, 3 *1901–1914* (Heinemann, 1969)

—, *Winston S. Churchill* Volume III *1914–1916* (Heinemann, 1971)

—, *Winston S. Churchill* Volume IV *1917–1922* (Heinemann, 1975)

—, *Companion* Volume III, parts 1, 2 *1914–1916* (Heinemann, 1972)

—, *Companion* Volume IV parts 1, 2, 3 *1917–1922* (Heinemann, 1977)

Green, David, *The Churchills of Blenheim* (Constable, 1984)

Greville, Daisy, Countess of Warwick, *Life's Ebb and Flow* (W. Morrow, 1929)

Hassall, Christopher, *Edward Marsh: A Biography* (Longmans Green, 1959)

Higham, Charles, *Dark Lady: Winston Churchill's Mother and Her World* (Virgin Books, 2006)

Kapla, Justin, *When the Astors Owned New York: Blue Bloods and Grand Hotels in a Gilded Age* (Plume, 2006)

Kehoe, Elizabeth, *Fortune's Daughters: The Extravagant Lives of the Jerome Sisters – Jennie Churchill, Clara Frewen and Leonie Leslie* (Atlantic Books, 2004)

Lee, Celia and John, *Winston & Jack: The Churchill Brothers* (Celia Lee, 2007)

Leslie, Anita, *Jennie: The Life of Lady Randolph Churchill* (Hutchinson, 1969)

Leslie, Shane, *Long Shadows* (John Murray, 1966)

Lough, David, *No More Champagne: Churchill and His Money* (Head of Zeus, 2015)

Lovell, Mary S., *The Churchills: A Family at the Heart of History* (Little, Brown, 2011)

Marsh, Edward, *A Number of People: A Book of Reminiscences* (Harper & Brothers, 1939)

Martin, Ralph, *Jennie: The Life of Lady Randolph Churchill* Volumes I, II (Prentice Hall, 1969)

Oldham, Our Heritage and History 1887–1987 (History Book Committee, 1987)

Pearson, John, *The Private Lives of Winston Churchill* (Viking, 1991)

Pilpel, Robert E., *Churchill in America 1895–1961* (New English Library, 1977)

Roberts, Brian, *Churchills in Africa* (Hamish Hamilton 1970)

Robins, Jonathan, *Cotton and Race Across the Atlantic* (University of Rochester Press, 2016)

Rose, Jonathan, *The Literary Churchill: Author, Reader, Actor* (Yale University Press, 2014)

Sandys, Celia, ed., *From Winston with Love and Kisses: The Young Churchill* (Sinclair-Stevenson, 1994)

Sebba, Anne, *Jennie Churchill, Winston's American Mother* (John Murray, 2007)

Soames, Mary, *Clementine Churchill* (Cassell, 1979)

—, *Speaking for Themselves: The Personal Letters of Winston and Clementine Churchill* (Doubleday, 1998)

—, *A Daughter's Tale* (Doubleday, 2011)

INDEX